WORKING TOWARD WHITENESS

WORKING TOWARD
Whiteness

HOW AMERICA'S IMMIGRANTS BECAME WHITE

The Strange Journey from Ellis Island to the Suburbs

David R. Roediger

BASIC
BOOKS

A Member of the Perseus Books Group
New York

Published by Basic Books,
A Member of the Perseus Books Group

Designed by Brent Wilcox
Text set in 11-point New Caledonia

Books published by Basic Books are available at special discounts for bulk
purchases in the United States by corporations, institutions, and other
organizations. For more information, please contact the Special Markets
Department at the Perseus Books Group, 11 Cambridge Center, Cambridge,
MA 02142, or special.markets@perseusbooks.com

Cataloging-in-Publication data for this book is available from the Library of Congress.

ISBN 0-465-07073-6

05 06 07 08 / 10 9 8 7 6 5 4 3 2 1

To Jean

CONTENTS

PART I: SEEING RACE IN NEW IMMIGRANT HISTORY

1 New Immigrants, Race, and "Ethnicity" in the
Long Early Twentieth Century   3

2 Popular Language, Social Practice, and the Messiness of Race   35

PART II: "INBETWEENNESS"

3 "The Burden of Proof Rests with Him": New Immigrants
and the Structures of Racial Inbetweenness   57

4 Inside the Wail: New Immigrant Racial Consciousness   93

PART III: ENTERING THE WHITE HOUSE

5 "A Vast Amount of Coercion": The Ironies of
Immigration Restriction   133

6 Finding Homes in an Era of Restriction   157

7 A New Deal, an Industrial Union, and a White House:
What the New Immigrant Got Into   199

Afterword: The Houses We've Lived in and the Workings
of Whiteness   235

Acknowledgments   245
Notes   249
Index   321

SEEING RACE IN
NEW IMMIGRANT HISTORY

Part One

New Immigrants, Race, and "Ethnicity" in the Long Early Twentieth Century

I had my fill of seeing people come down the gangplank on Wednesday, let us say, speaking not a word of English, and by Friday discovering that I was working for them and they were calling me nigger like everybody else. So that the Italian adventure or even the Jewish adventure, however grim, is distinguished from my own adventure.

JAMES BALDWIN, NOVELIST AND ESSAYIST (1971)

This pseudo "white" identity . . . was not something that just fell on us out of the blue, but something that many Italian Americans grabbed at with both hands. Many felt that their culture, language, food, songs, music, identity, was a small price to pay for entering the American mainstream. Or they thought, as my parents probably did, that they could keep these good Italian things in private and become "white" in public.

DIANE DI PRIMA, POET (1999)

One sideshow during the 1993 Wimbledon tennis tournament featured the defending champion, Andre Agassi, calling the eventual winner, Pete Sampras, a "monkey." The excitable press coverage that greeted Agassi's remark subsided quickly. When Agassi revealed that his own body hair had been removed to make him quicker, he provided a more photogenic story, overshadowing his characterization of Sampras.

Unlike former Atlanta Braves pitcher John Rocker's controversial reference to a dark-skinned teammate as a "fat monkey," Agassi's remark
lacked any apparently racial bite. Clearly he and Sampras are both white.[1]

At least now they are. Almost no U.S. tennis star in the past decade
would have been considered unequivocally "white" just a century ago.
Not Michael Chang, of course, since Chinese nonwhiteness was established by 1900 in court cases, naturalization proceedings, exclusion
laws, and pogroms. Certainly not Venus or Serena Williams, who would
have been Jim Crowed from tennis clubs and virtually all other privileged public and private U.S. spaces. But not Agassi either. And not
Sampras. And not Monica Seles. Agassi, Sampras, and Seles would have
embodied the "dark white" (and possibly not white) immigration "problem" that a century ago was thought to threaten the racial foundations
of the nation. The backgrounds of all three would have dictated their
being called "new immigrants" and doubly damned by the term. On one
hand it would have connoted an inexperienced recent arrival, a greenhorn. But new immigrants were also new because they represented a
different source of migrants—the streams from southern and eastern
Europe that overtook the streams from northern and western Europe as
the century turned and furnished the great majority of the more than 14
million newcomers coming in the first two decades of the twentieth
century. As an Armenian American, Agassi would have been part of the
immigrant group most singled out for ridicule by Henry James in his
writings on race and immigration. He would have seen the whiteness,
and hence the fitness for citizenship, of immigrants from his homeland
challenged by U.S. attorneys before and after an early twentieth-century
federal court decision finding them naturalizable as white. The 1911
Dictionary of Races or Peoples, a U.S. Senate document compiled by
the Immigration Commission, credited Armenians as the "Aryan race
. . . of Asiatic Turkey" before noting with alarm their "remarkable short-
ness and [the] height of their heads," as well as a "flattening of the back
of the head" which "can only be compared to the . . . Malay." Seles, Yu-
goslavian born but of Hungarian ancestry, would have been a *hunky* in
the early twentieth century. Sampras's Greek background would have
excluded him from jobs, housing, unions, and public places along with
other "Asiatic" nonwhites, especially in the West where his tennis game
matured. In the United States of a century ago people did not talk

about race in the way we do. To understand their history, we need to learn some of their language.[2]

In his 1907 contribution to travel literature, *The American Scene*, Henry James reflected at tortured length on his 1905 "look in" at arriving immigrants from the observation areas at Ellis Island and on other contacts with new immigrants. His account eerily anticipated contemporary debates over race and immigration, though the descendants of those he watched are now considered definitively white. Most of the time James's tone presaged the panic of the current English Only and anti-immigration movements over the possibility of a racially changed country. At other junctures he less convincingly staked out prematurely multiculturalist hopes that immigration would lead to bigger and better things. James conjured up many images, from cauldron to amalgam, which suggest a melting away of immigrant differences. But he also betrayed sharp anxiety that the numbers and kinds of immigrants and the "hotch-potch of racial characteristics" they brought to the United States would cause the concept of American to lose any sure meaning. For long passages, he scarcely described anything he actually saw but rather his sense of "unsettledness" in proximity to new immigrants. Worrying especially over "Italians, of superlatively southern type" and the "swarming [of] a Jewry that had burst all bonds," James feared an immigrant "conquest of New York." He struck fretful chords "no different," as Alan Trachtenberg aptly writes, "from any other high-toned, prejudiced WASP, save in the elegance of his writings." Indeed at times James's reactions to immigrants were so overwhelming that even his customary elegance was excruciatingly undermined:

> The Italians, who, over the whole land, strike us, I am afraid, as, after the Negro and the Chinaman, the human value most easily produced, . . . meet us, at every turn, only to make us ask what has become of that element of the agreeable address in them which has, from far back, so enhanced for the stranger the interest and pleasure of a visit to their beautiful country.

But on other levels, James's gaze at "new immigrants"—a racially inflected term that categorized the numerous newcomers from southern and eastern Europe as different both from the whiter and longer established northern and western European migrants to the United States and from the nonwhite Chinese and other "Asiatics"—opened for him new possibilities and alien dramas. He briefly wrestled with the possibility that the U.S. scene was always one of unsettledness. He raised the prospect that the immigrant accent would be America's "very ultimate future." Though it would be one we "shall not know as English," it might nonetheless become "the very music of humanity." By turns hopeful and despairing regarding the racial assimilation—what he tellingly called the "mitigation"—of new immigrants, James also registered fears that the "huge white-washing brush" of Anglo-American culture would render them "colourless."[3]

Others made more categorical predictions. The "special expert on foreign-born population" to the 1910 census, Frank Julian Warne, issued a jeremiad titled *The Immigrant Invasion* in 1913. Warne relied heavily on the views of the British socialist and science fiction writer H. G. Wells. In "The Future in America" Wells spoke of native-born U.S. society developing "above a racially different and astonishingly fecund" working class made up of Slavs and Italians. In importing this "darker-haired, darker-eyed, uneducated proletariat from central and eastern Europe," Wells continued, U.S. industry had undertaken a process that little "differs from the slave trade" and that would add "another dreadful separation of class and kind" to the ranks of the "'coloured' population" in the United States.[4] Like Warne, Austin Lewis relied on British socialist futurology. In his fascinating tract *The Militant Proletariat* (1911), Lewis argued for revolutionary industrial unionism and charged that by adopting the strategy of narrowly organizing skilled workers based on their craft, affiliates of the American Federation of Labor (AFL) had "segregated themselves from the . . . mass of their fellow workers." His long, approving quotation from *Problems of Modern Industry* by the English socialists Sidney and Beatrice Webb made it clear that this segregation was increasingly a "racial" one:

A few thousands of millionaire capitalist "kings," uniting the means of a few hundred thousands of passive stockholders, and served by, perhaps an equal number of well-salaried managers, foremen, inventors, designers, chemists, engineers and skilled mechanics, will absolutely control an army . . . of practically property-less wage laborers, largely Slavonic, Latin, or Negro in race.

On this view, the AFL unions—zealous as they were about rallying workers around organizing to defend "white men's wages"—might succeed in their narrow project and still leave the great mass of the working population not only unorganized, but racially distinct.[5]

And yet evocations of an invasion by nonwhite "Slavonic," "Latin," Italian, and Jewish races resonate strangely for modern U.S. readers. The typical U.S. history survey course might mention President Theodore Roosevelt's popularization of the term "race suicide" and his call for a higher "American" birthrate. However, the fact that Roosevelt admiringly borrowed "race suicide" from Edward A. Ross's 1901 article "The Causes of Race Superiority" is seldom emphasized. Ross, the pioneering sociologist and reformer, not only used the language of race to draw lines between "Asiatics" and whites but also policed divisions among European groups we would today regard as clearly white.[6] The spread of the critical study of whiteness and the rediscovery of brilliant works by James Baldwin and other writers of color on southern and eastern Europeans have begun to generate a growing literature on race and the "new immigrants" of the late nineteenth and early twentieth centuries. Contemporary debates over whether some Asian Americans, Arab Americans, and Latinos are or might become white have given this literature an urgency and edge. However, there is still too little awareness, beyond and within academia, that the nineteenth century ended with predictions that the United States was about to lose its racial moorings, and there is little work comparing the dynamics of race, fear, and immigration at the turn of the twentieth and the twenty-first centuries.[7] One necessity in any writing of the history of "new immigrants" and racial formation is that the account must be jarring enough to keep us from slipping back into easy assumptions that all European immigrants were simply white and that their stories were always ones of assimilation (or not) into American rather than specifically white American ways.

The recent work of Matthew Jacobson in *Whiteness of a Different Color* makes a bold move in necessary directions. Jacobson takes seriously the racial language that courts, reformers, academics, and others applied to new immigrants and provides an elegant narration of how Italian, Slav, Greek, German, French, Irish, and other European races were gathered under the term "Caucasian" in the twentieth century and thus unified as "conclusively" white.[8] However, the elegance and drama of Jacobson's account comes at some cost. In order to generate a neater narrative of movement toward whiteness, Jacobson assumes at times that the key sites of racial transformation are legal and intellectual. To summarize the triumph of the myth of a common "Caucasian-ness" in those venues represents a formidable task but avoids the welter of further problems raised when we think of whitening as a process in social history in which countless quotidian activities informed popular and expert understandings of the race of new immigrants, as well as new immigrant understandings of race. Those problems introduce messiness to the plot of how new immigrants became fully white.

Organized into three parts, *Working Toward Whiteness* preserves some of this messiness while imposing order on widely varied sources and advancing a story chronologically. Part 1 recasts what is typically regarded as white ethnic or "immigrant" history as part of the history of race in the United States. It especially concentrates on race as a category into which the social and intellectual structures of the United States placed new immigrants. Part 2 asks what it was like to "live in between" the stark racial binaries structuring U.S. life and law in the years from 1890 to 1945. It focuses on race as a form of consciousness that new immigrants developed in the United States and to some extent brought with them. The last section considers how, when, and why the racial "inbetweenness" of new immigrant communities gave way to a firmer acceptance of their position, as well as their identity, as white. Although World War II was a watershed, Part 3 argues for a gradual series of changes in urban race relations, housing, and state policies causing new immigrant communities to want and win a firmly white identity. Ironically, the nadir of new immigrant existence—the racial attacks culminating in restricted immigration in the 1920s—ushered in a period in which the "immigrant problem" seemed relatively settled and assimilation to whiteness could occur; at the same time, the great liberal mobilizations of the New Deal and industrial unionism in the 1930s made space in which new immigrants could mobilize as whites and exclude others. As they lived with race and called on the state for aid, the immigrant house, increasingly defined as a "white" house, became a key site for the making of race. As houses were constructed, so too was the idea—validated by popular campaigns for segregation of neighborhoods in the 1920s and then by New Deal housing policy—that African Americans were "antineighbors" and that all Europeans could unify around that realization.

The high ambitions of this book reflect a belief that much is at stake here for how we look at all of U.S. history in what I am calling the "long early twentieth century"—the period from 1890 to 1945. In a celebrated comment made more than half a century ago, Oscar Handlin remarked, "Once I thought to write a history of the immigrants in America. Then I discovered that the immigrants were American history." As a member of the first generation of influential non-Anglo-Saxon Protestant historians, Handlin was delivering an arresting manifesto, drawing confidence that he could change America's story because he had lived through the increased acceptance of southern and eastern Europeans in national life. However, the truth he told was a partial one and the acceptance of his new departure was fragile. Immigration history opens onto the critical issues of the entire U.S. past in some eras more than others, and all attempts to write U.S. history as immigration history have risked marginalizing the centrality of slavery, settler colonialism, and race. Moreover, Handlin wrote at an ebb of immigration from Europe; by the 1960s civil rights, new immigration, and further democratization of higher education would make race a powerful alternative axis on which to organize the story of the United States. This book seeks to work on both axes.

More than 100 million U.S. residents trace some of their heritage to Ellis Island, the main processing center during the period of the new immigration. The crucial role it played in "remaking" the nation's working class during the consolidation of U.S. industrial expansion makes the new immigration very important.[9] So too do relationships to the state, since southern and eastern Europeans and their children were the main objects of Progressive reform and nativist hatred, as well as the backbone of the New Deal political coalition. In many ways a "long early twentieth century" was defined by the mass arrival of new immigrants beginning in the 1890s and by their victories and defeats in struggling for full political, cultural, and economic citizenship. Moreover, the drama of new immigrant history turns significantly on how migrants were categorized racially and on contacts with people of color. *Working Toward Whiteness* asks what happens when we think of assimilation as whitening as well as

Americanizing, and when we view the deeply gendered clash between first-generation immigrant parents and second-generation children as being in part about who commanded knowledge of the U.S. racial landscape. It seeks to change the whole story of a crucial period in U.S. history without losing track of the wrenching dimension of race experienced by the new immigrants who were at its center.

MEETING INBETWEEN PEOPLES: CONNECTING AND DISCONNECTING TWO MEANINGS OF RACE

As national debate over restricting the numbers of "new immigrants" from southern and eastern Europe resounded in 1922, Sinclair Lewis's novel *Babbitt* featured the racial commentary of white riders on a train approaching Pittsburgh. One passenger contrasted the "fine" civility of "the old-fashioned coon" who knew his place in society with the supposed surliness of "these young dinges." Speaking without "one particle of race-prejudice," he prescribed, "We ought to get together and show the black man, yes, and the yellow man, his place." He further urged defense of "the rightful authority . . . of the white man." A "man in a velour hat" then shifted the ground of the discussion, thanking God for immigration restrictions, especially on Italians and Slavs. "These Dagoes and Hunkies," he reasoned, would have "to learn that this is a white man's country, and they ain't wanted here."[10] In his post–World War II novel, *Kingsblood Royal*, Lewis returns to the same subjects. His central character, Neil Kingsblood, lives in Sylvan Park, Minnesota, which boasts that it is "just as free of Jews, Italians and Negroes . . . as it is of noise, mosquitoes, and regularity of streets." But Kingsblood's opening conversation with his wife identifies racial nativism of the sort preached by the "man in the velour hat" as now class-bound and dated. His boss at the bank is "too conservative," Kingsblood holds. "He thinks only people like us, from British and French and Heine stock, amount to anything. He's prejudiced against Scandinavians and the Irish and Hunkies and Polacks. He doesn't understand that we have a new America." But the new America has its limits. Kingsblood continues, "Still and all and even hating prejudice, I do see where the Negroes are inferior and always will be." Shortly thereafter, Kingsblood discovers his own partially Negro ancestry and "resigns from the white race."[11]

The dialogue in Lewis's novels challenges our understanding of race and immigration. On the one hand, as the defender of the "rightful authority" of whites in *Babbitt* has it, race follows color (white, black, yellow) and separates humanity into "grand divisions" in which Europeans stand together as white. On the other hand, in the reckoning of the velour-hatted speaker, "Dagoes and Hunkies" are not wanted in a "white man's country." They are not "people like us" to Kingsblood, who nevertheless accepts them into his "new America," from which his boss would exclude them. The man in the velour hat and Kingsblood's boss engaged in ethnic prejudice, as opposed to the race prejudice that the first passenger and Kingsblood directed against blacks. But the distinction between the ethnic and the racial was scarcely available to scholars or train passengers when the first novel appeared and was only gaining prominence at the publication of the second. How then do we think about the categorization of those 13 million so-called new immigrants from southern, eastern, and central Europe (excluding Germany) who arrived between 1886 and 1925, with 70 percent of that number coming between 1901 and 1915 alone?[12] How do we think about their children's position? How do we take the measure of the identities adopted by new immigrant communities partly in reaction to their racial categorization?

The problem raised by the railway passengers in *Babbitt* recurred at the level of social scientific expertise. In 1888, according to experts, there were between two and sixty-three races. In 1924, an exasperated U.S. Supreme Court hearing a case on race and naturalized citizenship complained that various scientific authorities placed the number of races at between four and twenty-nine.[13] These wide gaps reflected, on the low end, a division of humanity into a few "color races," as the historian Reynolds Scott-Childress puts it. On the upper end, the many races listed were mostly what Scott-Childress calls "nation-races," subdivided much more zealously in Europe than anywhere else. The terminology Scott-Childress proposes was not extant in the early twentieth century. However, it remains useful—if we remember that the categories are frayed at the edges and the color of new immigrants as well as the cultural characteristics of color-races sometimes crept into discussions—in capturing how race served as the ruling terminology and how the meanings of that word bifurcated.[14]

This book keeps in mind the hard, exclusionary, and often color-based racism of Jim Crow segregation, Asian exclusion, and Indian removal as it retells the drama of European "new immigrants" and their children in, to use a freighted metaphor, "learning the ropes" of the racial system in the United States. It does *not* argue that new immigrant communities were subject to this hard racism in the way people of color were. Neither did they live outside the system of terror through which the idea of a "white man's country" was enforced. As new immigrants assimilated to whiteness, what the African American novelist James Baldwin has called "a vast amount of coercion" shaped their trajectories. The double meanings of race, in *Babbitt* and beyond, made new immigrants "conditionally white," to use Karen Brodkin's apt phrase. The context in which they were most securely white took shape when the stark differences between the rights of people of color and of Europeans were at issue. When the "race" of Europeans came under discussion, the deficiencies alleged to plague new immigrants were frequently connected to their fitness for certain kinds of jobs or for American citizenship—to precisely the areas that also defined hard racist exclusions in the United States, though on different frequencies.[15]

The argument pioneered by the eminent historian John Higham and the scholar of religion Robert Orsi, that new immigrants experienced racialization at times as "inbetween peoples," must therefore proceed on several fronts. "Inbetween" hard racism and full inclusion—neither securely white nor nonwhite—new immigrants were also chronologically inbetween the sharply posed calls for their racially based exclusion typified by *Babbitt*'s post–World War I dialogue and the far greater acceptance signaled by the post–World War II exchanges in *Kingsblood Royal*. To argue for inbetweenness necessarily involves a willingness to keep both similarity and difference at play. As the historian Patrick Wolfe has observed, the new immigrant experience was "not of the same order as the racialization that insulted black people." Nonetheless it was an experience of racialization. Thus *Working Toward Whiteness* both illustrates and complicates Thomas Guglielmo's recent insistence that Italian Americans, and by implication other new immigrants, were categorized as "white on arrival" in the United States. In some ways their ability to naturalize as citizens and other advantages made them such. However, the racial grounds on which they could claim naturalization remind us that the separation between race and color that Guglielmo posits (when he argues that Italian immigrants were securely white in the critical category of color but vulnerable to intra-European rankings of races) is difficult to sustain.[16]

Other attempts to find an alternative terminology regarding the new immigrants' racial position have tried to capture a distance from full inclusion in the white race as well as a trajectory toward such inclusion. The sociologist John Dollard's quaint references to "our temporary Negroes" and the historian Barry Goldberg's discussions of "not-yet-white" immigrants are striking examples.[17] Other labels, such as "situationally white," "not quite white," "off-white," "semiracialized," and "conditionally white," convey the ambiguity and uncertainty of an immigrant racial status that was constantly under review. This book prefers Orsi and Higham's "inbetween peoples" as the term most likely to reproduce the resonance of new immigrant experiences.[18] The term should not fix our attention solely on black or white racial divisions. New immigrants often existed between nonwhiteness and full inclusion as whites, not just between black and white. Comparisons to Chinese, Japanese, and Mexican Americans were sometimes as telling as those with African Americans. "Inbetweenness" also carries a useful expectation of possible change over time, much as "new immigrant" did.

Arguing for such complexity, and withal for the centrality of "race" to the new immigrant experience, exposes a historian to the charge of playing the race card in a way that reflects current "politically correct" preoccupations but not the realities of a century ago. However, race is far from a recent preoccupation imposed on a history in which immigrants and the host society thought in terms of ethnicity; indeed, as we shall see, very nearly the opposite is true. Contemporary politics has often kept us from reading the historical record clearly in this regard. Although the multiple meanings of race in the early twentieth century leave some room for saying that "race" as applied to new immigrants at times meant something akin to what is now understood as "ethnicity," we should hesitate before anachronistically applying the latter term. The striking absence of a term for ethnicity in the early twentieth century underlines the fact that the two meanings of race in *Babbitt* were not sufficiently far apart to be regarded as distinct by experts or society in general.

THE GOVERNMENT AND (NOT) COUNTING BY RACE

The racial politics of immigration made strange bedfellows. Terence Powderly, the Irish nationalist, Grand Master Workman of the Knights of Labor, and former abolitionist, wrote in the 1880s of the "menacing irruption" of "semibarbarous hordes" coming from Hungary and elsewhere to the United States. He insisted—none too convincingly in light of the similarities of his hysterical opposition to new European immigrants and his organization's clearly race-based support of Chinese exclusion from the United States—that his position was not motivated by "race hatred."[19] The personification of the Boston "Brahmin" elite, Henry Cabot Lodge, seemed as distant from Powderly as possible. However, Lodge, the first political science Ph.D. from Harvard and a Massachusetts congressman, used Powderly's expansive language. In an article written for a popular journal in 1891, Lodge quantified the "distribution of ability" by "race" in U.S. history. Counting biographical encyclopedia entries as proof of ability, Lodge tallied 10,376 excellent Americans from the "English race" as against 1,439 of the "Scotch-Irish race." The English race furnished 1,482 times as much excellence as the Italian race, and 3,458 times as much as the Greek race. One able Pole graced Lodge's charts.[20]

Powderly and Lodge would curiously come together in a series of bureaucratic and political battles revealing how poorly our conception of race as "color" and as an attribute mainly of non-Europeans survive time travel. They grappled with the ambiguities of race as a term that eclectically described the alleged divisions of humanity. Enumeration of such divisions took off from German anatomist Johann Friedrich Blumenbach's long-established fivefold schema identifying races by names and also by color: red, white, black, brown, and yellow. Others added refinements and sometimes included two white races: "chocolate brown, brown black, yellow, fair white and dark white." Race further named hierarchical divisions in Europe (Teutonic, Alpine, and Mediterranean, according to the widely influential 1898 study The Races of Europe by William Z. Ripley, who at times denied the existence of an overarching "white race"), as well as many intra-European microdivisions (such as the northern and southern Italian races).[21] However ill specified, race functioned to distribute the right to full citizenship and access to good jobs. Race clearly defined the disabilities of excluded Chinese workers, Jim Crowed African

Americans, American Indians confined to reservations, and Puerto Rican and Filipino subjects denied self-government. It also counted among Europeans in the United States. At least it did for Lodge and Powderly, who by the turn of the twentieth century were positioned to see to it that race *was counted* in new ways.

In 1898, just as the Spanish-American War and the validation of segregation in *Plessy v. Ferguson* helped solidify Deep South–style white supremacy nationally, collecting "race" statistics among European immigrants took a decisive step forward. The U.S. commissioner-general of immigration was none other than Powderly, reborn as a campaigner for Republican politicians and an immigration expert. Along with AFL veteran Edward F. McSweeney, by then assistant commissioner of immigration at the Port of New York, Powderly devised a new system of enumerating by race. His 1898 report, quoted in Joel Perlmann's important study of "federal race classifications" from 1898 to 1913, promised:

> With the beginning of the new fiscal year, there will be inaugurated a compilation of reports of immigration that will throw much additional light upon the subject. The new reports give . . . arrivals of immigrants by race. . . . Such a distribution by race appears much more rational than the present one, which simply reports the countries whence the immigrants respectively come, and gives no clue to their characteristics and their resultant influence upon the community of which they are to become members.[22]

On the one hand the policy change had a simple rationale. The older system of counting by "the recent geographical or political origin of aliens" under the category of nationality worked poorly. Many immigrants had moved inside Europe before coming to the United States or came from "multinational empires" whose hegemonic powers did not reflect the identities of those actually migrating (e.g., Jews from Russia and Slavs from Austro-Hungary, Germany, or Russia). Nonetheless the new procedure was bold and revealing. Powderly instituted the change despite the striking fact that there was no question on the passenger lists determining race. From 1898 through 1902, in most immigration stations, officials apparently reviewed lists, looked perhaps at the migrants, and made a notation about the "race" disembarking. In New York City, officials used a supplemental form providing information on "color," "country and province of birth," "mother tongue," and "religion" to divine the "race" of those arriving. For example, Russian birth plus Yiddish mother tongue plus Jewish religion equaled "Hebrew race." The resulting data were sometimes grouped under the heading "Race" and sometimes under "Race or People." Powderly emphasized that race was used "in its popular rather than in its strict ethnological sense," as if either sense were or could be specified. In 1903, new passenger lists added a "Race or People" heading "to be determined by the stock from which they spring and the language they speak." "Stock or blood," not language, was to be the determining factor, though how to arrive at such a determination stayed unclear.[23]

The race counting by immigration authorities sparked immediate opposition from elite Jewish organizations and individuals. In 1899, one column of Powderly's annual report counted immigrants by religion. Lobbying by Jewish opponents apparently stopped this practice in its tracks, but objections to the Hebrew "race or people" category continued, on the grounds that counting by religion was un-American and that the coincidence of "Jewish religion" and "Hebrew race" was so overwhelming as to make racial counting in effect religious counting. From 1907 to 1909 the stakes were raised for opponents of race counting. In the former year the United States Immigration Commission, headed by Vermont's proimmigration restriction senator, William P. Dillingham, began its massive study. The Dillingham Commission's work appeared in the 1911 publication as a multivolume report prominently including the *Dictionary of Races and Peoples*, which counted thirty-six races "indigenous to Europe" among forty-five races entering the United States. In 1909, the immigration commissioner played a prominent role in proposing an amendment to the 1910 Census Bill "to insert . . . 'race'" among the items to be enumerated. With the organizational clout of the American Jewish Committee (AJC) and floor leadership from Colorado's Senator Simon Guggenheim, the "race or people" classification was decisively defeated. One top AJC leader worried aloud that "ignorant census takers" controlled racial statistics, charged that the "schedule of races" to be used by the census was arbitrary, and wondered aloud, "What can they do if a Jew answers that he belongs to the Caucasian race?" Investigating "the great divisions of the human family,—

white, black, American Indian and others" was seen as permissible, but for the state to count intra-European racial distinctions threatened to end in "justifying discrimination against certain classes of citizens." The race amendment was struck in conference committee.[24] When the same set of issues emerged late in 1909 in hearings regarding the Immigration Commission, Henry Cabot Lodge proclaimed the striking of race from the census bill a "great mistake." Lodge, by then a Massachusetts senator, allowed that Europeans did not differ as to "scientific race" but held that they were nonetheless "historically racial." Census returns on the "great divisions like the Mongol, the Negro, the North American Indian, the Aryan, the Semitic" carried "no value whatever," but the counting of "historic races" mattered greatly. Lodge added, "I should be the last man to favor any discrimination. . . . This is purely an attempt to get at the ethnology of it."[25]

Given that Lodge was a long-standing proponent of racial nativism against southern and eastern European immigrants, whose presence he regarded as threatening to make "a great and perilous change in the very fabric of our race," his reassurances regarding discrimination were more than questionable.[26] Slovak immigrants, Lodge had commented in 1891, were "not a good acquisition" because they appeared to share "so many items in common with the Chinese." More broadly, division of European immigration into Teutonic, Iberian, Celtic, and Slavic "races or peoples, or more properly subdivisions of race" during critical years was, as Perlmann puts it, "partly political" in that it "provided a way of distinguishing racially the old [mostly northern and western European immigration] from the new immigration," a stratagem that particularly appealed to restrictionists such as Powderly and Lodge.[27] Nonetheless, organized opposition to race counting remained largely confined to Jewish groups, mostly relatively well-to-do German Jews who perhaps had the additional motivation of not wanting to be racially enumerated along with more recently arrived East European Jewish "greenhorns."[28] Even those protesting retreated by 1909 as the immigration bureaucracy incorporated Jewish officials, especially in New York, where the political power of naturalized Jewish immigrants was significant. In the run-up to an important 1906 New York gubernatorial election President Theodore Roosevelt appointed Oscar Straus, the nation's first Jewish cabinet member, as secretary of Commerce and Labor, with oversight regarding immigration.[29]

Thus invidious race counting and the immigrant's power as a white citizen could triumph together. No language to smooth tensions over race counting by enumerating new immigrants as "ethnic" rather than "racial" groups yet existed, and the worldview of a Powderly or a Lodge hardly allowed for softer terminology.

THE NEW IMMIGRANT AND THE RIDDLE OF THE ABSENT ETHNIC

"Most European peasants who migrated here," wrote the sociologist Richard Sennett, "had no consciousness when they came of being 'ethnics.'" Ethnicity was cobbled together, Sennett adds, out of "the badges of cultural inferiority American society forced the agrarian immigrant to wear."[30] If Sennett's latter generalization is one-sided, the former is an apt and unassailable reminder. Indeed, virtually nobody else in the early-twentieth-century United States thought of eastern and southern European immigrants as ethnics. The massive Cornell University Library Making of America database now contains over a million pages, concentrating on leading U.S. journals and magazines from 1815 to 1926. "Ethnicity," so vital to our interpretations of immigration in these years, does not appear once. "Ethnic group" likewise does not appear. Indeed as late as 1940, "ethnic" did not appear in the authoritative *Dictionary of American English on Historical Principles,* by Sir William Craigie and James R. Hulbert. It does appear with some frequency in the Cornell database but as an adjective, not a noun.[31] "White ethnic" comes up not at all. That term, according to the anthropologist Micaela di Leonardo, did not gain currency until about 1970, with the *Oxford English Dictionary* noting a 1964 first usage. This absence of ethnicity should concern us for two reasons. First, it permits us to reenter the actual ways that race and immigration were discussed in the early twentieth century. Second, the commitment of so many current scholars to using the term in discussions of that period—despite its nonexistence—reminds us of the historical forces that caused us to forget the racial history of new immigrants.[32]

Before examining the protracted and telling evolution of the language of ethnicity, we need to consider the riddle of the absence of a noun form of "ethnic" during the first half of the twentieth century. If new immigrants were "white on arrival" but also suspect in certain ways, why did a term to convey this doubleness not emerge? The federal courts urgently needed such a term—they virtually begged experts for one—in deciding naturalization cases turning on the question of who was white. Why were there no "white ethnics" for most of white ethnic history? The answer, at least partly, lies in the extent to which immigrants were slotted into unskilled jobs and subjected to sharp questioning as to their racial fitness for citizenship. They were not securely identified with the dominant race in many situations, and the language of experts reflected the extent to which new immigrants suffered undue scrutiny and exclusion.

Another explanation for the riddle of the absent ethnic is that a term doing some of the intellectual and cultural work later done by "ethnic" was "new immigrant" itself, a category that was remarkable for its ability to describe simultaneously the simple fact of recent arrival and the ways in which those recently arriving were singled out as racially different. It was a term encompassing history and biology, culture and "stock." Consider, for example, the words of Professor Ellwood Cubberley, whose *Changing Conceptions of Education* (1909) illustrated the expanse of what made a new immigrant new:

> About 1882, the character of our immigration changed in a very remarkable manner. Immigration from the north of Europe dropped off rather abruptly, and in its place immigration from the south and east of Europe set in and soon developed into a great stream. . . . These southern and eastern Europeans are a very different type from the north European who preceded them. Illiterate, docile, lacking in self-reliance and initiative and not possessing Anglo-Teutonic conceptions of law, order and government, their coming has served to dilute tremendously our national stock, and to corrupt our civic life.[33]

Cubberley later drew a policy lesson from these distinctions: "Our task is to break up their groups or settlements, to assimilate and amalgamate these people as part of our American race and to implant in their children, so far as it can be done, the Anglo-Saxon conception of law and order and popular government." This magic was to be worked on distinct "racial" groups, as well as inferior ones.[34]

Cubberley's emphasis on the children of new immigrants suggests that time and education might change the racial characteristics of new immigrants' descendants. Indeed some institutions and leaders acted at times as if this assimilation to the "American race" were more or less foreordained. The U.S. census, for example, counted the foreign-born and the children of the foreign-born as white, but in separate categories from whites whose parents were U.S.-born. However, the third-generation immigrant disappeared into the "white American" census category. During early-twentieth-century debates over whether the government might enumerate European immigrants by race, W. W. Husband, secretary to the U.S. Immigration Commission, emphasized the revealing limits of such counting: "Beyond the second generation the Commission made no reference to race except in the case of Orientals, negroes, and American Indians." As Perlmann observes, race thus "disappears in the third generation," but not for people of color. That the descendants of new immigrants were bound for full membership in the white American race was even more apparent after the 1924 immigration restrictions, which ensured that the third generation would not coexist with a large new generation of immigrants. Indeed the rise of a language of ethnicity interestingly follows on the wholesale restriction of immigration, a policy change that undercut the usefulness of "new immigrant" as a social category. Still the timing and even the outcome of the new immigrant's "mitigation" were unpredictable. In a book titled *Immigrants and Their Children* (1927), the sociologist Niles Carpenter sharply felt the need to find measures to quantify the different "grandchildren of the foreign-born." In 1932, Donald Young's mammoth study of "racial and cultural conflicts" prescribed education to remedy the handicaps of "language and traditions" plaguing the immigrant child. Training in "the English language and American ideals" was undertaken, according to Young, because it was "dimly realized that in a few generations he will be absorbed into the total white population."[35] Young's imprecision, like Cubberley's caution that the descendants of new immigrants might prove to be racially unfit to assimilate, reminds us of a strain in nativist and social scientific thought assuming that the racial progress of immigrants and their children was not simply a matter of time.[36] Since "new immigrant" nowadays simply refers to a recently arrived immigrant, using it to describe the eastern and southern European migrant of a century ago would lose some of the complex ways in which the term brought the race of immigrants into question. "Inbetween" referred to the situation in which the new immigrants had to live and one they might transcend. Both the living and the transcending are the concerns of this book.

INVENTING ETHNICITY, INVENTING ETHNICS, FORGETTING RACE

When "ethnic" was used as an adjective before and during the 1920s, its meanings scarcely differentiated "color-races" from more and less white European "nation-races." "Ethnic" was most often used in historical works describing the ancient world and migrations of Indo-European peoples. Its dominant meaning in the *Oxford English Dictionary* was (and remains) heathen, reflecting ancient Greek and Hebrew language designed to sort out nonbelievers from the chosen. Only in the United States did the leading meaning change, according to the *Oxford American Dictionary* of 1980, to "of a racial group" or, as a noun, to "a member of an ethnic group."[37] Thus Henry James's early essay "Spiritualism: Old and New" contrasts Christianity with "ethnic religions." In theological writings, however, a broader meaning for ethnic as having to do with a particular sect or group also emerged. "Heresies are at best ethnic; truth is essentially catholic," wrote one expert in 1875.[38]

With distinctions between cultures and belief systems thus loosely portrayed as "ethnic," it is not surprising that more modern and American uses made "ethnic" an adjective identifying "new immigrants" as well as established groups. Indeed, the Greek root word *ethnos* possessed a curious double meaning, as Werner Sollors has pointed out. It usually meant "others" but could also refer to any "nation" or "people," including one's one people. In general the word was used so promiscuously that it seemed to offer little prospect of sorting out questions of race and immigration in the United States. When James used "ethnic" in a discussion of immigrants in *An American Scene* in 1907, he set it off in quote marks as an unfamiliar term in that context. Theodore Roosevelt's article "The Roll of Honor of the New York Police" (1897) described the dominant "ethnic strains" of the New York City police force as Irish, German, and "Native American" (meaning native-born white, presumably going back for generations). Matthew Arnold's ideas on the "ethnic distribution of the civilizing powers" circulated in the United States, perhaps informing Lodge's enumerations of "ethnic" ability. The Dillingham Commission spoke mainly of "races or peoples" in describing new immigrants but also used idiosyncratically and very episodically "ethnical." The brilliant 1916 lectures of the African American philosopher Alain Locke branded race an "ethnic fiction" but shifted from one term to the other without firm differentiation.[39]

In one important milieu a a new conception of ethnic matured during and after World War I. Largely Jewish and often Zionist intellectuals coalesced around small publications, especially the *Menorah Journal*. Victoria Hattam's challenging studies of the group detail its loose organization and developing ideas. Hattam shows that such figures as Horace Kallen, Julius Drachsler, Isaac Berkson, and Maurice Fishberg began to experiment with new (to the United States) uses of "ethnic" in a specific, if many-sided, context. They drew on European precedents such as the Russian-born French anthropologist Joseph Deniker, who early in the twentieth century advanced toward the idea that race divisions were "zoological" while "ethnic" differences had "linguistic" or "social" markers. The creativity of Jewish scholars was shaped by intersections in U.S. cities of migrations from Europe with those from the African American South, the grim realities and memories of the world war, and patterns of material progress among Jewish immigrants. Anti-Semitic pogroms internationally, Klan organization in the United States, and assimilative pressures on immigrants seemed to threaten Jewish survival. In such crosscurrents, claiming white racial status was axiomatic for Zionist intellectuals, but such a claim was insufficient to define what made Jewishness distinctive and viable. New terms and new meanings for old terms seemed required, and Kallen produced them with uncommon fecundity: ethnic group, ethnic faction, and ethnic type, for example. Jews were white (or Mediterranean white) according to Kallen and the others, but with a difference defined by spirit or culture and termed "ethnic." Drachsler's 1921 doctoral dissertation on intermarriage in New York City kept "racial groups, black (Negro) and yellow" analytically distinct from European-language groups, which he termed "ethnic." Likewise, Kallen "defines ethnicity against race," to borrow Hattam's trenchant phrasing. Such a view claimed whiteness but identified its salience as receding in a modern order that made claiming ethnic difference a matter of crucial importance. Berkson's *Theories of Americanization* (1920) further elaborated a highly original synthesis of "theories of ethnic adjustment." Writing with "special reference to the Jewish group" but clearly counting other European immigrant groups as "ethnic," he offered a searing critique of intellectuals who attributed "inferiorities and evils" to the "'race' of the immigrant." He added an important conclusion whose parenthesis anticipated the selective application of "ethnic" to Europeans in the United States: "The one fact of racial origin (at any rate, with reference to all white races) means nothing."[40]

Although Hattam rightly stresses that formulations of ethnicity by Drachsler, Kallen, and Berkson were strikingly similar to later ones, their direct influence remained modest. Writers before 1930 seldom used "ethnic" to suggest that race and ethnicity were competing concepts or that "ethnic" might clarify the difference between the nation-race of new immigrants and the color-race of, for example, blacks and Asians. Nor did the term signal a firm reorientation to culture instead of biology as a source of difference among Europeans. Again and again authors at the time used race and ethnicity so inconsistently that a coherent separation of the terms was impossible. The *Encyclopaedia of the Social Sciences* enumerated "chink," "nigger," "sheeny," and "bohunk" as "ethnic tags."[41] The geologist Nathaniel S. Shaler wondered in print whether African American slavery might not someday be looked back on as "the most wonderful ethnic experiment that the world has known." The travel writer Lafcadio Hearn learned to appreciate "the dignity of a white skin" in the West Indies, where "white faces" were rare compared with those of "black and fantastic ethnic background."[42] The anthropologist Albert Jenks wrote in 1921 in *Scientific Monthly* that "ethnic groups differ from each other [because of] heredity resident in the reproductive germ cells." Any "boss of a gang of mixed foreigners on any American railway job" allegedly knew of these differences, which began "inside the seeds of the breeds." In the classic *Black Metropolis*, Horace Cayton and St. Clair Drake divided a key population table "by ethnic group." The groups were "Native-White," "Foreign-Born White and Other Races," and "Negro."[43]

The firmest signs that "ethnic" was evolving in a way presaged by the Zionist writers came after immigration restriction in the early 1930s with the use of "ethnic groups" in several key works. In 1933 the President's Research Committee on Social Trends published *Races and Ethnic Groups in American Life,* by T. J. Woofter Jr. Key sections turned on distinctions between "the European foreigner and the Negro." Thus there is some justification for James B. McKee in *Sociology and the Race Problem* seeing Woofter's work as a turning point in the language of race and ethnicity which recognized "that blacks and European immigrants were too different in social origin, historical development, visibility, and contemporary status to subsume them wholly under the encompassing concept of race." However, Woofter lacked full consistency in this regard. The first section of his book concerned "The Ethnic Pattern" but nonetheless incorporated a discussion of blacks and Mexicans. Following it came material on "Racial Contributions to American Development," which nonetheless included both "immigrant and non-white groups." Woofter's index of "racial heterogeneity" tellingly tabulated all counties with a thousand or more "aliens or colored people." Using this measure, he found that two-thirds of all U.S. counties suffered under "community problems cross-sectioned by race."[44]

Far more significant and brilliant was Caroline Ware's lengthy 1931 entry on "ethnic communities" in the comprehensive *Encyclopaedia of the Social Sciences*. Ware codified and extended earlier usages in ways that strikingly anticipated modern definitions of "ethnicity." She began with the flat allowance that in "its strict meaning the word ethnic denotes race" and then proposed a looser usage where "ethnic communities" were concerned. Such communities were "bound together by common ties of race, nationality or culture, living together within an alien civilization but remaining culturally distinct." Ware characterized ethnic communities as willed and self-conscious creations, thriving especially where acceptance by the host society was lacking. For Ware, the "chief base for [ethnic] cohesiveness is race," but "nationality, language and religion" also structured ethnic commitments. The separation of race from culture highlighted a specifically physical dimension where race was concerned. In seeking to explain why "the Chinese who seeks to leave his Chinatown is under a severe handicap not experienced by the Italian who emerges from Little Italy," Ware focused squarely on the role of color. Others soon joined in emphasizing that culture and not "stock" set new immigrants apart. A year after Ware's encyclopedia essay appeared, Young's massive *American Minority Peoples* argued that while the "white immigrant [is] patently handicapped by foreign language and tradition," the "Negro however is looked on as more of a biological problem." Robert Park's essay "The Nature of Race Relations" (1939) distinguished between the "ethnic unit and genetic group" in an influential discussion of what makes race visible. That same year Irvin L. Child enclosed "race" in quotation marks in describing the Italian Americans he studied.[45]

Ware, Park, and Young incorporated many of the key elements defining how "ethnic" came to be used in contradistinction to race. Nonetheless it was only in World War II, Sollors has argued, that the definitions offered by Ware became more or less systematized around the term "ethnicity," which eventually removed "nation-races" from meaningful connection to the world of biology. An early articulation hesitantly moving in this direction emerged from studies by W. Lloyd Warner and Paul S. Lunt of Newburyport, Massachusetts, in their Yankee City series. In *The Social Systems of American Ethnic Groups* (1942) Warner and Lunt posited "ethnicity" as a "trait" generated "almost entirely on a biological basis or upon purely social characteristics." They added that "Negroes tend to be at the first extreme" as "the most physically variant of all groups in the community" while the Irish define the other extreme, "since they are the most like the native white stock," though socially different. Other groups, they added, "fall in between these two extremes." By now the inbetween groups seemed to exist outside of the world of race. Anglo-Saxons apparently were off the charts where race or ethnicity was concerned. These founding ambiguities in the modern definition of ethnicity created enormous implications by leaving open the question of whether all whites had ethnicity and whether African Americans did not simply continue to be defined by race and color. This was not simply a matter of imprecision. The ambiguities spoke to how ethnicity tortuously emerged as a term registering uneven and unpredictable changes in how new immigrant communities and communities of color existed in a changing social structure.[46]

Tellingly the new language of ethnicity matured during the anti-Nazi war.[47] "Race," Sollors writes, had been "discredited by the emergence of fascism," but the question of whether this applied to both ethnic nation-races and color-races, or only to the former, remained. The Yankee City authors thought assimilation of new immigrants was assured. Ruth Benedict clarified that Jews, Italians, and Aryans were "not races" in her widely circulated pamphlet *The Races of Mankind* (1943). Her fellow anthropologist Ashley Montagu argued in 1946 for scrapping "the term 'race' altogether" in favor of "some non-committal term like 'ethnic group.'" However, these significant intellectual advances, as Jacobson shows, generally divided humanity into three races—Caucasian, Negroid, and Mongolian—concentrating attention on the former two and expressing far more confidence that full inclusion across "ethnic" lines was assured than across the starkly remaining racial ones. When Benedict's *Races of Mankind* became the basis for a popular 1945 exhibit at Walker Art Center in Minneapolis, the show taught that Jews and European national groups were not races but continued to affirm white, black, and yellow races. Ethnicity became "less a substitute for race than a way of distinguishing between ethnics of European origins and other racial . . . groups."[48]

Useful as it was, the term "ethnicity" was not sweepingly adopted to distinguish consistently between race and other forms of categorization and identification. Its coinage and spread did not reflect a breakthrough in pure knowledge so much as an evolution in immigration patterns and social structure. Language reflecting its sway took hold gradually, if impressively. *American Sociological Review* articles used the term by 1950, and the sociologists Everett and Helen Hughes immediately issued a perceptive critique, warning that the term dulled self-reflection by supposing that only those "unlike ourselves" possess ethnicity. The reach of the new term remained so narrow that a 1953–1954 *American Scholar* article by David Riesman is "customarily credited for the introduction of 'ethnicity.'" Widespread use among anthropologists took another decade. Handlin's classic work of immigration history stuck to older categories in its title: *Race and Nationality in American Life* (1957). Nor did all usages of "ethnicity" immediately banish the notion that southern and eastern Europeans might be different biologically. Even Warner stopped short of allowing ethnicity to fully replace "racial" divisions among whites, positing a division between easily assimilable "light Caucasians" and the harder cases of "dark Caucasians."[49]

"Ethnic" took even longer to become a noun. In *The More Perfect Union*, Robert MacIver noted that there was "no English noun corresponding to the adjective 'ethnic'" in 1948. When "ethnic" did become a noun, it was selectively applied in a way leaving little doubt that it emerged mainly from thinking about new immigrants and their descendants. The Yankee City series regarded Jews and Irish as "ethnics" in what the *Oxford English Dictionary* identifies as the first usage of "ethnic" connoting "a member of an ethnic group or minority." However, the Irish often dropped out of the category. They were marginal in Michael Novak's manifesto of the "new ethnicity," *The Rise of the Unmeltable Ethnics* (1971). A 1961 account called "ethnic" a "polite term for Jews, Italians and other lesser breeds."[50] The earliest dictionary reference to usage of "white ethnic," citing Irving Louis Horowitz's *New Sociology* (1964), included the Irish, Jews, and Italians under that heading, which it interestingly linked to their achievement of power in the United States. This neatly encapsulated the way in which loss of a racial classification represented a gain in social status. By 1980, William Petersen wrote that "many American writers now distinguish 'racial' from 'ethnic' minorities, the former being Negroes, Asians and other 'nonwhites,' the latter the European nationalities." He further observed that "white ethnics are Italians and Poles, for example, but usually not Scots or Norwegians."[51] However, such clarity in setting ethnic versus race as a way to demarcate nation-races from color-races was a long time in coming, and was immediately complicated by new migrations and by the rise of ethnic studies programs concentrating on racialized groups. Whatever clarity we believe we possess in distinguishing between race and ethnicity was unavailable to those who labored in colleges or factories in the first forty years of the twentieth century.

WHY WE DON'T UNDERSTAND THE ROLE OF RACE IN "WHITE ETHNIC" HISTORY AND WHY IT MATTERS

Much scholarship of the past four decades simply ignores the long, circuitous process by which "new immigrants" became "white ethnics." Such scholarship substitutes "ethnic" for "racial" in describing that past. One recent study, for example, specifies that when Henry Cabot Lodge wrote of "race-extraction," he "meant what we would now refer to as nationality or ethnicity." The leading scholar of the evolving language of migration and minorities, Philip Gleason, has written that the "most important point about the period 1860–1924 is that ethnicity assumed greater salience as an element in national identity than it has at any time before or since."[52] Thomas Guglielmo, after rejecting the idea that ethnicity can be substituted for race in discussions of Italian Americans in the early twentieth century, proposes two terms for the divided meaning of race in those years, partially reviving anachronistic language: "color race" and "ethnic race."[53] Carrie Tirado Bramen, in her provocative book *The Uses of Variety,* makes race in the early twentieth century a "sign of white ethnicity." Talk of European racial varieties, even by such bitterly anti-immigrant, racist intellectuals as Henry Pratt Fairchild, was supposedly a way to "consolidate the new immigrants into the already established white population." The new immigrants did not in this view really suffer from "race hatred." They were "what are today known as 'white ethnics.'"[54] Doubtless the most dramatic example of reading ethnicity back into an earlier period was Stow Persons's generally adroit study of Robert Park, the Chicago School of Sociology, and "ethnic relations." Park famously wrote of the "race relations cycle," but Persons changed all that. Allowing that Park used the term "ethnic group" in a modern sense only in one unpublished paper, Persons nonetheless made wholesale switches of "racial" or "race" to "ethnic" in discussing Chicago School work, beginning with his title. He reasoned that "the Chicago sociologists used 'race' where 'ethnic group' would now be preferred."[55]

The prevalence of studies that read later uses of ethnicity back across the decades perhaps reflects less on that term's ability to illuminate the lives of new immigrants than on its utility in supporting mainstream ideas about contemporary race relations, liberal and conservative. Although it came on the scene codifying differences between new immigrant "ethnics" and colored "races," from the start ethnicity carried the further promise that it might *eventually* expand to take in all "minorities." Some left liberals, especially around Louis Adamic's journal *Common Ground,* hoped that a "more colorless" term like ethnicity would apply broadly, providing a less "emotional" alternative to the category of race. The most widely read early deployment of ethnicity was surely in *An American Dilemma,* the lavishly publicized and funded 1944 study of the U.S. "Negro problem" by the Swedish sociologist Gunnar Myrdal. Myrdal's insistence that the American creed of fair play and equal treatment would eventually apply to blacks domestically and to the decolonized but U.S.-dominated world took comfort in what had already occurred:

> To make a homogenous nation out of diverse ethnic groups, the immigrants were to abandon their cultural "peculiarities"—or to contribute

them to American culture as a whole, as some would have it—and to take on the cultural forms of America. There could be diversity, to be sure, but this diversity was not to have a strictly ethnic basis; individuals should be free to be part of any community they wished.

Recent arguments by the historian David Gerber effectively recapitulate Myrdal's logic. "It is difficult to imagine . . . that we are not better off as a consequence of the liberal's hostile reaction [in the early twentieth century] to the racialization of white Others," he writes. Such liberal interventions came at a time when "calling the very concept of race into question" was impossible. However, Gerber continues, the clarification that European immigrants were *ethnic* and not *racial* groups ultimately served racial minorities as well: "Perhaps these limited doubts cast decades ago about the integrity of the race concept ultimately helped to pave the way for the larger doubts . . . serving to undermine it completely today."[56] Thus the spread of ethnicity, and not the acknowledgment that U.S. history has brutally turned on race, becomes the key to progress.

Milton Gordon's enormously influential *Assimilation in American Life* (1964) serves as a fair barometer of why and how loose modern meanings of ethnicity have been smuggled back into discussion of the period of the new immigration. Gordon's work summarizes how the term came to be used. Ethnicity, for Gordon, served as a "convenient term [for] a shared sense of peoplehood." It was overwhelmingly a matter of voluntary belonging and not exclusion. When Gordon reduced the "ethnic identity of an American" to a diagram, "self" was the core of four concentric circles. Nearest "self," but not necessarily most important, was "national origin," which only whites seemed to possess. Next was "religion" and then "race"—for Gordon the choices "ethnicity" had left largely undisturbed: "White, Negro, Mongoloid." The largest circle was "nationality," with "American" as the lone option. "Race," he added, "technically refers to differential concentrations of gene frequencies [and] has no intrinsic connection with cultural patterns and institutions." It is the category from which "one may not voluntarily resign." Although it differs from the cultural categories, race takes its place in Gordon's model as yet another intermediate ring in the tree of "ethnic" identity. "This American is a white Protestant Anglo-Saxon; this one is an Irish Catholic (white race understood), this one is a Negro Protestant (African background understood), that one is a Russian Jew (white race understood)," wrote Gordon.[57]

But spokespersons for those identified as ethnics in the post–World War II United States—eastern and southern Europeans and sometimes the Irish—often failed to share the optimism cherished by heirs to Myrdal's evocations of the ethnic. Aggrieved by the fact that the civil rights movement allegedly did not address *their* pain, they distanced themselves from that movement. If *ethnicity* was, for such writers as Andrew Greeley, Milton Gordon and John Higham, a voluntary option of self-organization—Greeley called it simply solidarity with "our own kind"—*white ethnics* often united around a sense of grievance born of the perception that others defined and dismissed them in favor of embracing racial minorities.[58] At their worst, such sentiments coalesced into a "white ethnic immigrant narrative," as the legal scholar Sylvia R. Lazos Vargas terms it, which stressed the overcoming of ethnic prejudices by virtuous new immigrant grandparents and chided African Americans and Latinos for failing to properly choose ancestors and/or get on with the cultural tasks of ethnic uplift. Ironically such a conservative narrative also gave a twist to Myrdal's hopes that ethnicity might provide a model of how the nation could expand to take in African Americans and Latinos. The argument was made that racialized communities had to shape up in terms of habits and values, not that an oppressive system had to change.[59] The scholarship of Nathan Glazer and Daniel Patrick Moynihan, which helped define the limits of 1960s liberalism and the rigidity of later neo-conservatism, thus famously allowed ethnicity to cross the color line, only to then query what cultural deficiencies kept communities of color from succeeding as white ethnic Americans had and as all ethnic Americans should. Glazer insisted, writing in 1974, that "we cannot separate ethnic and racial groups into two classes: those who have suffered . . . and therefore deserve redress, and those who have not."[60] This view has found its way into popular writing as well. For example, the columnist and fellow at the conservative American Enterprise Institute, Ben Wattenberg, recently branded Poles, Jews, Slavs, and, improbably enough, Italians, as AEEAs (American of Eastern European ancestry), the largest "minority group" in the United States. Here the Whiggish narrative of progress comes into the service of a conservative agenda. Wattenberg recalls that a century ago "the pillars of the American elite, including most eminent social scientists, thought that AEEAs were inferior . . ." His purpose is partly to add another cheer to the literature of American celebration—from shtetl to WASP in a hundred years—but also to gain ground in a running war against affirmative action with a reassurance that injustice need not be addressed for miraculous progress to occur.[61]

Responding to such views, radical antiracist scholars of the past three decades have rightly perceived a need for a sharp separation between European new immigrant history and the past of Latino, African American, Native American, and Asian/Pacific Island peoples in the United States. Michael Omi and Howard Winant thus acknowledged that Europeans' "race" was historically an issue but stressed that it was settled by the 1890s, periodizing with as unfortunate a choice of decades as possible. Robert Blauner inventively acknowledged some of the historical record while yielding nothing on the particular horrors of *racial* oppression. "White ethnics," he held, had been "viewed racially" but were not victims of racism.[62] Historian Alexander Saxton carefully demolished Glazer's use of ethnicity to oppose affirmative action and, cutting to the core of the matter, charged that Glazer "consistently blurs . . . distinctions by tending to equate ethnic or cultural difference with racial difference." Such imprecision makes it possible, Saxton continues, for groups that "historically were excluded from white democracy [to] be lumped together with groups which were racially . . . included."[63]

Demystifying "white ethnic immigrant narratives" required distinguishing between the historical oppression of people of color and that of new immigrants. Language that arrays race against ethnicity is commonly used to make such a distinction. This distinction has its uses, for example, in defense of affirmative action. However, where historical writing is concerned there are powerful reasons to insist on honoring the past usages. If attempts to do so are rare, they are also powerful and include some of the most challenging writings on immigration in the recent past. For example, Gwendolyn Mink's remarkable *Old Labor and New Immigrants in American Political Development*, light years ahead of its time on many fronts, insisted (to the puzzlement of critics) on sticking to "the concept of race . . . as it was articulated in the politics of industrializing America." For Mink, "Blacks were clearly central to race theories and the 'race problem,' but by the late 1870s race thinking covered European ethnic and national differences as well." Jacobson's *Whiteness of a Different*

Color is the existing study most like this one in its emphasis on taking seriously both the absence of ethnicity and the varied uses of race in the period of the new immigration. Jacobson could scarcely be clearer in asserting that the oppression and exclusion suffered by people of color was of an entirely different order than what the European new immigrant experienced. His refusal to explain those differences by ahistorically invoking ethnicity allows him, also to the puzzlement of critics, to show how decisive the role of race was on both sides of the color line.[64]

Writing as an anthropologist, historian, and activist, Micaela di Leonardo cautions that some writers of history "describe racial groups as genuinely oppressed in distinguishing them from ethnics . . . but this topology prevents us from understanding the economic-historical process through which the dichotomy has emerged."[65] In other, less grand ways as well we lose appreciation for historical processes—and for the real lives and terrors of immigrants—by facilely reading separations between race and ethnicity back in time. Mary Waters's recent *Ethnic Options*, for example, makes an important contemporary point when it argues that a Polish American worker was "less able to understand the experience of being black in America precisely because of being 'in touch with his own ethnicity.'" But if readers transport her assessment of Polish ethnicity ("lacking in social costs, providing enjoyment, and chosen voluntarily") into the past, they will significantly misunderstand the history of immigration and race. Among other things, such a view keeps us from understanding a deep tragedy with important lessons for today: that proximity to oppression could also lead new immigrants to distance themselves from black Americans.[66]

The firm separation of race-as-genes from ethnicity-as-culture that underlies, unexamined, distinctions between race and ethnicity also misleads us in apprehending the ways race was at once about "stock" *and* culture—heredity *and* environment—in the early twentieth century. For Powderly, race was a "moral," "mental," and "physical" inheritance. W. Z. Ripley wrote of the Jews as preserving their "Semitic brunetness" over centuries in Germany ("darker by 30% than their gentile neighbors") because of their sedentary indoor occupations and isolation. For Israel Cohen, exile and oppression had over centuries produced changes in "the organism of the Jew." They had "bent and stunted his body . . . sharpened his mind . . . given him a narrow chest, feeble muscles, and a pale complexion; they stamped his visage with a look . . . ever brooding upon the wrongs of ages."[67]

However, the larger objections to transporting ethnicity backward in time go beyond the fact that it puts a layer of mystification between us and the past. They focus on the political cost of not mounting a fundamental challenge to the idea that voluntary ethnic choices and inclusive state policies tell the central story of U.S. history. As writings by Gordon, Glazer, and more interestingly David Hollinger suggest, the proliferating use of ethnicity to subsume race is part of a process that has led to anything but a sharp awareness of the different experiences had by European immigrants and others of African, Latino, Asian, and American Indian ancestry. Those writings call on a potent mixture of liberal and conservative concerns to raise once again Myrdal's hopes that ethnicity differed from race, but only in the short run. Even when such differences are acknowledged, the silent lesson is that they do not rise to the level of structuring categories of analysis. The central U.S. story is, in this view, inclusion and race (for Myrdal's work meaning almost exclusively black people) enters as a subplot, a temporary exception and a passing dilemma. In that sense, the rise of ethnicity as a term in the 1940s and its proliferation come in the context of antifascism and increasing inclusion of new immigrants by the New Deal state. Moreover, it arose in the context of a left that fervently wished to embrace Americanism, of renewed demands for black freedom, and of a Cold War liberalism that answered those demands by emphasizing that the main elements in U.S. history predicted an end to racism.[68] The extent to which U.S. history has turned on race and oppression, not voluntary belonging, for huge numbers of residents who were not black can disappear in a search for optimism. The ways in which race broadly and deliberately structured competition for jobs and shaped ideas regarding who was a fit citizen or neighbor can get lost in a story that uplifts ethnics and premises the uplift not on addressing injustice but on Americanization.

The historical drama through which European immigrants and their children gained inclusion in the United States as whites and as participants in a process of excluding other races is thoroughly muddied when historical references to race are replaced with the language of ethnicity. The answer to conservative uses of white ethnic immigration narratives lies not in flattening the story of race and immigration but in examining the material and state-sponsored underpinnings of categories of the past and carefully analyzing how the new immigrant experience was different by probing where and how racially stigmatized European immigrants could claim white rights, as well as measuring the extent to which gaining fuller humanity could require participation in inhumanity. Such a confrontation with the historical record best affords us the opportunity to come to grips with the extent to which, as Toni Morrison has written in a striking essay, becoming American required the European new immigrant to "buy into the notion of American blacks as the real aliens."[69]

CHAPTER 2

Popular Language, Social Practice, and the Messiness of Race

The racial feeling is very strong. The Irish hate the Italians ("Dagoes")
and the negroes ("niggers"), and the North Italians hate the Sicilians.

LOUISE BOLARD MORE, SOCIAL RESEARCHER,
ON A GREENWICH VILLAGE NEIGHBORHOOD (1903)

The latter day employer resembles the old time planter in his blind-
ness to the effects of his labor policy on the blood of the nation.

EDWARD A. ROSS, SOCIOLOGIST (1914)

The racial landscape discovered gradually by new immigrants to the United States was a mess. As already noted, expert opinion divided the world into either a handful of races or several dozen. The range reflected the practice of making racial designations on at least two axes. One sorted the world's population into a few broad categories, invidiously separated, and the other divided Europe into many fragments, also invidiously separated. Race was at once biological and cultural, inherited and acquired. Race identified, depending on context, both a category and a consciousness. At times and to some it appeared to determine what could be expected of its bearer and her children. In more cheerful moments it could be molded and mitigated by reformers and by the virtues of America herself.

If, for example, an immigrant from Sicily walked about in a city long enough or frequented universities and governmental institutions, she could accumulate racial labels indefinitely, finding herself part of the

Latin, mixed (with Africans), new immigrant, southern European, Mediterranean, Italian, south Italian, Catholic, non–English speaking, Caucasian, white, and dark white races. She might have heard the slurs "guinea" and "greaser" uttered more frequently and with greater emotion than any of the flatter designations. A similarly circulating east European might have learned himself to be a member of the Polish, Slavic, (semi) oriental, Asiatic, Catholic, new immigrant, non–English speaking, Caucasian, and white races. But he would have felt the sting of the slur "hunky" more often than any other racial label. Either immigrant might have been flattered, tutored, or threatened regarding entry into the "American race" or invited to become naturalized as a white citizen and vote. At the same time, they would have heard, especially through the immigration restrictions of 1924, persistent political invective putting their races among those whose unfitness for citizenship threatened the very racial fiber of the nation.

Scholars are no friends of such messiness. Present political motivations—from the right, center, and left—feed preferences for projecting the firm distinction between race and ethnicity back in time. But also important in framing how such big stories of the nation are told is the way that such a clear and simple distinction—one that helps authors reduce race relations to a black-white binary—makes historical material more manageable. Such stories capture drama by being leaner and easier to follow than those that describe the changing contours of a mess. Even the introduction to *Working Toward Whiteness* began with a discussion framed around a firm distinction between "nation-races" and "color-races," and largely trimmed its sources to intellectual and political ones that make it possible to reduce complexities to a pair of categories, at least for a while. As we now turn to consider how race was spoken about and lived on the ground, how such a binary unravels becomes just as compelling as how it is sustained.[1]

Fortunately for the historian, rich and varied evidence from popular speech, labor struggles, literature, mass culture and social service providers, immigrant letters, and more survives to remind us of the thoroughly complicated ways that new immigrants saw their racial fitness questioned, both through denigration of their place in the hierarchy of European races and through discrimination connecting them with African Americans, Native Americans, Asian Americans, Mexican Americans, and Puerto Ricans. In choosing to emphasize such variety, this book proceeds in frank defense of messiness as a central characteristic of the racial order in which new immigrants were placed and they placed themselves. Moreover, messiness contains its own uncertainties and dramas, and it is indispensable in helping us encounter the harrowing and confusing aspects of how new immigrants learned of race in the United States. Such trauma was not that of being made nonwhite but of being placed inbetween.

GUINEAS, GREASERS, AND HUNKIES: HOW RACIAL LANGUAGE TRAVELED

The hypothetical Sicilian and Polish immigrants who opened this chapter would have been taught their racial place in the New World with slurs like guinea, greaser, and hunkie (or hunky). The fighting words that did the teaching often gained their harshness in part because they applied promiscuously to racially despised people and intersected with the economic forces arrayed against the racialized poor. "Guinea," for example, began as anything but an anti-Italian epithet. In the late seventeenth century, guineas began trickling into British North America. The gold coins took their name from the African slave trade for which they provided currency. Guinea, that stretch of coastal West Africa extending roughly from modern Sierra Leone to Benin, also furnished its name to guinea merchants, or slave dealers. No object better symbolized the relationships among the primitive accumulation of capital, the commodification of black bodies, and the deep associations of whiteness and property than guinea currency. African Americans began to be branded as guineas or guinea niggers by the eighteenth century, with the word serving as either a generalized slur or a rough designation of particular elements of the slave population, based on their geographic origin in Africa. Sometimes the word applied to all Africa-born slaves, distinguishing them from those born in the New World. The African American section on Boston's North End in the 1700s was New Guinea; soon the city's black enclave would be Nigger Hill. Nineteenth-century slaves and free blacks sometimes employed the term as a badge of identity and a loose marker of origins in Africa, distinguishing guineas from gullahs, for example.[2] By far the most celebrated literary usage was Herman Melville's midcentury portrayal of "Black

Guinea," who begged for coins as either a blackfaced white trickster or as a black mountebank who would whiten up in subsequent disguises in *The Confidence Man*. While dictionary makers would know that "guinea" referred to gold or to blacks, Melville's characteristic sensibilities regarding the ambiguities of race would question its precision presciently.[3]

In the late 1880s, the African American novelist Frances E. W. Harper created Annette Harcourt's character in *Trial and Trouble* and transported "guinea" specifically into proximity with questions regarding the immigrant's whiteness. Annette complained to Mrs. Lasette, an embodiment of black middle-class virtue, that a schoolteacher seated her next to Mary Joseph, "the Irish saloon-keeper's daughter." Mrs. Lasette guessed the result: "Ireland and Africa . . . were not ready for annexation." The two confronted each other at lunch, with the Irish girl declaring that "she wasn't used to eating with niggers," and Annette asking if Mary Joseph's "mother didn't eat with pigs in the old country." Responding to being called "nigger," Annette called Mary Joseph "a poor white mick." After the saloon keeper threatened Annette, she described her repressed anger: "My Guinea was up, but I was afraid to show it." Here guinea echoes the common phrase "get my Irish up" (become angry), further blurring lines between African Americans and Irish Americans. Annette added, "Grandmother says that an Irishman is only a negro turned wrong side out." She "told Mary Joseph that."[4]

Guinea came to straddle the color line when it named a significant population in West Virginia and Maryland. Of "mixed," controversial, and despised origins, these partly African guineas claimed English ancestry dating from the Revolutionary War and status based on Indian roots as well. By 1946, they enlisted in the military as whites but went to separate "colored" schools in counties where they were most numerous. Arson greeted their attempts to attend white schools, and local opinion regarded them as mulattos. They sometimes called themselves "Malays" and, like "triracial isolate" (as anthropologists hideously identified them) groups elsewhere in the South, struggled to be seen as nonblack, though not as white. Long endogamous, the West Virginia–Maryland guineas did "not as a rule associate with Negroes or whites," although by 1946 they were "said to intermarry with Italians."[5]

Italians, as a leading account of "triracial" guineas noted, were "also called 'Guineas.'" The epithet applied especially to darker southern Italians (and sometimes to Spanish, Greek, Jewish, and Portuguese immigrants), connecting them with proximity to Africa and with African Americans. Such usage dated from the 1890s, and the connection it made between new immigrants and blacks was not an idle one. "In all sections," John Higham has observed, "native-born and Northern European laborers called themselves 'white men' to distinguish themselves from the Southern Europeans whom they worked beside." Union organizers attempting to organize Italians recognized "guinea" as a term of racist abuse that undermined racial unity among workers. In commenting on the force of "guinea" as a slur, the economist Robert F. Foerster wrote in 1924, "In a country where the distinction between white man and black is intended as a distinction of value . . . it is no compliment to the Italian to deny him his whiteness, but that actually happens with considerable frequency." On some New York City docks, Charles Barnes wrote in 1915, Irish workers quit rather than share work with "Ginnies."[6]

Guineas run through early twentieth-century American culture, "high" and "low," mocking simplified racial categories. They are Italian in *Happy Tho' Broke*, by Clifton A. Fox, and *The Hairy Ape*, by Eugene O'Neill. At times the slur was lengthened to "black guinea," even and especially when Italian Americans were its object. The railroad policeman pursuing young Gino Carbo at the beginning of Mario Puzo's historical novel of Italian immigration, *The Fortunate Pilgrim*, yells, "You little black guinea bastard, you don't come down and I'll break your hump."[7] The most layered and fascinating exploration of the vagaries of race making and the Italian guinea comes in a scene from William Attaway's proletarian novel *Blood on the Forge* (1941). Attaway describes the reaction of Irish foundry workers and petty bosses after a black worker, Big Mat, decked a "hayseed" poised to hit an Irishman. The title "black Irish" was conferred on Mat. One Irish worker "grins" that "lots of black fellas have Irish guts." Another chimed in, "That black fella make a whole lot better Irisher than a hunky or a ginnie [guinea]. They been over here twenty years and still eatin' garlic like it's as good as stew meat and potatoes."[8]

Although some lexicographers have argued that "with time" the term became "less derogatory" and less bitter, "guinea" certainly carried intense and tragic meaning in 1926 when an Italian American poet made it central to a wonderful sonnet on immigration, exploitation, and death on the job: "What is it worth, if by misfortune or by accident/your body falls and smashes to the floor below—/poor Guinea, poor Dago?" In 1943, Irvin Child's fine ethnography of the children of Italian immigrants in New Haven found that among the informants most anxious to claim American and lose Italian identification, guinea cut deeply. This "rebel" type at times fought when thus insulted, but "he does not fight to defend the honor of the Italian group: he fights because he is personally insulted." One rebel, on the other hand, held that he did not hear such epithets, "except from people I know, because the others don't guess that I'm Italian." (Child acutely added that the "fact that he passes as a non-Italian" did not actually immunize the informant from hearing racial slurs, but only from resisting them when they were applied to other Italians.) The group of second-generation Italian Americans Child typed as "apathetic" concerning identity included some who professed that being called "guinea . . . never bothered me, even when pressed on the issue." However, half of the "apathetic" group admitted "immediately that they do not like words like . . . 'guinea,'" except perhaps "among ourselves" or "among friends." One reported, "In case you're playing cards and your partner makes a wrong move, you call him 'nigger' [or] guinea. . . . But there's no thought behind it." Child's "in-group" type, strongly identifying as Italian American, took a harder line against such slurs.[9]

Guinea continued to be used occasionally with reference to African Americans in the twentieth century, and World War II military slang made Pacific Islanders guineas—perhaps, according to one source, from "contemptuous association with the outdated term *Guinea Negro*." This kept the association of Italians and "nonwhites" alive. The first section of Piri Thomas's *Down These Mean Streets* pivots on tense exchanges regarding who could call whom a guinea in clashes between Puerto Ricans and Italian Americans. Puerto Ricans are guineas in Irving Shulman's novel *The Amboy Dukes* (1948).[10] As late as the 1960s, Italian Americans campaigned to have "guinea" removed from place-names in New York. New York City Italian American youths influenced by hip-hop have attempted a fascinating rehabilitation of "guinea," using it proudly, mimicking the attempt in rap music and African American slang to rehabilitate "nigger."[11]

"Greasers" and "greaseballs" likewise crossed (and were crossed by) racial and national lines. Originally a class and occupational term, greaser named those who greased sheep in preindustrial England and those who lubricated ships and railroad machinery in the nineteenth century. Both James Joyce's *Ulysses* and the English translation of Emile Zola's *Nana*, for example, refer to greasers working on the rails. Apologists for U.S. slavery seized on the seeming anomaly of begrimed "free" labor in criticizing the proliferation of "greasy mechanics" in the antebellum North. But the term "greaser" acquired its ongoing status as what dictionaries have called a "real Americanism" in referring to Mexicans who came to be within U.S. borders during this period as the United States annexed land. Many stories of its racialized origins preserve association with dirty, manual work. Greasing oxcart and wagon wheels and the guns of Mexican War artillerymen was "Mexican work" in Texas and California when the word gained currency. Trade in tallow, which functioned at times as a kind of currency, also was said to mark Mexican teamsters as greasers in the vocabularies of whites attacking both their greasy jobs and greasy money. Poorer Mexicans were particularly racialized as greasers. Bret Harte, the writer of humor and racial tourism, identified greasers as the "lower class of Mexicans." The supposed presence of the "blood" of indigenous people gave a biological basis to the epithet. The 1855 Greaser Bill in California, for example, was an antivagrant, anti–Native American, anti-Mexican law passed at a time when the landholding *Californio* ranchero elite was legally, if tenuously, accepted as white. Other stories of origin are equally suggestive. In some cases the alleged greasiness of Mexican food, skin, and hair was connected to Indians who greased themselves and perhaps to black slaves who were greased when sold. Anglo settlers characterized the tejano Mexican American greaser population of Texas as mongrels with African American and Native American "blood." "Sketches" of the greaser appeared with tremendous frequency in the national press and constantly emphasized mixed-ness and proximity to other people of color. The fullest account, William R. Lighton's *Atlantic Monthly* article "The Greaser," introduced "the mestizo, the Greaser, the half-blood offspring of the marriage of antiquity with modernity" as its "sunbrowned for centuries" subject. J. W. DeForest's "Overland" has Texas Smith, "an American, a white man," bristle at a perceived slight from a greaser and worry that *he* was being treated as "an 'Injun' or a 'nigger.'"[12]

Lighton's "The Greaser" ends, appropriately enough, on the same 1899 magazine page as the reformer Jacob Riis's famous account of the life of the immigrant poor, "The Tenement House Blight," begins. In the twentieth century the terms "greaser" and "greaseball" were applied to many European immigrants, especially Italians and Greeks, as well as to Mexican Americans and to Filipinos. Indeed, the character Nick the Greek is a greaseball in the classic 1932 movie *The Smart Money*, while an early twentieth-century novelist could be sure his audience would understand his lampooning of grand opera as "a bunch of greasers [singing] a lot of Dago stuff." In John Fante's arresting novel *Ask the Dust* (1939), the connections between Italian American and Mexican American greasers are intricately sketched. The Italian American central character Arturo calls his Mexican American love interest a "filthy little Greaser" and then absolves himself. The slur, he reasons, came not from "my heart" but from the "quivering of an old wound." That wound, Arturo adds, opened during his childhood in Colorado, where "Smith and Parker and Jones . . . hurt me with their hideous names, called me Wop and Dago and Greaser, and their children hurt me, just as I hurt you tonight." Mobsters, especially "unassimilated Sicilian" mobsters, were greasers in San Francisco in the 1930s. William Foote Whyte's *Street Corner Society* suggests that some Italian Americans applied "greaser" to less assimilated countrymen. When Greenwich Village Irish used the epithet "greasy wops," the supposed physical greasiness of Italians, whether of hair or face, received emphasis as it sometimes did in the slurs of the socialist writer Jack London, regarding Russian Jews. For immigrants who traded, greasy could imply being "slippery" when transacting business, a characteristic the celebrated sociologist Edward A. Ross imputed to Jews. The *Dictionary of American Regional English* gives "a Mexican or Mexican American" as greaser's primary meaning and "a person of Mediterranean background" as the second meaning. For greaseball, Mediterranean origins are in the first meaning, with Mexican below. There is no doubt that greaser was a racialized "fighting word," as C. A. Barnhart put it. Indeed, in a letter to an editor of the *Oxford English Dictionary* in 1971, renowned student of U.S. language Peter Tamony identified greaser and greaseball as "barroom brawl words" in contrast to the class and occupational term "grease monkey," which can be "caressively" applied to workers in service stations and engine rooms. Attempts to embrace greaser identity awaited the 1950s and 1960s, when the term was conflated with Elvis, cars, gangs, motorcycles, Wildroot hair tonic, and ultimately Sha Na Na's music to connote white (and, in the Southwest, sometimes Latino) working-class ethnicity. Sometimes, as in Maria Laurino's fascinating recollection of growing up "labelled by [the] ethnic slur" in Short Hills, New Jersey, Italian American young men were the group most commonly identified with the term as they worked on "beat-up cars" and fashioned an image from "their faint gasoline scent and oiled-down hair." Stephen A. Buff's account of hanging with greasers in the 1960s centers on style and class. The neighborhood of Buff's ethnography includes mostly families of Slavic or Italian extraction. The greasers wore sleeveless undershirts called "dago-tees."[13]

"Hunky" has a simple derivation, though with arresting complications. *Criminal Slang* described it as a "corruption of Hungarian" in 1914. Fifteen years later, *American Speech* connected it to "Bohunk," a corruption of both Bohemian and Hungarian. Josephine Wtulich's *American Xenophobia and the Slav Immigrant* attempts interestingly to untangle bohunk and hunky. Wtulich allows that between 1900 and 1930, bohunk came to mean not only a Bohemian–Hungarian but also a "Pole, Slovak and even an Austrian" or "any uneducated, unskilled immigrant from central and east Europe." Thus when a Texas planter fretted that "Bohunks wanted to intermarry with whites," and added, "Yes, they're white but they're not our kind of white," it is by no means certain to whom he refers. Had he used "hunky," the meaning would have been even less clear. Moreover, Wtulich adds, Bohunk and hunky were at times "used interchangeably."[14] The 1911 U.S. Immigration Commission complained of hunky's "incorrect" application to "Slavs indiscriminately." In Nelson Algren's *Somebody in Boots* (1935), a Latvian is, or at least "looks like," a hunky. Other sources found the hunky to be a "Russian, Slav, Serbian or of an allied race," or perhaps a Magyar or Tyrolean, or even any "foreign laborer." John O'Hara's *Appointment in Samarra* (1934) spelled the word "hunkey" and had it naming the "non-Latin foreigner." Similar ambiguities characterized the relation of "Hun" to "hunky." The former term, whose marauding and "Asiatic" connotations resonated fittingly with the fear of an "invasion" by poor immigrants, applied specifically to Germans largely during and after World War I. But even amid the intense anti-Germanism of the war, the iconography of the brutish Hun as an ape partook of earlier anti-hunky/hun stereotypes focusing on eastern Europeans. The connection with hard work was strong, with hunkies typed as "physically strong [and] self-sufficient," if also "intrinsically dull and stupid." To be hunked meant to be disabled by an occupational accident, a condition disproportionately afflicting eastern European workers in some areas. Between 1907 and 1910, for example, almost a quarter of recent immigrants employed at Carnegie South Works suffered death or injury on the job. Thus "hunkie" described both the brawny and the broken, the inferior and the damaged. In Upton Sinclair's play *The Second-Story Man* (1912), a steel worker-turned-burglar describes seeing a fellow worker caught in a crane. To free the victim, he recalls, would have meant taking the crane apart and several days of lost time. Because the maimed worker was "only a poor *Hunkie* . . . there was no one to know or care. So they started up the crane and cut his leg off." Alois Koukol's marvelous 1914 essay "A Slav's a Man for All That" spends almost a fifth of its length describing disabled hunkies. Even so, the dangerous work they performed hardly established the white manhood or value of hunky industrial workers. One foreman totaled the number of industrial accidents in his workplace during a month as "five men and twelve hunkies." The "dirty work" they did suggested to *American Tramp and Underworld Slang* that they were named by their degradation to a status "little better than hunks or clods of dirt."[15]

Hunkies themselves had a role in shaping the word's meaning. Josef Barton's study of immigrants in early twentieth-century Cleveland finds, for example, that a remarkable (if fragile) sense of prideful hunky identity developed across lines separating Serbs, Croats, Slovenians, Slovaks, Poles, and Magyars. Such identity may suggest an attempt at rehabilitation of the slur by the children of immigrants. The newcomers themselves, Thomas Bell argues in his classic Slovak American novel *Out of This Furnace*, had an "ability to shrug" on hearing hunky, which "could not be handed on" to their children. Some adults learned of the word's hurt through a child's perceptions: "Daddy, why does Jennie call me a hunkie?" Bell emphasizes, in what remains the most perceptive commentary on hunky yet written, that the word stung children and bespoke "unconcealed racial prejudice." Nonetheless, *Out of This Furnace* dramatizes the fact that the experience of such prejudice did not translate into solidarity with African Americans. Back in the old Slavic neighborhood in Braddock, Pennsylvania, with his grandfather and his grandfather's close friend, the labor organizer Dobie hears complaints that "niggers" had ruined the area. Reacting to charges that blacks are dirty, Dobie offers another explanation: "They're poor." Making little headway, he adds, "I was just thinking that once it was the Irish looking down on the Hunkies and now it's the Hunkies looking down on the niggers. The very things the Irish used to say about the Hunkies, the Hunkies now say about the niggers. And for no better reason." The grandfather's friend shrugged "but didn't say anything."[16]

INBETWEEN NATIONALITIES:
FROM FIGHTING WORDS TO THE SOCIAL EXPERIENCE OF RACE

When Red, a character in Upton Sinclair's *Singing Jailbirds* (1924), brags that labor radical Joe Hill's songs were sung "in dago and Mex, in Hunkie and Wop, we even sing 'em in Jap and Chink," he deploys and disarms slurs in a combination unfamiliar to modern Americans. Red mixes categories that have come to be thought of as nonwhite with those classed as "white ethnic." The examples of Greeks and Italians particularly underscore the new immigrants' ambiguous position with regard to popular perceptions of race. When Greeks were victimized by whites in the Omaha "race" riot in 1909 and when eleven Italians died at the hands of a white Louisiana lynch mob in 1891, their less than white racial status mattered alongside their nationalities. In 1920, J. D. Goss ran for office in Alabama as the "white man's candidate," calling for Greek and Syrian disfranchisement. As Gunther Peck shows in his fine study of copper miners in Utah, the Greek and Italian immigrants were "nonwhite" before their tension-fraught cooperation with the Western Federation of Miners during a 1912 strike ensured that "the category of Caucasian worker changed and expanded." It did not so readily expand in the heavily unionized gold-mining town of Cripple Creek, Colorado. Southern and eastern Europeans were, like Mexicans and Asians, excluded from a "white man's camp" that admitted African Americans but segregated them. The work of Dan Georgakas and Yvette Huginnie shows that Greeks and other southern Europeans were often categorized and "bivouacked" with "nonwhite" workers in western mining towns. In Helper, Utah, a "White Only" sign in a Chinese café forbade Greeks to enter. They were Jim-Crowed in Pocatello, Idaho, in the early twentieth century; in Arizona they were not welcomed by white workers in "white men's towns" or "white men's jobs." Chicago's Court of Domestic Relations heard the troubles of the feuding

Deakas family during the Great Depression; the German American wife expressed regret over marrying a "half nigger," as she called her Greek American husband. African American slang in the 1920s in South Carolina counted those of mixed American Indian, African American and white heritage as "Greeks" instead of guineas. In his sprawling study *Greek Immigration to the United States* (1911), Henry Pratt Fairchild tried to explain why the glories of antiquity should not color expectations regarding modern Greeks as potential U.S. citizens. He focused on "the checkered career of the Greek race in the last twenty centuries" and especially on the "admixtures of foreign blood" from Asia Minor. The California reformer Chester Rowell was similarly certain that "your track-walking Greek" represented the result of "racial" mixing with Turks and Tartars. Isaiah McCaffery's fascinating oral histories show Greek Americans' great anxiety about race and their experience of being perceived as Puerto Rican, mulatto, Mexican, or Arab, as well as being seen as nonwhite. On Minnesota's Iron Range, employers referred to Greeks (along with Montenegrins, Serbs, South Italians, and Croatians) as "black." In Greenwich Village, Spanish immigrants were caught in equally complicated crosscurrents. Associated by Irish Americans with "Cubians" [sic] as well as Filipinos and Mexicans, they were also called niggers.[17]

Italians, involved in a spectacular international diaspora in the early twentieth century, were racialized as the "Chinese of Europe" in much of the Anglo-American world. In Detroit, an Italian American editor wrote in 1909, "Italians are maltreated, mocked, scorned, disdained, and abused in every way. The inferiority of the Italians is believed to be almost that of the Asiatics." Jack London paired "Dagoes and Japs" as the enemies of true "Saxon" Americanism. A leading German-language paper in Chicago credited the idea that Italians, concentrated on the Atlantic coast, were the "Chinese of the East" and hoped that Chinese exclusion would be a model for a "law against immigration from Italy." One Chicago social worker specified that "dago," a classic anti-Italian American slur, also applied to Mexicans and gypsies. Indeed the historian Michael La Sorte holds that the "Americans considered Italians much the same as gypsies." But in the United States generally, the racialization of Italian Americans was, as guinea's evolution suggests, especially likely to connect Italians with Africans. In Chicago, as the socialist activist Egidio

Clemente remembered, the largest daily papers "would put in parenthesis 'Italian' or 'Negro'" when reporting on perpetrators in crime stories. Alexander Irvine, a socialist minister who went undercover to write about peonage in Virginia in the early twentieth century, appealed to Jim Crow legalities to get European workers out of a "colored" railroad car. He asked whether Virginia's laws had no provisions for "separation of the races." An African American porter made the reply: "Dere sho' is boss—but you ain't no races. You is jes' Dagoes, ain't you?" During the debate over how to disfranchise blacks and which whites might be deprived of the vote at the Louisiana state constitutional convention of 1898, some acknowledged that the Italian's skin "happens to be white" even as they argued for disfranchisement. But others held that "according to the spirit of our meaning when we speak of 'white man's government,' [the Italians] are as black as the blackest negro in existence." In 1914 the Ponchatoula, Louisiana's White Farmers Association, forbade membership to "Italians, Sicilians, Japanese, Chinese, Mongolians, Asiatics, Africans, or descendants of African farmers."[18]

More than metaphor intruded on this judgment. In some southern educational systems Italian immigrants were for a time assigned to black schools. In Minneapolis, the Washington League of Knights and Ladies excluded "Negroes and Italians" in 1902. An ambitious survey of California industry in 1926 found instances in which "white women worked with Mexican and Italian women, but refused to work with Negroes." The one black family on the *Titanic* was until recently lost to history in part because "Italian" was used as "a generic term for all of the darker-skinned passengers" onboard (apparently including some who were Japanese). In the Siskiyou County, California, lumber industry in 1909, complaints from immigrants reached an Italian consular official who contacted the governor because Italian Americans were being treated as nonwhite. The governor replied frankly that the term "white" was one way people of that locality had of distinguishing "Americans" from Italians. A higher official, President Theodore Roosevelt, was surely half joking when he told an associate that he divided the world into "two great classes—white men and dagoes." Louisiana's Italian American sugar workers were sometimes called "niggers" by bosses. The hero of Constantine Panunzio's autobiographical novel *The Soul of an Immigrant* (1921), driven from his work, described feeling "the cutting threads of race prejudice" for the first time.

Panunzio's victimizers were Russian immigrants but he argued that such prejudice "lurks at every corner." One religious reformer noted "two Italy's" in the white popular imagination in the United States. One was the white land of classical Rome and the Renaissance city-states. The other Italy conjured images of "the poor, struggling, dark-skinned colony in every city of America; the Italy that stands behind the pushcart, and sprinkles an odor of garlic as it walks; the Italy that is hated by our workmen almost as much as the Chinese." When William Dean Howells needed a bittersweet ending for his novel *An Imperative Duty* (1893), in which lovers discover that the woman has "black blood," he concludes with their moving to Italy, where she "is thought to look so very Italian." In 1911 a journalist asked a young assistant manager on a railway construction site in New Jersey if any workers had died on the job. The reply puzzled him: "There wasn't any one killed except wops." The reporter pressed for a clarification. He got one, which produced an expanded definition of an anti-Italian slur: "Wops. Don't you know what Wops are? Dagos, niggers, and Hungarians—the fellows that did the work. They don't know anything, and they don't count." One telling Alabama antimiscegenation prosecution ended in acquittal in 1922 when it was ruled that the Italian American partner to the relationship was not "conclusively white" and that therefore the color line had not been crossed criminally. The African American scholar Ralph Bunche made the same case in *A World View of Race* (1936), specifically mentioning Italians, along with Jews, Poles, and Greeks, as victims of "racial persecution."[19]

Supporters of Nicola Sacco and Bartolomeo Vanzetti, the celebrated anarchist Italian American political prisoners executed in 1927, worried that that the two were not white enough to be saved. As the radical poet Jim Seymour wrote at the time, "They're only a couple God Damn Dagoes!/I don't see how anyone can expect white people/to do anything for the likes of them." Eugene Lyons's popular story of their trial on robbery and murder charges found that Vanzetti was scarcely "reckoned a white man" on coming to the United States.[20] One key element in the case was contradictory eyewitness testimony concerning whether those committing the crime were "dark Italian-looking" men or were "awful white." Thirty years after the case, defense committee supporter Elizabeth Gurley Flynn still recalled that as "foreigners" Sacco and Vanzetti were held in the same regard by "New England Yankees" as "Negro people" were by southerners. Flynn would also have remembered the titanic Lawrence textile strike of 1912, in which a Boston newspaper greeted news of the arrest of Italian American labor leaders by enthusing over the renewed "ascendancy of the white-skinned races."[21]

The racialization of east Europeans was likewise striking. "Only hunkies," a steel industry investigator was told, worked blast furnace jobs, which were "too damn dirty and too damn hot for a white man." The African American United Mine Worker leader Richard L. Davis enthused in an 1892 report over cooperation among races in one southern locale. Davis could tell that "these people mean business" from their selection of officers: "one Hungarian, one [Negro], one Polander, one Slav and one white." While racist jokes mocked the black servant who thought her child, fathered by a Chinese man, would be a Jew, racist folklore held that Jews, inside out, were "niggers." Henry Ford's massively circulated anti-Semitic tract, *The International Jew* (1921), insisted that the "Jewish question" turned on race and nationality and charged Jewish promoters with bringing an "oriental infection" to American culture. The goal of elite Jewish reformers, according to education scholar Isaac Berkson's 1920 study, was the "complete de-orientalization of the Russian Jew." Management at the nation's best-studied early-twentieth-century factory divided the employees into "white men" and "kikes." On the Iron Range in Minnesota, towns were disqualified as "white" ones if they had substantial numbers of southern European immigrants. After a bitter 1910 strike by largely Polish oil refinery workers, native-born residents who were interviewed divided the city into two classes: foreigners and white men, a distinction John Fitch also found in steel production. As Fitch put it, in the Pittsburgh survey study, "By the eastern European immigration the labor force has been divided into two." The first group included "English-speaking men." The second contained the "Hunkies" or "Ginnies." ("Ginny," he added in a twist on typical usages, "seems to include all the Hunkies with the Italians thrown in.") Alternatively, Fitch wrote, the cleavage divided the "white men" from "the foreigners." The fascinating autobiography of Daniel Trees, *How Columbus and I Discovered America*, describes the life of a Yugoslav immigrant who was called hunky and was excluded in one Midwestern city after another on the grounds that "You ain't white and you was born wrong." In Butte in 1910 the local press complained of "Bohunks" getting jobs while many "white men . . . are seeking employment." In 1926 Serbo-Croatians ranked near the bottom of a list of forty "races" that 1,725 native-born, largely younger and middle-class "American" respondents were asked to order according to the respondents' willingness to associate with members of each group. They placed just above Mexicans, Negroes, Filipinos, and Japanese. Clustered above them, all radically more subject to being excluded than "old immigrants," were Syrians, Greeks, Hungarians, and Poles.[22] The literal inbetweenness of new immigrants suggests what popular speech affirms. The state of "conclusive" whiteness was approached gradually and messily.

INBETWEEN AND IN-AMONG

The travels of words like guinea, hunky, and greaser, along with the racialization of new immigrants, makes the racial categorization and consciousness of race among new immigrants seem dauntingly complicated. Such complication reflects the experience of migrants and the receiving society, not the confusion of historians. For example, at the level of legal and academic expertise, in the first quarter of the twentieth century, there was broad agreement that eastern and southern Europeans were white, though arguments raged about the relative merits of various white "races," such as southern Italians, Greeks, and Poles. A Senate report on immigration in 1911 revealed that Poles were "darker than the Lithuanians [but] lighter than the average Russian" white, while being "more high strung" than either.[23] Groupings of European nationalities into Nordic, Mediterranean, Alpine, and Semitic "races" existed alongside references to individual groups as "races" and Johann Friedrick Blumenbach's division of the world into five "races" (Caucasian, Mongolian, Ethiopian, Malay, and American). The courts complained on hearing anthropological testimony that sometimes enumerated a handful of "races" and sometimes ten times that many. [24]

Popular language and thought exposed new immigrants to still more complicated racial inbetweenness than expert ethnological opinion did. If, as Jacobson argues, intrawhite racial divisions mattered greatly among experts, social experience and popular terms like greaser, hunky, and guinea associated new immigrants with nonwhiteness on such multiple fronts that "in-among" may be a more apt, if cumbersome, term than inbetween in identifying their racial positions. If guinea connected blacks, Italians, and later Asians, greaser brought new immigrants into proximity with Mexicans and Puerto Ricans. Italians and Jews were far from alone in being conflated with "orientals." So too were the slowest to become white of the "old" immigrants, the Irish. The "Bohunk invasion" of the copper industry in Butte was seen as one of "European Chinamen." Warne offered extended Slovak–Chinese comparisons and French Canadians were *les Chinois de l'Est*. Slavs, Finns, and Syrians were contemptuously styled Asiatics. Henry Pratt Fairchild wrote of the "Alpine stock" of Italians as "essentially mongoloid in its racial affiliations." The social survey *Wage-Earning Pittsburgh* found Russians ugly because they were allegedly products of a "mesalliance, absorbing many Urgo-Finnish tribes." Moreover, anti-Asian and anti–new immigrant nativist organizations at times cooperated institutionally, as Erika Lee's superb work shows. Southern legislators were especially likely to regard new immigrants as "the degenerate progeny of the Asiatic hoards [sic] which, long centuries ago, overran the shores of the Mediterranean," to see "the Sicilian, the Southern Italian, the Greek [and] the Syrian" as living in the north of a "belt" including those areas "of Africa and Asia surrounding the Mediterranean Sea, and further east, including all Mongolians and Hindus." The J. Walter Thompson Company, a major advertising firm, grouped Armenians, Assyrians, Greeks, Persians, Syrians, Turks, Albanians, Letts, Chinese, Japanese, Filipinos, and Hindus together racially in a 1924 memorandum to employees. Since the development of gatekeeping strategies of immigration restriction first involved the control of Asian migrations, links of new immigrants to "orientals" were especially meaningful. As Erika Lee writes, "In terms of immigration restriction . . . new immigrants were more closely racialized along the Chinese immigrant model" than in counterpoint to African Americans. The often medicalized metaphor of "unwanted invasion" applied to both groups, though at differing frequencies.[25]

Likewise complicating inbetweenness was the total lack of clarity regarding whether the racial categories being bridged were biological or cultural ones. The eating, sweating, sun-darkened, dirty, working, groomed, sexually commodified, perfumed, hulking, and occupationally injured bodies that terms like hunky and greaser connoted were not necessarily fixed biological entities. Indeed the notion that the late twentieth century invented a new racism turning on mutable cultural norms rather than fixed biological categories cannot survive even passing acquaintance with historical sources from a century ago. Thus when Italian Americans suffered a group lynching in Louisiana in 1891, the press justified the atrocity by pointing to southern Italian biology and habits. The lynched Sicilians' "brutal natures" manifested themselves in their "low, receding foreheads, repulsive countenances and slovenly attire." The historian Richard Weiss wrote of the race thinking of Henry Cabot Lodge but captured far broader late-nineteenth- and early-twentieth-century assumptions:

> The concept of race . . . was not simply a biological concept. It did not encompass only physical and anatomical differences such as color, brain size, and facial features. It included those . . . but covered much more. . . . Differences in language, the arts, social organization, and aspiration were part on the "souls" of peoples, and soul was just as much a part of a person's inherited propensity as was size or skin color. Physical and cultural attributes were linked under the heading of race.[26]

Complicating matters further was the fact that joining the "American race" could transform habits and souls. Soap, a haircut, money, or new diet could make the greaser less slick. Learning a new language could do likewise. Thus the term "English-speaking races"—so at odds with presumed connections of race and biology—recurred again and again. Theodore Roosevelt, social reformers, steel mill workers, immigration officials, and sociologists all regularly used it.[27] Warne's jeremiad against the "invasion" of new immigrants denominated the "foreign-born from [northern and western European] countries supplying the earlier immigration as English-speaking" and the arriving "Slavs and Italians" as not "English-speaking." In fact, as Isaac Hourwich showed at the time, data from the Dillingham Commission suggested that, controlling for length of U.S. residence, immigrants from Poland may have been more "English-speaking" than those from Germany. Warne was thus right to admit a certain absence of "scientific precision" in terming the Germans, French, Dutch, Swiss, Norwegian, and Swedish as English-speaking, but the idea that a language change could announce a racial transformation spoke profoundly to the biosocial definitions of race. Peter Roberts's revealing teacher's manual, *English for Coming Americans* (1912), counseled an alternative strategy for teaching Scandinavians, Germans, and Finns as against the "wholly different problem" of laborers from southern Italy, Slavs, Hindus, Chinese, or Japanese. Those born in "favored nations" should not, he warned, be mixed with new immigrants and Asians as both of the latter groups suffered from "a heritage of inefficiency and sloth . . . which will take more than a generation to slough off." The aural fixations of travelers' accounts describing immigrant areas—from the writings and celebrated photographs of Jacob Riis to the words of Henry James—repeatedly emphasize a welter of languages in capturing the appeal and threat of "ghettoes." In doing so, they show the immigrant's race as simultaneously labile and resistant to change.[28]

Two final complications also mattered. First, race was not only an imposed category but also an embraced identity for new immigrants. Racial terms like guinea, greaser, and hunky were, as we have seen, sometimes embraced, sometimes used against other immigrants, sometimes used to build connections to other immigrant groups, and sometimes campaigned against. The second complication involved change over space and hinged on differing demographics, immigrant and host populations. In largely Polish American areas, for example, the odd non-Polish eastern European might be called "Polack" instead of hunky. In some areas there were Greek as well as Italian "dagoes." A Yugoslav might be slurred as a hunky in Cincinnati and excluded from public events there—but not in Detroit, an immigrant stronghold. Living inbetween racial categories and finding ways to whiteness were thus uneven, many-sided, harrowing processes. As Trees's revealing *How Columbus and I Discovered America* shows, at times even after the strategic cleaning up of hair, clothes, skin, food, or speech, a new immigrant could still be called a hunky.[29]

To the immigrant who sought to mitigate his or her nonwhiteness, it could not have always been clear whether such a process was a personal or a group one, whether it entailed overcoming biology or changing habits, whether it was practicable or quixotic. Some exclusionary rhetoric directed against new immigrants stopped carefully short of condemning whole races and instead argued that the particular poverty-stricken segments of the population migrating were made unfit for citizenship by history as much as by biology. Warne cautioned against the arrival of peasants "made inarticulate by centuries of caste rule." The founding spirit of labor history, John R. Commons, thoroughly mixed race, class, and historical experience. For him, potential migrants were "the product of serfdom" and therefore the exact antithesis of the "typical American citizen whose forefathers have erected our democracy." Edward A. Ross, who incorporated and at times criticized hereditarian perspectives, offered the equally inbetween characterization of newcomers as "beaten members of beaten breeds."[30]

Nowhere was the interpellation of cultures of poverty with ideas about racial inheritance more striking than in discussions of the oiliness and dirt that made migrants hunkies and greasers in both expert opinion and popular language. Frequent references to the "filth" on and around those arriving easily turned into words that purported to capture the very essence of the new immigrant: "scum," "trash," "dregs," and so on. Photographs often show newcomers living amid, or scavenging in, trash. If an immigrant was dirty, she could wash; if she was "scum" incarnate, the prognosis was poorer. Nonetheless, faith remained in America's power to transform, as the Statue of Liberty put it, "wretched refuse." When Ross, perhaps the nation's premier sociologist, spoke of Slavs as "immune to certain kinds of dirt," opining that they "can stand what would kill a white man," the studied confusion, the messiness, was complete.[31]

"INBETWEENNESS"

Part Two

"The Burden of Proof Rests with Him": New Immigrants and the Structures of Racial Inbetweenness

A turmoil of organization and fulmination ensued, with the late Colonel [Theodore] Roosevelt in his usual role of drum-major and prophet. Protecting the immigrant; restraining him; keeping him out; compelling him to conform to ourselves; doing at least something to the immigrant, and especially talking all sorts of phantasies about him, became the order of the day.

HORACE M. KALLEN, CULTURAL THEORIST (1924)

Indeed the slang terms for recent immigrants, such as "wop" and "hunkie" are commonly associated with . . . types of work—as the word "nigger" has been for three-quarters of a century.

NILES CARPENTER, SOCIAL SCIENTIST (1927)

The bulletin of Gads Hill Center settlement house featured a theater review in 1915. The head resident at Gads Hill, which served immigrants living on the lower west side of Chicago, wrote in praise of the recent blackface minstrel show performance at the center. The triumphal performances of young immigrants like Joseph Kraszewski, Frank Pletcha, and Ignac Chimielewski, he enthused, had quite transcended their singing of "Clare De Kitchen" and "Gideon's Band." Their "splendid sense of freedom . . . without the least touch of vulgarity" was the real triumph. Many in the crowd of 350, according to the reporter's judgment, knew so little English that they could only "enjoy the music [and] appreciate the really attractive costumes."[1]

In 1980, Joseph Loguidice, an elderly Italian American from Chicago, sat down to give his life story to an interviewer. His first and most vivid childhood recollection was of a race riot that had occurred on the city's near north side. Wagons full of policemen with "peculiar hats" streamed into his neighborhood. But the "one thing that stood out in my mind," Loguidice remembered after six decades, was "a man running down the middle of the street hollering . . . 'I'm White, I'm White!'" After first taking him for an African American, Loguidice soon realized that the man was a European, perhaps Italian, coal handler covered in dust. He was screaming for his life, fearing that "people would shoot him down." He had, Loguidice concluded, "got caught up in . . . this racial thing."[2]

New immigrants like Kraszewski, Pletcha, and Loguidice came into a society in which they and others were judged on the basis of race. From Henry James's "look in" on Italians, Jews, and others, to muckraking travelogues of immigrant neighborhoods, to serving as guinea pigs in the development of intelligence tests, to shape-ups outside factories in pursuit of work, to inspections on entering the country, immigrants were repeatedly scrutinized, tried, examined, and ranked against other races. Henry Pratt Fairchild's extended and direct 1911 comparisons of new immigrants to "the case of negroes in the United States" were atypical, but his conclusion was not. Fairchild answered those who argued that Greek immigration had caused no disaster by offering a comparison to the importation of slaves to the United States. The presence of slaves, he held, initially seemed no problem but ultimately brought "terrible and bloody conflict." Fairchild allowed that the new immigrants were "for the most part white-skinned" but added that they were "generally regarded as inferior." Such immigrants held jobs "Americans" avoided. In all of this, they were "like the negro." But, as Fairchild concluded, the judgment was provisional and the scrutiny would be extended: "If he proves himself a man, and . . . acquires wealth and cleans himself up—very well, we might receive him in a generation or two. But at present he is far beneath us, and the burden of proof rests with him."[3] This chapter tells the dramatic story of how courts, reformers, employers, and unions consistently slotted new immigrants in inbetween racial spaces and begins an account of what it was like to live there.

NATURALIZATION, THE STATE, AND NEW IMMIGRANT WHITENESS

In 1923 the U.S. Supreme Court necessarily gave up on using expert testimony to decide who was "white" and therefore eligible for naturalized citizenship in the *Thind* case. The shifting, contested, and often incomprehensible opinions of experts had posited that forty-five or more different "races" had migrated to the United States. Some groups that the Court felt sure were nonwhite seemed to have better ethnological claims to whiteness than Europeans whose naturalization as white Americans had long-established precedents. In denying citizenship to Thind, who as an Asian Indian and had strong claims to Aryan whiteness, the justices therefore took a new tack, reversing the logic used the prior year to deny naturalization to a Japanese litigant in the *Ozawa* case. Unable to demonstrate intellectually his nonwhiteness, the justices told Thind that everyone (or at least the "common" American) simply knew that he was not white. "Common speech" and "popular understanding" were to be the new tests for whiteness, at a time when the most ambitious social scientific study of "race attitudes" of the native-born middle class found almost identical percentages wishing to exclude Japanese and Serbo-Croatian "races" from citizenship. In both cases about 70 percent were in opposition. A majority also opposed naturalization of the Czecho-Slovak, Russian Jewish, and Bulgarian "races" and more than 40 percent opposed citizenship for Russians, Portuguese, Greeks, Poles, and "Roumanians." When the great African American writer Jean Toomer commented in 1929 that no "profit" would come from "giving scientific questions [on race] into the keeping of the 'average man,'" he was surely right that no special liberality or acuity would be gained. However, a certain inconsistency that would have been useful at least in undermining *Thind*'s assumption of a common understanding was surely present.[4] In the 1920s immigrant greasers, guineas, and hunkies were being racialized as less than white in common speech, and Congress was being flooded with appeals for racially based restrictions on the immigration of southern and eastern Europeans to the United States. The president, the labor movement, the National Industrial Conference Board, and a Ku Klux Klan swelling to a mid-1920s membership of 3–5 million all questioned the racial fitness of such newcomers, as detailed in Chapter 5.[5]

There was little consensus understanding of race beyond the near certainty among whites that African Americans were at or near the bottom of any racial hierarchy and that Asian exclusion was unassailable as public policy. Indeed, when attorneys for the Asian Indians denied naturalization rights later brought before the courts evidence that some popular ethnology writings led to the conclusion that their clients were at least as white as Mediterranean and Alpine Europeans, the judges were not interested.[6] "Race, to the man in the street," Ralph Bunche wrote in the 1930s, "is neither biological, cultural, linguistic, religious or political—it is all, any or none of them. This irrational view of race is and will continue to be held in the United States . . . a thousand . . . anthropologists notwithstanding." Likewise, he might have added, Supreme Court justices and major political leaders held such a view.[7]

The power of the national state was crucial in this context. It gave new immigrants their firmest claims to whiteness and their strongest leverage for enforcing those claims. The courts consistently allowed new immigrants, whose racial status was ambiguous in the larger culture, to be naturalized as white citizens and almost as consistently turned down non-European applicants as nonwhite. Political reformers therefore discussed the fitness for citizenship of new immigrants from two distinct angles, producing, through the beginning of World War I, a largely benign and hopeful discourse on how to Americanize (and win votes of) those already here. A debate on fertility rates and immigration restriction conjured up threats of "race suicide" if this flow of migrants were not checked and/or the fertility of the native born did not increase. A figure like Theodore Roosevelt could stand as both the Horatio warning of the imminent swamping of the "old stock" racial elements in the United States and as the optimistic Americanizer to whom the play that popularized the assimilationist image of the "melting pot" was dedicated.[8]

Such anomalies rested not only on a political economy in which the need for immigrant labor fluctuated, but also on peculiarities of U.S. naturalization law. If the "state apparatus" told new immigrants that they both were and were not white, it was clearly the judiciary that produced the most affirmative responses. From the first Congress in 1790, the law required that an immigrant seeking citizenship be a "free white person."

The political scientist Rogers Smith has demonstrated the foundational importance of such laws, which "literally constitute—they create with legal words—a collective civic identity." As Rachel Buff has written, "In the case of naturalization . . . citizenship becomes a narrative of ascent, where the legitimating body of the nation stands in for actual bodies and genealogies of subjects in bringing already existing individuals into the national fold."[9] In the United States the law made this ascent racial as well as civil. The original law, as post–Civil War court decisions argued, may well have intended to make no statement about the fitness for citizenship (or the whiteness) of Europeans other than those who were already arriving in considerable numbers, mainly Anglo-Saxons, Celts, Germans, and Scandinavians. Indeed, its main purpose was probably to codify the obvious fact that imported slaves were not to be naturalized.[10] But the statute, restated in 1802 and revised in 1870 to technically allow the naturalization of African-origin immigrants, nonetheless turned out to have momentous consequences. When much of the citizenry doubted the racial status of European migrants, the courts almost always automatically granted their full whiteness in naturalization cases, and legislators respected the precedents that naturalization decisions set. Even the often racially based campaigns against Irish naturalization in the 1840s and 1850s and against Italian naturalization in the early twentieth century aimed to delay, not deny, citizenship. The lone exception in this regard is a case in which U.S. naturalization attorneys in Minnesota attempted briefly and unsuccessfully to bar radical Finns from naturalization on the ethnological grounds that they were "Mongolian" and therefore not white. Even that case ended with the ruling that if they were "originally Mongols [Finns] have continued until they are now among the whitest people in Europe."[11]

Indeed, in the welter of late-nineteenth- and early-twentieth-century litigation in which Chinese, Japanese, Afghanis, Asian, Indians, Syrians, and other non-Europeans claimed whiteness, the courts took special care *not to raise* the issue of the racial status of European new immigrants, rejecting legal arguments in part because they might lead to questions about the fitness of "Russians, Poles, Italians, Greeks and others." The Marxist journalist Kiyoshi Karl Kawakami's 1914 riposte against racist naturalization policy identified this Achilles heel, declaring that "all this talk of Mongolian descent is laughable," since Hungarians and "many of the Russians" had more "Mongolian blood" than did the Japanese.[12] Observations regarding color might be made in cases such as that of Abdullah Dolla, an Afghani whose rolled-up sleeves revealed to a federal court in 1909 that "where protected by his clothing his skin was several shades lighter than that of his face or hands." But such tests, as appeals courts especially maintained, could not be a real standard since they conflicted with the clear eligibility for naturalization of the "southern Portuguese," for example. Similarly, the court's attempts to follow scientific race theories ran aground on such problems as complexity and mutability of the theories, as well as their tendency to call into question the citizenship of European immigrants earlier courts had naturalized. When experts spoke of the "non-Caucasian" status of "Magyars, Finns . . . Basques and Lapps" (and of the "white" status of Asian Indians), the judges lost their appetite for ethnology.[13]

The legal equation of whiteness with fitness for citizenship shaped the process by which race was made in the United States. Ian Haney-Lopez has aptly written that while *Thind* and related cases "directly address the racial identity of relatively few nationalities, they are relevant to our understanding of the racial identity of every 'white person' in this country." Worth emphasizing here is the extent to which the equation between legal whiteness and fitness for naturalizable citizenship helps predict which groups would, in law, *not* be made nonwhite in an ongoing way. Not only did the Irish, whose whiteness was under sharp question in the 1840s and 1850s, and later the new immigrants, gain the powerful symbolic argument that the law declared them white and fit. They also gained the power of significant numbers of votes, even if naturalization rates for new immigrants were not always high. During Louisiana's disenfranchising constitutional convention of 1898, for example, the bitter debate over Italian whiteness ended with a provision passed extending to new immigrants protections comparable, even superior, to those which the "grandfather clause" gave to native white voters. New Orleans's powerful Choctaw Club machine, already beneficiary of Italian American votes, led the campaign for the plank. In the Maryland referenda on disfranchising African Americans in 1905 and 1909, both major parties courted Baltimore's Italian American votes, with pro-disfranchisement Democrats attempting unsuccessfully to write a 1909 grandfather clause that would reassure recently arrived immigrant voters concerned about their own potential loss of the right to vote. The most significant Democrat to break party ranks to oppose the 1905 disfranchisement initiative as a threat to Italian Americans continually prefaced speeches with, "There's no man in the state that hates the darky more than I do," teaching sinister but portentous lessons in racial politics to his immigrant constituents.[14]

When Thomas Hart Benton and Stephen Douglas argued against Anglo-Saxon superiority and for an all-white "American race" in the 1850s, they did so before huge blocs of Irish voters. When Theodore Roosevelt, Benton's biographer, extolled the "mixture of blood" making the American race, a "new ethnic type in this melting-pot of the nations," he emphasized to new immigrant *voters* his conviction that each of their nationalities would enrich America by adding "its blood to the life of the nation." When Woodrow Wilson retreated from his 1912 campaign hints that Chinese immigrants were in some ways less undesirable than European new immigrants, he did so in the context of an electoral campaign in which the "foreign" vote counted heavily. *L'Italia* angrily editorialized, "Let him go to the Chinese . . . for votes." More established immigrants, especially the Irish, often led political machines that mobilized newer immigrants to take advantage of the political rights whiteness conferred and to beat back reform efforts that made cultural and racial arguments aimed toward limiting immigrants' political power.[15]

Nonetheless the case of the radical Finns mining in Minnesota remains revealing. The attempt to challenge the naturalization of left-wing Finns—to deny their voting rights and to leave them subject to further repression by casting them as Asian—fell predictably flat. Even with the nation's leading sociologist placing them as descendants of the "Finno-Tartar branch of the Mongolian race," the federal courts were not about to entertain challenges to the rights of Finns to become citizens as whites. But this is not the whole story. On the other hand, looser and more local racializations of Finnish labor militants did matter, even at the level of government policies toward them. Labor radicals in the United States had since the nineteenth century suffered from (and occasionally embraced) comparisons of their behavior with that of "Indian savages." Newspapers harped on these connections even as the same troops that victimized Indians also broke strikes. In Minnesota, where memories of the violence attending settler colonialism were fresh and where immigrant miners lived near Indians, the charge that Finnish labor radicals culturally resembled and consorted with the "countless savages bent on slaughter, rapine and plunder" circulated freely. What Gerald Ronning has called the "conflation of native and new-comer" in northern Minnesota took shape around supposedly constitutional affinities to alcohol abuse and to militant resistance the two groups shared. Both of these required close policing. After 1906, special (anti) Indian agents began a concerted campaign to close saloons and arrest bootleggers on and near the Iron Range. With the Mesabi iron strike of 1916, these "Indian bulls" went after saloons used by "red Finns"—the term connoted socialism in contrast to the churchly "white Finns," but also resonated with comparisons to Indians—and other immigrants to recreate and organize. The pretext for these incursions was to keep liquor from finding its way across "racial" boundaries to Indian customers. However, the "jackpine savage" stereotype connecting Finns and Indians enabled the police crackdowns to sprawl beyond any specific evidence regarding the liquor trade. The repression that eventuated on the Iron Range was nothing short of savage.[16]

THE U.S. STATE, PROGRESSIVE REFORMERS, AND THE "AMERICAN RACE"

Of course, the new immigrant voted alongside the Americans who racialized him as a guinea, a greaser, and a hunky. And the same federal government that in its naturalization policy made southern and eastern Europeans white generated a protracted debate over immigration restriction which called their racial fitness for American citizenship into question. The contributions of the state to the inbetween racial categorization of new immigrants were therefore as complex and contradictory as they were consequential. Francis Amasa Walker, bureaucrat and Ivy League professor, transformed the late-nineteenth-century census and identified southern and eastern Europeans as new immigrants peculiarly unable to be assimilated into the "American race." Theodore Roosevelt believed that their full assimilation as white Americans was possible in the space of two generations.[17] Ironically, it was not just the opposition between the nakedly reactionary tradition represented by Walker and the optimistic progressivism represented by Roosevelt that left the new immigrant racially inbetween whiteness and nonwhiteness. Rather it was the affinities and interplay between Walker's and Roosevelt's views on biology and culture that were decisive. Neither Walker nor Roosevelt directly challenged the legal status of new immigrants as whites, but both powerfully connected race and culture in ways raising profound questions about whether and how such immigrants could find a place in the "American" race. Walker answered such questions negatively and Roosevelt affirmatively, but each represented wings of a political discourse that left southern and eastern Europeans as objects of debate, their racial status on trial as they lived, poised inbetween nonwhiteness and a white Americanism that was seen as a racial as well as a national category.

Walker, already the chief of the U.S. Census Bureau in 1870, worried that the census predicted an increasing Catholic and Irish population. He reasoned that the numbers and fecundity of immigrants combined with declining trends of native-born birth rates to ensure dramatic and disastrous demographic change. During the next quarter century, Walker fretted over each new census and eyed the role of "foreign stock" in labor strikes. He meticulously developed his theory that contact with inferior people somehow caused lower birth rates among the native born, who responded to lower standards of life by decreasing family size.[18] Over time, his anxieties grew more urgent and changed focus. Walker soon acknowledged that Irish Americans had joined the dominant race, admitting his previous errors and arguing for religious tolerance. The new enemy was the new immigrant, whom Walker could differentiate racially from the old, using studies from that inveterate citadel of academic racism, Harvard University. "The ignorant and brutalized peasantry from the countries of eastern and southern Europe," Walker found, would undermine "American standards" with a "contact so foul and loathsome." "Centuries are against them, as centuries were on the side of those who formerly came to us," Walker concluded.[19]

No other statistician has had a more decisive impact on U.S. history and politics than Walker. While his racial anxieties typified those of his fellow New England patrician intellectuals, Walker's theories laid the groundwork for a nativist politics that far transcended appeals to that narrow group. Breaking anti–European immigrant initiatives from their sometimes unproductive moorings in anti-Catholic bigotry, Walker focused nativism squarely on race, as John Higham has brilliantly shown. He helped make the New England elite-led Census Bureau an ongoing source of dry statistics and alarmist predictions regarding the U.S. racial character, providing to politicians and the public "the language to debate the sources of social turmoil."[20]

That language resonated powerfully with the popular language of race because it insisted that race was *both* biological and cultural, both "inherited" and "achieved."[21] Just as greasers, for example, were racialized in various times and places on the basis of their poverty, jobs, speech, diet, and other "environmental" characteristics, Walker evoked images of disease, degradation, ignorance, squalor, and "habits of life" to establish the racial unfitness of new immigrants. Their problems were those of race, but also of class and history. Their diseases and deficiencies, as Alan Kraut has recently shown, were traced both to "germs" and "genes." The sociologist Edward A. Ross mixed the medical, biological, and moral in characterizing the alleged tendency of Italian Americans to insist on "relief as a right" as a form of "spiritual hookworm." Walker held, in a phrase borrowed by Ross, Samuel Gompers, and other twentieth-century advocates of immigration restriction, that southern and eastern European immigrants were "beaten men of beaten races." Deficient as individuals, as a class, and as a race, they represented "the worst failure in the struggle for existence" and earned discredit as "races of . . . the very lowest stage of degradation."[22]

This loose, state-endorsed linkage of biology to culture, history, and class can mislead modern historians of race who characteristically attempt to disentangle the biological from other rationales for oppression, regarding the former as underpinning racism and the latter as underpinning other kinds of prejudice. But what was so striking about restrictionist and racist thought at the beginning (and, indeed, at the end) of the twentieth century was its very entanglement of the biological and the cultural. Thus Walker's contemporary, the nation's leading evolutionary biologist, E. D. Cope, counted four inferior forms of humanity: "non-white races, all women, southern as opposed to northern Europeans and lower classes within superior races."[23] The sponsor of the first serious restrictive legislation directed against new immigrants, the Contract Labor Law of 1885, derided "ignorant, brutal Italian laborers." He premised exclusion on the "moral tone" of the newcomers. But, like the late-twentieth-century race thinkers who slide from moralistic indictments of African Americans' "underclass" cultural values onto the bell curve of biological racism without a second thought, he cast culturalist arguments in terms of color and biology. Immigrants with a "lower moral tone," he warned, "will cause general moral deterioration as sure as night follows day. The intermarriage of a lower type with a higher type certainly does not improve the latter any more than the breeding of cattle by blooded and common stock . . . improves the blooded stock."[24]

Such crude biologism and opposition to "race" mixing as degenerate figured strongly in immigration restriction arguments, especially between 1916 and 1924. As early as 1912, congressional hearings on immigration restriction debated whether Italians were "full-blooded Caucasians." Madison Grant's 1916 classic and fully racist attack on the mixing of Nordics with "lesser" Alpine, Mediterranean, and Semitic people represented an important strain in nativist attacks on new immigrants. Ross interestingly called the new immigrants he feared the "Caliban type," and opined that they were "hirsute, low-browed, big-faced persons of obviously low mentality." Ross believed he could predict intelligence by noting the "sugar-loaf heads, moon-faces, lantern jaws, and goose bill noses" among those arriving in such alarming numbers. But the opposition of employers to restrictions on immigration joined with the presence of a strong immigrant vote and other factors to keep anti–new immigrant racism from finding successful direct political expression before the 1920s. Advocates of literacy tests, control of contract labor, and other restrictions might allude to the positive effects of their policies on the "stock" of the United States. But the logic of their policy reforms until the 1920s argued that the problem with immigrants lay in their lack of education or intelligence, their sexuality, diseases, or oppression by labor contractors, not simply in their "race."[25]

Race-based, anti–new immigrant hatred was held at bay politically through 1921 in large part because industrial capital opposed restrictions on workers whom they saw as loyal and cheap. Capitalists allied with an optimistic strain in progressive reform that embraced immigrant voters, immigration, and even the mixing of European "races." It kept open, however the possibility that new immigrant "stock" might, in some circumstances, be found damaging. Among such reformers, no one was more influential, insistent, and effective in his incoherence regarding the consideration of race and immigration than Theodore Roosevelt. Roosevelt's almost laughable proliferation of uses of the word "race"—one careful account explores at least five variations and intimates that there were many more—did not serve him poorly but well, according to his various needs as reformer, imperialist, historian of the West and, above all, as political candidate. He tacked effectively and sincerely, undertaking seemingly contradictory embraces of Charles Darwin's evolutionary theory and of Lamarckian biology's insistence on the hereditability of acquired characteristics, of melting pots and of race suicide, of an adoring belief in Anglo-Saxon and Teutonic superiority alongside professions of awe at the grandeur of a "mixed" American race. His soaring patriotic hopes for an invigorating process of manly assimilation existed hard by his acknowledgment of the possibility that immigration was, as the cultural historian Mark Pittenger puts it, drawing the nation into a "suffocating devolutionary mix." Roosevelt, like the Census Bureau, thought in terms of the biological "stock" (a term that called forth images of Wall Street as well as the farm) of the nation. That stock was for him directly threatened less by high immigration rates than by low birth rates among the nation's "English-speaking race." But races could also progress over time and the very experience of mixing and clashing with other races would bring out, and improve, the best of the "race stock." Thus the "Kentucky race," to use Roosevelt's term for those he considered the best embodiment of the American frontier's fighting virtues, had repeated the drama of Teutonic progress in the New World, and moved by conquering others from an amalgam of "Scotch Saxons," "Scotch Celts," and "true . . . old Irish" to become a distinct *race* with an exalted place in the hierarchy of races. The "American race" could absorb and permanently improve the less desirable stock of "all white immigrants," perhaps in two generations, but only if its most desirable "English-speaking" elements were not swamped in an un-Americanized Slavic and southern European culture and biology. Even John Fiske, reputedly the nation's most popular historian at the turn of the century, and a figure so obsessed with Anglo-Saxon achievements and progress that one critic has called him an "ethnic" historian of English immigrants to the United States, believed that such assimilation was possible. Thus not just the "fitness" of new immigrants but also their "fit" with the existing native stock was at issue. Opinions on the proper mix of immigrants could change over time. Even Ross opposed immigration restriction for a time, arguing that the "psychic whirlwind" provided by U.S. conditions could elevate "lowly men" and that "dilution need not spell decline."[26]

With a firm faith in their own capacity and that of their race to reorder U.S. society and the world, Roosevelt and his cothinkers challenged

Walker's pessimism less by emphasizing the racial merits of new immigrants than by extolling the uplifting power of progressive reformers and of existing, racially fit American stock. If Walker preached that native-born white Americans would meekly cut their birthrates in the face of the new immigration, Roosevelt insisted that his educative efforts could turn the tide against "race suicide" by increasing native-born birth rates rather than by turning back the flow of immigrants, although he also advocated restrictions on European immigration based on political beliefs and intelligence tests.[27]

Professional Americanizers and politicians appealing to immigrant constituencies for a time seemed to marginalize those who viciously racialized new immigrants and even to develop images of utopian European race mixing as striking as they sometimes were chilling. Big business generally gave firm support to relatively open European immigration and sometimes funded reform efforts. The Ford English School literally sponsored the melting pot image, with the car manufacturing giant holding a pageant of rebirth for new immigrants. After nine months of classes in English and assimilation, graduation consisted of a ceremony in which variously costumed Europeans descended into a giant pot. Stirring the pot produced new men who emerged in American clothes holding American flags. The influential anthropologist and critic of race, Franz Boas, argued in 1910 to Congress that "melting" was physical as well as cultural. His "Changes in Bodily Form of Descendants of Immigrants" tried to document the changing size, brain capacity, and hair color of children of Jewish and Sicilian immigrants. Brains and bodies grew and hair lightened. A "new human race," as Sander Gilman puts it, seemed capable of evolving under "American conditions."[28]

Progressive reformers in politics even showed the potential to rein in their own Anglo-Saxonist tendencies, especially when votes were up for grabs. Woodrow Wilson, when he was a southern academician, wrote of the dire threat to "our Saxon habits of government" by "corruption of foreign blood" and characterized Italian and Polish immigrants as "sordid and hapless." Later, as a presidential campaigner in 1912, Wilson reassured immigrant leaders that "we are all Americans," offered to rewrite offensive sections on Polish Americans in his *History of the American People*, and found Italian Americans "one of the most interesting and admirable elements in our American life."[29]

But even with these hopeful strains acknowledged, Progressive reform failed to place new immigrants beyond the pale of racial attack. The Progressive project of imperialist expansion and the Progressive nonproject of capitulation to Jim Crow segregation ensured that race thinking would retain and increase its potency. Where empire was concerned, Pedro Cabán's indispensable comparative study of progressive attempts to Americanize immigrants in the United States and colonial subjects abroad rightly insists on the simultaneity and similarity of the two enterprises even as it pinpoints difference. Cabán writes, "Despite the bigotry and racism the Southern Europeans encountered, they were subjected to an Americanization process that was designed to incorporate them into the dominant culture." He contrasts this process with "the Americanization of Puerto Ricans and Filipinos [which] was an element of a campaign to . . . socialize them into becoming loyal wards of the empire." At home, if industrial leaders backed open European immigration and funded Americanization projects, the corporate model stressed standardization, efficiency, and speedy results. In following corporate logic and in pursuing their own electoral interests, many Progressives came to support local and state "good government" reforms bound to curb immigrant political participation.[30] In Progressive thought, eastern and southern Europeans remained "on trial" racially. As Philip Gleason's superb history of the "melting pot" metaphor shows, the term raised more questions for reformers than it answered. What was the source and heat of its flame? Who stirred it and how vigorously? Who watched for cracks? What proportions of "slag," "dross," "scum," and "gold" eventuated? Even those expressing provisional faith in the possibility of European "race mixing" in the United States shared and popularized much of the viewpoint of those who advocated restriction on racial grounds. Roosevelt is again the best example. The founder of a Harvard student society that invited Francis Walker to speak on campus when the future president was an undergraduate, Roosevelt supported harsh immigration restrictions early in his career and lost confidence in the Americanization of immigrants late in it.[31]

Far from being a believer in the decisive influence of environment, Roosevelt was utterly obsessed—from the U.S. frontier to New York City to the Philippines—with racial traits, stocks, and hierarchies. When he used the presidential bully pulpit to rail against "race suicide," he demonstrated a capacity to fret over census returns quite as insistently as Walker and other experts who foresaw "the Jew, the Russian, the Hungarian [and] the Italian . . . darkly outshading the Americanized descendants of the English, the Irish, and Scotch, the German and the Swede." Choosing to campaign for increased fertility among English-speaking races, Roosevelt trumpeted the idea that an apposite "racial" mix was necessary to make experiments in Americanization work. More importantly, the "race suicide is curable" argument made "old stock" women white in a new way, as citizen/custodians of the American racial character. It exalted their critical role even as it vilified them for failure to breed enough to live up to their procreative duties. If the censure of Walker fell on "beaten" men of inferior races, that of Roosevelt and his cothinkers fell on "restless" women of the "best stock." Indeed Roosevelt once used his annual message to Congress to declare that "willful sterility" led to "race death." It was not only a "sin for which there is no atonement" but "more dreadful exactly in proportion" to the extent that it was committed by "those whom for the sake of the state it would be well to see . . . mothers of many healthy children."[32]

It is hard to demonstrate that presidential appeals swelled the maternity wards, but women reformers responded favorably to the call to preserve the "American race." Remarkable middle- and upper-class women working at settlement houses for immigrants taught and witnessed Americanization. Jane Addams, for example, learned much from immigrants, and extolled not only assimilation but also the virtues of ongoing cultural differences among immigrant groups. These women, as Gwendolyn Mink has recently shown, believed that "with proper instruction and protection, women from different backgrounds could become . . . mothers of fully American children," approximating the cultural pluralism of Horace Kallen.[33] Although some feminists critically answered "race suicide" arguments, which at times singled them out as the cause of low fertility, others took racial responsibilities most seriously. For all their pluralism, settlement house workers both believed and taught that race was crucially important. As Elizabeth Lasch-Quinn has recently shown, their leading theorists invoked a racial continuum that ended "farthest in the rear" with African Americans and often goaded new immigrants to change cultural habits by referring to Old World traditions as atavistic repositories of "racial consciousness." The literary scholar Valerie Babb concludes that Hull House, which conformed to Jim Crow ostensibly because new immigrants would stay away from integrated facilities, introduced clients "to the benefit of skin color as an aid to social and economic success." Prominent feminists such as Lydia Kingsmill Commander (who enjoined "intelligent Americans" to have six children per family) and Charlotte Perkins Gilman bought fully into the logic of the "race suicide" argument.[34]

The campaign for women's suffrage at times traded tragically on the perceived affront and the supposed peril caused by the presence of black and new immigrant voters while the "best" of American women suffered disfranchisement. Promising to be active citizens and voters, white middle-class suffrage proponents at times came dangerously close to transposing the logic of "race suicide" arguments to voting rights. Aileen Kraditor's study of the suffrage movement shows that common participation in reform with immigrants mitigated biases but also that the new immigrants' inbetween position was sometimes mirrored by contradictory perceptions that "coexisted in the minds of individual suffragists." Thus Florence Kelley could castigate pro-suffrage speakers for their frequent references to "ignorant immigrants," even as she complained that state-by-state suffrage amendments were "an ignominious way to treat us, to send us to the Chinamen in San Francisco, to the enfranchised Indians of other western states, to the Negroes, Italians, Hungarians, Poles, Bohemians and innumerable Slavic immigrants in Pennsylvania and other mining states to obtain our suffrage."[35] Similar patterns of racial acceptance and rejection would follow immigrants to work.

INBETWEEN JOBS:
CLASS, MANAGEMENT, AND THE NEW IMMIGRANT

Even as the world of work mercilessly taught the importance of being "not black," it also exposed new immigrants to frequent comparisons to African Americans and at times to close competition with them. Management created an economics of racial inbetweenness that instructed new immigrants on the importance of racial hierarchy while leaving their places in that hierarchy open to judgment. The ways in which capital structured workplaces and labor markets contributed to the ideas that competition would be cutthroat and should be racialized. In the early twentieth century, employers preferred a labor force divided by race and national origins. As radicals understood at the time, and as the labor economists Richard Edwards, Michael Reich, and David Gordon have reaffirmed, work gangs segregated by nationality and/or race could be made to compete against each other in a strategy not only designed in the long run to undermine labor unity and depress wages but also to spur competition and productivity every day. New "Taylorist" systems of scientific management coexisted quite comfortably with the simpler pitting of workers of different nationalities against each other. At other junctures, the preference was to divide each work group on "racial" lines to forestall development of solidarity. As late as 1907 the pioneering labor economist John R. Commons regarded not scientific management but "playing one race against the other" as the only "symptom of originality" in U.S. management. During industrial conflicts, fostering such division had a special appeal. In the Great Steel Strike following World War I an antilabor detective agency told its operatives, "Spread [information] among the Serbians that the Italians are going back to work. Call up every question you can in reference to racial hatred between these two nationalities." At Pittsburgh's Central Tube Company, a personnel manager produced an analysis of the "racial adaptability" of no fewer than three dozen nationalities of workers. His care reflected the fact that the purported ability to place and "handle" nonwhite workers was itself a marketable commodity for managers during this period. Other employers connected specific national origins to specific job classifications far more offhandedly. Want ads could end "Syrians, Poles and Rumanians preferred." When the "Greek menace" organized a strike in the coal mines of Utah in 1911 (characteristically the strike included Italians and Slavs as well), a state mine inspector and a coal company official both blamed departures from the time-tested policy of "guard[ing] against union troubles by installing workmen of different nationalities." The cause, in this view, was "a perponderance [sic] of the Greek element" in the mines. The government offered statistics, however egregiously inaccurate, breaking down the propensity toward unionism of various races. According to Dillingham Commission figures, 6 percent of Slovak miners of bituminous coal who had been in the United States for less than five years were union members; the comparable figures for Magyars, Poles, and southern Italians were 8 percent, 13 percent, and 19 percent respectively. Employers, one historian observes, "were no doubt interested" in these figures. Industrial Commission reports on

Jewish immigrants identifying them as the "instigators" of protest among "satisfied" coworkers.[36]

On the other hand, management made broader hiring and promotion distinctions which brought pan-national and racial categories into play. In some workplaces and areas, the blast furnace was a "Mexican job"; in others, it was a pan-Slavic hunky one. The race of the workers could define the race of the work. Although in one study 15.9 percent of Irish immigrant males over age ten worked as laborers around blast furnaces in 1920, those jobs remained tied to Mexican immigrant men (47.6 percent of whom labored around the furnaces) and hunkies (with 22.4 percent of Slovak immigrant men so employed). When a native-born labor investigator asked for a "hunky job" on the blast furnace, he was told that "only hunkies work those jobs, they're too damn dirty and too damn hot for a 'white' man." In a smelter in Black Eagle, Montana, work in the tank house was so undesirable in the early twentieth century that one employee recalled "it was hard to get a white man to do it." Slavs did the tank house jobs that "white men" refused. Lumber companies in Louisiana built what they called "the quarters" for black workers and (separately) for Italians. For white workers, they built company housing and towns. The distinction between white native-born workers, sometimes termed Anglos, and nonwhite new immigrants, Mexicans, and African Americans in parts of the West rested in large part on the presence of "white man's camps" or "white man's towns" in company housing in lumbering and mining. In some mines the blanket term "Mexican" referred to nonwhite Slavs and southern Europeans as well. As Antonio Ríos Bustamante has written, mine management sometimes mixed Italians, Spaniards, and Mexicans in neighborhoods segregated from Anglo workers. In the early twentieth century, such neighborhoods "had no more amenities than the entirely Mexican *barrios*," although in some camps Italians could work below the ground while Mexicans could not. In the Southwest, Linda Gordon has written, those who sought to preserve whiteness were so intent on barring Mexicans, Chinese, and "new immigrants" that in some instances black miners were seen as acceptable and could even identify themselves as "white." When the principal railroads running through Chicago issued a 1914 report on track laborers, they divided the workforce into two parts. The "hoboes," or "white laborers," were "the Irish, English and American survivals of the time when all this work was done by English-speaking immigrants or native Americans." On the other hand, there were "foreigners" from southern and eastern Europe. An employer on the Brooklyn docks outlined a simple division of labor: "in discharging [the ship] we employ all Italians and in loading all white men." Croatian Americans in the Kansas City stockyards complained that German American foremen "called them 'Hunky' rather than by their own names." Poles registered strikingly similar problems with German American foremen in Buffalo. In the mines around Monessen, Pennsylvania, the fact that bosses would issue orders by referring to "hunkies" or by saying "Hey Polack," or "Hey Dago, come here," was recalled with sharp resentment.[37]

Indeed as Herman Feldman acutely observed in 1931, it was in many cases "supervisors, section heads, foremen and other minor functionaries" whose racial opinions mattered most immediately. Foremen, according to Feldman, were especially tempted "to vaunt . . . superiority by speaking of . . . immigrant employees as 'wops', 'bohunks' or 'mutts.'" The sociologist Niles Carpenter's 1925 interviews with "group leaders" in the immigrant communities of Buffalo drew extended responses from seventeen Italians and Poles. Eight were of the opinion that employers discriminated against their group. Five thought fellow workers discriminated, but a dozen reported discrimination by foremen. In Johnstown, one general foreman admitted as much: "When they had a list of names for promotions . . . they tended to scratch out the 'Hunky' ones." One prerogative of foremen was, as Gabriela Arredondo's rich research shows, to decide whether immigrants' claims to skills would be honored in the United States. In making such decisions, the foreman was often "solidifying his own position of belonging and of American-ness."[38]

In the 1930s southern and eastern Europeans, sometimes lumped together as "racials," suffered employment discrimination in industry. They were at times acutely aware of this discrimination. Thus one informant among the Italians in the Chicago Oral History Project referred to the historical concentration of Italian Americans in unskilled labor while "the other races were something else." Another recalled being treated "like blacks here" after his 1926 arrival, and a third allowed that African American workers had been the most exploited but added that "the Italians and the Polish were just a few steps above them." WASP, through the early 1960s, referred to white Anglo-Saxon Protestants, to be sure, but not necessarily to those of elite status with whom we associate the term. Instead it marked the working class, often southern migrant, whites whom employers of less skilled labor sometimes preferred to (or preferred to balance against) new immigrant "racials." Indeed WASP may have gained currency in part as an employment agency acronym that identified nonracial workers. As late as 1957, *Life* could write that the cartoon hillbilly Lil' Abner typified the WASP.[39]

There was also substantial fascination among managers in the specific comparison of new immigrants with African Americans, and less frequently with each other, as workers. These complex comparisons generally favored new immigrants over blacks. African Americans' supposed unreliability ("especially on Mondays"), intolerance for cold, and incapacity for fast-paced work were all noted. But the comparisons were often nuanced. New immigrants, as Herbert Gutman long ago showed, were themselves counted as unreliable, "especially on Mondays." Some employers regarded black workers as more apt and skillful "in certain occupations," and as cleaner and happier than "the alien white races."[40] A very occasional blanket preference for African Americans over immigrants surfaced, as at Packard in Detroit in 1922. One manager in the steel town of Granite City, Illinois, professed to prefer two Negroes to three Macedonians. In iron and steel mills in Alabama, the federal Immigration Commission reported in 1911 the "practically universal opinion among employers that South Italians are . . . the most inefficient of all races, whether immigrant or native." Comparisons carried a provisional quality, since ongoing competition was not only desired but also, as one employment agent told Commons in 1904, "systematized." In 1905 the superintendent of Illinois Steel threatened to fire all Slavic workers. He reassured immigrants that no "race hatred" motivated the proposed decision, which was instead driven by a factor that the workers could change: their tardiness in adopting the English language (and thus, presumably, in joining the "English-speaking races"). As the social scientists Everett Cherrington Hughes and Helen MacGill Hughes observed, research analyzing actual performance by race was as rare as opinions were numerous. Indeed the disparity made Hughes and Hughes wonder if "modern society is really guided by the impersonal concepts of the market and efficiency in choosing and assigning its labor force." In the 1920s and 1930s, Feldman and the social researcher T. J. Woofter anticipated the Hughes's argument, agreeing that "manufacturers, ordinarily very careful of the grades of raw material used in their products, rely on hearsay and rumor as to the grades of the labor hired."[41]

The fact that the new immigrant was relatively inexperienced on the job vis-à-vis African American workers in the North in 1900 and (given immigration restriction and mass black migration from the rural South) relatively experienced by 1930 makes it difficult for economic historians to measure the extent of discrimination by employers. Melvyn Dubofsky's provocative claim that "only the Negro's presence kept the Italian, the Pole, and the Slav above society's mudsill" likely overstates the extent of contact between blacks and new immigrants and oversimplifies wage differentials. New immigrants themselves suffered wage discrimination, receiving as much as 10 percent less than natives with like skills in the same industry. As Paul McGouldrick and Michael Tannen put it, new immigrants experienced "moderate but certainly nonnegligible discrimination" in securing jobs for which they were qualified. Some of the best evidence in this regard comes from copper mining in Arizona and involves differentials among Mexicans, Italians, and "whites." At the Detroit Copper Company in the Clifton-Morenci copper area in 1903, for example, only 6 percent of Italians received $3 a day or more while 11 percent of Spanish-surnamed workers did. Among Anglo miners, 43 percent made $3 or more daily. With 47 percent of Italians earning less than $2.50 daily, the group fell between white workers (24 percent) and the Spanish-surnamed (70 percent). Among a group of New York tunnel workers in the early twentieth century, the more racially accepted Irish Americans reportedly made $3 to $5 a day while Italian Americans received $1.75 to $3.00 daily. In another instance the Irish American unskilled made $2 for a ten-hour day while Italian, Slavic, and Hungarian workers were paid $1.46. In rare cases typically before 1915, black workers were paid on average more than new immigrant groups. A 1910 survey of iron and steel workers gave evidence of such a differential. Richard Gambino cites one 1896 advertisement for "common labor" which quoted rates as "white $1.30 to $1.50 . . . colored $1.25 to $1.40 [and] Italian $1.15 to $1.25." However, as immigrants gained language and job skills, this advantage proved fragile, especially since Slavic workers were more successful at passing on relatively well-paying jobs to their compatriots and children. By 1927, Niles Carpenter would write in his excellent statistical study of Buffalo that "color and nationality, especially color, unmistakably do count for or against an individual" on the job market. Woofter wrote that "quite effective 'dead lines' as to the limit of Negro work are set by tradition." He found the job opportunities of "the children of Oriental immigrants" even more circumscribed. Such handicaps—in using "dead lines" Woofter appropriated a term used to apply to boundaries defining where racial minorities could not go in cities—applied "to a lesser degree" to European immigrants. Clearly timing and demographic change mattered alongside anti–African American racism in structuring a situation in which the new immigrants quickly came to occupy spaces on the job ladder between African Americans below and those who were fed into the economic historians' computers as NWNPs (native-born whites with native-born parents) above. Indeed Steward Tolnay's new statistical research on race, immigration, and "occupational standing" in 1920 finds that African Americans were "much more segregated, from immigrants and third-plus generation men . . . than the latter two groups were segregated from each other." Tolnay further argues that African American men found themselves far more concentrated on the lowest rungs of job ladders already by 1920. He adds the fascinating observation that "new immigrants" were relatively better off in cities with higher proportions of African American population, lending some support to Dubofsky's "mudsill" hypothesis. As one study of steel labor in Gary, Indiana, observes, "Steel company employment practices not only reflected institutionalized racism, but helped to socialize other steel city newcomers . . . to the Jim Crow values and attitudes of the city's corporate elite." One of the most careful students of this process, Stanley Lieberson, uses the image of a queue to help explain the role of discrimination against African Americans in leading to such results. Such results not only structured new immigrants' lives but also their learning about race in the United States.[42] In describing an industrial system in which workers often lined up for jobs so that bosses could pick among them, the image is wonderfully apt. In the queue of workers ordered by employer preference, as in so much else, new immigrants were inbetween.

RACE, UNIONS, AND THE TRIALS OF NEW IMMIGRANTS

While organized labor exercised little control over hiring outside of a few organized trades, its racialized opposition to new immigrants reinforced their inbetweenness on the job, in politics, and in unions. The unions in the largest wing of the organized labor movement, the American Federation of Labor (AFL), also provided an important venue in which "old immigrant" workers interacted with new immigrants, teaching important lessons in both whiteness and Americanization. They offered harsh criticism of immigrants along with some provisional opportunities to join the labor movement, almost as trial members.

As an organization devoted to closing skilled trades to any new competition, the craft union's reflex was to oppose outsiders. In this sense, most of the AFL unions were "exclusionary by definition" and marshaled economic, and to a lesser extent political, arguments to exclude women, Chinese, Japanese, African Americans, the illiterate, the noncitizen, and the new immigrants from organized workplaces, and, whenever possible, from the shores of the United States.[43] So clear was the craft logic of AFL restrictions that historians are apt to regard it as simply materialistic and to note its racism only when direct assaults were made on groups traditionally regarded as nonwhite. Thus Higham argues that it was only after 1916 that Samuel Gompers and "the men around him" supplemented "strictly materialist" rationales for restriction of new European immigration with new reasoning based on the threat of migration overburdening "the nation's capacity to unify and Americanize." Only in the last moments of the major 1924 debates over which immigrants to restrict did Gompers, in this view, reluctantly embrace "the idea that European immigration endangered America's racial foundations."[44]

The remarkable recent work of Robert Lee, Gwendolyn Mink, and Andrew Neather fully demonstrates that appeals to craft and race in AFL campaigns to restrict European immigration separate less easily than Higham implies. Trade union opposition to the Chinese stressed the connection between their "slavelike" subservience and their alleged status as coerced "coolie" laborers, schooled and trapped in the Chinese social system and willing to settle for being "cheap men."[45] Dietary practices (rice and allegedly rats rather than meat) symbolized Chinese failure to seek the "American standard of living." All of these are cultural, historical, and environmental matters. None of them prevented the craft unions from declaring the Chinese "race" unassimilable nor from supporting exclusionary legislation premised largely on racial grounds. The environmentalist possibility that over generations Asian "cheap men" might improve was simply irrelevant. By that time the Chinese race would have polluted America.[46]

Much of labor's anti-Chinese rhetoric was fastened onto the Hungarian immigrant in the 1880s and then recycled in the AFL's campaign to restrict the "new immigrant" generally over the next four decades. The "filthy Huns" from eastern Europe, the Pittsburgh-based *National Labor Tribune* charged, "lived in a manner that would disgust any crescent-eyed leper on the Pacific Coast, and if they do not breed a pestilence it will not be their fault." Pasta, as Mink demonstrates, joined rice as an "un-American" and uncivilized food. The railway unionist and later socialist leader Eugene V. Debs wrote in 1891 that the Italian "fattens on garbage" and lives "far more like a wild beast than the Chinese." W.E.B. Du Bois held in 1915 that "the European and white American working class was practically invited to share" in the "new exploitation" of racial capitalism and imperialism. Furthermore, he added, those same white workers "were flattered by popular appeals to their inherent superiority to 'Dagoes,' 'Chinks,' 'Japs,' and 'Niggers.'" In sometimes accepting such an "invitation" to connect the Italians and other new immigrants specifically with the Chinese, the AFL also signaled that its anti–new immigrant racialism carried policy implications, as the Chinese were the group on which the law and bureaucracy of exclusion cut its teeth.[47]

Far from abjuring arguments based on "stock," AFL leaders supported literacy tests designed, as Catherine Collomp puts it, "to reduce the numbers of Slavic and Mediterranean immigrants." They allied with the anti–new immigrant racism of the antilabor Senator Henry Cabot Lodge, hoped anti-Japanese agitation could be made to contribute to anti–new immigration restrictions, emphasized "the incompatibility of the new immigrants with the very nature of American civilization," and both praised and reprinted works on "race suicide."[48] They opposed entry of "the scum" from "the least civilized countries of Europe" and "the replacing of the independent and intelligent coal miners of Pennsylvania by the Huns and Slavs." They wrote of fearing that an "American" miner in Pennsylvania could thrive only if he "Latinizes" his name. They explicitly asked, well before World War I, "How much more [new] immigration can this country absorb and retain its homogeneity?" Those wanting to know the dire answer were advised to study the "racial history" of cities.[49]

Robert Asher is undoubtedly correct in arguing that (1) labor movement reaction to new immigrants was "qualitatively different from the response to Orientals" and (2) AFL rhetoric was "redolent of a belief in racial inferiority" of southern and eastern Europeans.[50] Neather is likewise on the mark in speaking of "semiracial" union arguments for restriction directed against new immigrants.[51] Subtle distinctions and outright contradictions continually operated, with new immigrants scored at once for their poverty and their race. United Mine Workers leader John Mitchell made a firm separation between new immigrants and the "English-speaking" race. Gompers's characterization of them as "beaten men of beaten races" followed that of racist social scientists and perfectly captured the tension between fearing that southern and eastern Europe was dumping its "vomit" and "scum" in the United States and believing that Slavic and Mediterranean people were themselves scummy. Labor sometimes cast its ideal as an "Anglo-Saxon race . . . true to itself." Gompers was sometimes more open but equivocal. He found that the wonderful "peculiarities of temperament such as patriotism, sympathy, etc.," which made labor unionism possible, were themselves "peculiar to most of the Caucasian race," but still suspected many of that race. In backing literacy tests for immigrants in 1902, Gompers was explicit. Such tests, according to Gompers, would leave British, German, Irish, French, and Scandinavian immigration intact but "shut out a considerable number of Slavs and other[s] equally or more undesirable and injurious." He took such positions despite data, massively compiled by the great debunker of anti–new immigrant stereotypes, Isaac Hourwich, that eastern and southern European workers joined unions in as great a proportion as native-born whites. (Interestingly Hourwich's figures show African Americans, the most excluded group, as having the highest union density.) Likewise adding complexity were the facts that labor was almost never in a position to enforce discriminatory hiring and promotions on its own and that AFL policy was sometimes less vital than quite varied local practices.[52]

Such "semiracial" nativism most obviously impacted on AFL politics but it also led to exclusion of new immigrants from many unions. When the iron puddlers' poet Michael McGovern envisioned an ideal celebration for his union, he wrote: "There were no men invited such as Slavs and 'Tally Annes' [Italians], Hungarians and Chinamen with pigtail cues and fans." Craft unions in the building trades were likely to exclude Italians, Jews, and other new immigrants. The hod carriers union, according to Asher, "appears to have been created to protect the jobs of native construction workers against competing foreigners." The shoe workers, piano makers, barbers, hotel and restaurant workers, and United Textile Workers likewise kept out new immigrants, whose lack of literacy, citizenship, English-language skills, apprenticeship opportunities, and initiation fees effectively barred them from many other craft locals. In Boston, as Howard Kimeldorf writes, Irish-controlled waterfront unions successfully enforced "long-standing membership prohibitions against 'blacks'— aimed at keeping out Italians and African Americans." As late as 1932 the sociologist Donald Young wrote in his *American Minority Peoples,* "Immigrants and Negroes have little reason to trust the unions which, taken by and large, have done their best to keep them from better jobs and to relegate them to . . . crude labor." This "internal protectionism" apparently had lasting results. Lieberson's research through 1960 shows new immigrants and their children having less access to craft jobs in unionized sectors than did whites of northwestern European origin.[53]

On the other hand, new immigrants had more access to unionized and skilled work than African Americans, and unions never supported *outright* bans on their migration, as they did with Asians. A. T. Lane's useful history of labor and immigration, though overly eager to see AFL opposition to the new immigration as based on culture and labor markets and not "genetic" factors, acknowledges a hard core of union opinion seeing eastern and southern European immigrants as mirroring the biological unsuitability of Asians. Gompers, he argues, represented the norm in the movement, using race to describe new immigrants only because it was fashionable. Gompers, and the labor leadership generally, according to Lane, "agreed that the Chinese and the new Europeans were not identical and could not be treated in exactly the same way. Yet there were similarities between them." Reflecting this view of eastern and southern Europeans as "inbetween," the AFL insisted on outlawing Asian immigration and restricting European "new immigration." Organized labor's opposition to the Italians as the "white Chinese" and "padrone coolies," or to new immigrants generally as "white coolies," usually acknowledged and questioned new immigrant whiteness at the same time, associating "lesser" whites with nonwhites while leaving open the possibility that contracted labor, and not race, was at issue. A strong emphasis on the "brotherhood" of labor also complicated matters. Paeans to the "International Fraternity of Labor" ran in the *American Federationist* in fifteen pages of anti–new immigrant hysteria such as A. A. Graham's "The

Un-Americanizing of America." Reports from labor leaders in Italy and poems like "Brotherhood of Man" ran hard by alarmed predictions of "race suicide."[54]

Moreover, the very things which the AFL warned about in its anti–new immigrant campaigns encouraged the unions to make tactical decisions to enroll Southern and Eastern Europeans as members. Able to legally enter the country in large numbers and to become voters, hunkies and guineas had clear social power, which could be used to attack the craft unionism of the AFL from the right or, as was often feared, from the left. To restrict immigration, however desirable from Gompers's point of view, did not answer what to do about the majority of the working class, which was by 1910 already of immigrant or second-generation origins. Nor did it speak to what to do about the many new immigrants already joining unions, either in the AFL, in language and national federations, or under socialist and anarchist auspices. If these new immigrants were not going to undermine its appeals to corporate leaders as an effective moderating force among the whole working class, the American Federation of Labor would have to consider becoming the Americanizing Federation of Labor.[55]

Most importantly, changes in machinery and relations of production made real the threat that craft skills could be undermined by training of unskilled and semiskilled immigrant labor or by deskilling work generally. While this threat could give force to labor's nativist calls for immigration restriction, it also strengthened initiatives toward a "new unionism" that crossed skill lines and organized new immigrants. Prodded by independent, dual-unionist initiatives by Italian socialists and the United Hebrew Trades, by the example of existing industrial unions in its own ranks, and by the left-wing multinational, multiracial unionism of the Industrial Workers of the World, the AFL increasingly, if reluctantly, got into the business of organizing and Americanizing new immigrant workers in the early twentieth century. The logic, caught perfectly by a Lithuanian American packinghouse worker in Chicago, was utilitarian:

> . . . because those sharp foremen are inventing new machines and the work is easier to learn, and so these slow Lithuanians and even green girls can learn to do it, and the Americans and Germans and Irish are put out and the employer saves money. . . . This was why the American labor unions began to organize us all.

Even so, in some cases, and especially those in which new immigrant women were the potential union members and skill dilution threatened mainly immigrant men, the Gompers leadership refused to incorporate dual unions or initiate meaningful organizing efforts under AFL auspices. When organization did occur, "racial" attitudes could yield only slowly. Regarding the Chicago stockyards, for example, a 1905 *Bulletin of the Bureau of Labor* article quoted Irish unionists who had seen the necessity of common organization: "however it may go against the grain, we must admit that common interests and brotherhood must include the Polack and the Sheeny."[56]

Although self-interested, wary, and incomplete, the AFL opening to new immigrant workers initiated a process that could transform "semira-cial" typing of already arrived new immigrants. In a sense, AFL organizing openings mirrored Theodore Roosevelt's willingness to take on new immigrants as trial members of the social compact. Although specifically defending (and equating) "white" and "American" standards of wages, consumption, and working conditions, the more hopeful came to regard it as possible that some new immigrants could be taught those standards. Unions and their supporters at times treasured labor organization as the most meaningful agent of democratic "Americanization from the bottom up." "The only effective Americanizing force for the southeastern European," Commons argued, "is the labor union." Frank Julian Warne's *The Slav Invasion and the Mine Worker* (1904) saw the 1900 and 1902 anthracite strikes as "mere episodes in [the] great conflict of races." The conflict pitted the "English-speaking race" (of which Germans were somehow the largest group in some major anthracite fields) and the "Slav" race (which somehow consisted of up to 20 percent Italians). English-speaking unionists used language and residency requirements for licenses to work as a miner to stem the "Slav invasion" in the 1890s and then made the United Mine Workers of America "an instrument of defense against the Slav" in the 1900 strike. Strike successes, however, both necessitated having "Slav" members and created confidence among the "English-speaking race" that they would not be driven from the mines. By 1902, English-speaking miners were, according to Warne, "optimistic" enough to use the union to reshape "Slavs." Warne went even further than Commons in articulating a vision—which he later recanted—of the

union as a peacemaker among races: "The union is socializing the hetero-
geneous mass; it is making it over from the individualistic and race point
of view to that of the industrial group." The union could teach "Americanism and bind more closely the heretofore antagonistic . . . races."
Warne worried, however, that the presence of immigrants would force
"the American workingman in self-protection to resort to . . . industrial
unions—to the closed shop, boycotting, strikes, and the like—thus bringing to our people a long train of evils." Industrial relations expert William
Leiserson was more optimistic, writing in 1924 that a "trade union needs
to engage in no Americanizing or proselytizing campaigns to make Americans of immigrant workmen. If it is efficient and successful as a union, it
unites all the workers and imperceptibly fuses native and foreign born
into a common folk." After all, Leiserson argued by favorably quoting the
Harvard professor and race theorist William Z. Ripley, the assemblies and
conventions of the unions imparted to immigrants nothing less grand
than "the primitive character of the Anglo-Saxon folkmoot."[57]

In struggles, native-born unionists came to observe not only the common humanity but also the heroism of new immigrants. Never quite giving up on biological/cultural explanations, labor leaders wondered which
"race" made the best strikers, with some comparisons redounding to the
disfavor of Anglo-Saxons. When they went into much detail, as in Industrial Workers of the World (IWW) leader Covington Hall's reports from
Louisiana, their words remind us that we know little about how unionists,
and workers generally, conceived of race. Hall took seriously the idea of a
"Latin race," including Italians, other southern Europeans, and Mexicans, all of whom he thought put southern whites to shame in their militancy. As a southerner and a labor editor, Hall would have known of
stirring examples of solidarity among Italian and Cuban immigrants in
the cigar industry in Tampa. He may also have been aware of pan-Latin
working-class mobilizations in the Arizona copper industry. Mexican and
Mexican Americans shared low wages, occupational hazards, parishes, and
love of soccer—Phoenix boasted a Mexican/Italian Yellow Kids Football
Club—with many Italian (and some Spanish) immigrants. As Phylis Cancilla Martinelli shows, Italian Americans in Arizona often chose to speak
Spanish in preference to English. During and after the 1903 copper
strike at Morenci, a Latin racial identity took shape around self-activity in

unions, mines, and mutual aid organizations. Italian Americans held places among the leadership of such organizations as the Alianza Hispano Americana, functioning as "honorary Mexicans" at times.[58]

The labor investigator Peter Speek reported similar comparisons in popular speech in western rural areas where the IWW organized. A "white man," Speek wrote, "is an extreme individualist, busy with himself," a "native or old-time immigrant" laborer, boarded by employers. "A foreigner," he added, "is more sociable and has a higher sense of comradeship" and of nationality. Answering the derogatory use of "hunky" to describe Slavic miners at a mine workers convention during World War I, a speaker recalled an Illinois coal strike and credited hunkies for a militancy that made unionization possible. One socialist plasterer offered a specific critique of native-born unionists who used "guinea" to describe Italians. He pointed out that the Italian's ancestors "were the best and unsurpassable in manhood's glories; at a time when our dads were running about in paint and loincloth as ignorant savages." Many Italian Americans, he added to bring the argument up to the present, "are as manly for trade union conditions as the best of us; and that while handicapped by our prejudice."[59]

While such questioning of whiteness was relatively rare in AFL publications, the "new unionism" provided an economic logic that could furnish space for progressive unionists wishing to unite the whole working class. With their own racial status less open to question, new immigrants were at times brought into class-conscious coalitions with whites and at times with African Americans. The great success of the packinghouse unions in forging such unity during World War I ended in victory and spectacularly improved conditions. The diverse new immigrant and black workers at the victory celebration heard Chicago Federation of Labor leader John Fitzpatrick hail them as "black and white together under God's sunshine."[60] If the Irish American unionists had often been bearers of "race hatred" against new immigrants as well as against blacks, they and other old immigrants also could act, in the person of Fitzpatrick, William Haywood, or William Z. Foster, as the bearers of the lesson that class unity transcended race and semirace.[61]

But even at the height of openings toward new unionism and new immigrants, labor organizations taught contradictory lessons regarding whiteness and race. At times, overtures toward new immigrants coincided with renewed exclusion of more fully racialized workers, underlining Du Bois's point that the former were mobbed to make them join unions and the latter to keep them out. The Western Federation of Miners (WFM), whose episodic radicalism coexisted with its anti–new immigrant nativism and a consistent anti-Chinese and anti-Mexican racism, gradually developed a will and a strategy to organize Greek immigrants in some camps, even as it encouraged exclusion of all southern and eastern Europeans elsewhere. By including Greeks, the WFM reaffirmed exclusion of Japanese mine workers and undermined impressive existing solidarity between Greeks and Japanese, who often worked similar jobs.[62] The fear of immigrant "green hands" was balanced against a fear of black hands, so that one historian of immigrant Chicago has suggested that the desire to limit black employment generated the willingness to organize new immigrants. On the other hand, the Irish-dominated Boston waterfront witnessed the erection of color bars against "blacks," meaning both African American and Italian American workers. Much gentler but full of multilayered meaning was the tale found in the papers of Chicago settlement house leader Mary McDowell regarding one of the first black women in a stockyards local, her Irish American local president, and her new immigrant union sisters. After a meeting, members were asked, "Have you any grievances?" The crowd, described as "black and white, Polish, Bohemian, Irish, Croatian and Hungarian" was silent for a time. Then a "morbidly shy black girl" rose to say, "A Polish girl was always taunting her on her color." The two young women were then told to stand together. The Polish worker explained, "Well I did tease her, but she called me a Polack, and I won't stand that." A "hearty, good-natured" collective laugh cleared the international atmosphere. "Ain't you ashamed of yourselves?" the president asked. "Now shake hands and don't bring any more of your personal grievances here."[63]

In 1905, Gompers promised that "Caucasians are not going to let their standard of living be destroyed by Negroes, Chinamen, Japs, or any others."[64] Hearing this, new immigrant unionists might have reflected on what they, as "Caucasians," had to learn regarding their superiority. Or they might have fretted that guineas and hunkies would be classified by organized labor along with "any others" undermining white and American standards. Either way, and many listeners would surely have heard it *both* ways, new immigrants would decidedly have to consider learning about race as part of their labor education.

More complicated still was the relationship between anti-immigrant racism and craft unionism itself. If the logic of Taylorism led to new and broader union initiatives, the logic of whiteness powerfully favored the recrudescence of narrow craft organizations and weakened alternatives to it. The latter logic took several forms. One was to see new immigrant workers' radicalism as "racial," irrational, and dangerous rather than class conscious. In 1907 in Buffalo, for example, between four hundred and a thousand organized Italian laborers paraded behind the union's flag from the Italian quarter to Main Street. After an altercation between a street-car operator and a parade marshal, brief skirmishing with police led to four arrests for incitement to riot. This small and tame protest took on, as Virginia Yans-McLaughlin's vivid account shows, inflated importance in the eyes of white, native-born Buffalonians, for whom "Italians symbolized a double threat" of working-class violence and racial difference. Buffalo's white citizenry saw the demonstration as "a racial disturbance" (the local press headlined it "Race Hatred") because, as Yans-McLaughlin observes, "swarthy Italians" from Calabria and Sicily marched.[65]

This same dynamic took place tellingly in the great strikes after World War I, especially in the 1919 steel strike, rightly termed "an unprecedented display of immigrant defiance" by the labor investigator David Saposs. Saposs recognized that Slavic workers saw the union as a vehicle to combat racial discrimination. He reported that the immigrant workers "feel the discrimination against them as hunkies very keenly and emphasize it more than any of their other grievances." While the leading report on the steel strike described a working-class community as containing "twenty or thirty distinct mental worlds, belonging to as many different races," class unity brought many such world views into effective coalition. At the shining moment of hunky solidarity during the strike, employers responded with successful appeals to "English-speaking" skilled workers. Such appeals included the widely circulated figure of a strikebreaking Uncle Sam—complete with a craft union label. The appeal of the employers went out to native-born whites who, as one pioneering social researcher put it, believed that immigrant workers "are 'Hunkies,' that is all" and who, even if earning just pennies a day more, "look[ed] upon them with an utter absence of kinship." As David Brody wrote in his excellent history of "the nonunion era" in steel, "Eager to dissociate himself from the Hunky, the skilled man identified with the middling group of small shopkeepers and artisans, and with them came to regard the merchants and managers as his models. Whatever his interests may have been, the English-speaking steelworker had a psychological commitment in favor of his employer." One white native-born skilled worker told Saposs that "hunkies" were nothing but "cattle," and that he would not "sit next to a hunky or a nigger as you'd have to in a union." Another asked, "How would you like to shake hands with niggers and foreigners, and call them brothers?" The so-called Greek strike (actually a pan-national one involving a variety of new immigrants for a time cooperating with native-born skilled workers) around Grays Harbor, Washington, in 1912, offered a similar scenario. In that case, the native born backed away from class politics after securing concessions for "white" workers at the expense of "nonwhites" who were sometimes Asians and sometimes "undesirable" Europeans. [66]

Seen as acting tribally when they unionized as workers, new immigrants threatened to undermine the manly American respect alleged to exist between capital and labor. The celebrated historian Frederick Jackson Turner complained early in the twentieth century that "the sympathy of employers with labor has been unfavorably affected by the pressure of the great numbers of immigrants." Moreover, when immigrants mobilized it was far easier for the press and the government to hitch the rhetoric of race to antilabor violence. Thus anti-immigrant racism made craft unionism, with largely native-born members, seem a much safer form of organization and in fact did expose craft unions to less danger than industrial unions.[67]

If the stick of state-sponsored antilabor violence greeted attempts, especially those organized by the radical Industrial Workers of the World, to organize the new immigrant "races," the carrot of jobs in the government's immigration bureaucracies awaited those defeated and conservative labor leaders who espoused xenophobia. Although unable to win decisive legislative victories for immigration restriction, the union bureaucracy enjoyed its greatest pre–World War I legitimation by the state precisely by questioning the rights of immigrants. Terence Powderly's move from the Knights of Labor to U.S. Commissioner General of Labor at the turn of the century was emblematic of this acceptance. Brotherhood of Locomotive Firemen leader Frank Sargent succeeded Powderly as commissioner general. Powderly, described by the historian of Chinese exclusion Delber McKee as having "a free hand to make policy and place men who saw matters as he did in strategic positions" in the recently formed bureau, opposed both Chinese immigration and much of the "new immigration" from Europe. Opposition to Asian immigration and to "new immigration" also gave the divided and loosely federated AFL a common national project. As the German historian of North American immigration Dirk Hoerder has recently written, "From Chinese to east and south European exclusion, the American Federation of Labor made use of the state not only to deal with the issue of 'cheap labor' but also to determine the ethnocultural composition of the nation." He might have added that the state bureaucracy with which labor dealt was in this instance also one in which it held important positions.[68]

Equally powerful in discouraging egalitarian industrial unionism was the fact that many native-born workers had, in their life choices, divorced themselves from doing hunky work. Thus during the 1919–1920 steel strike, appeals to skilled U.S.-born workers to break ranks with new immigrant strikers could play on the idea that the families of the native born had already written off sections of the plants as racially different. The dynamics here substantially transcend anything so simple as the native born constituting a privileged "aristocracy of labor."[69] Certainly some contemporary observers identified elements of such a native-born white racial aristocracy. Grace Abbott's astute study *The Immigrant and the Community* (1917) quantified the extent to which the white native born dominated skilled jobs and positions in the best-paying and most unionized sectors. In the building trades, when she wrote, there were 2,257,506 native-born wage earners and only 850,875 foreign born. In the blast furnaces, the foreign born predominated by 202,512 to 180,089. On steam railways, the native born furnished roughly a million workers and the foreign born about 400,000, but there were over 228,000 unskilled foreign-born laborers on the railways as against 146,000 native born. In the sweatshop-dominated ready-made clothing industry, 65 percent of the workers were immigrants. The British writer H. G. Wells saw the "older American population . . . being floated up" by the new immigration. John Griswold, a Scotch-Irish furnace boss, explained what had driven Irish immigrants and their children out of blast furnace jobs: "It ain't the Hunkies—they couldn't do it—but the Irish don't have to work that way. There was fifty of them here with me sixteen years ago and now where are they? I meet 'em sometimes around the city, ridin' in carriages and all of them wearing white shirts." John Fitch, the Pittsburgh Survey investigator who took evidence from Griswold, was fascinated by the disappearance of "American boys" from whole categories of mill work. Fitch recognized, however, that "those American boys who fancy that they degrade themselves by entering into competition with a Slav for a job" did not automatically prosper. Instead they often ended in dead end "pencil jobs" where "pay is poor." Moreover, the white native born continued to compose a third or more of the unskilled labor force in the United States as a whole in the early twentieth century.[70] But native-born whiteness did make some "white" workers draw a sharp line, based on a mixture of what Fitch called "false pride" and real privileges, between themselves and new immigrants. In Steelton, Pennsylvania, when a plant manager offered to move skilled "white" workers into "hunky" jobs during the depressed conditions of 1908, most preferred to stay jobless.[71]

Teaching Americanism, the labor movement also taught whiteness. The scattered racist jokes in the labor and socialist press could not, of course, rival blackface entertainments, the "coon songs" in the Sunday comics, or a blockbuster film like *Birth of a Nation* in teaching new immigrants the racial ropes of the United States. The socialist movement, largely native born, provided a widely circulated literature of popularized white supremacist ethnology, editorial attacks on "nigger equality," and warnings of "race annihilation" resulting from European immigration. Jack London, a major left-wing cultural figure, taught amid some contradictions that it was possible and desirable to be "first of all a white man and only then a socialist," and excoriated the "dark-pigmented things" migrating from Europe.[72]

But the influence of organized labor and the left as instructors in whiteness focused on popular language more than on literature and on picket lines rather than lines on a page. Unions that discriminated but opened to new immigrants more readily than to African Americans, Mexican Americans, and Asian Americans reinforced the "inbetween" position of southern and eastern Europeans. For example, of the twenty-eight unions in which black workers might have sought membership in Buffalo in the 1920s, three formally practiced Jim Crow and nine others readily admitted doing so informally. Investigators strongly suspected that other unions in the city likewise excluded African Americans informally.

Meanwhile only one union in five in Buffalo practiced any exclusion of new immigrants and those that did directed exclusion specifically at those not naturalized. Unions also exposed immigrants to intricate and spurious associations of race, strikebreaking, and lack of manly pride. Even as AFL exclusionism ensured that there would be black strikebreakers and black suspicion of unions, the language of labor equated scabbing with "turning nigger." Warning all union men against "slavelike" behavior, unions familiarized new workers with the ways race and slavery had gone together to define a standard of unmanned servility, sometimes using pageants to do so. The unions organized much of their critique of working-class quiescence around a critique of "slavish" behavior that could be mobilized against ex-slaves or against Slavs, but indicted the former more fiercely than the latter.[73] In confusing situations, with scabs coming from the African American, new immigrant and native-born working classes as well as from college campuses (and with craft unions routinely breaking each other's strikes), Booker T. Washington identified one firm rule of thumb: "Strikers seem to consider it a much greater crime for a Negro who had been denied the opportunity to work at his trade to take the place of a striking employee than for a white man to do the same thing."[74]

Inbetween at work, in looking for work, in unions, in the popular mind and in the eyes of the state, new immigrants were racially scrutinized in ways as painful as they were numerous. Their trials made certain that race would enter the consciousness of immigrants from eastern and southern Europe in forms different from the race thinking of their homelands. The contradictory structural positions that they inhabited ensured, as we shall see, that their evolving consciousness of race would be anything but simple.

CHAPTER 4

Inside the Wail: New Immigrant Racial Consciousness

Only a super-ass would see even the slightest comparison between the Negro's degraded position in this country and the favored position of the English, the Irish, the Germans, the French, the Italians, and the Russians, all of whom are admittedly within the charmed circle of the dominant race.

THE CRUSADER, RADICAL AFRICAN AMERICAN PERIODICAL (1920)

I wasn't even born in America. I had no prejudice.

**JEWISH IMMIGRANT RECORDER OF
AFRICAN AMERICAN SONGS LAWRENCE GELLERT,
ON HIS SUCCESSES COLLECTING IN THE SOUTH
(1966, REFLECTING ON THE 1920S AND 1930S)**

Racism, according to the legal theorist Patricia J. Williams, "is aspiration as well as condemnation."[1] Early in the twentieth century, it was by no means clear that immigrants from southern and eastern Europe would escape the condemnations of white supremacists. Nor was it certain that these immigrants would aspire to do so. In reflecting on a visit to her Hull House settlement by W.E.B. Du Bois, the social reformer Jane Addams suggested in 1909 that the interests and aspirations of the "Mediterranean immigrants" attending did not include being white. They listened to the "scholarly address" of the eminent African American intellectual and activist with "respect and enthusiasm." The Chicago crowd watched with "apparently no consciousness of the race difference which color seems to accentuate so absurdly." In Addams's view the listeners did not experience being part of the master race. Physically assaulted "simply because they are 'dagoes,'" and, in the case of the Greeks "filled with rage when their very name is flung at them as an opprobrious epithet," they seemed to Addams to share a fate with African Americans. Anti-immigrant hatred, she held, "would be much minimized in America, if we faced our own race problem with courage and intelligence, and these very Mediterranean immigrants might give us valuable help." Those in the audience, Addams implied, also sensed this linkage. Du Bois spoke as he was launching the National Association for the Advancement of Colored People. Addams described his raptly listening southern European audience as having a sharp personal interest precisely in "the advancement of colored people."[2] Addams's remarks carry considerable hyperbole, and her remarks about color and race are curious since Du Bois would have been no darker than many Greek and south Italian immigrants. Moreover, Addams tragically joined the typical settlement house practice of accepting Jim Crow and consequently barring African American participation, on the theory that bringing in black residents would cause immigrants to withdraw.[3]

Nonetheless, Du Bois was not without dreams similar to those Addams attributed to the new immigrant audience. Writing in 1922, he branded postwar "Americanization" campaigns as nothing more than "a renewal of the Anglo-Saxon cult; the worship of the Nordic totem, the disfranchisement of Negro, Jew, Irishman, Italian, Hungarian, Asiatic and South Sea Islander—the world rule of Nordic white through brute force." He reminded readers of *The Crisis* that "the majority of people in the United States" were not Anglo-Saxon, and he sought to unify that majority:

> The same forces south and east that are fighting democracy in the United States are fighting black men and fighting Jews. The great alliance then between the darker people the world over, between disadvantaged groups like the Irish and the Jew and the working classes everywhere is the one alliance that is going to keep down privilege as represented by New England and Old England.[4]

That year, Du Bois began work on *The Gift of Black Folk* (1924) as a contribution to a projected series published by the Knights of Columbus of the Catholic Church. Offering positive accounts of the "gifts" of various immigrant groups, the series aimed to combat pending racist immigration legislation. The volume included a long introductory essay by Dr. Edward McSweeney detailing immigration law proposals and called specifically for defense of Italians and Jews. In the year before *Gift of Black Folk* appeared, when Du Bois told the socialist newspaper *Jewish Daily Forward* that "the Negro race looks to Jews for sympathy and understanding," he was both describing and prescribing with regard to black–Jewish relations. These questions were never easy ones. At other junctures, Du Bois offered more somber assessments of possible solidarity between African Americans and new immigrants. He suggested that aliens became white over the bodies of black Americans, who in turn were "silently elated" at the "inhumanity" of "Nordic fanatics" who restricted immigration from southern and eastern Europe in 1924.[5]

Knowing how the twentieth century turned out, we may regard Du Bois's pessimistic words as judicious and his optimistic ones as romantic, if not reckless. However, there were strong reasons at times for optimism. New immigrants were capable of hesitating to embrace a white identity and even of forging unity with African Americans. In the most ambitious early study of race in the United States, Swedish sociologist Gunnar Myrdal suggested exactly this point. Writing in *An American Dilemma* in 1944, Myrdal asserted that new immigrants held an "interest in solidarity with Negroes" for a time after arrival or at least lacked "the intense superiority feeling of the native Americans educated in race prejudice." The very idea of securing a pure white, "Anglo-Saxon" nation with such a diverse population could appear ridiculous to them. Many immigrants firmly rejected any imperial Anglo-Saxon mission abroad. The Irish American humorist Finley Peter Dunne showed why they hesitated to join the "Anglo-Saxon 'lieance'" during the Spanish American War. Such an alliance, his title character Mr. Dooley held, impossibly gathered together the "Rooshian Jew," the "Ancient Order iv Anglo-Saxon Hibernyans," "th' Dago Anglo-Saxons," the "Bohemians an' Pole Anglo-Saxon," "th' Pollacky Benivolent Society" and "th' Afro-Americans," all united in "common hurtage." Dooley mockingly counted himself as willing to sign up as "wan iv th' hottest Anglo-Saxons that iver come out iv Anglo-Saxony." At home, Chicago's Polish-language *Dziennik Zwiazkowy* gloried in the presence of a contingent of black workers in the funeral procession of packinghouse union leader Jan Kikulski in 1920. After a brief history of African American life, that same paper asked, during the 1919 riots, "Is it not right they should hate the whites?" Houston's Greek Americans developed, and retained, a language setting themselves apart from *I mavri* (the blacks), *I aspiri* (the whites), and Mexican Americans. In New England, Greek immigrants worked in coalitions with Armenians, whom the courts were fretfully accepting as white, and Syrians, whom the courts found nonwhite. Workers in the large Greek American sponge fishing industry in Tarpon Springs, Florida, fought the Ku Klux Klan, accepted Polish immigrants, and employed black workers on an equal, share-the-catch system. Nor did Tarpon Springs practice Jim Crow in public transportation.[6]

In Louisiana and Mississippi, southern Italians learned Jim Crow tardily, even when legally accepted as whites, so much so that native whites fretted and black southerners "made unabashed distinctions between Dagoes and white folks" treating the former with a "friendly, first name familiarity." In a Mississippi town whites wrecked an Italian American restaurant and drove away its owner after he defied Jim Crow by serving a black customer. After a Louisiana lynching of three Italians in 1896, so many African Americans showed up to mourn that local whites fretted about the possibility of interracial revenge. Three years later, the lynching of five Italian Americans at Tallulah, Louisiana, resulted in part from fraternization with blacks. In McCloud, California, black and Italian American workers struck together and stuck together in 1909. Italian and Italian American radicals, as Rudolph J. Vecoli puts it, "consistently expressed horror at the barbaric treatment of blacks," in part because "Italians were also regarded as an inferior race." *Il Proletario* denounced not only lynchings but also "the republic of lynchings," branding the rulers of the United States the "savages of the blue eyes." It ridiculed as well the civilizationist pretensions of Italy's invasion of Tripoli in 1911. In a 1905 essay the Italian American lawyer and activist Gino Speranza questioned how an Italian immigrant could place faith in "American justice when he . . . learns of it through the lynchings of his countrymen or the burnings of negroes." The Paterson, New Jersey–based anarchist Il Gruppo Diretto all' Esistenza (The Right to Exist Group) criticized racism, colonialism, and even whiteness in *La Questione Sociale* and its successor *L'Era Nuova*. The latter newspaper ran "The Crimes of the White Race" in 1909, denouncing the "systematic destruction of the races of color" and specifying the oppression of American Indians, blacks, and Asian immigrants. "The white race," the article held, "has acted against all other races like a predatory animal." After the Russian Revolution, Italian American anarchists, who signed their manifesto The Bandits of All Laws, dreamed of returning to a revolutionary Italy and exposing U.S. crimes, especially "the pale flames of the race hatred" that produced massacres in East St. Louis and the "insisting lynchings," year after year. In 1934, Local 89 of the International Ladies Garment Workers Union, New York City's Italian American local, reprinted "Le Razza di Colore e il Colore il Socialismo" by Arturo Labriola. In it the Italian antifascist charged "those with white skins" with complicity in racism, slavery, and imperialism. He neatly if ambiguously positioned Italians in reminding readers that "those with European stock" are a small minority in a world largely "black, yellow, olive [and] mixed." These politically pointed analyses coexisted with a broader and fascinating Italian American cultural critique of mainstream white Americans as belonging, by virtue of their extreme acquisitiveness, to "another world, another race." "To my people," Pietro Di Donato wrote, such white Americans were "colorless, unsalted baloney munchers." As late as the 1940s, rock music star Frank Zappa would later recall, his Italian immigrant parents puzzled over how odd and lamentable the behavior of "white people" in the United States was.[7]

The socialist-leaning Polish paper *Dziennik ludowy* bespoke the egalitarianism of sections of the eastern European immigrant press when it editorialized in favor of complete equality "regardless of skin color or languages" as early as 1907. In 1928 *Dziennik Chicagoski* denounced the adoration of all things "Nordic" as "malignant and harmful just as the German 'Deutschland uber alles.'" "Nordic" was a "thought-up term" that could "excuse . . . anything" but "not explain anything." In mounting this critique, the paper pointed not only to "dago" and "hunky" but also "nigger" as terms that "immediately darken our brain." Elsewhere it asked readers to critically dissect racist propaganda: "If the words 'superior race' are replaced by the words 'Anglo-Saxon' and instead of 'inferior races,' such terms as Polish, Italian, Russian and Slavs—in general—not to mention the Negro, the Chinese, the Japanese—are applied, then we shall see the political side of the racial problems in the United States in stark nakedness." In 1912, a Lithuanian paper in Chicago expressed sympathy for the victims of racism and distance from whites: "There is no Negro problem in Europe because, it is apparent, things are done differently there. The Negro problem in

America has been created by the Americans themselves." The article warned, "Sooner or later one has to pay for trampling moral principles and the truth of that must now be felt especially by the whites." The Slovak American Communist organ, *Rovnost L'udu* (Equality for the People), denounced lynching as "the worst form of barbarism." Another Slovak American paper reacted to racist atrocities by counseling that African Americans "need some strong defensive society." [8]

The Jewish press at times identified with both the suffering and the aspirations of African Americans. In 1912, Chicago's *Jewish Daily Courier* concluded that "In this world . . . the Jew is treated as a Negro and a Negro as a Jew" and maintained that the "lynching of the Negroes in the South is similar to massacres on Jews in Russia." Two years later the same paper held that anti-Jewish pogroms in Poland and hate crimes in the United States were essentially the same: "In Poland when a crime of this sort occurs, you can hear them utter these words 'It does not matter, it was only a Jewish home.' And in this country when a Negro's house is burned the white people say 'Why this is nothing; it was only a Negro's house.'" The New York *Call*, with the largest circulation of any socialist paper in the United States and a huge readership of immigrant radicals, echoed the Italian American radical press in denouncing racist atrocities in a way that hoped to puncture myths about American capitalism and American democracy. Its 1919 response to postwar race riots charged, "American capitalism is about as foul as will be found anywhere in the world. Of pogroms we have the most atrocious in the world." In 1899 the Yiddish-language *Freie Arbeiter Stimme* ridiculed the "civilizing" mission of the United States in the Philippines in light of domestic racist atrocities. Joseph Opatoshu's novella *Lincherei* (Lynchers) (1923) offered an indictment in Yiddish of a "hysterically happy southern white roasting a black man alive for a crime he did not commit." When the Hungarian Jewish American blues collector Lawrence Gellert strode around Boston Commons in 1932 with the black poet Sterling Brown and the revolutionary heiress Nancy Cunard, they cherished what Gellert regarded as a common goal: "the full equality of the black race." When Gellert commented that the key to effective collection of blues music was having "no white sons of bitches around," he was only probably joking. As late as 1928 Louis Wirth's classic study *The Ghetto* argued that many immigrants in Chicago's Jewish areas "have as yet not heard of the color line." Earlier that same decade the anthropologist Albert Jenks drew the point more worriedly and broadly: "The foreigner coming fresh to our shores almost entirely lacks the racial prejudice which is native to America." The memoir of the South Carolina African American community leader Mamie Garvin Fields recounts working with "Italian and Polish girls" in the needle trades during a Massachusetts sojourn in 1913. Communicating largely in "sign language," the immigrants showed the African American workers the work process and at times even threw sleeves they had sewn on the piles of neophyte black workers, to ensure that some piece rates were earned. As Fields put it, "Those immigrant girls made us feel at home, in America, in a foreign-speaking place."9

These affinities found political and organizational expression, as, for example, in Jewish participation in the National Association for the Advancement of Colored People and in fragile pan-immigrant coalitions opposing Anglo-Saxon bias in school textbooks. As the Socialist Party debated immigration just prior to World War I, it was the black preacher George Washington Woodbey who attacked its nativism and insisted, "There are no foreigners." At times, as the industrial relations expert Herman Feldman wrote in 1931, it was possible to assemble alliances of "Scandinavians, Italians, Czechoslovaks, Poles, Slavs of all groups [and] Negroes" who rallied against the Anglo-Saxon symbol of King George. That symbol, Feldman held, stood "for all kinds of injustice and persecution to which they have been subjected under the impulse of race prejudice; for artificial racial discrimination in our immigrant policy; for . . . indignities in naturalization; for Klan outrages and police brutalities." It further symbolized all of the "opprobrious epithets . . . hurled in their faces . . . 'wop,' 'dago,' 'kike,' 'hunkie,' and 'nigger.'" In labor organizations alliances of European and African "races" achieved some successes. The early Jewish-led ILGWU supported interracial organizing and even, in the case of the Waist and Dress Makers Union in 1923, the radical African Blood Brotherhood. Lisa McGirr's fine study of Marine Transport Workers Local 8, the successful, racially mixed Industrial Workers of the World affiliate in Philadelphia, describes it as an example less of black–white unity than of black–Polish–Lithuanian unity—a solidarity whose tensions Howard Kimeldorf's new study suggestively explores.10 In Grant Town, West Virginia, a "hoary old Negro" miner found African Americans and new immigrants to be the "mainstay of the union," cooperating under largely black leadership in the face of the Jim Crow social practices and the "100 percent Americanism" of native-born whites. Nativist-inspired contract language kept workers who had not filed for citizenship (and nonspeakers of English) from serving as union committeemen. The U.S. Department of Labor found "miners of foreign birth" open to representation by blacks in West Virginia while "native white" miners were likely to refuse to serve on mixed committees or accept orders issued by "colored committeemen."[11]

In many ways the World War I–era experiments in packinghouse trade union organization were likewise examples of black–hunky unity.[12] In the wake of the Chicago race riot of 1919, according to C. L. R. James, unionized workers refused to go to their jobs until the police withdrew from the stockyards. When they did return, blacks and Slavs "met as old friends" on the shop floor; many "put their arms around one another's necks." James summed up an official report on the strike: "There was nothing in the contact of the Negro or the Pole or the Slav that would indicate that there had ever been a race riot in Chicago, and there was nothing from the beginning of the race riot to the end that would indicate there was any feeling started in the stockyards . . . that led to the race riots."[13]

In the post–World War I maritime strikes in New York City, a black–Italian–Irish alliance was, at least temporarily, sealed by African American support for direct actions supporting Irish freedom, sometimes referred to by black and by Irish unionists as a "race" issue. In 1933, the *Irish People Monthly* offered consecutive articles opposing the framing of the Scottsboro Boys, African American defendants in a celebrated case of alleged rape, and then praising their Jewish lawyers and denouncing anti-Semitism. The historian of the Scottsboro defense, James Goodman, has described early appeals to Alabama authorities on their behalf as being headed "We the members of the Lithuanian Working Women's Alliance" or "We the Ukrainian Labor Temple," or again "We" the "Russian," "Finnish," "Scandinavian," "Croatian," "Hungarian," and "Jewish" workers.[14]

INSIDE WHICH WAIL?

The possibilities of black solidarity with new immigrants found expression in a particularly lyrical, rich, and tragic tradition developed by African American creative artists, who were, significantly enough, the U.S.

thinkers most consistently attuned to questions regarding the racial position and consciousness of southern and eastern European newcomers.
That tradition reached its highest expression in William Attaway's stirring
1941 novel, *Blood on the Forge*. In that work of proletarian fiction,
Melody and his half brother Chinatown disagreed on the merits of the
music made by Slavic immigrants with whom they worked in Pittsburgh's
steel mills. Chinatown heard nothing in it but a "yowl," adding that "a
man can't understand one word they yowlin'." But Melody, who lived to
play the blues and could "hear music in a snore," knew better. He

> had heard some of these people from the Ukraine singing. He hadn't un-
> derstood one word. Yet he didn't have to know the words to understand
> what they were wailing about. Words didn't count when the music had a
> tongue. The field hands of the sloping red hill country in Kentucky sang
> that same tongue.

Hearing the wails of his old Kentucky home in Ukrainian music, Melody
echoed Frederick Douglass's observations of almost a century earlier.
During his 1845–1846 tour of Ireland, Douglass heard the "wailing
notes" of the music of the oppressed and famished Irish people as close
kin of the "wild notes" of the slaves' sorrow songs.[15] As late as 1974, white
bluesman Mose Allison would be agreeing with Attaway, insisting to
Melody Maker that Bartok's collection of Hungarian and Romanian folk
songs featured "a lot of blues."[16]

For the Jewish jazz musician Mezz Mezzrow, weeping and wailing
united black and new immigrant music. In a remarkable section of his autobiographical *Really the Blues*, Mezzrow recalled a prison term he
served for selling drugs. Having convinced himself that he was in fact
black, he likewise convinced prison officials, who allowed him to be confined in the segregated African American section of the prison. Nonetheless, when white Catholics in the prison organized Christmas caroling,
the response of Jewish prisoners was to ask Mezzrow to lead them in
song. Professing surprise that he, "a colored guy," would be chosen to direct a Jewish chorus, Mezzrow learned "once more how music of different oppressed peoples blends together." He did not "know the Hebrew
chants," but a "weepy blues inflection" made his interpretation of the
"wailing and lament" a huge success. Elsewhere Mezzrow described "an

old Jewish man with a long beard" listening in Chicago to Blind Lemon Jefferson's "Black Snake Moan" playing on a Victrola in the Jewish Maxwell Street market district. The man "kept shaking his head sadly, like he knew that evil black snake personally." Paul Robeson's language struck a similar chord, in explaining to the Yiddish publication *Morgan Journal-Tageblatt* why he eschewed singing in French, German, or Italian but did sing "Jewish opera." The former three groups, he held, lacked parallel histories with his enslaved ancestors while the "Jewish sigh and tear" made Jewish music accessible.[17] Others also believed (or as Jeffrey Melnick's evocative *A Right to Sing the Blues* hints, wanted to believe) that Jewish music emanated from inside (or at least alongside) the African American wail. The journalist/novelist/funnyman Ben Hecht offered the most damning portrayal of the relationships—for Hecht thoroughly market-mediated ones—among suffering, race, and song. In his 1931 novel *A Jew in Love* Hecht wrote of Jewish jazz bands whose "songs quiver with self-pity [and] are full of the unscrupulous wailings of ancient Jew griefs tricked out in Negro, Russian and oriental rhythms." *Forward*, on the other hand, posed the question, "Is there any incongruity in this Jewish boy [talking film pioneer Al Jolson] with his face painted like a Southern Negro singing in the Negro dialect?" It answered, "No, there is not. Indeed [there is] a minor key of Jewish music, the wail of the *Chazan*, the cry of anguish of a people who had suffered. The son of a line of rabbis well knows how to sing the songs of the most cruelly wronged people in the world's history." In *The Jazz Singer*, blackface Jolson was said to perform "just like his papa, with the cry in his voice."[18]

On one level, these African American commentaries on the soul of the music of oppressed Europeans underline the affinities between blacks and "inbetween" immigrants suggested by Jane Addams's look at Hull House residents looking at Du Bois. But Mezzrow, Douglass, and Attaway were as intent to invoke tragedy as possibility in discussing new immigrant relations with nonwhite Americans. Mezzrow disdained appeals to Jewish "racial" solidarity in the entertainment world, seeing such "jive" as a betrayal of "colored musicians" who were his "real brothers." Douglass lingered over the wails of the Irish to emphasize the tragedy of Irish American racism, seconding Irish nationalist leader Daniel O'Connell's long-standing point that this "cruelty" was not learned in Ireland but was a bitter product of U.S. experience. Toni Morrison makes much the same point in describing her own innocent and wrenching relationship with a schoolmate during her Ohio youth. The immigrant child learned to speak and read English in large part from Morrison, with whom he was paired in one of the "two seaters" common at that time in grade school classrooms. Very quickly he also learned the word "nigger" and racial ground rules in the United States. His U.S. education taught him (but not his sister, who stayed close to Morrison) to turn his back on Morrison's friendship and tutoring. Country music's biggest African American star, Charley Pride, wrote similarly of Latvian refugees brought to the "Mississippi Cotton Pickin' Delta Town" he was living in just after World War II. When the Latvians socialized with African Americans and dating relationships seemed on the horizon, the white southerners built houses for the immigrants at a distance from African Americans. Pride remembered, "The Latvians weren't Americans but they were white and the townsfolk wanted to get them away from the blacks as quickly as possible."[19]

James Baldwin's indispensable essays on the whitening of new immigrants share the attuned-to-tragedy humanism of Attaway and Douglass as well as their lack of illusions. In "On Being 'White' . . . and Other Lies" and "White Man's Guilt," Baldwin pairs the embrace of whiteness with the immigrants' loss of contact with land and community. Baldwin makes the adoption of whiteness a product and a cause of the loss of humanity by new immigrants. Regimented into the disciplines of industrial work, these new immigrants also "chose" to enter the imprisoning confines of whiteness, which Baldwin suggestively terms a "factory." At times Baldwin describes a blanching process that "took generations and a vast amount of coercion." Joining in acts of racism against people of color made immigrants white over time. Elsewhere he posits an almost immediate sea change to a white identity.[20]

The idea of an immediate embrace of whiteness by new immigrants occurs repeatedly in African American thought, though typically alongside more complicated scenarios. Indeed the simplest and perhaps most celebrated answer to how the whiteness of new European immigrants can be historicized comes in the epilogue to Malcolm X's *Autobiography*. His collaborator on the book, Alex Haley, describes being in a U.S. airport with Malcolm and admiring an arriving family of European immigrants. They are, Malcolm predicts, about to learn their first word of English: "nigger." Malcolm's one-liner is precisely repeated (without credit) or presaged in the works of black artists from John Oliver Killens to Richard Pryor, which raises the possibility that they drew it from black folk humor. Morrison deftly counts "nigger" as the second word in the immigrant's English vocabulary, with "okay" coming before. St. Clair Drake and Horace Cayton added detail when they wrote that African Americans in Chicago generally "grumbled [that] foreigners learn how to cuss, count and say 'nigger' as soon as they get here."[21] Like much enduring folklore, such a line distills a sharp point and operates on a variety of levels. Pessimistic to the point of rancor, the joke's logic resembles that of African American usages of "hunky" and "honky," which imply that the eastern European new immigrants slurred by the former term could come to exemplify the white oppressors identified by the latter term in a remarkably short time.[22] However bitter, the joke does not make immigrant racism a product of the essential "white" characteristics of the newcomers. Pryor, for example, applies it to Asian immigrants. The weight of U.S. racial division must be learned—and the immigrants' beauty or as Baldwin has it, "soul," must be lost.[23] The tragedy arises from the knowledge that U.S. realities were brutal, effective teachers of racial division and immigrants were ready learners. "It is quite remarkable," the New York *Age* wrote, "how easily foreigners catch on to the notion . . . to treat Afro-Americans disdainfully and contemptuously."[24]

Often a single piece of evidence reflects both the possibility and the implausibility that blacks and new immigrants cohabited inside the wail. While the Jewish socialist Baruch Vladeck visited Virginia in 1910, white rioters descended on black communities to avenge Jack Johnson's heavyweight boxing victory over a white champion. Vladeck refused to identify with the "great white hope." He compared the riots to anti-Semitic pogroms in Russia and urged his Jewish listeners in Norfolk to protect African Americans from attack. Vladeck's plans excited no response, other than being informed by some in the Jewish community that he knew nothing of the situation and that blacks were "nothing but animals." Vladeck's ill-starred antiracist appeal illustrates the potential of European experiences to generate a sympathy with victims of racism and even a standing aside from whiteness. His listeners, in their opposition and inaction, demonstrated that egalitarian logic never prevailed automatically. Immigrants in different times and places drew widely different conclusions from the lessons regarding race that they learned in

Europe and the United States. The hope that "common oppression" would spark interracial solidarity materialized at times; so did its opposite with dreary frequency.[25]

Each side of the Vladeck incident is strongly, indeed too strongly, reflected in the scholarship on race and immigration. In his introduction to a recent collection on blacks and Jews, Paul Berman argues that the latter group has experienced the former as "The Other and Almost the Same." Insofar as historians and cultural critics have investigated interactions between African Americans and new immigrants—the literature in this area is shockingly sparse except for Jewish/black studies, where quantity considerably exceeds quality—they have tended to pick one side or another of Berman's dichotomy. Some, like Michael Lerner and Ze'ev Chafets, find the new immigrant group of interest to share a "nonwhite" past with African Americans. Some stress the presence of "common enemies" in accounting for new immigrant–black cooperation in the past. Others elide the question of race by imagining a similar "ethnic" experience shared on differing frequencies by all newcomers to the United States. Far less sanguinely, some join Herbert Hill and Stephen Steinberg in emphasizing otherness and hostility, marking the new immigrant the "deadly foe" of African Americans. Berman's work holds special interest because it decisively moves in both directions. Blacks and Jews, he observes, disregarding studies by Sander Gilman, never appeared physically similar. But what they shared was unspeakably dramatic, a common "boot press" on the neck. Such vulnerability makes Berman take seriously the idea of "almost the sameness." But he quickly retreats from it, finding even the boot on the neck experiences to be scarcely comparable after all.[26]

For some groups, such as Poles and Jews, the experiences that put them in a position to understand life "inside the wail" resonated more intensely in Europe. Thaddeus Radzialowski's ruminations on Polish American identity go far toward showing how centrally important a sense of oppression in Poland has been even into the third and fourth immigrant generations in the United States. When Lerner maintains, as in a fascinating recent exchange with Cornel West, that Jews are "not white," his strongest evidence focuses on Jewish history in Europe. When commenting on the United States, he grudgingly allows that, through struggle and at great psychic cost, Jews gradually secured the benefits of whiteness. His spectacularly revisionist claim of Jewish nonwhiteness thus deflates into one not so different from James Baldwin's. For Baldwin, it was precisely the success and the cost of Jews becoming white (or as Ralph Ellison had it, "passing for white") in the United States that fueled tension on both sides of the black–Jewish divide.[27] The European background could, of course, leave memories that would combine with experience of class inequalities and of inbetween status in the United States to produce a general critique of oppression. Thus the Jewish American poet Emma Lazarus wrote, "Until we are all free, we are none of us free," and immigrant radicals rallied their communities to activism in support of black civil rights around her aphorism. But a Jewish immigrant from Poland to the southern United States would recall in a 1971 interview that he had "heard the term 'nigger' used by Jewish sons of immigrant parents with the same venom and contempt as the term 'Zhid' was used in the old country."[28] Many immigrants did not hear the wails of other groups or, hearing them, turned away.

In the United States, no European immigrant group suffered anything like the terror that afflicted people of color. One 1930s study put the number of Italian Americans, the new immigrant group most victimized by extralegal violence, to die from lynching in U.S. history at twenty-eight. Richard Gambino's more expansive compilation suggests only slightly higher estimates of Italian Americans lynched. A handful of Jews were lynched, from a Reconstruction-era radical civil rights advocate in the South through accused murderer Leo Frank.[29] But these patterns of violence were utterly incommensurate with the racist violence visited on thousands of Native Americans, Latinos, Asian Americans, and African Americans in the late nineteenth and early twentieth centuries. The number of Chinese Americans killed in the Rock Springs (Wyoming) massacre alone in 1885 probably exceeded that of all new immigrants lynched. African American lynchings outstripped those of new immigrants by perhaps a factor of 75 to 1 or more. During and after World War I, as racist immigration legislation of the 1920s took shape and as Ku Klux Klan physical attacks on new immigrants increased, a series of pogroms against entire African American communities in Tulsa, Omaha, Longview (Texas), East St. Louis, Chicago, Elaine (Arkansas), Rosewood (Florida), and elsewhere took many hundreds of lives. To find comparisons to such experiences, Jews and Armenians, for example, had to look to what they had fled in Europe, not to what they found in the United

States. By the time of the East St. Louis riot of 1917, one Jewish spokesman was arguing that the U.S. perpetrators of racist violence were still more pitiless. Oscar Leonard, superintendent of the Jewish Educational and Charitable Association in St. Louis, found that the Russians "gave the Jews a chance to run while they were trying to murder them. The whites in East St. Louis fired the homes of black folk and either did not allow them to leave . . . or shot them the moment they dared attempt to escape the flames."[30] The emphasis on transatlantic passage in the psychoanalytically informed work of C. Fred Alford is therefore telling: "Jews and blacks are not only not in the same boat but they never were, not even—or especially—when they crossed the Atlantic to the U.S." Baldwin's observation that Jews escaping European persecution knew so much about life in the wail as to be "unwilling to imagine it again" suggests that however proximate in character, black and Jewish oppression were separate *in the United States* and that if many Jews bridged that separation it was by no means easy or natural to do so.[31]

The extended account of the life of David Pearlman, gathered from oral family traditions by Louis Schmier, captures some of the contradictions in the Jewish case. Pearlman sought to build Jewish–black bridges in the U.S. South over several decades. Sent to the United States from Russia in 1884 in the face of fierce oppression, Pearlman heard his mother's very guarded optimism about his migration. "Here, there, what's the difference? A *goy* [Gentile] is a *goy* no matter where he is. But, at least if our David is going to be persecuted, he will be better dressed for the occasion." Arrived in Americus, Georgia, David joined his cousin's peddling enterprise and complained that carrying a hundred-pound sack hardly seemed to signal a "successful business." His cousin replied, "Anything not near the Czar is a success." In visiting black customers, David adopted an easy familiarity, in part because they helped teach him English as he imparted bits of Hebrew and Yiddish to them. His longer-established relatives wasted no time in acquainting him with the dangers of treating blacks like "long-lost *mishpoche* (relatives)." His cousin spoke slowly: "The *schwartzers* (blacks) here are like we are in Russia. Do you understand? They are to *goyims* Jews—outcasts, nothing, dirt!" To befriend them was to court disaster from the "*goyishe cossacks*" of Georgia. David replied that buying into white supremacy would make him a cossack. "It is easy," he told his cousin, "for you to forget how to feel and what it is like to be hurt and stepped on when you think of yourself as white today and forget what it was like being a Jew yesterday." The cousin did not deny David's parallels but counseled, "Let the *goyim* tell you how to handle these people." The cousin wondered aloud, "Is it so bad that they should hate someone else for a change?"[32] There was logic in both David's position and his cousin's. So too was there logic in some Jewish leaders, most of them earlier-arriving German Jews, charging that making comparisons between the bloody 1903 Kishineff pogrom and U.S. lynchings was a backhanded attempt "to break the force of world-wide public opinion against Russia," even as other Jewish leaders found good reasons to forward such comparisons. It made sense, in 1919, for a Jewish subway conductor to be the only person to express sympathy for a black hobo hoping to warm up in the conductor's rest house. After other workers mocked the conductor with "Perhaps he is a friend of yours?" it made sense for the conductor to lapse into silence.[33]

In other cases proximity to racialized minorities in the United States led to a desire to establish distance rather than a sense of common purpose. Greek workers in the West, often segregated, mistaken for blacks or Mexicans, and victimized, responded positively to belated overtures from the Western Federation of Miners. When that union began to regard Greek miners as white fellow workers, the Greeks did not rock the boat by demanding admission for Japanese American mine workers with whom they had previously allied themselves. In the 1920s in northeastern Colorado, a Greek American restaurateur may have forgotten, or may have remembered, his group's experiences with exclusion in the West when he barred Mexican Americans from eating. Greek and Italian Americans were, not surprisingly, often tempted to use appeals to the roots of "European civilization" to establish themselves as "the highest type of the caucasian race."[34] Italians, as Robert Orsi has shown, feared being associated with African Americans, Asians, and Latinos, depending on time and place, and at times decisively practiced exclusion so that there could be no mistake. In the wake of World War I, young Stjepan Mesaroš, on his first day at a Philadelphia slaughterhouse job, noticed the torrents of abuse heaped on a black coworker. A Croatian, Mesaroš sat on a break with a Serbian radical who worked in the plant. "You soon learn something about this country," the Serb explained. "Negroes never get a fair chance." The exchange sparked a series of conversations that helped transform Mesaroš (renamed as Steve Nelson) into a socialist and an antiracist. But for many immigrants, caught in a world of dog-eat-dog competition, the lesson would likely have been that African Americans were decidedly among the eaten, and thus to be avoided. Robert Zecker's study of the many short articles in the Slovak American press recounting lynchings of blacks captures an important dynamic. The accounts, translated from wire service articles, sometimes carried approving headlines like "People's Justice." Even when they did not they functioned to "naturalize" lynching and served as cautionary tales.[35]

Recently arrived Jewish immigrants on New York City's Lower East Side in the early twentieth century sharply and vocally resented reform efforts which implied that they should make a common cause with African American *schwartzes*. Matthew Frye Jacobson's study of the Jewish "diaspora imagination" in the United States ably discusses the Yiddish-speaking left's fragile anti-imperialism but also notes its embrace of the idea of the "yellow peril" *(gelersrek)* Asian immigration represented to U.S. labor. In New Bedford, "white Portuguese" angrily reacted to perceived racial slights and sharply drew the color line against "black Portuguese" Cape Verdeans, especially when preference in jobs and housing hung in the balance.[36] When labor reformer Carroll D. Wright cast the French Canadians as the "Chinese of the Eastern States" in an 1881 Massachusetts Bureau of Labor Statistics report, he precipitated a firestorm of protest that lasted more than a decade. At hearings on the report, a Quebecois spokesman declared, "We are a white people." In Oakland, Azorean "white Portuguese"—whose children were once said by "experts" to have an average IQ of 80—were constantly victimized by other Europeans, but the result was not necessarily solidarity with people of color. Stan Weir, an organizer in the Chevrolet plant there, recalled, "Most of the people in that local were Portuguese-Americans from East Oakland. There was a great deal of Jim Crow amongst them because American society was constantly trying to put them in the position of American blacks." In Hawaii, the pressure for Portuguese agricultural workers to attempt to achieve *haole* (white) status by distancing themselves from Asians was great but so too were interracial labor organizing initiatives including the Portuguese.[37]

Radzialowski's work on black and Polish workers brilliantly suggests that the latter group may have developed its self-image and honed its reputation in more or less conscious counterpoint to the stereotype of the "niggerscab." "Poles who had so little going for them (except their white skin—certainly no mean advantage but more important later than earlier in their American experience)," Radzialowski reasons, "may have grasped this image of themselves as honest, honorable, non-scabbing workers and stressed the image of the black scab in order to distinguish themselves from . . . the blacks with whom they shared the bottom of American society."[38]

WHITE ON ARRIVAL? WHITE BEFORE COMING?

So thoroughly did the wails of new immigrants at times find places in a chorus of U.S. racism that it is tempting to accept the "first word" joke as the *Cliffs Notes* adumbration of the history of racial consciousness among new immigrants and to regard the wails of the inbetween as background noise. Thomas Guglielmo's provocative argument that Italian immigrants in early twentieth-century Chicago were WOA (white on arrival) articulates this position forcefully. Guglielmo principally refers to the racial (or, as he puts it, color) categorization of Italian Americans as white, but the phrasing is also potentially useful where their consciousness is concerned.[39]

A possible reading of the WOA characterization would be that new immigrants were white before coming (WBC) and therefore carried racism in the cultural baggage that they brought across the Atlantic. Recent scholars, rightly taken up with the drama of immigrants learning the "lie of whiteness" in the United States, have been slow to consider this possibility. In *The Good Life*, Loren Baritz quoted a Hungarian newspaper editor of the Progressive Era as complaining that he was not embraced in the United States as "a white man as he used to be on the other side." Baritz added, "This man's racism, however, revealed that he had already made a key adjustment to the new land."[40] The possibility that the editor identified with white supremacy "on the other side" falls out of the analysis. So does the possibility that he and others came with patterns of race thinking, if not a full-blown sense of whiteness, which made them perhaps RTBC (race thinkers before coming) and facilitated speedy learning of racial systems in the United States. In at least one immigrant autobiography there is explicit comment on this matter. In *How Columbus and I Discovered America* Daniel Trees describes growing up as a Yugoslav under Austro-

Hungarian rule and learning that there "are four skin colors among people" just as "there are four skin colors among potatoes." Trees was taught that there were "four races of people—white, black, red and yellow," as well as an overarching sense of Christian brotherhood. In the United States, "We were simply hated because we were not of an Anglo-Saxon character, were not considered to be white." Trees wrote that "it did cause me to wonder why I had been told, as a school boy [that] I was white."[41]

Those who follow James Baldwin in seeking to learn how immigrants "became white" have not investigated the WBC/RTBC possibilities. And yet even the Irish whom Douglass heard wailing hardly lacked awareness of people of color. A large percentage had signed abolitionist petitions. Many had migrated to Britain—London's black population far exceeded Boston's—before crossing the pond to the United States. To a tragic extent they foot-soldiered for British imperialism, and at times they made appeals for fair treatment based on that service and on their being European, civilized, and white.[42]

In the period of the new immigration the case of the Italians raises the WBC/RTBC issues with special force and underscores the possibility of being victims of race thinking before coming as well. Italians had long experiences of exchange with, and exploration of, Africa. They participated in the trans-Saharan slave trade and the worship of black Madonnas and other dark saints at religious shrines. At least one migrant prayed to black saints to get money for passage to the United States. Letters home from earlier immigrants spread negative images of African Americans while occasionally teaching that they were *bravi*—good people. Interestingly, Jane Addams once attributed a lack of racism among Sicilians in Chicago to their long-standing proximity to Africa and familiarity with "the dark-skinned races." On the other hand, Italy had been an aggressive imperialist aspirant in Africa since the 1890s and later nurtured a huge fascist movement. It was hardly innocent of the idea of racial distinction. Although Jennifer Guglielmo is likely right to point out that before fascism, southern Italians were slow to buy into anti-African racism, she also observes that service in imperial armies in Africa was among the claims of the region to "civilization." In Chicago in 1936, "4000 daughters of Italy married their husbands anew," according to a *New York Times* account. They did so "in celebration of their homeland's conquest of Ethiopia," donning "iron of empire" rings Mussolini provided in exchange for their gold wedding bands, which they sent to the fascist state. The lessons of the Ethiopian crisis clarified Italy's place for Du Bois, who wrote in *Foreign Affairs* in 1935, "Economic exploitation based on the excuse of race prejudice is the program of the white world. Italy states it openly and plainly." Although in some cases Italian American youth apparently let the adults play army and sustained existing relationships with black schoolmates, Italian American gangs in Minneapolis threatened African Americans with special zeal in the wake of the Ethiopian conflict. James Baldwin's childhood memories included fighting "every campaign of the Italian-Ethiopian War with the oldest son of the Italian fruit and vegetable vendor who lived next door to us." "I lost. Inevitably," Baldwin continued, "he knew who had the tanks." An Italian immigrant track laborer in New Haven told an interviewer during the Depression that Mussolini was destined to "fix up" black Americans as well as Ethiopians, breaking them of the habit of loud and "crazy" laughter and making them "civilized." As Stefano Luconi demonstrates, Italian Americans lobbied with remarkable success against the Pittman-McReynolds bill in 1936, arguing that its limits on arms sales to Italy threatened fascist successes in Ethiopia. This imperialist cruelty was hardly learned in a specifically American context, although there is evidence that southern Italians in the United States warmed to the war in Ethiopia more than did the people of southern Italy. Moreover, justification for Italian empire led some Italian American editorialists to dismiss African American grievances in the United States and to imagine that both Italian and U.S. ventures in white supremacy brought blacks into the "school of progress."[43]

Moreover, as the research of Alessandro Triulzi, David A. J. Richards, and Robert Orsi has shown, Italian contacts with North, East, and West Africa fed the racialized prejudices of northern Italians against Sicilians and other dark, poor southern Italians.[44] As the African American cultural critic Albert Murray has written, "Long before there were Southerners in the U.S.A. . . . there were Southerners in Italy." The "southern problem," as the Marxist theorist Antonio Gramsci and others called it, was often cast as not only underdevelopment but also racial inferiority and lack of civilization. The race lore holding that Europe "ends at Naples" and "all the rest belongs to Africa" dates from at least 1806. In 1893, Cesare Lombroso, a leading Italian anthropologist, proposed classifying southerners as Semitic or Afro-Asiatic. Alfredo Niceforo's classic *L'Italia barbara con-*

temporanea (*Barbarian Italy Now*) (1898) described southerners (Nice-foro was himself one of their number and provides an apt reminder of what Rudolph J. Vecoli calls the "collusion" of elites from the region in the "racialization" of peasants from the south) as "still primitive, not completely evolved." Niceforo's work informed U.S. census classifications racially dividing the people of the north and the south in Italy.[45] In a recent homage to Kym Ragusa, the director of important films on race in Italy and Italian America, Edvige Giunta recalls hearing "Africani" yelled at Sicilian children exhibiting poor table manners. "Tenemmu l'africa vicunu," Giunta adds—We are close to Africa. The Buffalo-area Italian immigrant railway workers who forced an African American track inspector from his job in one of the first recorded "hate strikes" by new immigrants may have been fast learners of U.S. racism, but they may also have arrived knowing something of the importance of drawing racial lines.[46]

. The racial slur *tutsún* was deployed against African Americans by Italian Americans. American studies scholar Margot Fortunato Galt described her father as having "picked up the virus of racism first in Pittsburgh," where he was born in 1909 to immigrant Italian parents. Late in his life, suffering from dementia, he pointed to a black couple and said *sutsunis* (a variant of *tutsún*). But *sutsunis* was not just a Pittsburgh virus. When Lou De Caro Jr. sat on the lap of his aunt as a small child and she repeatedly (and good-naturedly) teased that he was born a little *tutsún* whom the doctor rescued by turning him inside out, the noun central to the gag came from Italy. More than that, it has its uses in intra-Italian racism. The word, as Andrea di Tommaso wrote, came from "*tizzone*—a burning log or piece of wood which is black from being charred." Northerners in Italy, she continued, "sometimes refer to southerners as *tizzoni* (or *Marrocchini*—that is, Moroccans)." The slur *tutsún* is "vicious," far more negative than *melanzana*, the racial slur derived from the Italian word for eggplant, which was also used as an imported immigrant term for African Americans.[47]

In the United States, social scientists, census takers, and immigration officers were not alone in making sharp "racial" distinctions between northern and southern Italians. Italians themselves pressed the distinction. In 1901 in St. Louis a northern Italian bragged to a reporter that Italians living in "The Hill" neighborhood had remained white. "Plenty them little black fellows here," he explained, "but they all downtown."

The "black fellows" were Sicilians. Other St. Louisians from northern Italy emphasized that "they want the world to know that they did not come from the South or Sicily" and that they therefore were of a "lighter complexion" and were "further advanced in intelligence." They were "Holy Ghosti" as against the "devils" from southern Italy. In 1932, an Italian staff person at the International Institute suggested not only the persistence of such views but their internalization by some immigrants from southern Italy: "A Southerner stands in awe of a Northerner." More benign, but suggestive of the extent of tendencies to connect shade of skin and peoplehood, were Adolfo Rossi's recollections of viewing the immigrant masses in Castle Garden (Rossi was a middle-class northern Italian immigrant). He remembered guessing their nationality on the basis of their clothing and their "white, brown, yellow and copper colored faces." Like peasant populations generally, Italians connected color and class, with sun-baked darkness serving as a badge of field labor.[48]

Nor were Italians exceptional. Jews in the United States used *die schwartze* to refer to and castigate African Americans. Norman Podhoretz's troubled racial memoirs, for example, describe his mother cursing both the *schwartzes* and the *goyim* (Christians). German Americans brought the usage in the nineteenth century, if not before. H. L. Mencken suggested that it may have been used to discuss black servants in their presence. The German-language press in Philadelphia used it to racialize crime reports, although "nigger" quickly slipped in as an Americanism. *Schwartze* had German, not German American, origins, a fact that undercuts one scholar's recent insistence that the word "originated in the [Jewish] ghettoes of New York's Lower East Side." In common use in German states in the eighteenth century, by the nineteenth century it was clearly pejorative, conflating blackness, an almost militant ignorance, and the devil.[49]

Images of Africa abounded in Europe and some people of African descent were physically present. The immigrant Hungarian Jewish family of the artist Hugo Gellert and his blues-collecting brother Lawrence remembered a "Negro doorman" whom children touched for good luck at a Budapest hotel. When they arrived in the United States, they met a Hungarian-speaking African American who had learned the language while traveling in Europe. Africans were displayed in wildly popular and degrading European exhibitions during the nineteenth and early twentieth centuries. Russia, like Italy, attempted to establish colonial power in East Africa in the late nineteenth century. Portugal was, of course, such a power and in general an idea of colonialism as a "European" project was extant. By the time of the new immigration, a Czech genius, Franz Kafka, had marvelously portrayed a fictional West African displayed as an ape and had detailed the specimen's scientific strategies for gaining humanity. The Polish-born Joseph Conrad had already produced the most celebrated story of race and colonialism in Africa, *Heart of Darkness*.[50] As Anne McClintock's challenging work on cleanliness, advertising, and race shows, the "soft-soaping of empire" was well under way in an early twentieth-century Europe awash in racist logos and ads for cleaning products. Many of these European advertisements traded on jokes concerning beliefs that blackness could be rubbed (or scrubbed) away. This widespread "commodity racism" was only a small part of the panoply of racist imagery that ran through European culture, high and low, especially in the imperialist powers, at the height of "new immigrant" migration to the United States.[51]

Examples of European-on-European racism, like that which split Italians on geographic and color lines, can be easily multiplied. The historian of apes and Irishmen, L. Perry Curtis, has written that "virtually every country in Europe has had its equivalent of 'white Negroes' and simianized men, whether or not they happened to be . . . Slavs, gypsies, Jews or peasants." In their massive immigration study, *The Polish Peasant in Europe and America*, William I. Thomas and Florian Znaniecki framed much material in terms of "the problem of the fight of races" and noted Poland's long and wide experience in this fight. Polish nationalists had to fight oppressors "at every moment for the preservation of her racial and cultural status" and shared space with Europe's "highest percentage of the most unassimilable of races, the Jews." Discriminated against in his early travels in eastern and central Europe because he was thought to be a gypsy or Jew, Du Bois recognized an "old tale," familiar to him from experiences with antiblack racism in the United States. In Romania, *tigan* meant both "slave" and "gypsy." The Slovak word for "gypsies" from eastern Europe came into service as an antiblack slur in the United States. While Slovak Americans embraced "yellow peril" rhetoric of anti-Asianism in part to protect themselves against charges that they were "Asiatics," they did so also to press long-standing intra-European grievances against Magyars, whose language made them especially vulnerable

to the charge of having "oriental" origins. Not only were many Jews identified and victimized partly on the basis of their dark skins in Europe, but
also, as Michael Lerner writes, the category "Jew" was itself singled out
for racial hatred. Lerner writes that "to be 'white' is to fit into the social
construct of beneficiaries of European imperialism. . . . Far from being
such beneficiaries, Jews have been [in Europe] the primary 'Other,'
have been socially and legally discriminated against, have been the subject of racism and genocide." U.S. magazines referred to European
anti-Semitism and other conflicts in central and eastern Europe as instances of "race hatred" or "racial hatred."[52]

Slavic nations regularly suffered under the hegemony of great and not
so great powers. Donna Gabaccia reminds us that Poles and southern
Slavs who emigrated had been "colonized minorities—already disparaged
for their backwardness and racial difference—at home." Eastern Europe
itself, as Larry Wolff's excellent study of the "invention" of that region
demonstrates, was commonly and not idly referred to as the "Orient of
Europe." Maria Todorova's important *Imagining the Balkans* has similarly
developed evidence of the application by Europeans of "semicivilized
and semioriental" labels to that region and to the southern Slavs and others in it. When the German American press in Chicago prefaced its attacks on the alleged perfidy and backwardness of Slavs during World War
I with racial characterizations of East Europeans as "Asiatic" or "semi-
Asiatic,"[53] it was not gerry-building arguments based solely on American
racial categorizations.

Not surprisingly, the great migrations to the United States in the early
twentieth century included many of those racially persecuted in Europe:
southern Italians, Jews, and Poles, for example. Interesting complexities
emerge when we acknowledge that many immigrants practiced racism
while being victimized by it, and had experience with inbetween racial
positions in Europe. Slavs at times generated strong anti-Semitic movements even as they themselves suffered from racial slights. Northern Italians saw southern Italians as Africans while southern Italians looked
down on Africans. Ashkenazi Jews used *schwartze* to refer to Africans as
well as Sephardic Jews. In many ways and for many immigrants the experiences of race and race thinking in Europe were thus not of the sort to
make them white before coming but rather inbetween before arrival.
Michel Foucault and Ann Laura Stoler have analyzed the emergence of

the modern European state as connected, at the very time of the new immigration, with a death-dealing "state racism" purportedly defending the health of the nation against not only its external but also its *internal* enemies, especially the disabled, the poor, the sexual minoritized and the religiously, culturally, or physically different, making people citizens and potential objects of genocide simultaneously.[54]

Strong, if complicated, evidence from African Americans observing new immigrants and from new immigrant populations themselves casts doubt on whether the weight and shape of European racism prepared migrants for what they would find regarding white-on-black racism in the United States. Thus when the African American poet and novelist Claude McKay encountered vicious U.S.-style racism in the south of France, he carefully emphasized that its source was an Italian who "had lived somewhere in America" and attempted to apply Jim Crow overseas. "You have sucked off so much America," McKay charged the Italian, who had kept him from taking a vacant spot on a bus, "that you need some fascist castor oil to purge you." McKay, greeted as *Schwartz' Mohr* (black Moor) in Berlin in the 1920s, nonetheless found that he was "treated much better and with altogether more consideration" than in the United States. He noted significant racial tensions in the south of France. W.E.B. Du Bois was perhaps the most cosmopolitan U.S. intellectual of the 1920s and the most insistent on seeing American whiteness in the context of broader international racisms shaped by the slave trade and by imperialism. Nonetheless, he wrote of the United States as an exporter of its own special brand of white supremacy: "She trains her immigrants to this despising of 'niggers' from the days of their landing, and they carry and send the news back to the submerged classes in the fatherland." The black sociologist E. Franklin Frazier wrote in the 1920s of Italian American longshore workers taking on "the prejudices of white men" toward African Americans in order to "insure their own standing." In 1928 Jane Addams quoted a young Italian doctor making much the same point. Reacting to reports of Italian Americans lynching an African American for speaking with "a young Italian girl" during the 1919 race riot in Chicago, Addams noted "prejudice and lynching on this score are alike unheard of in Italy." The doctor added, "I guess they are getting Americanized." The Swedish visitor and investigator Gunnar Myrdal accepted this point, finding that race prejudice was "one of the lessons in Americanization." For the Japanese American Communist Katayama Sen, the United States was "the country of race prejudices and racial hatred."[55]

Much more difficult to interpret are immigrant sources reporting on early encounters with African Americans who were said to be utterly beyond imagination in European frames of reference. For example, Stefan Winkowski, a Polish immigrant butcher in Michigan, was in trouble with his mother in 1908. He had not found a way to tell her that he intended to marry the "not Polish" but "Catholic just as we" Bronislawa Dronskowska and had let too much time pass between letters home. His "great trouble" financially as he prepared to marry precluded his sending money back to Poland. In writing the difficult letter bearing this news, Winkowski excused his failure to keep in touch with a diversion that lends support to the view that race was learned dramatically in the United States. The experience with African Americans he had just undergone, Winkowski wrote, was impossible to write about in a letter. "I cannot describe to you my lot where I was," he observed. "It is likely that if my acquaintances knew it they would never believe it." With regard to the African Americans he had encountered, Winkowski exclaimed, "What a nationality there is in America! If such a man were brought to your village then all people would run away from fear."[56] A ninety-one-year-old Slovak American woman interviewed by the historian Robert Zecker offered even more dramatic recollections. Passing through Ellis Island in the 1920s, she screamed with horror when an African American porter tried to carry her baggage at the train station. She thought, or remembered thinking sixty years later, that he was a monkey. The mistake occurred, she further recalled, despite the fact that an earlier-arriving sister had written to describe *èiernis* (blacks) in the United States. The terrified woman had assumed that the sister referred to gypsies.[57] In Cleveland's Little Italy, an informant told of her mother. While pregnant, the mother needed to run to a nearby bakery to pick up a "start" (leftover dough) to use for a new batch of dough in her own bakery. On the errand she saw her first black person and was so frightened that she came home repeating "Madonna Mia mi scanza" ("My lady protect me"). Her fear, preserved in a family history that fairly begs for psychoanalytical interpretation, was that the baby would be born with Negro features.[58]

Such individual stories are perhaps less important than the ones that are repeated so often in a tradition that they attain the status of what the

anthropologist Robert Orsi calls "myth." Whether or not literally accu-
rate, Orsi argues, such stories possess "credibility," "authority," and "paradigmatic truth." Among Irish Americans, tales recounting seeing a black
person for the first time after immigrating to the United States and leap-
ing overboard from the ship in fright rise to the level of "myth." The myth
dramatically trades on Irish folklore regarding the devil turning people
inside out.[59] Among Italian Americans, Orsi describes a myth that informants all over the country told him, "always with the same details," which
he regards as one of Italian America's "fundamental moral tales." In it a
newly arrived (greenhorn) Italian immigrant sees an African American
man. Mesmerized, the immigrant stares, hesitates, agonizes, and finally
"approaches the stranger, grabs the startled man by the arm, and starts
rubbing his skin furiously to see if the black color comes off."[60] Given
what we know about Irish exposure to black people and racial images, the
literal truth of the Irish "first encounter" myth is unlikely. In the Italian
case it is still more implausible as an often repeated experience. And yet
the marking of the "paradigmatic truth" of a sharp break between home
country experiences of race and U.S. experiences remains compelling evidence against a pat conclusion that the immigrants were simply white
before coming.

WOA/USA AND THE ATTRACTIONS OF INBETWEENNESS

The emphasis among African American writers on how quickly new immigrants proved "apt students" of white supremacy and on how tellingly
the host society "trained" them to racism suggests a second sense in
which white on arrival might apply to new immigrant consciousness.[61] If
not white before coming, they may have been so quickly engaged by the
clear advantages of being white in the United States as to be virtually
WOA. Five leading historians of immigration have recently concluded as
much in their magisterial article on "the invention of ethnicity" in the
United States. They write that new immigrants and the children of immigrants quickly learned that "the worst thing that one could be in this
Promised Land was 'colored.'"[62]

Some contemporary white observers shared this conclusion. In northern West Virginia after World War I, for example, one mine superintendent faced the threat of a wildcat strike by white workers and the "foreign

element" when he attempted to hire African Americans. He sounded very much like Malcolm X later would in reflecting on how unlikely it was that black workers would "turn 'red' with hunkies and Russians whose first words in English are usually 'I won't work with a _____ black ___ of a _____.'" The socialist novelist Alexander Irvine added complexity and a tragic tone but still regarded the coming to race consciousness (and "not the slightest hint of class consciousness") of an Italian American character as the result of a simple American learning process: "They call him a 'Dago.' He in turn calls the black man a 'nigger.' They told him to keep his place . . . exactly what he learned to say of the colored man." In her work at Greenpoint Settlement in New York City in the late 1890s, the radical reformer Mary White Ovington took fifteen young boys of eight immigrant nationalities on an outing to a park. From the trolley they spied a black woman and suddenly "as at a signal, every boy jumped to his feet and yelled 'Nigger, Nigger, Nigger!'" The shouting was in this case a learned "ritual" among boys with "no race prejudice," according to Ovington, but a few pages later the same shouts accompany an armed attack on African American children. One Slovak American historian writes that "nigger" was "the one word in English old Slovaks almost certainly knew." But evidence regarding how they learned it can contain fascinating twists and hard interpretive challenges. Anna Kikta, a Slovak who immigrated to Cleveland's East Side in 1928, for example, remembered many decades later that a low point in her experience as a greenhorn came when a knowing but cruel boy told her to approach a black girl on the street by saying, "Hi, nigger." She was slapped by the girl and then laughed at by white children in on the "big joke." For Kikta, the story spoke to the "pretty rough" experience of newcomers, not to antiblack racism.[63]

Certainly there were compelling reasons to conclude that being white was far more advantageous than being African American, Asian American, or Latino. In emphasizing the new immigrant's inbetween racial status it has proven all too easy for scholars to suppose, as some advocates of the "white ethnic" did thirty years ago, that southern and eastern Europeans "overcame" an oppression closely analogous to that experienced by people of color in the United States. The political scientist Jennifer Hochschild has recently written that "'whites'—that is, earlier European immigrants, were as vicious toward members of the Irish, southern Italian, and eastern European 'races' as towards blacks, Chinese and Japanese." A more considered conclusion would stress that new immigrants often heard the racial structure of the United States described as a line (or a ladder) with African Americans at the far back (or very bottom) and that their experiences in jobs, schools, unions, and elsewhere quickly confirmed this view.[64]

Victimized, but not in the same way as African Americans or immigrants of color, the new immigrant could claim whiteness via naturalization and naturalization via whiteness. This tie of race with fitness for naturalized citizenship mattered greatly, as we have seen, in giving immigrant groups political power. As an African American educator put it in 1909, "It didn't take [the Irish] Pat long after passing the Statue of Liberty to learn that it is popular to give [the black] Jim a whack." The denial of black civil rights powerfully taught this lesson.[65] In a nation that commonly denied citizenship rights and naturalization to those who were classed as not white, the racial privilege of naturalized citizenship also taught an important symbolic lesson. Moreover, any enduring "nonwhite" alliance would almost certainly have proceeded from an awareness of exclusion from the benefits of citizenship. The revolutionary labor leader William "Big Bill" Haywood caught some of this possibility when he described how he opened the founding 1905 convention of the Industrial Workers of the World (IWW) and coined the organization's most famous term of address for working people:

> I turned over in my mind how I should open the convention. I recalled that during the French Commune the workers had addressed each other as "fellow citizens," but here there were many workers who were not citizens so that would not do. I didn't want to use the old trade union form, "brothers and sisters," so, picking up a piece of board that lay on the platform and using it for a gavel, I opened the convention with "fellow workers."[66]

The hope of the IWW and other syndicalist-influenced organizations that workers would fight as "labor" and not as "citizens" reflected real possibilities. The immigrant population always included large numbers not yet eligible for naturalization, and still more shuttling back and forth to Europe as "birds of passage" or remigrating to Europe permanently. The citizenship rights of African Americans, virtually nonexistent in the South, were precarious everywhere. In African American slang from the

1890s to the 1930s "citizen" meant prosaic white person.[67] Mexican Americans, entitled by treaty rights to naturalization, if not to whiteness, became citizens in very small numbers. Valuing Mexican citizenship, these immigrants were also aware that the benefits of "America" could be elusive after naturalization. They reasoned, as Gabriela Arredondo has emphasized, that "our looks cannot be changed by our nationality."[68]

Some "new immigrant" groups also had extremely low naturalization rates. Desmond King has recently estimated, using figures from Department of Labor sources, that in 1920 almost 83 percent of immigrants from Greece were not naturalized. For Albanians and Bulgarians the figures were over 88 percent and 92 percent respectively. Southern Italians, who had ample reason to suspect that looks mattered as much as nationality, were particularly unlikely to take out citizenship papers. Indeed at times *not* being a citizen seemed to offer protection against the racial victimization of new immigrants. In 1908, some blacks were freed from peonage when Italian and Greek diplomats successfully demanded investigations of their countrymen's treatment by landowners and lenders in the South and broader inquiries ensued. The 1910 lynchings of two Italian Americans in Florida led Du Bois to remark, tongue not entirely in cheek, "The Italian government protested, but it was found that they were naturalized Americans. The inalienable right of every free American citizen to be lynched without tiresome investigation and penalties is one which the families of the lately deceased doubtless deeply appreciate." When we add that a significant section of the poor white population in the South had recently been disfranchised along with blacks by poll taxes and other devices, and that the civil liberties of immigrants suffered under steady assault from the state and "100 percent American" organizations during and after World War I, the syndicalist strategy of claiming that industrial, and not legal, citizenship mattered had some purchase on lived experiences. In the Great Steel Strike of 1919, nativist appeals to American-born citizen workers mattered at least as much as the introduction of African American strikebreakers in leading to defeat. David Brody chose his words carefully in observing that "the citizenry of the [steel] mill towns aligned with the steel companies."[69] However, in the longer run, many new immigrants who stayed in the United States did largely come to be naturalized as white and their U.S.-born children were full citizens.

More generally the consciousness of new immigrants often remained "inbetween," rather than fully white, for a considerable period. The best frame of comparison for discussing new immigrant racial consciousness is that of the Irish Americans in the mid-nineteenth century. Often eagerly, militantly, and loudly white, even and especially when not broadly accepted as such, Irish Americans could insist that politicians acknowledge them as part of the dominant race. Changing the political subject from Americanness and religion to race whenever possible, they challenged anti-Celtic Anglo-Saxonism in part by becoming leaders in the cause of white supremacy.[70] New immigrant leaders never approximated that path. With a large segment of both political parties willing to vouch for the possibility of speedy, orderly Americanization and with neither party willing to vouch unequivocally for their racial character, southern and eastern Europeans generally tried to change the subject from whiteness to nationality and assimilation.

Inbetween consciousness had several material connections to the labor of new immigrants. As discussed in the previous chapter, patterns of hiring and wage discrimination placed southern and eastern Europeans between the native-born and African Americans. Especially in the first quarter of the twentieth century, employers used strikebreaking and managerial favoritism to keep new immigrants apart from black workers in what one historian has called a "conscious corporate strategy" of division. In addition, immigrant workers often depended, at least in an immediate way, on other non–Anglo-Saxons for access to employment. Because of the presence of a small employing, or subcontracting, class in their communities, new immigrants were far more likely than blacks to work for "their own." In New York City in 1910, for example, almost half of the sample of Jewish workers studied by Suzanne Model had Jewish supervisors. About one Italian in seven had an Italian supervisor. Model added, "The study sample unearthed only one industrial match between laborers and supervisors among blacks."[71]

Even as new immigrants relied on family and community networks to hear about and secure work, Irish American bosses often hired them. In shrugging off being called hunky, the novelist Thomas Bell wrote, Slovak immigrants in steel took solace that they "had come to America to find work and save money, not to make friends with the Irish." But getting work and "making friends with" Irish American foremen, skilled workers, union leaders, and politicians were often connected, and the relationships were hardly smooth. In isolated work camps for miners, quarrymen, railroaders, and timber workers, Irish Americans brutally enforced work discipline against Italians. But over the long run, a common Catholicism (and sometimes common street gang or political machine affiliations) gave new immigrant groups access to the fragile favor of Irish Americans who were in positions to rearrange the hiring queue that African Americans could not achieve. Sometimes such favor was organized, as through the Knights of Columbus in Kansas City packinghouses. Over time, as second-generation marriages across national lines but within the Catholic religion became a pattern, kin joined religion in shaping hiring in ways largely excluding African Americans.[72]

Many new immigrants, especially Greeks, Italians, and Jews, went on to peddle goods or sell food, often in their own communities. Some sold especially to African American customers. Their "middleman minority" status in trading with blacks rested on physical proximity, necessitated cultural accommodations, and, as in the case of bargaining over prices, was built on cultural affinities. Some accounts, as we have seen, suggest a conscious choice about how far to go in the direction of courting and even befriending customers. The immersion of small new immigrant businessmen in black culture typically did not lead to a decision like that made by Johnny Otis to become black "by persuasion." Otis, the black-identified rhythm and bluesman born Johnny Veliotes, the son of a Greek immigrant grocer in a mixed but largely African American Berkeley neighborhood, was singular in many ways.[73] Far more common was a dynamic in which a middleman minority lived in communities of color, in close, tense relationships that situated them in racially inbetween contexts. An 1897 *Harpers Weekly* article reporting on a Jewish shopkeeper in New York City balances anti-Jewish and antiblack stereotypes and suggests how the middleman minority's day-to-day relations included contact with and distance from blacks. "For a student of race characteristics," the reporter wrote, "nothing could be more striking than to observe the stoic scorn of the Hebrew when he is made a disapproving witness of the happy-go-lucky joyousness of his dusky neighbor." The early-twentieth-century Italian immigrant Michael Califi bought into practically every southern racist stereotype but developed elaborate strategies to gain African American business. One turned on posting a sign offering credit: "Trust Everybody, Niggers Too."[74]

If some shopkeepers traded from an inbetween identity, it also functioned in that way for the great popular culture stars coming from new
immigrant communities. Many new immigrants learned to deploy and
manipulate white supremacist images from the vaudeville stage and the
Hollywood screen. Blackface minstrel shows occurred in churches serving immigrants, in voluntary immigrant organizations, and in settlement
houses. In them, and in paid venues, immigrants stepped in and out of
conventional gender and racial roles via blackface. Sophie Tucker's racy
blackface act, for example, ended with her removing a glove to "prove"
her whiteness. The Jewish "impersonator" of "orientals," Tiny Kline, went
from that disguise early in her career to the apex of theatrical whiteness,
as Tinkerbelle's incarnation at Disneyland. Michael Rogin's exciting work
on blackface in film argues that immigrant entertainers like Eddie Cantor
and Al Jolson overcame "nativist pressure that would assign them to the
dark side of the racial divide" via minstrelsy. He sees them as having
"Americanized" and whitened themselves by "crossing and recrossing the
racial line" in disguise.[75]

However, the equally provocative work by Jeffrey Melnick shows that
by loving African American music, Jewish entertainers of the early to
middle twentieth century worked out a Jewish identity as well as a white
American one. The insistent comparisons of black and Jewish musical
transitions gave voice to such a search. Entertainers from immigrant
backgrounds claimed both whiteness and proximity to the appeal of the
exotic and dark. What was called at the time the "Chameleonic blood" of
Jews was thought to impart "an absolute fluidity that somehow maintains
its mark of difference." This two-ness, however mythical, could animate
highly marketable cultural productions. From Rudolph Valentino's het-
erosexually and homoerotically charged Arab-face disguise in *The Sheik*
to Jolson's *Jazz Singer*, such appeals were best negotiated from an inbetween but white-ward moving position. Melnick shows that Jolson, Cantor, and others saw blackface as an apprenticeship to be abandoned on
reaching mature stardom and suggests that in leaving blackface behind,
stars became less identified with Jewishness as well.[76]

In terms of social and political mobilizations, new immigrants also were
"inbetween" in important ways for a considerable period of time. They
came together beyond their national groups in coalitions with others
not yet fully admitted to Anglo-whiteness but not racialized as definitely

"colored." In Utah, a violent 1911 strike sought to unite Greek, Austrian, and Italian miners against favoritism for the native born. In places, a hunky identity cut across national lines that were far more firmly drawn, and blood spattered, in Europe. In urban politics, new immigrants were often brought into participation by machine leaders from old but not Anglo-Saxon groups, especially the Irish. In a city like Chicago, the machine at times achieved unity by sounding alarms regarding Anglo-Saxon threats. In the Chicago race riot of 1919 the politically connected Irish street gang Ragen's Colts apparently dressed in blackface to burn down homes in a new immigrant neighborhood in Back of the Yards. They hoped that new immigrants would blame blacks for the arson and then engage in racial terror. Next, the Colts organized a militant demonstration against the anti-Catholicism of the Ku Klux Klan. In both settings Ragen's Colts acted as what James Barrett has called the "military arm of the Irish political machine." More generally, an identity of "Catholic whiteness," discussed in detail in Chapter 6, brought new immigrant groups together, without and at times against African Americans and often under Irish American tutelage. Indeed the new immigrant did not negotiate his or her racial identity with entities as abstract as the state, the host society, or even the labor market. Instead they confronted the policeman, the ward committeeman, the church leader, and the straw boss. Often these critical day-to-day contacts were not with Anglo-Saxons but representatives of older immigrant groups—German Jews, Scandinavians, Germans, and, above all, the Irish. These older groups sometimes taught lessons of unity across "racial" lines. The Manasseh Clubs (Motto: Equal Rights for All) played highly visible roles in upper Midwestern cities in organizing massive interracial social events for the Scandinavian immigrant and African American families (most of whom came together while working in domestic service). But by and large, the lessons taught by contact with the petty powers of non–Anglo-Saxon old immigrants (again, especially the Irish) focused on the fact that race was volatile and momentous in the United States and that new immigrants themselves could experience violent attacks, exclusion, or precarious acceptance by the old. In Hoboken, New Jersey, however, it was German American dockworkers who were seen as, to use Michael La Sorte's nice pun, "harbor[ing] an intense hatred for those small, swarthy people from southern Europe." A child of Lithuanian and Polish parents, interviewed in Connecticut in 1939, "hated the Irish kids" and remembered, "We used to fight with them for calling us names like 'Hunkies' and 'Polacks.'" In and around New York City's Greenwich Village Italian Americans did not need to find Anglo-Saxons in order to be slurred as "greasy wops." The Irish American parish priest could provide that. So too could the Irish American truant officer who lectured a single mother on the "guinea bastard" she was raising. In Buffalo in the 1920s Italian Americans recalled fighting "racial battles" with the Irish. In Maramoneck, New York, an Irish American mob drove out members of a small working-class Italian American colony who fled to the Bronx. Auto worker Antonio Margariti, a Calabrian who immigrated to the United States in 1913, wrote in his 1980 memoir of the special burden caused by "the harsh, negative, uncompromising attitudes of the members of the Celtic race who are convinced that we are of a lower social order and treat us accordingly." Indeed the "special hatred" of the Irish for Italians was something of a trope in memoirs of the latter group. At times, that special hatred was interlaced with admiration for the Irish as those who had learned to navigate urban life, politics, and race relations and who represented "the image of what an American looked like."[77]

"Inbetween" consciousness also profited from the fact that too full an identification with whiteness threatened to cut against the strong national/cultural identifications as Jews, Italians, Poles, Slovenians, and so on, which many early-twentieth-century immigrants held. At times, the strongest tie might be to a specific Sicilian or Slovakian village. To become "white" could also put new immigrants into uncomfortable proximity with bitter European rivals (e.g., Lithuanians with Poles), though the same rivalries also impeded pan-nonwhite coalitions. The extent to which (and the grounds on which) new immigrant groups in Chicago abstained from the 1919 race riots—as did new immigrants in other riot-torn cities at the time, to a far greater extent than theories connecting racial violence and job competition at "the bottom" of society would predict—is instructive on this score. The Chicago riots, important Polish spokespersons and newspapers emphasized, were between the "whites" and "Negroes." Polish immigrants had, and should seek to have, no part in them. Indeed, the *Jewish Daily Courier* staked out its people's position as "between them" where black–white relations were concerned before the riots. Italian Americans, at the center of some of the most hideous and high-profile bloodshed in the Chicago race riot, present a more complicated case and one that shows how white violence could incorporate new groups. Jane Addams observed at the time that "before the riot Italians held no particular animosity toward Negroes" but that "antipathy" developed in the context of disorder. Even so Italian Americans were apparently underrepresented among "white" rioters. The city's popular Italian American press did not enlist firmly on the white side, with *L'Italia* showing remarkable sympathy for black riot victims. Such abstention from whiteness also characterized the practice of rank-and-file east Europeans. "Slavic immigrants," Rick Halpern writes, "did not play a role in the racial violence," though by 1921 the evidence becomes more mixed. Jews, James Grossman has observed, also viewed these events from a neither white nor black vantage point.[78]

While the blackface arson by Ragen's Colts moved the immigrant press from an attitude of disinterested sympathy for black riot victims to one of distancing itself from the fray, the consistencies in immigrant press coverage of the riot are more suggestive. Polish American accounts of the race riot, an event vital to the future of Slavic packinghouse workers and their unions, were sparse. Coverage occurred only when editors "could tear their attention away from their fascination with the momentous events attending the birth of the new Polish state." Slavic nationalism, which Robert Park had intriguingly discussed in 1914 as a movement that had "run parallel" with the changes in consciousness of African Americans since emancipation in the South, framed reaction to the rioting. Both in hesitant sympathy with mobbed blacks and in hesitant defense of the logic of mobbing African Americans, comparisons with pogroms against Jews in Poland framed the discussion. *Narod Polski* held, for example, that both Jews in Poland and blacks in Chicago had done much to bring violence on themselves. That the defense of Poland was as important as analyzing the realities in Chicago emerges starkly in the convoluted expression of sympathy for riot victims in the prolabor organ *Glos Polek*:

> The American press has written at length about the alleged pogroms of Jews in Poland for over two months. Now it is writing about pogroms against blacks in America. It wrote about the Jews in words full of sorrow and sympathy, why does it not show the same today to Negroes being burnt and killed without mercy?[79]

Viewing race in the United States through the lens of nationalist struggles and prejudices in Europe could also cut in another direction. Two of the most dramatic examples of immigrant press cartoons drawing on stock mainstream U.S. antiblack images deployed those images in reaction to their homelands being treated "like negroes," or occupied partly by black troops, during and after World War I.[80]

Finally, both "becoming American" and "becoming white" could imply coercive threats to European national identities. Even as antiblack prejudice warmed during the invasion of Ethiopia in the mid-1930s, South Philadelphia Italian Americans opposed a "whites only" housing project because they saw it as potentially bringing other Europeans into the neighborhood. *Dziennik Zwiazkowy* in Chicago charged in 1911 that "Americanism . . . is systematically trying to pour all races, all nationalities, into one mass." National pride in Italian nationality—a pride often made in the United States and carrying a hard masculine edge—could function as an alternative to whiteness. The 1906 remarks of an Italian government official investigating Sicilian sharecroppers in Louisiana illustrate the intricate, interrelations of Americanizing and whitening. The official found that "a majority of plantation owners cannot comprehend that . . . Italians are white," and instead considered the Sicilian migrant "a white-skinned negro who is a better worker than the black-skinned negro." He patiently explained the "commonly held distinction . . . between 'negroes,' 'Italians' and 'whites' (that is, Americans)." He tellingly added that the "American" in the South

will not engage in agricultural, manual labor; rather he leaves it to the negroes. Seeing that the Italians will do this work, naturally he concludes that Italians lack dignity. The only way an Italian can emancipate himself from this inferior state is to abandon all sense of national pride and to identify completely with the Americans.[81]

Thus 100 percent whiteness and 100 percent Americanism carried overlapping and confusing imperatives for new immigrants, but in several ways the former was even more uncomfortable terrain than the latter. Such pursuit of white identity, consistently tied to competition for wage labor and to political citizenship, was coded largely as male, and it tended to apply awkwardly to the immigrant mothers whom both Americanizers and immigrant leaders recognized as key figures in identity formation.[82] More cast in determinism, the discourse of race also produced fewer openings to inject class demands, optimism, and cultural pluralism than did the discourse of Americanism.

In a fascinating quantified sociological study of Poles in Buffalo in the mid-1920s, Niles Carpenter and Daniel Katz concluded that their interviewees had been "Americanized" without being "de-Polandized." Their data led to the conclusion that Polish immigrants displayed "an absence of strong feelings so far as the Negro is concerned," a pattern "certainly in contrast to the results which would be sure to follow the putting of similar questions to a typically American group." The authors therefore argued for "the inference that so-called race feeling in this country is much more a product of tensions and quasi-psychoses born of our own national experience than of any factors inherent in the relations of race to race." Their intriguing characterization of Buffalo's Polish community did not attempt to cast its racial views as "pro-Negro" but instead pointed out that "the bulk of its members express indifference towards him." Such "indifference"—the term was perhaps borrowed from a typology of general immigrant responses to U.S. culture used by Robert Park—also struck observers of other groups. It was the product not simply of unfamiliarity with, or distance from, the U.S. racial system. It reflected Old World loyalties compounded by intense, harrowing, and contradictory U.S. experiences inbetween whiteness and nonwhiteness. In an era of immigration restriction, the white house would come to have greater appeals, and the discourse of Americanization would generate deeper anxieties.[83]

ENTERING THE WHITE HOUSE

Part Three

CHAPTER 5

"A Vast Amount of Coercion": The Ironies of Immigration Restriction

Now everybody knows that a black man is inferior to a white man (except, of course, Jews, Italians and Slavs).

W.E.B. DU BOIS, FREEDOM FIGHTER (1924), WITH RICH AMBIGUITY

There is much of similarity between the case of the negroes and that of the modern immigrants. To be sure, the newcomers of today are for the most part white-skinned instead of colored, which gives a differ- ent aspect to the matter. Yet in the mind of the average American, the modern immigrants are generally regarded as inferior peoples— races he looks down on, and with which he does not want to associ- ate on terms of social equality.

HENRY PRATT FAIRCHILD, EUGENICIST (1911)

The second prize in the Pepsi-Cola Portrait of America art competition for 1944 went to Philip Evergood's *Wheels of Victory*. The artist
was born Philip Blashki, the son of a Jewish father who migrated from
Poland to New York City. As a child raised in Britain by his wealthy English mother, Blashki suffered anti-Semitic exclusion from schools before
his name was changed, on the advice of none other than Winston
Churchill, to the promising Evergood, as whom he gained admission to
the elite halls of Eton. Back in the U.S. during World War II as a radical

painter of the "proletarian grotesque," Evergood took exclusion as a central theme in *Wheels of Victory*.[1] Alongside powerful images of war-winning men and machines, another drama plays out in the painting. Four centrally located and well-illuminated white workers huddle, exchanging words and the time of day. Looking wistfully at them from a catwalk is a patrolling black guard. The painting strikingly captures what civil rights leaders at the time called the need for a double V—victory over the Nazis abroad and victory over racial exclusion at home. But what the painting assumes is perhaps as important as what it argues. The four foregrounded figures, checking watches, stand for the included white worker. But just a quarter century before, during the World War I era, the dress and the sometimes orientalized and sometimes "hunky" features of the four would have signaled their "inconclusive" whiteness.[2] Indeed, synchronizing watches, they might easily have been construed during World War I as new immigrant saboteurs rather than as cogs in the "wheels of victory."[3] Clearly, important processes of inclusion were occurring, shaped by continuing exclusion of people of color.

COMPLICATING CHRONOLOGIES OF WHITENESS

If the racialization of new immigrants was messy—varying widely across time, space, and circumstance—we would hardly expect the change that Evergood's painting registered to be easily summarized or dated. As the "whitening" process is considered from many angles in Part 3, the complicating question "According to whom?" deserves consistent foregrounding. Where large public processes were at work, courts, naturalization bureaucracies, army recruiters, and executive orders on fair employment left considerable paper trails, though they hardly led in only one direction. Unions and employers likewise spoke volubly, as we have seen, to the question of which immigrants were acceptable, but their utterances created crazy-quilt patterns, with wide local variations based on the demographics of particular workplaces and industries, patterns of strikebreaking management strategies, language acquisition, and labor markets. Popular cultural images abounded, but questions of audience reception remain vexed. Academic discourse was uneven, changing from a language of race in its discussion of new immigrants to a language of minorities in and after the 1930s and ethnicity in and after the 1940s. But the broader influences of such scholarly writings are difficult to gauge.[4]

The messy micro-encounters in which whiteness was and was not made best illustrate how important the question "According to whom?" is when looking at racial categorization. Nelson Algren's novel *Never Come Morning* (1942), for example, forcefully captured the ways in which new immigrants judged each other racially, even as they were judged, and showed how situational whiteness could be. Early in the novel, a Greek tried to join a gang rape and was told "Beat it, Sheeny, this is a white man's party." He replied to the Polish Americans excluding him, "Make half those gorillas stay out of it and I'll show you who the white man is." He was murdered shortly thereafter. Later in the novel "sheeny" found its more conventional slurring application, to Jews, but Mama Tomek ended her anti-Semitic tirade by turning to her Jewish janitor and exempting him from the racial insult: "Not you, Snipey. You're a white sheeny." A Jewish bar owner esteemed by eastern Europeans was "the only white kike in the business." New immigrant "white hopes" abounded in the boxing sequences in Algren's novels. An ethnic contender, hardly secure in his racial place, happily heard applause on entering the ring. The "white men" in the audience cheered him on "for bein' white too." The "whole white man's house" roared him to victory: "The Polack had made it a white man's evening after all."[5] Similar judgments of situational whiteness were reported by sociologists, oral historians, and their immigrant informants. The Jewish playwright Israel Zangwill wrote of Sicilians as "dark white" but also as "crossed with the sons of Ham from [the Mediterranean's] southern shore." Irish Americans, so often the teachers and arbiters of race, could make Italians "guineas" and Jews "kikes." Native-born whites, even at their most anti-Italian or anti-Jewish, took care to admit the possibility of the occasional "high-class" new immigrant amid the "trash."[6] Indeed discrimination almost always involved making choices about merit within as well as across "racial groups."

At the level of racial consciousness, the coming of whiteness likewise presents difficult problems regarding periodization and evidence. Particularly important is the extent to which immigrants' assertions of their own difference, often in the late nineteenth and early twentieth centuries of *racial* difference, could occur in perverse and even inverse relationship to the lived experience of U.S. racism. Thus, as Eric Goldstein's work shows,

Jews in the last three decades of the nineteenth century often spoke of a Jewish race, distinguished "not only in cultural particularity but in biology, shared ancestry and blood." During this period, Jews "felt confident that they could employ a racial self-description without being subjected to demonization on racist grounds." Middle-class Jewish American women were particularly apt to speak in the language of race. However, in the early twentieth century, immigration of east European Jews "swelled to unprecedented numbers," and Jim Crow, Asian exclusion, and empire tightened racial distinctions in the United States. In these new conditions, Goldstein finds, Jewish use of the language of race declined in the interests of self-protection. Viewed as both "dark-complected and alien in custom," new immigrant Jews faced "racial" perils but did not necessarily experience "racial" consciousness. Goldstein writes, "If in the late nineteenth century, Jews' claims to racial distinctiveness cast them as a variation of the 'Caucasian' race, in the twentieth century their perceived racial peculiarities threatened to place them beyond the pale of whiteness." Jewish race talk, though far from disappearing, declined: "Not until . . . 'ethnicity' was coined . . . would American Jews again have an emotionally satisfying and politically safe vehicle for the expression of their identity." On other frequencies, such as Americanizing of names, the same curious dynamic in which securing whiteness made it *more* possible to express difference also ensured complexity.[7]

Not surprisingly, given such a multiplicity of factors, no turning point can mark a definitive and universally accepted whitening of new immigrants, at the level of how they were seen or how they desired to be seen. Nonetheless, the search for patterns, processes, and turning points is instructive. To the extent that the question has been broached by historians, scholars have most often seen World War II as such a turning point. At about the time when Evergood painted *Wheels of Victory*, a number of barometers measured change in the racial status of eastern and southern Europeans. In an anti-Nazi war, intellectual space for antiracist arguments opened dramatically and the question of intra-European racism assumed exterminationist dimensions. Clearly the inclusion of new immigrant communities under the "Americans All" banner of antifascist mobilization was far more consistent than that of African Americans. The army, however, remained Jim Crow with black support troops often assigned to serve immigrants and the children of immigrants in combat. Italian Americans, whose support for fascism had been consequential before the start of the war, largely escaped being put in camps by the government, even as Japanese Americans were massively interned.[8] The substantial emphasis on the immigrants' record of heroism and on anti-Nazi resistance fighters in Europe created a very different picture from World War I, when the new immigrants' performance had sometimes drawn praise but often suspicion. Unlike the World War I–era race riots, when immigrants abstained from joining in white terror in crucial instances, in the 1943 Detroit race riots young members of the eastern and southern European immigrant communities mobilized decisively. One Italian American remembered the war years as a time when his friends went to Harlem to "beat up some niggers." He recalled that "it was wonderful. It was new. The Italo-American stopped being Italo and starting becoming American."[9] In popular culture, the music of Glenn Miller's band gave World War II a beat. The segregated "all-American team" of Miller, according to Lewis Erenberg, "included ethnic minorities" but not African Americans.[10]

Coming from the vantage points of political economy and political science respectively, Mike Davis and Jennifer Hochschild illustrate the ways in which inclusion and exclusion came together during World War II. Davis contrasts World War I, when suspicion of immigrants prevented development of "nationalist unity" among the working class, with a World War II nationalism "broadly inclusive of the *white* working class."[11] Hochschild finds that the "language" of race, still broadly applied to new immigrants in the 1920s, "disappeared over the next few decades in favor of an increasingly general category of 'white' or 'American.'" World War II stood out among historical circumstances that sped this process because it "blurred ethnic divisions into Americanness as the children of new immigrants worked and fought beside great-grandchildren of the old against the racist scourge of Nazism." People of color, Hochschild adds, were not just left out of this process. Rather, the move of some to full whiteness "arguably required the existence of a race which could *not* traverse the same path." The war and war shortages exacerbated tensions "between newly identified 'whites' and blacks, as well as between 'whites' and Asians." But such tension was also part and parcel of a long process "of solidifying the new category of 'us' against a category of 'them' who by comparison are even more different from whites than Slavs are from Italians or Anglo-Saxons."[12]

Both Davis and Hochschild posit the dramatic inclusion of the 1940s as part and parcel of a longer drama of the expansion of whiteness, one with especially important roots in the New Deal and the inclusive trade union mobilizations of the 1930s. Matthew Jacobson's attempts to construct a chronology of when intra-European "racial" difference receded ranges back still further. "Whether the critical decade is the 1930s (according to John McGreevey) or the 1940s (according to Michael Denning), the general trend between the 1920s and the 1960s is unmistakable."[13] Jacobson adds a fascinating, partially developed insight that proposes yet another turning point. Breaking promisingly from a commonsense history of the whitening process as a linear one leading to ever greater inclusion, he argues that the immigration restrictions of the 1920s, particularly 1924, marked a pivotal moment in the "ascent" of new immigrants and their progeny into the ranks of a "monolithic whiteness." In situating the coming of whiteness amid exclusion as well as inclusion, Jacobson's observations recall James Baldwin's contention that a "vast amount of coercion" helped make new immigrants buy into the "lie of whiteness." Jacobson's brief description of why the 1924 restrictions mattered so much develops one aspect of the legislation's impact. Seeing the restriction of immigration as the fevered triumph of the "racial science" of eugenics, Jacobson holds that the 1924 act in a sense "solved" the immigration problem as posed by eugenicists and paved the way for the triumph of the idea that the racial label "Caucasian" united all Europeans as white.[14] Apt as it is in many ways, Jacobson's discussion cannot fully explain why immigration restriction dissipated anti-immigrant racism. After all, the "threat" of southern and eastern European immigrants exercising political power was much greater in the 1930s than in the 1920s. Moreover, U.S. racism sustained a deep fear of genetic intermixture with African American, Latino, and Asian American populations that were relatively small in comparison to the "white" majority. To understand why 1924 so impacted the racial status of new immigrant communities requires a more sustained analysis, stressing social as much as intellectual history and attending not only to the hard racism of eugenic thinkers that came to the fore in the early 1920s, but also to softer variants of Progressive Era race thinking that demobilized during debates on immigration restriction.

Key

IN THE SHORT RUN: THE YEAR 1924 AS
A VERDICT ON THE RACE OF NEW IMMIGRANTS?

In 1924, the Johnson-Reed Act was passed and set the basis of immigration law for decades to come. The restrictionist legislative initiative originally set quotas based on the (alleged) origins of the population in 1890, since that mixture was vastly more northern and western European than had been the pattern of immigration in recent decades. "New stock" would not be allowed to destroy the "racial status quo."[15] That status quo continued as a viable mix but was under threat. Calvin Coolidge, the president who signed the bill, put himself firmly on record as endorsing this sense of racial peril. Writing in *Good Housekeeping*, he favored "the right kind of immigration." Citing "biological" laws that are "as great a necessity to a nation as immigration law," Coolidge held that "racial considerations too grave to be brushed aside" made it clear that "divergent people will not mix or blend." "The Nordics," he continued, "propagate themselves successfully. With other races, the outcome shows deterioration on both sides."[16]

As it deliberated, Congress was deluged with letters registering grave fears at the prospect that the "distinct American type," undergirded by the northern and western European "Nordic race," might be swamped. Ku Klux Klan membership swelled as Klan leaders promised "real whites" that the organization would defend the victimized "American race," a "mass of old-stock Americans . . . a blend of various peoples of the so-called Nordic race" against the "mongrelized." Nordic supremacist writers had unprecedented popularity. Grant's *Passing of the Great Race* enjoyed a vogue in the early 1920s that had eluded it when the book appeared in 1916. Moreover, as Matthew Pratt Guterl has shown, Grant occupied key policy roles in shaping restrictionist legislation regarding immigration. The best-selling U.S. magazine, *Saturday Evening Post*, praised Grant and sponsored Kenneth Roberts's massively mounted jeremiad warning that continuing the same pattern of immigration would yield "a hybrid race of people as worthless and futile as the good-for-nothing mongrels of Southeastern Europe," whose skulls, Roberts stressed, in opposition to the optimism of the antiracist anthropologist Franz Boas, were not destined to change shape in the United States.

Even so, eugenic biologism and hope for a monitored Americanization of new immigrants often coexisted in the skull of a single reformer. Thus Harry H. Laughlin, whom Desmond King calls "the eugenicist with the greatest influence on immigration policy," proposed in 1920 that a "national registry of aliens" be set up to follow the "naturalization and Americanization" of all immigrants.[17]

Coinciding with the *Thind* decision, and with massive racist attacks on African Americans, the restrictionist momentum was part of a pro-white tide that swept new immigrants, temporarily at least, to the wrong side of the line setting apart the master race. Albert Johnson, the Washington congressman who shepherded the restrictive legislation bearing his name through Congress, was a veteran anti-Japanese campaigner.[18] Gerard Leeflang, author of the marvelous *American Travels of a Dutch Hobo*, was set upon by a "big fellow" in rural Iowa in 1923 because Leeflang's companion announced that they were from Pennsylvania. "Lots of foreigners and aliens there," the Iowan countered, "too many—we don't like to have them here and to have our communities polluted with Negroes, Jews and other nonwhites like in Pennsylvania. . . . We sure have to take care that America remains white." Barney Keefe, a memorable character in a scene from James T. Farrell's novel *The Young Manhood of Studs Lonigan*, set in 1924, had virtually the same line, as he tellingly mixed race and culture: "You know, you can tell an inferior race by the way they dress. The Polacks and the Dagoes, and niggers are the same, only the niggers are the lowest."[19]

In many ways, then, immigration restriction represented the triumph of starkly reactionary, pro-Nordic racism against new immigrants. Clearly the sharp concerns over new immigrant loyalty, willingness to fight, and aptitude that World War I provoked helped legitimate this point of view. Robert Ward's contemporary commentary on the 1924 legislation traced its triumph convincingly to scrutiny (however jaundiced) of the behavior of the "various alien racial groups" during the war. Madison Grant's co-thinker, Lathrop Stoddard, reflected that the "late war" had conclusively demonstrated "the truth that the basic factor in human affairs is not politics, but race."[20] Although the national state made some wartime efforts to curb open displays of anti-immigrant hatred ("I mustn't call you 'Mikey' and you mustn't call me 'wop'/For Uncle Sammy says it's wrong and hints we ought to stop"), the coercive power of the nation worked to foster nativist racism. The government's wartime loyalty programs and its deportation of alien radicals in response to the postwar "red scare" resulting from the 1919–1920 strike waves furthered the conflation of race and immigration as threats. A battery of highly biased intelligence tests for soldiers added the issue of genetic inferiority to the mix. In one case the tests directly measured racial knowledge, asking how many legs a "kaffir" (the rough South African cognate of nigger) has. As Horace Kallen noted at the time, these tests became central to "racial theories descanting variously upon the magical superiority of the Nordic stock." Test results—like those obtained from 1912 examinations which "proved" that over 80 percent of a large sample of Jewish, Russian, Italian, and Hungarian immigrants being processed at Ellis Island were "feeble-minded" and even "moronic"—yielded easily to interpretations which argued that blacks and new immigrants were childlike and inferior, and constituted a threat to democracy.[21] The psychologist Robert Yerkes used these tests in a highly visible 1923 article in *Atlantic Monthly* to maintain that "races are quite as significantly different" in intelligence as are individuals and that differences among Europeans are "almost as great as the intellectual differences between negro and white." The "disquietingly low" intelligence of new immigrants could then be connected with "the dominance [in numbers] of the Mediterranean races, as contrasted with the Nordic and Alpine." Italians and Poles stood among the "worst" of the "races" from Europe and, like African Americans, on average lacked fifteen IQ points supposedly possessed by native-born white Anglo-Saxons. University of Texas educational psychologist William A. Sheldon published a noted summary of intelligence data purporting to show that Mexican children were far less intelligent than "whites." However, his study included a table showing Mexicans in fact ahead of the "Italian" and "Slavish," who were presumably considered nonwhite. The race science popularizer Henry Laughlin legitimated such swill as the "expert eugenics agent" for the House Committee on Immigration and Naturalization in the early 1920s.[22]

But as clearly as 1924 represented a triumph for race-based exclusion of new immigrants, it also signaled a loss of confidence among those who had accepted immigrants as trial members of the American Experiment. Henry Ford, a sponsor of the literal-minded melting pot pageant at Ford Night School before the war, endorsed massive spying on his foreign-born workers—spying as much directed at Slavic "Huns" as at German ones after U.S. entry. By 1919 his Dearborn *Independent* regularly serialized anti-Jewish exposés.[23] Ford was in every way an extreme case, but in general large capitalist concerns could no longer be counted on to support open immigration by the early 1920s. In responding to the postwar strike waves, as one historian put it, "employers inflamed the historic identification of class conflict with immigrant radicalism." To the extent that they convinced themselves that immigrant radicalism derived from "racial" tendencies, they equivocated on their opposition to immigration restriction. Capital's support for the conservative Americanization programs of the fascinatingly named Inter-Racial Council dried up quickly after the war. When the National Industrial Conference Board met in 1923, its chairman allowed that immigration restriction was "essentially a race question" (and one of proper "citizenship"). Delegates tried, as one of them put it, to balance "commercial purposes" that made immigration attractive against the threat of "deteriorated," "half-breed" children. As immigration restriction became law, Kallen wrote, the employers of immigrants consistently chose to see labor radicalism as "always an alien importation, never a home-grown product of the soil of exploitation they have themselves prepared and cultivated." By 1924, industrialists reacted to labor shortages by appealing for an immigration policy featuring both quotas and flexibility, but their once unified voice was divided and weakened.[24]

Nor did the heroism of new immigrants as "trial members" of labor unions in the postwar strike wave soften growing AFL opposition to immigration. The immigrant mobilizations of 1919–1920 had scarcely ended when the AFL publication, the *American Federationist*, incredibly featured disquisitions on "Americanism and Immigration" by John Quinn, the national commander of the nativist and intensely antilabor American Legion. Although new immigrants had unarguably proven the most loyal unionists in the most important of strikes, the AFL now openly supported exclusion based on "racial" quotas. Quinn brought together biology, environment, and his own highly racialized history of the United States, defending American stock against Italian "industrial slaves" particularly and against the "indigestion of immigration" generally. Completing his autobiography as the 1924 restrictions were passed, Samuel Gompers emphasized that the nation's future hinged on its "maintenance of racial purity and strength."[25]

Among professional reformers and politicians as well, the war and the postwar mass strikes led to a loss of confidence and an increasingly brittle and despairing insistence on immediate "100 percent Americanism." The phrasing of such a requirement, crucially supported by the long-time advocate of gentler assimilation programs, Frances Kellor, suggests the extent to which many progressives literally lost any sense of proportion where new immigrants were concerned and how thoroughly their earlier defense of immigrant races had been conditional and measured. Indeed Horace Kallen's classic *Culture and Democracy in the United States* (1924) counted Kellor's Inter-Racial Council as in step with the American Legion, the American Defense Society, the National Security League, the Daughters of the American Revolution, Chamber of Commerce, and the Ku Klux Klan in a bitter footnote describing those who fed frenzied stories about immigration to a "specious" press. Americanization, for many reformers, had long been not simply a cultural process but an index of racial change, which could fail if the concentration of "lower" races kept the "wondrous Americanizing alchemy" of racial transformation from occurring. Since "race" mixing never was regarded as unmitigated good but as a question of proportion that had a number of possible outcomes, the new immigrant's record was constantly under scrutiny. The failure of Americanization to deliver total loyalty in war and at work made the broader record one of failure. The sense that "virility," "manhood," and "vigor" would be injected into American "stock" by intermarriage had long coexisted with the emphasis on obedience and docility in the curricula of Americanization classes. At their most vigorous, in the 1919–1920 strike wave, new immigrants were most suspect. Nationalists, and many Progressive reformers among them, were sure, according to Higham's magisterial history of immigration restriction, that they had done "their best to bring the great mass of newcomers into the fold." The problem was not theirs, but a reflection of the "incorrigibly inassimilable nature of the material on which they had worked." The new immigrant, on this view, had been tried and found wanting, had been racially tested and failed. One top secret government response, the aptly named War Plans White initiative (1919), developed draconian plans to put down anticipated insurrections by African Americans and new immigrants. Security planners saw the latter group as not ever "entirely recasted in the American 'Melting Pot,'" and therefore "susceptible to hostile leadership against Anglo-Saxon Institutions."[26]

Yet the form taken by implementation of the 1924 legislation ensured that the racially excluded "new immigrant" groups would remain in some sense "inbetween." Here as elsewhere, the probing, precise work of the political scientist Gwendolyn Mink cuts to the heart of complex matters. Nativism, she writes, rested on the "overlapping characteristics of race, poverty, and dependency" that new immigrants were seen as sharing with African Americans. "Race and nationality" became the "new moral rachets of citizenship," casting doubt on the fitness of all except "old-stock white men." But such questioning took forms that were very different in kind and degree. The quotas for legal immigration ultimately were based on the "national origins" of the white population enumerated in the 1920 census. New immigrant groups, who would have acquired 45 percent of quota slots if a proposal to use the numbers of European immigrants according to the 1910 census as the basis for calculations had been implemented, were massively excluded. When quotas under the 1924 act were finally hammered out in 1929, the annual number of slots for Italy, Spain, Portugal, Poland, Albania, Bulgaria, Czechoslovakia, Greece, Hungary, Romania, Yugoslavia, and Russia *together* was 18,408. Great Britain, Northern Ireland, and the Irish Free State alone generated 83,574 places, 4.54 times as many as the total of the dozen southern and eastern European sources of immigrants enumerated. Germany alone generated an additional 25,957 slots. Nonetheless, the one slot in seven going to new immigrant groups meant that their blanket racial exclusion was avoided. Naturalization of new immigrants as white continued. Asian nations, meanwhile, received nominal quotas reserved "for persons who are eligible to citizenship in the United States and admissible under the immigration laws of the United States"—that is, for non-Asians! The 9 percent of the 1920 population of African origins generated negligible quotas for African immigrants. As Mae Ngai has put it, the 1924 act "differentiated Europeans according to nationality and ranked them according to desirability." In the 1920s, such a ranking was racial. At the same time, Ngai continues, the 1924 law helped to construct "a white American race, in which persons of European descent shared a common whiteness that made them distinct from those deemed not white." Even at a low point of their racialization, the new immigrants remained inbetween, or "conditionally white."[27]

The *Thind* decision on whiteness and naturalization was vital in maintaining this inbetween status. For years courts had worried that following ethnological arguments too closely would lead to questioning the "white-ness," and therefore the right to naturalization, of such "Asiatic" Euro-pean groups as the Magyars and the Finns. For the courts to try to divine the intent of the congressmen who framed the 1790 naturalization law threatened, as courts observed in 1909, 1913, and 1915 cases involving Middle Easterners and Parsees from India, to subject Russian, Polish, Italian, and Greek claims to citizenship to scrutiny. As Ian Haney Lopez has shown, the judicial move to exclusion based on a "popular" or "com-mon" understanding of who was white circumvented the uncertainty and the tendency to result in inclusion of some non-Europeans characterizing cases decided on ethnology. At the same time, *Thind* forestalled ques-tioning of new immigrant whiteness by simply asserting the popular un-derstanding. The Supreme Court simply ignored the larger debates concerning race, migration, and new immigrants' fitness for citizenship, despite the white heat of the debates in the early 1920s.[28]

THE LONGER RUN: 1924 AND THE DIALECTICS OF WHITENESS

For southern and eastern European immigrants who lived through that repressive decade, the 1920s seemed unlikely to catalyze their move from racial inbetweenness toward whiteness. To appreciate longer-run processes that connected the political triumph of anti-immigrant racism in the 1920s with eventual incorporation of new immigrant communities as white requires a long view and a sense of irony that the victims of im-migrant restriction doubtless would have judged misplaced. The 1926 *New York Times* obituary for the playwright Israel Zangwill captured the national mood: it pronounced Zangwill's dream of a "melting pot" as dead as the author himself.[29] That same year, the eugenicist Henry Pratt Fairchild's *The Melting Pot Mistake* seemed as much a postmortem as a jeremiad.[30] If the "new immigration" had been an off-white "flood," leg-islation had been put in place to slow it to a trickle. While the Johnson-Reed Act was not passed until 1924 and did not find a formula for full implementation until the decade's end, a combination of the restriction acts of 1921 and 1924 and the illiberal granting of visas by U.S. consuls in Europe produced a near decimation of immigration from Europe to the United States after 1921. The first decade of the twentieth century saw almost 9 million European arrivals. From 1922 until 1940, less than 3 million Europeans came. In the 1930s, 1940s, and 1950s together, European immigration to the United States did not reach 3 million. More importantly for the racist restrictionists, law and practice transformed the composition of immigration from Europe. Racial restriction directed against new immigrant populations worked. In the 1870s there had been seventeen times as many immigrants from northern and western Europe as from southern and eastern. In the 1880s, this figure fell to seven times as many and in the 1890s to roughly twice as many.[31] By the first decade of the twentieth century, the proportions were virtually even, according to official figures. Those figures counted all Austro-Hungarian migrants as being from northern and western Europe and thus concealed the fact that the "new immigration" already quite outstripped the old. By the 1910s, southern and eastern European immigrants came in about twice the numbers as those from the "English-speaking races." The sociologist Niles Carpenter broke down statistics on immigration from northwestern Europe as against that from the "other" Europe in his 1927 study and came to still more dramatic conclusions. The former category had outstripped the latter, he argued, by more than fourfold in the 1880s; in the 1890s, the two categories were roughly even. From 1900 to 1910, the "others" were migrating at three times the rate of northwestern Europeans and that figure increased further in the 1910s. Carpenter's estimate for 1920 was that "new" immigrant parents "furnished" four to eight times as many members of the next U.S. generation as the "old" immigrants did.[32]

Any projection of migration trends was bound to show a huge future preponderance of the "inbetween" races. The rapid entry of 1.5 million immigrants in the second half of 1920 and in 1921 came largely from "new immigrant" origins, especially Jewish, and alarmed predictions at the time of restriction debates focused specifically on trends in Italian and Jewish migration. Experts predicted several more years of immigration at 2 million per year. Federal policies reversed such patterns in their tracks. For that decade, old immigrant groups furnished 1.2 times as many migrants as the new. In the 1930s, when net immigration was negligible, the figure was 1.4 times; in the 1940s, five times as many "old immigrant" newcomers arrived and in the 1950s, three times as many.[33] Moreover, the numbers of second-generation births to parents at least one of whom was a new immigrant plummeted after the 1924 restrictions. For the birth cohort from 1921 to 1925, the figure was about 1,536,000, barely down from the 1916–1920 peak. By 1926–1930 the figure declined to less than 1.2 million and for 1936–1940 it scarcely exceeded 400,000. With visas more and more selectively distributed, the demography of immigration also shifted where skill was concerned. U.S. consuls in Europe, predicting which immigrants were likely to "become public charges," apparently favored skilled workers. Such workers made up half of all European immigrants to the United States in 1925 and 1926 as against a third a decade earlier.[34]

The quota system provided dramatic reassurances of the determination to keep the United States "white." Implementation of the 1924 act initially figured quotas based on the 1890 census, literally banishing southern and eastern Europeans from the demography and the history of the United States. The census, Mae Ngai has aptly written, became for the twentieth-century racist what "craniometric data" had been for his old school predecessors.[35] The mostly mechanical 1927 revisions of the law, which took the 1920 census as a base, kept the figures from the 1924 debates well in mind and produced only modest adjustments in the end results. From 1901 to 1920, Italians entered at the average rate of about 160,000 annually; the quota set in 1929 was less than 4 percent of that number. For Austria-Hungary, the 1929 quota did not reach 2 percent of average prewar levels of immigration.[36]

However, even such radical and ruthless policy changes could not immediately and automatically appease nativism, especially in its most irrational racist strains. Immigration restriction could only gradually make it more difficult to sustain a fever pitch of alarm regarding an immigrant invasion. For example, the antiblack, anti-Semitic, anti-Catholic, and anti-new immigrant Ku Klux Klan, several million strong, remained the largest voluntary political organization in the United States for a time even after the Johnson-Reed Act. A reform organization in Chicago declared in 1930 that "since the war and the quota acts," the city suffered under "far more prejudice against aliens." Other experts likewise endorsed the view that "race prejudice" against southern and eastern Europeans became more respectable and widespread in the short run after 1924. In that sense, Oscar Handlin's observation from a half century ago wears well. Handlin characterized the 1924 law as "a rejection of the foreign-born who aspired to come to the United

States [and] a condemnatory judgment of the foreign-born already long established in the country."[37]

Immigrants suffered massively from state laws restricting their access to jobs before and after the Johnson-Reed Act passed. In New York in 1924, for example, noncitizens could not get the licenses required to work as stationary engineers, marine engineers, master pilots, or movie projectionists. In Michigan they could not cut hair. After the Great Depression began to generate mass unemployment in 1930, the nation's 6.2 million aliens suffered new threats to their livelihoods. An Arizona law, invalidated later as unconstitutional, attempted to criminalize any employer of more than five workers, unless 80 percent of those workers were citizens.[38] The Detroit Common Council ordered dismissal of 748 "alien" municipal workers in February 1930. Their action, as Herman Feldman wrote, bespoke a trend in "various communities . . . to assail the 'foreigner' as one who took bread from the mouths of natives." The "problems" of alien labor and illegal immigration from Europe continued to excite public opinion throughout the Depression, providing a pretext to victimize even naturalized new immigrants and their U.S.-born children.[39]

However, given the magnitude of anti–new immigrant racism in the 1920s and its association with labor organizing among immigrants, a remarkable feature of the Great Depression in the United States, especially in contrast to Europe, was the relative absence of intra-European racism in response to the crisis. The campaigns for working-class unity mounted by the new unions in the Congress of Industrial Organizations (CIO) deserve much credit for this result. However, it could equally be said that the 1924 act created, however perversely, a sense of security that the immigration issue had been disarmed and helped the CIO succeed where its predecessors failed. Indeed there are few counterfactual scenarios more fruitful for U.S. historians to contemplate than to wonder what would have happened to the labor movement and to racial formation in the United States if the Great Depression had begun before effective immigration restriction was implemented. For example, what if a dozen years of depression had begun in 1920, not 1929? How powerful might the Ku Klux Klan and fascist organizing generally have then become? How widespread might the animus against existing immigrant communities have grown? How lastingly divisive to the cause of labor unity might the American Federation of Labor's embrace of anti–new immigrant racism have been under such conditions? As it happened, the Depression instead proved how well (from the restrictionists' viewpoint) the changes made in the 1920s actually worked. Though the economic crisis was global and political and racial persecution in much of Europe was dire, few of the persecuted could reasonably consider migration to the United States as a solution to their woes. The first four full years of the Depression saw the number of immigrant aliens in the United States decline by 22 percent. In 1934, those arriving in the United States outnumbered those departing by a mere 1,151 persons.[40]

The stark effects of the 1920s policy changes help flesh out the ironic connections of racially justified restriction with new possibilities for already arrived southern and eastern Europeans to claim whiteness in the longer run. The new demographics of immigration dramatically undercut political mobilizations based on fear of an "invasion" insofar as there was every indication that the invasion of "hunkies" and "guineas" had been decisively turned back. Subsequently experts reasserted the progressive views of Theodore Roosevelt and others that in the right proportions new immigrants could, properly digested, even invigorate U.S. "stock." If a million Slavs, Jews, and southern Europeans per year could not be Americanized, a few thousand perhaps could. Thus Herbert Hoover, the central political figure of the 1920s as secretary of commerce and then president, allowed that the nation could handle immigrants "if they behaved." As one expert put it, "Strange races . . . make no trouble if they are kept out of the way of our people."[41] The reduced numbers of immigrants could be "digestible." Dartmouth professor Herman Feldman quantified matters: "The problem of dealing with new Italians, for example, in any one year, is that of helping a maximum of 5802 new people to adjust themselves in this country." He added that the accusation that new immigrants threatened the standard of living was no longer tenable. The Presbyterian Church statement on "Foreign-Speaking Work" (1928) reflected a renewed, if hesitant, hope that the new arithmetic of restriction would let reform agencies nurture changes in a way they could not before. The church found the quota laws "furnished the community with a breathing spell. The constructive civic, social and religious agencies have been given a chance to catch up." A minor character in Sinclair Lewis's *Babbitt*—named Koplinsky—anticipated the logic: "And another thing we got to do is keep these damn foreigners out of the country. . . . When we've assimilated the foreigners we've got here now . . . and turned 'em into regular folks, why then maybe we'll let in a few more." He aired these opinions hard by a poisonous discussion of "niggers, nowadays." New immigrant inbetweenness had long been viewed by the native born as an admixture of biological and cultural deficiencies. Attitudes toward immigrants included panic over "mongrelization" but also a cheerful faith that the United States could change biology if immigrants did not "swamp" it. Restriction, although based on eugenic racism in its triumphant moment, allowed the more hopeful impulses to revive, albeit in a shrunken laboratory.[42]

The flip side of the 1924 immigration restrictions made an equally crucial but less noticed difference. With the main sources of immigrant labor suddenly shut off, capital turned to the recruitment of workers racialized as nonwhite, not as "inbetween." This trend began during the decline in immigration caused by World War I, with 400,000 African Americans leaving the South for northern cities and many more urbanizing in the South. By the late 1920s, more than a million Afro-southerners had followed pioneers in the Great Migration to the North. As Francis Brown and Joseph Slabey Roucek wrote in 1937, "The immediate result of shutting off the supply of labor from Europe was the influx of negroes from the south into northern industrial cities." In Chicago, for example, the African American population in 1910 was 44,000; by 1930 it stood at 234,000.[43] In Philadelphia, a city with fewer immigrants and fewer African Americans, the black population grew from about one in fourteen in 1910 to one in six in 1950. Meanwhile the proportion of the foreign born in Philadelphia declined from one in four to one in nine.[44]

As one expert put it in 1931, "the North has been placed in the position of securing its chief sources of new labor from Southern Negroes . . . unless Mexicans are permitted unrestricted entrance." Capital, especially but not exclusively agricultural capital, at times successfully championed the use of Mexican labor in the 1920s, though stopping far short of defending their fitness as citizens. Consequently a half million Mexicans entered the United States, a sixteenfold increase over the first decade of the twentieth century. With Filipinos briefly enjoying greater access to migration, Mexican American, Puerto Rican, and Asian/Pacific Island immigration reached two-thirds of the totals for southern and eastern Europeans for the 1920s. And some contemporaries estimated that illegal Mexican immigration outpaced documented migration. Although remigration to Mexico was significant in the 1920s, official figures put the population increase of Mexican immigrants at roughly threefold, from 220,000 in 1920 to 639,000 in 1930. Nearly 90,000 immigrants arrived in 1924 alone. In 1933, a study written under the auspices of the President's Research Committee on Social Trends worried that "in becoming less foreign white the country will become less white, while the Mexican and Negro groups increase" and confidently averred that Mexicans themselves were less than 10 percent white and over 89 percent Indian and mestizo. The sense that immigrant workers were dependent and unsuited for American liberty because of their recruitment by labor contractors became divorced from European "new immigrants" as their migration declined and attached to Mexicans.[45]

Whether African American, Asian, or Latino, newcomers often came from the countryside, sometimes after brief periods of urban life and proletarianization. Poor and typically unskilled or unable to get jobs commensurate with their skills, they often migrated back and forth between older homes and U.S. cities. Their movements put strains on family structures. They either failed to speak English or spoke it in an accent subject to ridicule. These racialized migrants, along with white "hillbillies" fleeing rural poverty and Okie refugees from the Dust Bowl in the 1930s, came to be seen as the city dwellers most foreign to urban life, displacing the new immigrant in the minds of experts and laypersons alike as prototypes of those suffering most acutely from a maladjustment resulting from ignorance and genetics.[46]

Southern and eastern European immigrant communities meanwhile lost many of the cultural attributes that marked them as unfit to enter the white house of U.S. nationalism as full equals. Restriction brought the emergence of a population in which the first generation of migrants bulked less large, and to which a third generation eventually began to be born. This change meant that even that central instrument of anti-immigrant racism, the United States census, could no longer easily mark the new immigrant as different. The census continued to enumerate the foreign born separately and to count their children (and the "mixed," who had one native-born parent) in yet another category. But there remained no category for the third generation, which had presumably merged with the "English-speaking races" over time.[47]

What David Montgomery has called the "stabilization" of immigrant working-class communities also assuaged fears. To the extent that immigrants were despised for their real and reputed links to radical labor organizations, the decimation of unions, and especially industrial unions, in the 1920s was a vital element in making a more stable image for the new immigrant working class. Moreover, remigration rates declined steeply after restriction, as the immigration bureaucracy "made any possible return home an irrevocable act." Because nativists harbored a particularly sharp animus to remigrants, this change was crucial. Indeed, as Gunther Peck has shown, transiency itself generally helped identify new immigrants with nonwhite workers in some regions.[48] Immigrants who did take the "irrevocable" step of going home were disproportionately unskilled. Applying for citizenship offered "some protection against deportation" (which increased by a factor of four and a half from 1923 through 1930) and the number of applications rose dramatically. In the wake of the 1924 law, 75 percent of citizens seeking visas to bring in relatives had recently been naturalized, suggesting another practical urgency shaping citizenship choices. Foreign-born wives of foreign-born men applied for citizenship in massive numbers, which surprised even supporters of the 1922 Cable Act making the process possible (and necessary, since a wife's citizenship previously followed from her husband's). The great reformer and investigator of foreign-born women's applications for naturalization, Sophonisba Breckinridge, held that the process "brings . . . security to the home." The overall results were dramatic. Poles and Italians in the United States, for example, had about the same naturalization rates in 1920, with just over one in four naturalized. Their 1930 rates were virtually identical, but with one in two naturalized. For Hungarians, the increase was from 30.0 percent to 56.2 percent during the 1920s and for Greeks from 17.4 percent to 45.1 percent. By 1930, 60.4 percent of the foreign-born white population held U.S. citizenship. Despite fears that the Cable Act would cut citizenship rates of foreign-born women, who tended to be isolated in homes, the percentage of citizenship—now a status autonomously achieved and including voting rights—increased substantially in the 1920s, passing the 50 percent mark with women almost as likely as men to be naturalized. By 1950 over 70 percent of the foreign born were citizens.[49] Thus as immigration restriction tightened, new immigrant communities actually gained in potential political power born in

CITIZENSHIP STATUS OF FOREIGN-BORN POPULATION

Year		Percent Citizens
1920	Males	44.9
	Females	48.7
1930	Males	57.1
	Females	54.2
1940	Males	67.6
	Females	57.4
1950	Males	76.7
	Females	69.4

SOURCE: Calculated from Bureau of the Census, *Historical Statistics of the United States: Colonial Times to 1957* (Washington, D.C., 1961), 65. These statistics include the "nonwhite" foreign-born.

part of their ability to be naturalized as "white." The 1928 presidential campaign of Al Smith, an Irish Catholic, offered a chance to mobilize that strength, which would become a bulwark of the New Deal's political coalition. Smith carried the twelve largest U.S. cities, benefiting greatly from votes of the naturalized.[50]

The 1920s saw a flowering of cultural organization in immigrant communities bent on retaining their heritage while increasingly cut adrift from remigration to and new immigrations from their homelands.[51] But inevitably these institutions were more U.S.-centered and more likely to conduct community life in English. The thriving pre–1920 movement of Chicago's new immigrants (along with Germans and Scandinavians) for foreign language instruction in public schools, for example, died for lack of support in the 1920s, and the foreign language press underwent decline. Joshua Fishman's major study of language loyalty in the United States is unequivocal in terming the 1920s restriction of immigration as "the major force in limiting language maintenance." Richard Alba's research using 1979 current population surveys tabulated the proportion of "U.S.-born South-Central-East European ethnics" who reported non–English language use in their childhood homes. For the cohort born before 1916, 76.8 percent reported such usage; for the 1916–1930 cohort the figure declined to 70.2 percent; by the 1931–1945 cohort, it was only 45.5 percent and for those born between 1946 and 1960, 24.9 percent.[52] World War I brought the first criminal penalties for "illegal entry" to the United States and in the 1920s border patrols were beefed up. Prosecution long after unlawful entry also became a fact of life. Finally, "stabilization" occurred in regard to sex ratios. The mostly male patterns of migration early in the century gave way to balanced second-generation sex ratios. In 1910, there were seventy-six "new immigrant" women for each hundred men, reflecting the fact that 75 percent of all immigrants from 1899 to 1910 had been male. As the world war hampered and the state then restricted immigration, the ratios became 81 to 100 in 1920 and 86 to 100 in 1930. Since, as Barbara Foley has shown, the "racist anti-radicalism" deployed against immigrants in the 1920s partook of rape fantasies in which the nation was "penetrated" and "violated" by male intruders, such gender changes were consequential symbolically as well as in communities.[53]

"Inbetween" rather than fully racialized, southern and eastern Europeans would have seen stark differences in ways in which they were categorized compared to Asians, blacks, and Latinos even at the nadir of their mistreatment in the 1920s. If, as argued in Chapter 4, immigrants were taught U.S. racism through witnessing white supremacy, the increasing black population in northern cities offered many more opportunities for immigrants to see hardening northern versions of Jim Crow. The *Thind* and *Ozawa* cases, as we have seen, conclusively ended the opportunity for naturalized citizenship by immigrants from almost all of the Asian continent at almost the same moment as new immigrants' entry into the United States—but not their ability to be naturalized as white citizens—was sharply curtailed.

The rise in Mexican immigration meanwhile generated an acceleration of efforts to separate Mexican Americans categorically from the white race, with the Census Bureau briefly making Mexican a "racial" category for the 1930 census. The immigration bureaucracy and immigration law amply demonstrated the racial vulnerability of Mexicans. The funding of the border patrol and the extension of the concept of "illegal entry" to make it an ongoing crime that authorities pursued beyond the border itself singled Mexican immigrants out for scrutiny. In the 1920s, deportations of Mexicans increased tenfold, accounting for 50 percent of formal deportations and 80 percent of voluntary ones. As Ngai has written, "European American communities had achieved a measure of political representation and could count on . . . settlement organizations to advocate their interest." One New York City study found European immigrants ten times more likely than Latinos to have counsel in deportation cases.[54]

The Deportation Act of 1929 offered a smorgasbord of circumstances justifying deportation. The law applied to "aliens of any race," but the specific provision making any alien who had entered illegally liable to deportation ensured that Mexicans were the people most greatly affected. Changing laws, consular policies, a historically suspect and porous border, inadequate record keeping, and aggressive agribusiness labor recruitment made the legal situation of many Mexican Americans unclear. In 1929, a law felonizing migration of a deported alien back into the United States also fell heavily on immigrants from Mexico. The whole issue of "illegal immigration," with its many implications regarding the history of whiteness and fitness for U.S. citizenship, became increasingly attached to immigrants from Mexico, who had long possessed the right to be naturalized. During the Depression, 400,000 or more Mexican Americans were expelled wholesale, many of them U.S.-born children who clearly were citizens.[55] As Ngai writes, "'Illegal' became constitutive of 'Mexican' . . . a wholly negative racial category." Repatriation of Filipinos was likewise widespread. More broadly, Ngai tellingly continues, "The Immigration Act of 1924 contributed to the racialization of immigrant groups around notions of whiteness, permanent foreignness and illegality—categories of difference that have outlived the racial categories created by eugenics and post–World War I nativism." The more ephemeral categories were, of course, those applied to "inbetween" immigrants from southern and eastern Europe.[56]

Even as they suffered near exclusion, new immigrant groups had greater opportunities to learn that they were categorized differently from people of color. The processes through which they calculated the costs and benefits of whiteness, and their chances of securing it, occurred in localities, lodges, unions, workplaces, churches, and households. These processes are examined more closely in Chapters 6–7. However, one important national manifestation of immigrant consciousness directly relates to the 1924 restriction law and merits consideration here. In 1924, a small band of legislators consistently opposed the law as un-American. As Montgomery has perhaps too breathlessly put it, they "despised the racist

logic that pronounced some Americans more desirable than others."
Often representing working-class immigrant constituencies and sometimes themselves part of the new immigration, these reformers articulated a "civic nationalism" broadly inclusive of Europeans. Based in New
York, New England, and Chicago, they courageously risked organized
labor's support in many cases to support such inclusion, which surely was
doomed to lose. Fully half of all members of Congress endorsed as
"friends of labor" by the pro-restriction American Federation of Labor,
broke ranks to oppose the 1924 law.[57]

However, theirs was overwhelmingly a white egalitarianism. As Gary
Gerstle's important recent work demonstrates, the antirestrictionists "did
not always stand up for their civic nationalist tradition. Indeed, on the
question of Japanese exclusion, they abandoned it altogether." (Another
reading of the evidence might emphasize that the Euro-inclusive civic nationalism they espoused had a long history of cohabitation with white supremacy.) Adolph Sabath, a leading antirestrictionist in Congress, aptly
summarized the group's viewpoint as "all in favor of exclusion of the
Japanese." New York's Samuel Dickstein, another antirestrictionist stal-
wart, interrupted the anti-Japanese rant of a California congressman to
emphasize that he shared the speaker's position in favor of total exclusion
of the Japanese. Fiorello LaGuardia, who came closest to questioning
Japanese exclusion but stopped short, endorsed a preference for European immigration over Mexican "peons." The antirestrictionists further
supported the view that a "vast gulf" separated the assimilable new immigrants from African Americans. They argued, according to Gerstle, that
their immigrant constituents "belonged to the same superior European
race as the English and Germans." When confronted with "an opportunity to place their constituents on the right, white side of the racial divide,
they grabbed it."[58] In 1924 in a single moment, new immigrants might
thus be victimized racially, still inbetween and bound for (and to) whiteness. Their less unequivocal admission into the white house of the United
States would not mainly occur at the level of symbolism and national affairs, but in urban neighborhoods and homes.

CHAPTER 6

Finding Homes in an Era of Restriction

When they say East Harlem . . . Harlem was never East Harlem, Harlem was Harlem. When the blacks started to come towards this area, in order for us to explain where we lived . . . we said we live in East Harlem, that's where the name East came into being, to separate the white and the black.

PETER PASCALE, HARLEM RESIDENT (1988)

A home was a complex of brick and fantasy, security and hazard, fact and fiction.

CHARLES ABRAMS, FAIR HOUSING ACTIVIST (1955)

The bitterest and the best poem in Alain Locke's celebrated anthology *The New Negro* (1925) was Claude McKay's "White Houses," which begins, "Your door is shut against my tightened face, and I am sharp as steel with discontent." He reflected on the results of an exclusion that "rends my vitals as I pass" and requires of the poet a Herculean effort to "hold me to the letter of your law." The poem played insistently on the twin images of the exclusionary white neighborhood and the seat of executive power in the United States. Indeed McKay wanted to call his contribution "The White House" and had earlier published the poem under that title. When he learned of the arbitrary retitling of the piece, McKay furiously wrote to Locke that the change "destroyed every vestige of intellectual and fraternal understanding" between them.[1] Capturing the relationship between the right-wing White Houses of the 1920s and the terror, law, and neighborhood organizations that made millions of houses white in that same decade was no small matter.

McKay's "White Houses" takes us straight to the themes of this chapter and the next. The process by which new immigrant groups came to a fuller sense of their own whiteness and a more secure footing as whites hinged on becoming at home in the United States. Houses of worship, movie houses, and the house of organized labor gradually made for the possibility of feeling at home. However, it was the house and the connections between white and immigrant neighborhoods that provided the most apt symbols of inclusion in the nation. The confluence of a new immigrant passion for home ownership, the inclusion of all whites in restrictive covenant campaigns to bar people of color from neighborhoods in the 1920s, and New Deal support for the idea that the private home structured white citizenship ensured as much. Moreover, the house provided the setting in which the generations and genders comprising new immigrant families tried to figure out how race worked in the United States, debated whether the young or the old knew more about the mysteries of race, experienced tensions surrounding intermarriage, and balanced preservation of old ways with an embrace of a U.S. culture deeply inflected by black styles.

THE NEW IMMIGRANT HOUSE

The evolution and intensity of new immigrant commitments to white neighborhoods must be understood. The explanation begins with the deep attachment to home ownership felt by many new immigrant groups. As the urban historian Arnold Hirsch observes, "Historians who have very often agreed on little else have all noted the ardent ambition on the part of Irish, Italian, and Slavic immigrants to own homes." With local variations, historians almost universally agree that new immigrants succeeded remarkably in making that ambition into reality. Monumental Works Progress Administration (WPA) studies enumerating every parcel of property on Chicago assessor's blocks in 1939, for example, found that only 21.7 percent of the city's native-born white residents owned their own homes, while 41.3 percent of the foreign-born did. Nearly 50 percent of Lithuanians and Poles and about 40 percent of Italians lived in owner-occupied homes. In some cities, where land was cheap and public transportation costs held down by progressive city administrations, the achievement of home ownership came very rapidly. In Toledo, for example, in 1900 63 percent of Polish American families owned their own homes. U.S. cities stood apart from European ones in terms of availability of land and particularly in terms of the "relatively low and affordable" cost of working-class homes in general.[2] Typical patterns featured modest rates of new immigrant home ownership early in the century followed by spectacular gains later. Ewa Morawska's excellent quantitative study of Johnstown, Pennsylvania, shows that in 1900, 8 percent of Croatian male immigrants to that city owned a home; for 1940, the figure was 38 percent; corresponding figures for Slovaks find a rise from 5 percent to 32 percent; for Slovenes from 4 percent to 33 percent. In Detroit by 1920 no "Polish block" sampled by Olivier Zunz had less than 30 percent home ownership and in some blocks 75 percent of heads of households owned a home. One 1913 Chicago study of the Back of the Yards meatpacking immigrant neighborhood broke down data to show how thoroughly any chance of home ownership was seized. About 30 percent of female heads of households with no husbands and 47 percent of male heads earning less than $2 a day owned a home. For the remainder of the male heads of households, 95 percent were home owners. In 1910 Polish Americans were only marginally less likely to own a home than the native-born white population, although heads of native white households outearned Polish Americans by 1.71 to 1.[3]

Clearly home ownership functioned as something other than a badge of the achievement of wealth for new immigrants. As Zunz boldly puts it, "Owning a home . . . was not a middle class phenomenon, nor was it a sign of any movement into the middle class." Instead it stood as "more an emblem of immigrant working-class culture than of established middle-class native white American culture." The new immigrant did not so much "buy into" the American Dream of home ownership as help create it.[4]

Immigrant working-class home ownership necessitated patterns of significant sacrifice. Reformers and social researchers recognized such sacrifices but often registered surprising ambivalence about them. Peter Roberts's 1914 study of Pittsburgh counted Slavic and Italian commitments to home owning as evidence that not all of their number "went to the bad," and Margaret Byington's 1910 account of Homestead linked Slavic home ownership to austere budgets showing respect for the home owning head of household as "a fair type of our new citizens."[5] But Louise Montgomery's *The American Girl in the Stockyards District* (1913) warned that the immigrant male was willing to "make the most unbelievable sacrifices of his own comfort and that of his wife and children" in order to own a home. Those in social services began to worry that commitment among immigrants to buying a home came "even if they have to starve their families to get the money." Social workers Jane Addams, Mary McDowell, and Sophonisba Breckinridge all fretted that hunger for real estate crowded out, in Addams's words, "all other interests." Keeping children in school became less a priority, in this view, than gaining an inadequate, unhealthy home. Some in new immigrant communities shared with reformers the knowledge that keeping up mortgage payments could come at the expense of the family's food budget, or even of shoes for children. In recessions and strikes, illness and old age, the mortgage payment loomed. In Johnstown between 1915 and 1930 on average one immigrant home-owning family in seven lost that status in each five-year interval of the period. The idea that home ownership represented the "highest form of prosperity" nonetheless remained powerful.[6]

The willingness to pay such a high cost for a home followed from its multiple meanings and uses for immigrants. The first, and in many ways still the best, study of white houses, Charles Abrams's *Forbidden Neighbors* (1955), frames its key chapter by discussing home buying as an "emotional experience." Abrams emphasizes peril—foreclosure, family disintegration, neighborhood decline—as part of the emotional history of home buying.[7] It is perhaps apt to start with the fantastic, psychological, and perilous before turning to the "bricks," the great functional utility of a house for working-class new immigrants.

The images of the home as hazard and as security capture much of the meaning of its ownership for new immigrants. One glory of *The Jungle*, Upton Sinclair's classic novel of immigrant life in the early twentieth century, lies in its exploration of the attraction of home ownership alongside the real threat of homelessness. Indeed ownership, amid fraud and disaster, turns out to have its hazards and homelessness has its redemptive moments in the novel. The immigration of the poor was ultimately, both figuratively and literally, a risky bid for a new home.[8] The central character in Mike Gold's immigrant labor novel *Jews Without Money* recalls his mother's first night in the United States by connecting her anxiety to race.

Lacking a place to stay, she ends trying to sleep amid "groans and confusion on the floor of a crowded cellar for immigrants. It was called the Nigger House."[9]

The circumstances of many new immigrants in coming to the United States located their decision to save for a home in a concrete set of historical dramas. Following Rudolph Vecoli's early insights, immigration historians have poetically branded immigrant desires for a home as a "transfiguration of the ancient peasant land hunger." The specific appeal of land—Poles in the urban United States self-identified as *polanie*, literally "dwellers of the fields"—captured one dimension of this transfiguration. Of course, little land came with the typical immigrant house in U.S. cities, but the opportunity to garden was sometimes present. More importantly, owning a home spoke to the problems many immigrants had historically experienced with absentee landlords in Europe and offered a way to avoid repeating them in the United States. Here again, the passion for home owning intersected with broadly defined questions of "racial" identity. It spoke to group values reflecting how immigrants thought about both sides of the Atlantic. When President Herbert Hoover characterized the desire for a home as a "racial longing," he implied that the Anglo-Saxon "race" was his point of reference. However, when the Lithuanian newspaper *Lietuva* editorialized on home ownership as a way to "honor" one's nationality, it referred to another set of complex, powerful, transnational "racial longings."[10]

The "bricks" from which a practical passion to own a home were constructed included the desire to never again pay rent, to eventually complete mortgage payments and escape the threat of eviction. Beyond these straightforward desires, however, lay concrete appeals that spoke profoundly to the economies, life cycles, vulnerabilities, and gendered labor divisions of immigrant families. While purchasing a home often brought immigrants into relationships with banks or building and loan associations, the house itself acted as a kind of bank, providing security when age made work in jobs requiring brute strength less possible. The constant threat of being "hunked"—injured or killed on the job—also enhanced the appeal of the security that home ownership seemed to provide. So did joblessness caused by seasonal and cyclical unemployment or strikes.

That the home served as a bulwark against the insecurity of irregular earnings had a flip side too. Home owners survived foreclosure in part because of their asset's status as a place of work as well as a domicile. The unpaid labor of caring for family and the paid labor of industrial home-work and taking in laundry also occurred in rented tenements, but home ownership offered a special opportunity and flexibility for wives and widows to take in boarders as the need arose. Collecting rent from boarders and providing them with food and cleaning services could yield from 25 percent to as much as 70 percent of the earnings of a male employed in a mill or mine, as Morawska estimates, with women sometimes working seventeen-hour days. Reformers especially lamented boarding, pointing out that a family often regarded the practice as temporary but ended always in need of income from boarders. Experts regarded even child mortality as linked to the presence of boarders, but the practice provided such strong links to kin, countrymen, and countrywomen, and especially to security in hard times, that attacks fell on deaf ears. Owning a home was not necessary to take in boarders—indeed in Johnstown renters engaged in the practice more often than owners. But to exercise a measure of control over the business of boarding and to have the process lead to optimal returns in emergencies and old age, buying a home made sense.[11]

Only home owners could profit from a second type of labor in and around a residence. If boarding and industrial homework represent well-studied forms of labor in the home, scholars have taken far less notice of labor on the house. "Not only did they invest their savings . . . in putting a roof over their heads and providing shelter for their families," Zunz writes, "they also invested their time." Richard Harris projects the term "sweat equity" backward to describe long-standing patterns of "home maintenance, extension and, at the extreme, self-building [as] substitutes for wage income." As the architectural historian Dianne Harris has shown, this dimension of "home/work" carried racial dimensions as well. Do-it-yourself magazines featured white handymen exclusively.[12]

To place the new immigrant house amid dreams, fears, mortgages, sweat equity, and the "business venture" of boarding is to underline how difficult it is to determine whether new immigrants principally saw their homes as commodities possessing exchange value or as shrines possessing use value. The "usefulness" of the home lay in part in its ability to generate income, and expenses were closely watched. Boarding was commoditized but often involved relatives. Both sides of this dual sense of the home's value would matter greatly in the new immigrant's embrace of the white house.[13]

IN THE GHETTO?

In the early twentieth century Jewish residents and some other new immigrants were said to live in "the ghetto" more often than blacks. Popular language borrowed the term from areas of European cities in which Jewish residents lived in isolated districts often under anti-Semitic laws and pressures. It applied in the United States to areas far more loosely segregated but containing large numbers of newly immigrated eastern European Jews. Those immigrants could read of the "spirit" of their ghetto and could hear (and join in) fretting over the boldness, dress, and bearing of young, unmarried "ghetto girls" in their neighborhoods. They could see films like D. W. Griffith's *A Child of the Ghetto* (1910), which took the immigrants' side against paternalistic charity workers and suspicious police. Subsequently, and largely through the efforts of social scientists from the University of Chicago, "ghetto" came to be a scholarly term, applied not only to Jewish enclaves but also to a variety of neighborhoods said to be dominated by one immigrant nationality. Louis Wirth's classic study *The Ghetto* (1920) treated Jewish Chicago but noted a tendency to refer to any immigrant quarters as ghettoes, including "Little Sicilies, Chinatowns and Black Belts" or any "section where the immigrant finds his home shortly after his arrival in America." University of Chicago studies came to include African Americans as ghetto residents, implying that for blacks, as for immigrants, this neighborhood form would be temporary. As Loïc Wacquant's marvelous account of the past "dark ghetto" makes clear, "Only after World War II did the semantic range of the 'ghetto' contract . . . to denote nearly exclusively the forcible relegation of African-Americans." This contraction marked "the contrast between the smooth residential dispersal of 'white ethnics' and the persistent seclusion of the descendants of slaves."[14]

When Chicago sociologists attempted to conflate African American and new immigrant "ghettoes," they were part of a well-intentioned scholarly effort to displace race from biology and characterize it as a fluctuating identity based on migration, culture, and history. However, as Henry Yu has provocatively shown, the idea of a ghetto could replace the ersatz physicality of the racialized body with the ersatz physicality of the obsessively mapped racial neighborhood. Cultures "became self-contained objects with clear physical boundaries." When it was used to describe African American ghettoes or study Chinatowns, this approach brought a new essentialism to race. With regard to new immigrant "ghettoes," the problem was of a different order. Insofar as those ghettoes were thought to describe enclaves in which an immigrant nationality suffered isolation of a sort akin to that experienced by Jews in parts of Europe or by blacks in a northern city, the concept did not even minimally fit demographic facts.[15]

Fittingly enough, the most withering assault on the Chicago sociologists' broad use of the term "ghetto" has come from research on Chicago itself. Humbert Nelli's 1970 study of Italian Americans in the city showed that though they were the most "segregated" immigrant group in Chicago, even the "very heart of 'Little Italy'" was 47 percent non-Italian in 1912. No single side of even one square block in the city between 1890 and 1930 was found to be 100 percent Italian. In 1978, in a spirited study reflecting the impact of the civil rights movement, Thomas Lee Philpott presented telling research on other national groups in Chicago and drew bold conclusions. New immigrants were not "ghettoized," either in the sense of being unable to move if and when they prospered or in the sense of actually living in unmixed neighborhoods. Philpott computed the extent of ghettoization for eight groups in 1930. The percentage of Russians, Czechs, Italians, and Poles living in "ghettoes" (Philpott seldom omits the quotation marks) ranged from 37 percent to 61 percent, but none of these groups except Poles (54 percent) constituted a majority in their own ghettoes. Almost 93 percent of blacks lived in ghettoes—the "only real" ones in Chicago according to Philpott—and those ghettoes included 82 percent of all African Americans. Philpott allowed that new immigrants often lived in poor neighborhoods isolated from native-born white Americans, but showed that they did not live in ghettoes like those inhabited by African Americans. The distinction gave Philpott the title of his book: *The Slum and the Ghetto*. Research on other metropolitan areas bears out this distinction. John Logan's recent study summarizes and reworks older research on more than a dozen cities and adds important new data breaking down New York City segregation by sanitary districts, a smaller unit likely to pick up on the presence of enclaves. Extremely nuanced in his analysis, Logan draws two central conclusions: "the disparity between the white ethnic and black experiences [with segregation] was stark and growing" between 1920 and 1970 and "the (relatively) optional character of white ethnic segregation [in contrast to] the involuntary imposition of segregation imposed upon blacks and Hispanics."[16]

The critical distinction between the slum and the ghetto, as drawn by Philpott, recapitulates a central point of *Working Toward Whiteness*. The racial experiences that blacks and Chinese had on the one hand and new immigrants had on the other differed qualitatively. However, to stop there, emphasizing only a firm and ahistorical difference between slum and ghetto, also carries liabilities, some of which Philpott anticipated. One liability lies in losing the ways in which segregation changed over time. The post–1914 years, when the Great Migration of Afro-southerners to northern cities intersected with restrictions on mass immigration from Europe, firmed up existing but looser distinctions between slum and ghetto. Moreover, the figures on the relative absence of segregation of Italians, Jews, Greeks, and Poles from one another does not mean that references to specific "foreign quarters" held no purchase on urban realities. What Logan anachronistically calls the "ethnic neighborhood" could exist without having the same levels of segregation that characterized ghetto formation. Indeed he shows that even beyond 1950 many new immigrant groups in New York City clustered voluntarily and self-consciously.[17]

Moreover, statistical proofs that new immigrant areas of cities were polyglot are fully compatible with the possibility that groups within them still *imagined themselves* as living in an Italian (or Jewish or Greek) quarter, neighborhood, or even ghetto. When Philpott used his own Irish American mother as an informant, he was in pursuit of a vital point. The mother recalled that in her neighborhood growing up, "everybody was Irish." But even in St. Columbanus parish, around which the mother's recollections centered, Irish Americans apparently constituted a minority. As Philpott explains, the "social world she experienced and kept alive in her memories was peopled with relatives and friends, and public characters . . . were Irish Catholics." The logic resonates beautifully with the recent writings of geographers who emphasize that place and space are "social constructions," not easily captured by census tracts or sociological maps. Social reformers and social scientists constructed distinct neighborhoods bounded by nationality—even when they sometimes realized that the facts were otherwise.[18] Immigrants likewise often made highly mixed places imaginatively their own. To see how the house took its place in an imagined immigrant community helps us understand on another level the enormous psychic importance of home ownership. Moreover, it warns against a simplistic conclusion that might flow from the realization that slums were not ghettoes. Although they moved into mixed neighborhoods unavailable to African Americans, new immigrants did not necessarily and immediately see themselves as building a home in a *white* community. That consciousness took time to develop alongside the belief that one lived in an immigrant neighborhood peopled by a specific group. The defense of the white neighborhood from "colored" outsiders became a defense of the "ethnic neighborhood."

To place the new immigrant house within such imagined neighborhoods requires an appreciation of the ways in which nationality and race resided in cities. Indeed in the case of new immigrants, as opposed to that of the Irish, the weight of the house in the imagination assumed special importance. As Stephen Steinberg has pointed out, all idealizations of the immigrant neighborhood run afoul of the reality that most new immigrant groups lacked any control over jobs and public schools in their communities. New immigrant imaginations of neighborhood had to look homeward more insistently.[19]

Indeed the home often stood at the very center of mental maps defining Little Poland, Little Italy, and more. The first-generation couple, seldom intermarried across national lines, sacrificed to buy the home, incorporating the wages of children and payments by boarders in the project of ownership. Especially among Italians, worship often occurred in the home. As children married, they often lived in the house while saving through building and loan associations based on nationality. Again the partner was likely, though less so, of the same nationality. Boarders too tended, even in a highly mixed neighborhood like Chicago's Back of the Yards, to be countrymen, often close or distant kin or migrants from the same region or even village. Newcomers ensured, especially before immigration restriction, that homes were sites of language preservation and sometimes learning, as well as of the decision to adopt English. New immigrants may have had far more time to imagine where they resided. "The foreign-born," Arnold Hirsch writes of Chicago in the 1920s and 1930s, "showed a greater inclination to endure at a single address." Four of ten such immigrants there had lived at the same address for a decade before 1939, twice the rate of the native born and four times that of African Americans.[20]

The mental maps of immigrant neighborhoods allowed the same territories to be coded as embodying several particular national communities. Shopping districts exemplified this complexity with the small triangle formed at the intersections of three major south side Chicago streets constituting the "'Italian downtown,' 'Greek downtown,' 'Bulgarian downtown,' and many other . . . groups' downtown."[21] An informal system of "deadlines"—the term was coined by an Irish American policeman to describe areas utterly off-limits to criminals—dictated where certain nationalities could safely walk. Irish American gangs often enforced these boundaries enthusiastically. Where African Americans were concerned, deadlines were often mapped by long streets. The movements of new immigrants were more likely to be confined in shifting microgeographies, with a block or a park or even the side of a park off-limits in the mixed neighborhoods.[22]

The most dramatic and complex examples of how the idea of a neighborhood defined by a specific nationality coexisted with the presence of many immigrant nationalities revolve around the connection between immigrant houses and houses of worship, especially Catholic churches. John McGreevy's important work details how ritualistically aware congregations were of the "parish boundaries" annually walked by parishioners. But those boundaries could significantly overlap with those of other parishes. In one square mile of Chicago near the stockyards, there were two Polish, one Lithuanian, one Italian, two German, two Irish, a Croatian, a Bohemian, and a Slovak Catholic church. Only the Irish parishes in the area were "territorial" ones, catering allegedly to all the Catholics in the area, regardless of origins; the rest were "national" parishes. But the Carnegie Foundation was clearly onto something in 1920 when it referred to such parishes as places gathering Catholics into "racial churches of their own." As an Italian American priest put it in 1922, "It is true that such idealists dream of an American millennium when all races will be found fused into one new American race—but in the meantime it is good that each think of his own."[23]

These "racial" churches faced a Catholic hierarchy increasingly inclined to apply instructions from Rome designed to expand the territorial parishes of a universal church. Such policies increased a sense of "shared victimization" among immigrants even as they produced only gradual change. Between 1918 and 1929, fully a third of Detroit's new parishes were "racial" ones, though the trend nationwide was in the other direction. Because these parishes often included schools providing instruction by nuns of the same "racial" group and committed to language preservation, the boundaries of the "racial" parish defined imagined neighborhoods. Moreover there was some residential concentration by nationality around churches and schools. The churches, which dominated the commanding heights of the skyline in new immigrant communities, grew to tremendous size and splendor as a result of parishioners' financial sacrifices.[24]

Embracing "Americanizing" (critics would call them "Hibernicizing") reforms, many Irish Catholic leaders exercised great influence in the Church hierarchy, where they could zealously denounce both the Polish American pursuit of national rights (and rites) in parishes and Italian American nonsupport of parishes and parochial schools. The rise of the territorial parish threatened to extend Irish influence at the very time the Great Migration brought masses of Afro-southerners into contact with new immigrants. The results included a curious strengthening of new immigrant commitments to the national parish and an accelerated use of the parish, national or not, to combat black movement into white neighborhoods. Partly because moving out of a changing neighborhood meant abandoning spectacular Church buildings, decisions to move were tense.[25]

Since the Catholic hierarchy had tightened the approval process for national parishes, entry into a territorial parish often loomed after migration to developing areas. Whether struggling to charter a new national parish, maintain ties to an old national parish distant from new homes, or put a national stamp on a territorial parish, new immigrant Catholics experienced the Americanization of the Church in ways that increased particularistic "racial" consciousness in the short term. The results of such struggles were uneven. As Italian Americans moved from areas in Chicago having national parishes, they often ended in territorial churches without marked Italian American influences. As Poles dispersed, they tended to maintain Polish American parishes. Hostility toward, and among, the "newer Catholic races" remained strong, as did Catholic anti-Semitism in some locales, but the attempt to keep neighborhoods white could generate new alliances.[26]

Defense of the parish, of the city within the city imagined by immigrant groups, and of the all-white neighborhood thus matured together. Moreover, Irish American clerics and parishes provided leadership where antiblack racism and segregation were concerned, even as they seemed to threaten new immigrant autonomy. Catholic parishes and schools sponsored blackface minstrel shows with distressing regularity, for example. Sometimes these shows had stars named Pietrangelo, Bastulli, Paolucci, and Fiorelli, but more often they appeared to be projects of established Irish American Catholics, who might then incorporate new immigrants into the festivities. Where direct action against black neighbors or aspiring neighbors was concerned, many of the same patterns applied. Even as hesitant Catholic initiatives for interracial harmony took shape, the Church taught by example that African Americans were different. Thus the turn to mixed territorial parishes conspicuously left out African Americans, consigning them to separate congregations. Catholic schools remained highly segregated, if not exclusionary, into the 1940s. Given all this, and the fact that blacks were also distrusted because they were overwhelmingly Protestant, it is unsurprising that rank-and-file Catholics and their parish leaders often aided agitation to keep neighborhoods white. In some instances, for example, efforts in the late 1920s and 1930s by the Italian American St. Philip Benezi parish on Chicago's north side to "defend" a "neighborhood [that] has always belonged to them" against "invasion . . . by the colored people," members of a new immigrant community provided leadership.[27]

WHITE PEOPLE OF THE COVENANT AND THEIR ANTINEIGHBORS

In the context of passionate new immigrant commitments to "racial" churches, imagined neighborhoods, and defense of the home, we now revisit the alleged arson by the Irish American street gang, Ragen's Colts, during the Chicago race riot of 1919. Apparently the gang disguised itself in blackface makeup and stole into a Polish and Lithuanian neighborhood to torch homes.[28] They hoped that eastern Europeans, who had not eagerly participated in anti-African American rioting, would believe blacks had attacked their homes and therefore rally to the banner of whiteness.[29] As hideous and unproductive as such an act would have been, its logic was unassailable on one count. New immigrant identification with whiteness would eventually turn on the defense of home and neighborhood. Grassroots mobilizations and the embrace of restrictive covenants to segregate housing, not simply the practice of terror, structured that identification.

The African American poet Langston Hughes summed up restrictive covenants in a few lines. Writing of that prototypical home of the covenant, Chicago's South Side, Hughes captured the African American experience of seeing pan-European "white flight" when a neighborhood did desegregate. He also described similar unity among otherwise divided whites in efforts to prevent integration. Hughes's narrator wrote that immediately upon his arrival in a neighborhood:

Folks fly.
Even every foreigner
That can move, moves.[30]

The work done by covenants, according to Hughes's verse, consisted both of restricting the ability of black homeowners to "breathe free," and of something more. The glory of Hughes's brief poem lies in its capturing two sides of a dialectical process. The first and more obvious involves the ways in which inclusion of "foreigners" in a racist community-building mechanism affronted African Americans.[31] But the other side of the process bears equal emphasis. New immigrants came to be *included,* via real estate agreements, in a white race that was, Hughes suggests, itself a broader restrictive covenant and one that could survive court decisions invalidating any particular legal mechanism of segregation.

The enormous power, real and symbolic, of the restrictive covenant lay in its range of appeal and its timing. Since 1890 experiments in "covenanting" property to keep it from being sold to Asians had failed to pass constitutional muster. But where segregation was legally enforced Jim Crow zoning laws had become the favored legal device. However, in 1917 the Supreme Court ruled in *Buchanan v. Warley* that such statutes also violated the Fourteenth Amendment—of whites wishing to sell property. Realtors, developers, and private citizens returned to experiments with restrictive covenants as a "constitution-proof" way to discriminate.[32] In their new and far more ubiquitous incarnation, such covenants won approval from state courts, and the U.S. Supreme Court, in a key 1926 decision, refused to abrogate them. With the Great Migration of Afro-southerners and in some places of Mexicans to cities, the "problem" of integration came to be seen as far more urgent as well. In a 1947 study hundreds of restrictive covenants then in force in St. Louis and Chicago underwent examination. Over 62 percent of those covenants dated from the 1920s.[33]

From the new immigrants' point of view, the spread of restrictive covenants in the 1920s came in a telling context. At the very moment when millions of Klan members decried their presence, when educational experts quantified the "retardation" of their children, when trade unions retreated from inclusive organizing campaigns, when progressive reformers insisted on "100 percent Americanism," and, above all, when a racist Congress decimated legal immigration from southern and eastern Europe on the grounds of the immigrants' unfitness as citizen workers, new immigrants were warmly welcomed as "white" and as fit neighbors in the grassroots campaigns to blanket whole urban areas with covenants. As "restriction" was shouted loudly at them in so many other venues, an opportunity to become active and accepted agents of restriction suddenly arose. In 1919, the light-skinned African American minister Archibald Carey "passed" as a white pro-restrictionist at a meeting of the Hyde Park–Kenwood Property Owners Association. He found "various nationalities" convened "to draw a color line." His commentaries bespoke bitterness: Jews attended, taking time out from charitable efforts to aid pogrom victims; Irishmen came straight from Free Ireland events; Italians left the "murder zone" in which they lived to victimize blacks; Poles, seen as having the blood of anti-Semitic massacres on their hands, showed up; Czechs and Slovaks, Russians and even "an honorable Japanese gentlemen" united against the "coon." In the Greater Pullman Property Restriction Association activists "had names like Perlman, Zimmerman, Korzeniecki, Birkhoff, Larocco, Hocksta, Teninga, Novak, and Bezdek."[34]

This willingness to incorporate diverse white voices did not bespeak a liberal impulse on the part of the realtors and developers who provided resources for the restrictive covenant campaigns. They suspected African Americans more, not immigrants less, but this ranking mattered. In 1924, the principal figure in the "progressive" reform of real estate, Nathan William MacChesney, drafted Article 34 of the Code of Ethics of the National Association of Real Estate Boards. As immigration restriction became codified, MacChesney's words enjoined realtors not to introduce "members of any race or nationality" into a neighborhood where they might lower property values. Since thirty-two state governments empowered state commissions to revoke licenses from realtors who were out of compliance with the Code of Ethics, the possibility of legal actions surrounding the free movements of new immigrants was real. Indeed the first two major texts on "minorities" and real estate value appeared in 1923. As Charles Abrams wrote, "One argue[d] that the Negro is the threat; the other the foreigner," who allegedly sucked the "life blood" from "pure and warm . . . citizens."[35] In later studies, the emphasis fell on the need for "temporary segregation" of "undesirable elements of Southern Europe and Asia." Charles Male's *Real Estate Fundamentals* (1932) cautioned against any "fine theory about quickly assimilating the white races" and made the case for keeping new immigrants "more or less segregated in sections by themselves for at least one generation." (For the "negro problem," Male added, only "rigid segregation" promised a satisfactory solution.) In the year following Male's publication, the economist Homer Hoyt issued a major study of land values in Chicago. It listed thirteen "races and nationalities," according to their favorable impact on neighborhoods. Northern Europeans topped the list, followed by northern Italians. Greeks, Russian Jews, and south Italians came in last among European groups but below them were "negroes [and, last] Mexicans." Hoyt held that "except in the case of negroes and Mexicans, however, . . . racial and national barriers disappear when individuals . . . conform to the American standard of living."[36]

Realtors' urgency in ghettoizing newcomers arriving during the Great Migration of African and Mexican Americans blunted attempts to restrict new immigrant home buying in cities. Although new housing developments could use deed restrictions to bar ownership and occupancy by non-Caucasians, restrictive covenants were made to order for enforcing segregation in established neighborhoods. To get 75 percent or more of owners in an area of several square blocks to sign away their right to sell to nonwhite buyers, and furthermore to pay a fee to lose that right, was a tremendous organizing task. It could take years to develop what Chicago's *Hyde Park Herald* called the "marvelous delicately woven chain of armor" keeping large parts of a city white. In most cases, the vulnerable neighborhoods bordering on the ghetto—the "racial frontier" as it was sometimes called—included many new immigrant home owners. Fine distinctions as to which European groups were most desirable and their relative levels of assimilation were incompatible with such organizing campaigns. Indeed in the frenzy of restriction organizing, neighborhoods with 45–60 percent "foreign stock" residents came to be called "American" districts, even "Yankeelands." By 1927, when MacChesney wrote his *Principles of Real Estate Law* and produced a standard form for realtors to use, the only "undesirable" population specified was "the negro." The following year *Housing* magazine took the same stance. "It is only with regard to the negro population," that reform-oriented publication specified, "that race segregation is suggested."[37]

Of course restrictive covenants did not utterly reorient housing discrimination along a black–white axis. Those excluded by covenants and deed-based measures sometimes included all who were not Caucasians and documents could go far in spelling out what groups were barred. A 1939 Minneapolis covenant, for example, forbade sale or lease "to any person or persons of Chinese, Japanese, Moorish, Turkish, Negro, Mongolian or African blood or descent." As new suburban developments came to regard exclusion as a status symbol, the list of those banned grew. In the West, covenants guarded against "invasion" by Asians and Mexicans with special zeal. Nonetheless, the extent to which covenants originated out of a specific fear of black residents and exempted new immigrants from restrictions bears emphasis. In Johnson and Long's sample from Chicago in 1944, for example, only 1.4 percent of covenants barred anyone else.[38]

Under law, the vast majority of new immigrants were secure in their Caucasian identities. Despite considerable memories of new immigrants being excluded under restrictive covenants, documents do not reflect such exclusions. The principal exception in this regard was the exclusion of Jews, especially from some new suburban developments and rental properties, but such situations did not produce urban ghettoization. Some property owners wished to discriminate more broadly. When Johnson and Long asked neighborhood improvement associations in Chicago and Detroit what "non-Negro" groups they "considered objectionable," one response in nine was "Jews" and one in sixteen included "Italians, Poles, and Greeks." However much it could contribute to more informal mechanisms of exclusion, such animus could not energize campaigns for broader restrictions. Where covenants were concerned, such immigrants and their children were participants in, not victims of, a campaign for segregation.[39]

In measuring the impact of that campaign on new immigrants, the range of its appeals and its forms deserves elaboration. By far the most important feature of the covenant was its firm linking of white racial status with property. The case for the constitutionality of restrictive covenants could rest on the "color-blind" argument that any property owner, regardless of race, could freely encumber his or her private property with restrictions designed to make it more desirable or valuable. But clearly it was the existing and potential value of the white house that was being protected and that value lay in large part in its whiteness. As one realty textbook put it:

> The colored people certainly have a right to life, liberty and pursuit of happiness, but they must recognize the economic disturbance which their presence in a white neighborhood causes and forego their desire to split off from the established district where the rest of the race lives.

Not surprisingly, the language of the marketplace was ubiquitous. Restriction constituted "insurance" and, on the word of *Good Housekeeping* no less, was "a great asset" to neighborhoods and suburbs. The real estate industry declared that the "liabilities" associated with new immigrants were diminishing and developed a "Gresham's Law" linking property value and "complexion."[40] Inviting the new immigrant, however grudgingly, to participate in what Cheryl Harris calls "whiteness as property" constituted a perfect appeal: it addressed a central immigrant concern with the home as an investment and posited the embrace of whiteness as an economic opportunity rather than a set of cultural coercions.[41]

But acknowledging the calculating appeals of restrictive covenants should not blind us to less quantifiable matters. Covenant, of course, had a deep and abiding meaning in the theology of Christian and Jewish new immigrants and in the history of colonization and nationalism in the United States. When new immigrants settled areas around "their" church, they drew on faith-based ideas of covenant and sometimes cast their activities as urban "pioneering." Thus the mass movement around covenants connected immigrants to old and new world values profoundly. More importantly, it connected them to a set of powerful and pervasive allies, some familiar and some not. Real estate interests led the campaign but corporate interests beyond the realty industry also gave firm support and lent gravity to their own understanding of how property values worked. In some cases the corporations employing new immigrants subsidized their attempts to buy Jim Crow homes. The meetings organizing covenant campaigns could include the familiar local priest and the less familiar Congregational minister. When the Central Uptown Chicago Association covenanted a large tract between 1928 and 1930, all ten churches and synagogues in the area helped defray the expenses. Youth gangs mirrored respectable organizations, patrolling areas deadlined against people of color, often with a wink from the police. (One Chicago study of 880 such gangs in the 1920s found two in five to be integrated by "race or nationality" but only one in thirty-five to include whites and blacks.) Terror and legality mixed in many restriction initiatives. Progressive reformers, who so often made new immigrants the objects of reform, gave vital support to campaigns for covenants, and court approval of restrictions put what Charles Abrams bitterly called a "moral" imprimatur on Jim Crow housing.[42]

As elite driven as they undoubtedly were, restrictive covenants also included a substantial component that one scholar has called "democratic," providing a sense of the debasement of that term when wedded to white supremacy. Certainly new immigrants received invitations to community meetings and grassroots organizations as well as to contractual fellowship. Mobilizing neighborhoods to sign covenants required the support of organizations, and their commitment had to be sustained over a period of years, since covenants typically had expiration dates after which a set percentage of those wishing to opt out could abrogate the agreement. The structure organizing support for restriction tellingly took the name "neighborhood improvement association." While such associations, taking up issues of zoning and safety, for example, predated the mania for covenants, their numbers spiked in the 1920s along with the restriction drive. As late as 1944, Johnson and Long found that seven neighborhood improvement associations in eight professed an interest in keeping the neighborhood white and three in five actively supported restrictive covenants. One scholar of race and Catholicism noted that "improvement association" meant "keep Negroes out."[43]

Of course these associations also organized projects to improve neighborhoods. It was precisely in the automatic connection of white and neighbor that restrictive covenants, and Jim Crow housing generally, most poisoned new immigrant attitudes regarding race. In the nineteenth century, people of color had been made to symbolize the category of "anticitizens"—unfit to participate in the republican experiment of the

United States. But new immigrants stood in such complex and uneasy relationships to citizenship that "anticitizen" worked less well in organizing working-class antiblack racism in the twentieth century.[44]

The arrival of hundreds of thousands of black southerners in urban areas in the North and West during the world wars, when housing was desperately short, conditioned new immigrants' receptivity to the idea that African Americans were "invaders." The fact that the Great Migration brought newcomers without homes just as war and then immigration restriction enforced a "settling down" among an increasingly home-owning new immigrant population contributed to the notion that the African American embodied the antithesis of the home owner. However, these factors, driven by demographics and timing, mattered enduringly because of purposeful cross-class, state-supported social action designed to maintain segregation. The sociologists Douglas Massey and Nancy Denton subtitled their classic study *American Apartheid* as *Segregation and the Making of the Underclass*. But such segregation—the processes used to enforce it and the social fact of its existence—also brought a white ethnic population into being. What sociologists call "indices of black isolation" trebled between 1910 and 1930 in the seventeen northern city studies by Stanley Lieberson. In cities like Chicago, Boston, New York City, and Buffalo, some new immigrant groups lived in greater isolation from "native whites" than African Americans did in 1910. This condition, Lieberson concluded, "completely reversed by 1920" and still more so by 1930. In Cleveland, the index of segregation for blacks in 1910 was 70.4 as against 86.9 for foreign-born Italians; in 1930 black isolation scored as 78.4 while foreign-born Italians stood at 53.6; in 1950 the figures were 85.3 for blacks, as against 48.4 for Italians. Such trends help explain how new immigrants could increasingly imagine their specific communities as distinct parts of a larger white community, and "ghettoes" as the opposite of neighborhoods.[45]

Most critically, what Hughes called the "hemming in" of African Americans worked powerfully to make black housing shortages an ongoing crisis, not just a wartime emergency. In St. Louis by 1944 covenants covered 559 blocks, including especially those nearest existing black communities. In Chicago and Los Angeles, and in New York City suburbs, estimates of even vacant land covenanted ranged upward of 80 percent.[46] The systems of exclusion produced by gangs, realtors, covenants, and churches effectively made orderly integration impossible, reinforcing the idea that "changing neighborhoods" were zones of desperation, replete with panicked sellers, social conflict, and renegade realtors. Moreover, integrated neighborhoods often came in the 1920s to be considered what Kevin Mumford has eloquently described as "interzones," in which illegal drinking, prostitution, and queer sexualities were deliberately concentrated and "hemmed in." For new immigrants, who had been much associated in the popular mind with prostitution and organized crime, and in the case of Italian American men at times with queer culture, such interzones were places to be avoided by the settled-down community, except perhaps on late weekend evenings.[47] Unable to build and expand, "ghetto" residents paid exorbitant rents for substandard housing. Concentrated poverty made it easy to draw unfavorable comparisons between the African American ghetto and the neighborhood. Shut out of skilled jobs in the construction trades, barred from land on which to build, and kept at a physical distance, African Americans did not seem a part of the remodel-it-yourself and in some cases build-it-yourself community of home owners. They stood as the very antithesis of "neighborhood improvement," as antineighbors.[48]

GENERATIONS OF WHITENESS (1): POPULAR CULTURE, MOVIE HOUSES, AND WHITE HOUSES

Restrictive covenants held out the seductive possibility that neighborhoods could be imagined both as white and as the property of a European "racial" group, even as experiences of new immigrants ensured that questions of identity would be painful ones. Immigration scholars have long discussed one key dimension of this pain as "the problem of the second generation." Born in the United States to immigrant parents, children in the second generation had to decide whether and how to assimilate and Americanize—to weigh whether to hold on to neighborhood and parish ties, language, the customs of their parents, and even to their names. In contrast to the assimilationist position taken by many in the second generation, Irvin Child's classic sociological study *Italian or American?* emphasized the "rebel" type, choosing that label to describe those most eager to learn "American" ways and reject traditions. At one self-hating extreme such a stance could generate a remark such as that quoted from a twelve-year-old son to a Sicilian father: "I'll take nothing off a damn Dago like you."[49] Eastern European Jews popularized the wonderful term "allrightnik" to name the analogous group within their ranks. Family dramas over the embrace of new identities were so highly charged that Howard Stein's intriguing "psychoanthropology of American culture" suggests that all reactions to nativist prejudices by new immigrant children must at once be considered also as deep encounters with the "idealized natal family."[50]

However, the ways in which we cast such choices as ones involving assimilation to an "American" identity can obscure the extent to which they were also lived as "racial" choices. Assimilation involved not just an embrace of American identity but specifically of white American identity, while the national ties being jettisoned connected immigrant children to groups still considered in the 1920s and 1930s to be racial ones. The central dramas in the classic 1927 film *The Jazz Singer* thus speak powerfully to questions of race, popular culture, and generational tension. The new technology of synchronized sound found its way into bits of dialogue supplementing written words flashed on the screen. The most sustained sound synchronization lay in Al Jolson's performance of jazz songs. Thus Jolson's Jakie Rabinowitz character existed in old and new worlds in a double sense. His cantor father tried to call a halt to both the new technology and the new music. As Jolson emoted, the father commanded "STOP!" Jakie's second-generation musical tastes threatened fundamentally patriarchal, first-generation control of the home: "How dare you bring your jazz songs into my house?" When Jakie chose American, secular, and modern music over—or perhaps in addition to—the chants and faith of the fathers, he also broke from traditional culture in other ways. Performing under the new name of Jack Robin, he found himself gravitating toward a "forbidden woman," a gentile who was probably seen by audiences as Irish American.[51]

On one level, all of these plot turns in *The Jazz Singer* can come together under the rubric of the Americanization of the second generation. The "jazz songs" Jakie's father deplores are more recognizable as Tin Pan Alley productions than as African American music. Jolson's transformation in the film crucially derives from his willingness—indeed eagerness—to perform in blackface makeup, and no analysis of the film can miss the way Jakie embraces a racially inflected American culture. This modernism is specifically marked by blackness as a creative impulse, a commodity, and a foil animating Jolson's character. The stage name Jack

Robin let no one forget Jim Crow, that signifier of both the nineteenth century minstrel character and the segregation- and ghetto-making racial system of the twentieth century. Indeed, the late Michael Rogin's brilliant account of race in *The Jazz Singer* shows how minstrelsy greased and grease-painted the path to commercial success, acceptance, and white intermarriage for new immigrant stars.[52]

The film invited viewers into "the ghetto," but it did not encourage them to stay there. Near its start, a title card set the scene: "The New York Ghetto, throbbing to that rhythm of music which is older than civilization." Jolson could have recalled his own "ghettoized" theatrical roots. In 1899, Israel Zangwill plucked the young Lithuanian Asa Yoelson from the streets of Washington, D.C. Zangwill had adapted a popular book of his own, *The Children of the Ghetto*, for production as a play. He hired Yoelson, later to be Jolson, as an extra, until the child's father, a rabbi, found out and ended the arrangement. *The Jazz Singer* in some ways recapitulated Zangwill's career, which climaxed when he coined the term "melting pot" to describe the magical and dissolving effect of U.S. culture on immigrant populations. The film appeared at virtually the same time as Louis Wirth's sociological classic *The Ghetto*. If it did not share Wirth's stance of being "negatively attuned to the Russian-Jewish immigrant world," it was equally "impatient for [the] dissolution" of that world.[53]

The Jazz Singer signaled a crisis in Hollywood's representation of recognizable Jewish characters, especially as portrayed by Jewish actors. However, this was no simple case of mass culture immediately and decisively producing homogeneity. As Lizabeth Cohen and others have shown, early radio and film often cultivated audiences by nationality. In its earlier and less imposing incarnations, the movie house reflected neighborhoods and marketed to particular European "racial" audiences. This trend so structured the business that early-twentieth-century films about Italy's past, pitched to Italian American audiences, appealed to a firmer sense of Italian unity than the deeply divided immigrant population in the United States in fact possessed.[54] On the lower East Side in New York City, films did not, in the short run, supplant live Yiddish vaudeville productions but rather revitalized them, with nickelodeons increasingly incorporating such entertainment on their programs about 1910. As this dual programming abated, cinemas in the neighborhood featured such titles as *Samson the Hero* and *Joseph's Trials in Egypt*, in what one film historian calls an "overkill of Jewishness [as] a planned marketing strategy."[55]

But if immigrant groups formed marketing niches for the film industry, movie houses also taught the lessons of the color line wordlessly and effectively. To see a film was to experience Jim Crow, with blacks and sometimes Mexican Americans excluded or banished to balconies or other restricted areas. David Nasaw acutely specifies that such Jim Crow practices were part and parcel of the "democratization" of "movie palaces" for whites. Moreover, the content of cinema reinforced the lessons imparted by seating. Blackface performances by white actors were ubiquitous, whether for comic effect or, as in *Birth of a Nation*, to terrify white audiences. A pioneering U.S. film lampooned Chinese American workers, setting in motion an enduring "yellowface" tradition. Films about the U.S. West provided another genre in which a white audience was created as the plots rehearsed triumphs over people of color.[56]

The industry's wooing of European immigrant audiences contrasted with its treatment of "nonwhite" ones. A Jolson or a Rudolph Valentino could be marketed as a Hollywood star—with racial impersonations leading to the rise of both of their careers. Griffith's *Birth of a Nation* benefited from the endorsement of President (and historian) Woodrow Wilson as its exhibitors faced down civil rights protests against its racist depictions of interracial governments during Reconstruction and its broadcasting of beast-rapist stereotypes regarding black men. It likewise profited from Griffith's long track record of producing sympathetic films catering to a new immigrant working-class audience, famously among them *A Child of the Ghetto*.[57]

Blackface as presented in early silent cinema and in vaudeville allowed for racial (mis)education to occur among those knowing very little English. Just as settlement houses and churches could use minstrelsy to "Americanize" immigrants who did not know the words to songs and skits, popular culture did likewise. Race was in part a sight gag and films were accessible on very different levels to those with greater and lesser exposure to English and to racial masquerades. Minstrelsy educated newly arriving adults, migrants who (like Jolson) came as children, and the children born into the second generation. Its complexities were most accessible to second-generation adults.[58]

Education in U.S.-style racism also took on nonverbal (or minimally verbal) forms elsewhere in popular culture. The "comics" and cartoons on sheet music featured racist and imperialist caricatures. Their images and simple texts were perfect early reading experiences for immigrants destined to join the "English-speaking races." Harry Houdini, the wildly popular turn-of-the-century escape artist—a rabbi's son who escaped his Jewish name and ancestry—made the Chinese water torture cell escape his "most compelling" stage act. He publicized his peril with a poster of himself menaced by the "oriental" device and by a huge African "brute." When new immigrants ventured to amusement parks, they saw "hit the nigger" ball games testing throwing accuracy. Dolls, banks, and other popular toys lampooned black and orientalized images. Advertising cards circulated racist images and one-liners. Tobacco, flour, molasses, cereals, and a host of other products used black or Indian names, images, and even live spokespeople in their marketing.[59] The stereotypical pickaninny Gold Dust Twins, advertising the soap powder of that name, existed as artwork and as live spokespersons. Their presence resonated with endlessly repeated transnational sight gags in soap ads showing a black child being washed white.[60] The most famous black advertising icon, Aunt Jemima, sold pancakes to largely middle-class audiences. But variants of ads featuring her could also turn up in the foreign-language press.[61]

The display of people of color in world's fairs, circuses, museums, traveling shows, and even zoos provided another telling example of how racist pedagogies were at once simple and sophisticated. The immensely popular fairs displayed captive, conquered, and exoticized people, sometimes in official buildings and sometime on the entertainment-oriented midways. Government officials and anthropologists collaborated after the imperial adventures of the United States in 1898 to show that the conquered Philippines contained a range of types, some ripe for uplift and other fated to die out. The St. Louis World's Fair of 1904 featured over a thousand conquered Filipinos and also displayed American Indians, Africans, African Americans, and a host of others. Filipino nudity and near nudity, as well as stories of dog eating, undoubtedly made a larger impact on popular consciousness than the ethnological lessons being drawn. Those displayed existed in "native" houses, sometimes on stilts, contrasting sharply with the white houses of the European world. After the fair, officials staged games, the counterpoint to the "civilized" 1904 Olympics, among those racialized as "barbarians." That the fairs themselves sometimes patronized African American attendees with "darky days" and segregated facilities underlined the lessons of racial hierarchy being imparted. After those days, press caricatures might ridicule black fairgoers' misadventures with their "po' relations" in the village of "Dahomeyans" and with the better spoken South Sea Islanders on display.[62]

The great comedian Jimmy Durante, son of an Italian immigrant barber, held out the possibility that music, dance, and fun at night held out a possible exception to the ways that popular culture taught racism. "Nightlifers," he claimed, reflecting on clubs he knew from his early career as a piano player, "don't know there is such a thing as a color line." Since Durante saw his patrons as "husky men and pretty girls in cheap finery," such a remark would imply that the new immigrant working class, at least in the second generation, crossed the color line effortlessly in search of pleasure.[63] Some caution should apply as we consider such a possibility, however. Urban youth adopted African American dance styles in the 1910s and 1920s, often in direct preference over the "racial" dance of their immigrant group. Similarly, eastern European Jewish parents complained that "ragtime" displaced Yiddish songs and religious music in the preferences and purchases of their children. However, the dire finances of many immigrant families and the weak claim of children, especially young women, to their own wages left many in the second generation stuck at home without music. One Pittsburgh social survey asked young women in the second generation, "What do you do with your evening?" The modal reply was, "Nothing."[64] Moreover, in most cases dances were learned in a certain kind of nightspot in which the color line gave way, as David Nasaw writes and as Durante was aware. Even in Harlem, respectable clubs bowed to the preferences of authorities and the expectations of white customers that Jim Crow would prevail. "Except for the notorious 'black and tan'" establishments, Nasaw writes, "segregation on the dance floor was an essential constituent of the entertainment experience." The African American music on the bandstand combined with the exclusion of the black dancers from the floor to "celebrate the 'whiteness' of the audience." Even in "animal dances" and in one brief dance craze that was called "the Nigger," white youths knew that "when the music stopped, the play-acting also did."[65]

Given what Kevin Mumford calls the increasing "racial segregation of vice," black Americans could decisively impact the culture of the interzone. However, in cities where "jazz" meant both hot music and illicit sexual intercourse, the vice districts were off-limits to many second-generation youths, points of episodic attraction to many others, and home to very few. Some posh clubs strove to present jazz purged of its racial inflections. When the Jewish heroine of Anzia Yezierska's *Bread Givers* thrilled to the "fiery rhythm of jazz," she thought the music and dance "burst loose the shut-in prisoner in me." She felt tempted to enter nightlife as an "excitement eater," but that world was raceless in the novel.[66]

In some cases sustained contacts with people of color in nightlife did transform children of new immigrants. As Rhacel Salazar Parrenas and others have shown, the "taxi dancers" in U.S. cities who sold time to male customers often were eastern European women. Out of admiration for the style, steps, hygiene, and generosity of Filipino customers, taxi dancers often preferred Filipino over white (and also new immigrant) customers. The relationships that developed ranged from friendship, to solidarity, and even to love, all of which developed in the shadow of racist violence.[67] More famously, such jazz legends as Louis Prima, Mezz Mezzrow, and Chicago's Austin High gang inhaled and sometimes mastered African American musical forms, at times developing close relationships and fierce identifications with the black community. Two fascinating complications bearing on the problem of the second generation deserve mention here. The first is that the "rebellion" expressed by some musicians who identified with African American culture and music was cast in opposition to both the fathers' "old" culture and their desire for upward mobility in their children, which required elements of assimilation. Maria Damon brilliantly reads Mezzrow's recollections of stealing his sister's fur coat after she put on "fancy high school airs" and critiqued blueswoman Bessie Smith, connecting his stance toward "the upward mobility he scorns" with his desire to use money from the theft to leave the "white house" of his family.[68]

But the move away from the house introduces a second complication. In his arresting memoir *Lots,* the Jewish writer S. Oso describes a boyhood spent apprenticed to black workers who wedged cars into downtown Philadelphia parking garages. In flight from a middle-class upbringing and high expectations, Oso tried hard to become "a black male," a status he connected to "sexual revolution" as insistently as Mezzrow linked blackness to drug culture and music. Ultimately Oso came to suspect that his "compulsion" reflected not a desire to fit into black culture, but to be "independent of all culture" for a time. If African American culture was for

Oso a "fulcrum to detach from white society," it may have functioned in much the same way for Mezzrow. As such it could signify not so much the rejection of the "white house" forever as of all houses for a time. This multiplicity of meaning suggests that the differing views of the embrace of African American culture by second-generation musicians provided by Werner Sollors and Burton Peretti do not exhaust all possibilities. Sollors sees such an embrace as an attempt to "defy assimilation," while Peretti finds musicians seeking "to incorporate themselves into a new kind of American life." Both dynamics surely applied, as did an attempt to move nowhere for a time.[69]

Marshall Berman's recent discovery that the shooting script for *The Jazz Singer* offered a different ending for one of the film's key lines provides an opportunity for summation regarding the swirling cross-currents affecting race, generation, and popular culture discussed above. In the film, Yudelson the "kibitzer" from the ghetto falters on seeing Jakie in blackface. "Jakie, this ain't you," he begins, before turning to comment to the audience, "It talks like Jakie, but it looks like his shadow." In the shooting script, Yudelson's lines ended instead with, "but it looks like a nigger." The dialogue of the immigrant and his or her shadow was a vital one within the new immigrant second generation. Blackface, blackness, and black culture was often useful as a symbol of freedom and as a commodity, but rarely as an enduring or vigorously sought identification.[70]

YOUTH, WHITE HOUSES, AND GENERATIONS OF RACE

As genders and generations in the new immigrant community contested who would control spending decisions and what was brought into the house, they also made distinct and differing claims to racial knowledge in the United States. Folk and family stories provide a good vantage point to help us see how such claims were made. For example, in the family of the historian Thomas Sabatini, lore survived concerning a new immigrant ancestor working as a cop. Approaching a distressed black woman, the young policeman had troubles understanding race, sex, and English. When the walking woman insisted that she wanted "a push," he thought that she was a prostitute propositioning him. Only as the two mounted a small rise did the woman's stalled car appear and clear up the confusion. Conflating "greenhorn" inexperience regarding race with imperfect knowledge regarding sex, the story carries a self-effacing tone. But its original teller also positioned himself as one who had then learned the ways of the racial and sexual world. More widely shared tales involved a wife's horrified initial reaction when a husband brought a black man to visit the immigrant family's house. On learning that the visitor is an exception—a dedicated union brother or, as in a remarkable scene in Gold's *Jews Without Money*, a black coreligionist—the wife softens and perhaps comes to conclude that the visitor is not so different after all.[71] Such tales were designed to teach much about African Americans. They might be prostitutes, suspects, fellow workers, car owners, or Jews. But they also provided instruction on who could claim to know race by virtue of experience in the world.

The second generation, male and female, had its own claims to such knowledge. Young people experienced with great force the ways in which racialization applied to new immigrants and connected them to people of color. Child's classic work on "types" in the second generation of Italian Americans counted resistance or acquiescence in the face of slurs such as "guinea" or "wop" as one index of division. Sometimes the slur was nothing short of the word "nigger" itself. Individuals, especially males, whose physiognomy, color, or hair texture made such a branding possible had that name (or "Blackie") fastened onto them in "white" working-class communities. Babe Ruth, whose appearance left him vulnerable to epithets in this regard despite the fact that his roots were Swabian, brawled as a child when he heard the repeated taunt "nigger lips." As a superstar, Ruth still heard the slurs. As one biographer observed, "Ruth was called nigger so often that many people assumed he was partly black." He once went after a Giants pitcher who had directed the word at him and then explained, "I don't mind being called a prick or a cocksucker. . . . But lay off the personal stuff." Mezzrow was called "nigger" in Missouri because of his appearance, not his affectations.[72] In *Jews Without Money*, "Nigger" led the neighborhood's Jewish youth into a series of gang battles. The naming often persisted into adulthood among inhabitants of interzones. After an anti-Asian riot at one taxi dance hall in 1926, a white patron held that "no really white guy" would dance where women were dancing interracially unless he had "a little nigger in him."[73]

At the other extreme, the second-generation youth who grasped the ideal of presenting himself as assimilated and bound for success could fasten a different name on his goal. The "specially favored" up-and-comer—the "man destined for . . . reward," the teacher's pet—was the "fair-haired boy." One second-generation Italian American working in iron and steel remembered life in the 1920s and 1930s in Pennsylvania. He stressed that bosses "had what they called the 'fair-haired' boys; they paid them at a certain rate. And the rest got a lower rate." The "fair-haired boy" could get a mortgage to buy a house from the company-controlled local bank. Envisioning clearly oneself as a "fair-haired boy" was harder for some than it was for others.[74]

The threat to second-generation girls, on the other hand, lay in being classified as "oriental" and therefore ugly and available for sexual exploitation. For first- and second-generation young women, the threat of racialization intersected with appearance, at times in harrowing ways. Mae West, the Irish American star who taught and transgressed color lines, once quipped, "I used to be snow white, but I drifted." The new immigrant woman, often having darker hair and skin, was unlikely to be seen as snow white, and powerful forces taught her to watch closely how far she drifted. The "immigrant girl," wrote Grace Abbott of the Immigrants Protective League, was vulnerable to sexual abuse by employers because of her isolation (Abbott saw small Greek restaurants as especially perilous), overwork, language disadvantages, crowded housing, and poverty. However, Abbott also blamed "the stupid race prejudice which leads many Americans to conclude that she suffers less from shame and humiliation than do other women and girls." At times, awareness of the vulnerability of female children of new immigrants drove reformers into alliances with family patriarchs to keep young women off the streets. Jane Addams, for example, saw the difference between "Italian fathers" and "fathers of colored girls" precisely in terms of the knowledge the former had as to the need for "protection" and the alleged failure of the latter to provide it. The Italian American had the ability to call on "the inherited resources of civilization," which from slavery had allegedly separated African Americans.[75]

In the early twentieth century, the erroneous view that prostitution was a new immigrant "racial" problem—though it was called white slavery—further exposed immigrant women to sexual exploitation, police harassment, and sometimes deportation. The battles over Filipino men socializing with new immigrant women in taxi dance halls suggest another

dimension to this problem, one in which new immigrant men sat in judgment of the "wildness" of "their women." Of course Old World strictures
against single women going out continued in the new world, but the discredit associated with daughters "sneaking" out now applied to the whole
"race" as well as to the patriarch and his family. After 1920, the association of prostitution and immigration abated as vice districts came to be
associated with an African American presence and as the number of migrants from Europe declined. However, many inexpensive rooms for single working-class women—Joanne Meyerowitz brilliantly discusses them
as "women adrift"—were located in or near interzones, making drifting a
problem well into the second generation.[76]

Blond and fair to a fault, West could playfully descend from snow
whiteness. Her contemporary, the Jewish American singer Sophie
Tucker, enjoyed no such advantage. Her immigrant "ugliness" caused one
producer to predict that audiences would ridicule her: "Better get some
cork and black her up." Tucker later pled, "Let me work in whiteface. . . .
Really I'm not bad looking." To be seen as "oriental" carried connotations
of sensual abandon, lack of beauty, and unfitness for citizenship, as Janice
Okoomian's fine studies of Armenian American women immigrants show.
Readers of the Yiddish–English newspaper *Day* learned in 1930 that because "many Jewish girls are of the Oriental type of physique," they had
to present themselves with great care in "an Occidental Gentile country"
like the United States. "Her graceful curved nose . . . vivid coloring [and]
full well-developed figure" might be "very beautiful in [their] proper setting." However, in the United States these very virtues could cause her to
be typed as "blowsy," "common" and "vulgar," if she did not wear "the
simplest clothes possible."[77]

Not surprisingly, many young new immigrant women desired to lose
"racial" markings. During the first twenty years of the twentieth century,
as Julie A. Willett's history of beauty shops shows, immigrant women
were likely to "simply [have] their hair washed or combed instead of cut,"
but younger women broke from that old-world style by the 1920s. The
hair that was cut or bleached platinum was often "foreign" hair, very dark
or curly. The wider culture embraced the blond as pure and Aryan, with
Physical Culture Magazine publishing predictions that chivalry and
democracy had their fates assured only so long "as the blond race lasts"
and with Madison Grant's influential racist propaganda warning that the

"Great Blond Nordic race" was being "bred out by the lower types of the brunette races." For sociologist Edward A. Ross, the "humble races" of southern and eastern Europe were also the "brunet nationalities." Within immigrant groups, fair-haired young women were seen as having an easier time but were also suspected of being lazy, stupid, and corrupted by their advantages. Thus the Russian Jewish immigrant Mary Antin wrote of idolizing the "glory of golden curls" among native-born girls sent to perform for the immigrants' uplift. But golden-haired Mashah in *Bread Givers* was seen as trapped in superficialities. "She lived in the pleasure" of her looks, Yezierska wrote. One part of the second-generation experience, ironing curly hair to straighten it, also could reflect a desire for Anglo conformity. Rose Romano made poetry of this choice in her powerful "Dago Street." She recalled ironing the texture out of her hair, attacking:

Mediterranean curls, Greek
curls, African curls, Sicilian
curls, Neopolitan curls.

The periodic fashion vogue for perming hair presented another level of complication.[78]

With regard to color, new immigrants sometimes showed awareness regarding the advantages lighter-skinned community members had over darker-skinned ones. Alisa Zahller, a curator at the Colorado Historical Society, recalls that her Italian American grandmother "had a white face powder she used so that she didn't seem so dark." One blue-eyed Italian American from Chicago looked back on his life declaring, "I was lucky. . . . See my kids, all of them have brown eyes like my wife. Very dark skin, olive." Literal whiteness could not be the sole commoditized standard of beauty in the cosmetic industry, in part because European women of various skin tones constituted the market for beauty products. As immigration restriction passed, Pompeian Beauty Powder ran ads cautioning against the faulty understanding that "we are white women and therefore must use white powder." Pompeian specifically marketed to those with "olive skin . . . the clear dark skin we frequently see on beautiful Spanish or Italian women." However, the other four skin types to which the company pitched powder shaded beauty away from darkness:

white, peachy, medium (between "milk white" and "peachy"), and pink. No mainstream marketing to those darker than olive occurred. A generation later, Woodbury marketed three shades of "color-controlled powder." One was for "ivory" skin, another "tropic," and a third "cameo" for "very fair" beauty.[79] Immigrant women may have wished for "lighter" skin for various reasons. Rural Europe associated dark skin with peasant labor and immigrants may have connected lightness with upward mobility and Americanization. Antin, for example, linked looks, polish, opportunities, and "glimpses of a fairer world" on seeing native-born women perform. In *Old World Traits Transplanted* (1921) Robert Park and Herbert Miller reported that many migrants from Cinisi, Sicily, to New York City saw shading skin from the sun as an unseemly form of striving but some (perhaps especially in the second generation) did not: "Look at the [serf]! In the old country she used to carry baskets of tomatoes on her head and now she carries a hat on it." Or "Gee! Look at the daughter of so and so. In Cinisi she worked in the field and sun burnt her black. Here she dares to carry a parasol."[80]

Married new immigrant women faced the pressures of racialization from a position of isolation. The threat of being judged racially was inscribed on their persons, but also on the homes in which they spent so much of their time. As Katrina Irving has recently emphasized, the "immigrant mother" focused the anxieties and hope of reformers who saw her as the key to Americanization efforts and of nativist opponents of immigration, who saw her reproductive capacity as the very embodiment of the "race suicide" of Anglo-Saxons they feared. Both groups operated on the premise that "woman is the race."[81]

Despite relative poverty, 1930 figures show that first- and second-generation homemakers worked outside the home less often than did native-born homemaking women with native-born parents in all seventeen major cities studied. Their labor force participation rates typically were one-third to one-half those of black homemakers. On the other hand, foreign-born women worked for wages "at home" as often or more than did native-born women of native-born parents in thirteen of seventeen cities. Moreover, new immigrant wives performed the unpaid labor of social reproduction in gritty cities and for relatively large families. Such patterns of labor did not lead to significant cross-racial experience. Company housing policies and racism kept homemakers from knowing each other, though at times limited sources of water for washing could foster contact.[82]

That the immigrant mother worked so hard to keep her family thriving amid smoke, dirt, and lack of services, that she sometimes suffered from spousal abuse, that she often bargained over prices and foraged for fuel or clothing, and that she sometimes did domestic service in middle-class homes racialized her in the minds of reformers. Thus Frank Julian Warne's *The Slav Invasion and the Mine Workers* observed that Slavic women could be seen "picking coal from the culm-bank, [and] carrying driftwood from the forest nearby." Warne added that "English-speaking women" would not think of doing such work.[83] The home served as the locus of judgments regarding the new immigrant's Americanization and his or her racial characteristics. The "starched" young worker from the settlement house, Oscar Handlin wrote, "Took stock from the middle of the kitchen. Were there framed pictures on the wall? Was there a piano, books? He made a note for the report: *This family is not yet American-ized; they are still eating Italian food.*"[84]

Low wages, industrial accidents, and the immigrant husband who "made" his wife work all seemed to be parts of a general problem to many reformers. But ultimately it was the wife's "neglect of housekeeping" that reflected ill on the community and highlighted her, and its, status as "one less favored in training and mental development." David Saposs, an academic researcher with an ear to hear working-class new immigrants, showed how fully such judgments could merge lifestyle and beauty, writing that native-born and mostly skilled workers "had the best-looking women as wives. Best-dressed women as wives. The contrast was extraordinary in the way that they lived . . . the way their women were." In particular the charge that new immigrant groups were dirty ran through efforts to racially type them and to reform them, with mothers particularly implicated.[85]

When new immigrant women insisted on having white curtains in industrial enclaves, they were claiming respectability and hope. Writing of white curtains in Braddock and Homestead, Pennsylvania, the labor journalist Mary Heaton Vorse keenly observed, "There is not a woman so driven with work that she will not attempt this decency." Vorse claimed she could write a tragedy about these window curtains. As the historian Stephen Sage Burnett remarked, such curtains were "flags of whiteness" at the same moment that they flagged cleanliness and respectability. Such white flags, and an obsession with cleanliness generally, showed to neighbors and to social workers that the American standard of living, and the lessons of women's acculturation that made "whiteness visible" in homes, were being absorbed.[86]

While the statements that white curtains made to families and communities were more important than statements made to welfare workers, the latter group's impressions did matter. With welfare reserved for the deserving poor, a group racialized as "white," new immigrant mothers faced judgments that had material consequences. Although some had trouble securing benefits, the patterns of pension outlays to mothers shows a broad achievement of racialized respectability. In 1911 in Chicago, for example, Italian Americans got aid to mothers four times their proportion of the population and Polish Americans two and one-third times. Black Chicagoans, deemed undeserving, generally received no mothers' pensions.[87]

Several of these dynamics came together dramatically over the question of whether new immigrant children should play with African American children. Again and again, parents and others reported on such play and on efforts to end it. In Chicago in the early 1920s, the commission looking into the 1919 riots found the color line wavered in Little Sicily, and the Urban League cited some interracial contacts inside homes. However, by 1925 the sociologist Esther Quintance was told by residents that they needed her help to "chase the niggers out" of the area. The resistance to having black neighbors focused on teaching that "no decent Italian family" would "let their children play" interracially and on the more general stricture, "Don't visit the niggers in their houses." In Homestead, the very lack of space to play in tenement areas forced sharing, in this case by "Polish, Slavic . . . Hungarian, Jewish and Negro" youngsters.[88]

The oral history given by a Slovak American to an Italian American government investigator in Bridgeport, Connecticut, in 1939 captures the hostility toward interracial play as well as the children's persistence:

The colored kids in this section seem to be all right. I know a lot of the people here, both Slovaks and Italians, don't like the idea of the colored kids playing with their own children. In spite of this the kids play together, and they don't seem to mind what the parents have to say. I personally don't like this playing around among the different kids . . . they should live apart from the white people and have a section of their own.

As Jennifer Guglielmo's study of Italian American women in New York City argues, the complaints of an older generation about the "criminal" behavior of black youths—a stereotype from which Italian American youth were scarcely exempt—similarly betrayed a larger anxiety about the persistence of "socialization" across the color line among children when they mixed in neighborhoods and schools.[89]

Typically the enforcer of bans on interracial play was the immigrant mother at home all day. Thus when Emory Bogardus described the attack on child's play in a 1928 study, he constructed this generic description: "Frequently a child plays with a boy or a girl of another race, and is entirely happy in his new-found playmate, until he hears his mother exclaim, 'What? . . . playing with that nigger! I won't have it!'" Viola Mellone, an Italian New Yorker, wrote to the educator Leonard Covello in 1945, spelling out the contradictory fears at play in opposing children interacting across the color line. Mellone characterized black youths as "beyond control in their viciousness towards the White Race," but also as able to form interracial bonds enabling them to allegedly teach "White Boys . . . stealing, using vile language, no respect for elders, disobedience[and] not abiding law and order." A Slovak woman in a Connecticut area where "colored and white [were] often seen playing together" offered testimony to a researcher that speaks to her own uncertain position as an "immigrant mother" vulnerable to the charge that her own people's dirtiness made them less than fully white:

> I always tell my children not to play with the nigger people's children, but they always play with them just the same. I tell them that the nigger children are dirty and that they will get sick if they play. I tell them they could find some other friends that are Slovaks just the same. This place now is all spoiled, and all the people live like pigs because the niggers they come and live here with the decent white people and they want to raise up their children with our children. If we had some place for the children to play here I'm sure that the white children they would not play with the nigger children. . . . All people are alike—that's what God says—

but just the same it's no good to make our children play with the nigger children, because they are too dirty.[90]

THE WHITE SCHOOLHOUSE?

If young new immigrant children often disobeyed parents to play with friends of a different race, self-organized clubs and gangs of adolescent and young adult second-generation new immigrants tended to mix European nationalities but draw and enforce color lines. In accounting for such a change, teaching by parents is important, but it is also necessary to assess the influence of the school on the second generation's racial learning, especially since education is so often accorded a central place in the progressive narrative of the assimilation of immigrants. Certainly the school system, public and Catholic, taught powerful lessons implicitly by segregating students of color, South and North. However, the same schools also institutionalized practices of self-separation, isolation, and discrimination against new immigrants to a degree that ensured that they could not rival the imagined neighborhood as a site in which a specific immigrant "racial" consciousness could coexist with a secure sense of white identity.

School attendance by immigrant children skyrocketed by 1930. In that year, 91.3 percent of second-generation members age 14 and 15 were in school. This proportion, up from 36 percent twenty years before, slightly exceeded that of native-born whites with native-born parents (90.0 percent) and far outstripped black school attendance by fourteen- and fifteen-year-olds. For sixteen- and seventeen-year-olds, second-generation members were closer in attendance at 54.4 percent to native-born children of native-born parents (61 percent) than to blacks (46.3 percent). The same was true of eighteen- to twenty-year-olds. Such figures hide a great deal, however. For example, the presence of older students was far from predicting the numbers of students at the grade level appropriate to their age. Figures on "grade retardation" were telling. One study showed that 34.1 percent of white children with native-born fathers were "retarded," in the sense of having been held back. For south Italians, the rate was nearly 50 percent, as it was for Poles. Such figures, as well as alleged new immigrant IQ deficiencies, were emphasized in the education literature, and the National Education Association's close ties to eugenicists ensured that teachers were schooled on the constitutional deficiencies of new immigrants.[91]

Not surprisingly, schools could be harrowing places for the second-generation new immigrant. The teachers, overwhelmingly native-born women with native-born parents, could "casually," as Handlin wrote, "twist the knife of ridicule in the soreness of [students's] sensibilities: there was so much in their accents, appearance and manners that was open to mockery." The characterization of students as "savages," "dirty little Russian Jews," and "little animals" could cut deeply against any sense of shared "white identity."[92] Louis Adamic's superb *What's Your Name?* (1942) regarded it as a frequent practice in the 1920s "to humiliate pupils with 'difficult' names." Johnny Rodzinski became Johnny Sneeze-it. Another student became known as "The Boy with the Long Name"—ten letters—and dropped out largely in response to such ridicule. Teaching cleanliness especially blurred the line between tough love and humiliation. In the Bronx, one Polish American girl recalled being sent to a brother's classroom. The teacher, with the full class looking on, pulled at the brother's collar, revealing dirt. "See that he washes better" was the day's lesson. Of five hundred school leavers interviewed in a Chicago packinghouse neighborhood in a 1909 study, an astounding 269 opted for the factory as a place where, unlike the school, they were not hit.[93]

A school attached to the national parish of a Catholic Church offered some protection against some forms of abuse. At times nuns taught in the European language of the group and were immigrants themselves. Parishes turned back efforts of the Church hierarchy, often Irish American, to curb such instruction. However, in no major city studied in the 1920s did the foreign born exceed 9.5 percent of the teaching labor force, and the national figure was 5.8 percent. Over four in ten teachers were native born with foreign parents. But the huge majority of this group was of "old immigrant" stock, over 40 percent of them Irish Americans. Only "Hebrews" combined dramatic strides to gaining teaching positions with southern or eastern European origins. Moreover, Catholic school attendance varied greatly from group to group and according to age level. In Cleveland, for example, Slovaks sent students to parochial elementary schools well over 80 percent of the time but Italians and Romanians did so less than 10 percent of the time. By middle school, four in five Slovaks were also in public schools.[94]

If the native-born teacher was aware of her students' "racial" distance from her, the students reciprocated that awareness. Doc, a central informant in William Foote Whyte's *Street Corner Society* (1943), described the school's hidden curriculum:

> You don't know how it feels to grow up in a district like this. You go to the first grade—Miss O'Rourke. Second grade—Miss Casey. Third grade—Miss Chalmers. Fourth grade—Miss Mooney. And so on. . . . When the Italian boy sees that none of his own people have the good jobs, why should he think he is as good as the Irish or the Yankees? It makes him feel inferior.

In some Catholic schools, especially in mixed territorial parishes, the presence of Irish American nuns was a bone of contention. One Connecticut Catholic remembered that the Sisters of Mercy used "a crack in the face" to suppress Italian language use. A Polish–Lithuanian student regarded her school's prizes, top grades, and "honorary jobs" as reserved for Irish Americans. Carmen Leone's fictionalized family history of early-twentieth-century Youngstown featured the Vitullos, who were willing to attend mass in an Irish American–dominated parish—they saw the liturgy as universal—but refused to "even consider sending a daughter to the parish's 'Irish' school."[95]

Leonard Covello, the pioneering New York City Italian American educator, remembered his own miserable experience in Harlem public schools early in the century as still more problematic:

> Throughout my whole elementary school career, I do not recall one mention of Italy or the Italian language or what famous Italian had done . . . with the possible exception of Columbus, who was pretty popular in America. We soon got the idea that Italian meant something inferior.

Covello persisted in school, chanting cheers for the "Red, Watzum Blu" long before he divined their meaning. What he was taught, he later wrote, led to the erection of "a barrier between children of Italian origin and their parents." He attributed this barrier, as Adamic did, to aggressive Americanization. "We were becoming American," he reflected, "by learning to be ashamed of our parents."[96]

WHITE BY INTERMARRIAGE?

In November 1969 Current Population Survey data showed that slightly more that half of queried respondents listed "Other" or "Don't Know" when asked their national origins. At that time the proportions of husbands with different nationalities than their wives was listed—technical matters make these overestimates—at 59 percent for Polish Americans, 47 percent for Italian Americans, and 53 percent for Russian Americans. The immigration scholar David Herr has reasonably concluded that many unable or unwilling to pick a national origin group had "such mixed ancestry" as to problematize any such choice.[97] The category "white" proved a useful catchall for such mixed people, who could readily answer the demographer's questions about their race. Indeed by the 1960s and, certainly by the 1990s, the number of hyphens among those who descended from new immigrants via at least one great or great-great grandparent was in some cases so daunting that even if specific, often symbolic connections with several ethnicities persisted, "white" held appeal as a matter of convenience. Knowing this end might predispose us to regard intermarriage as a key to the appeal of white identity. As John Bukowczyk puts it, "White . . . afforded white ethnic groups an ingenious and rather comprehensive solution to the problem of dissolution of ethnic ties 'of blood' through . . . white ethnic intermarriage." Since new immigrants and their children married into "whiter" old immigrant groups with some regularity in the 1920s, such mingling created a pan-white and not just a "pan-new immigrant" identity.[98]

However, reading backward from the later twentieth century on these matters carries dangers. New immigrants became parents of the largest cohorts of the second generation between 1911 and 1930. Those children were born at a time when intermarriage across national lines was by most measures rare. Although the second generation far exceeded their parents' rates of intermarriage, marriage within the national group was the norm. Growing rates of intermarriage only gradually produced significant numbers of "mixed" European children over the generations. Joel Perlmann's fascinating work on the intermarriage of Italian Americans, for example, finds that in 1960, 58 percent of the third generation had at least one parent or grandparent not of Italian origin. (They thus may also have been fifth-generation Irish Americans, complicating the whole notion of generation.) Even so, this leaves 42 percent with all-Italian grandparents and parents, an impressive index of endogamy. Indeed Perlmann shows that the growth to a majority of mixed status within the partly Italian American population in 1960 occurred despite a large majority of Italian Americans marrying others in their group.[99]

Such figures underline the importance of considering the lived experience of the first and second generations as well as the results by the time of subsequent generations. By 1920 some scholars were already predicting the eventual amalgamation of almost all European immigrants into the U.S. population. Julius Drachsler's *Democracy and Assimilation*, for example, spoke in 1920 of the "facts of intermarriage" as leading "inevitably . . . to the amalgamation of European nationalities in the United States, with the possible exception of one or two groups." It was in this context that he most confidently described new immigrants as ethnic, rather than racial, groups. But most new immigrants doubtless considered intermarriage in ways far different from those suggested by sociological and government statistics. For example, migrants whose families had married within a village or small area for generations would have thought of any union beyond those circles as a kind of intermarriage. When a daughter of Italian parents, for example, tried to keep her parents from knowing the Sicilian origins of a suitor, she (and they) clearly saw marriage with him as an intermarriage every bit as much as the father who tried to break up a Croat/Slovenian wedding.[100] Indeed statistics on intermarriage can be broken down to show large or small numbers. Josef Barton's research on second-generation Romanians and Slovaks in Cleveland, for example, finds 35 percent of males in each group marrying women of "other immigrant" origins. For women, the figures were 20 percent and 27 percent respectively. A majority of Romanians and Slovaks outmarried. But if Barton had followed the lead of an early twentieth-century researcher like Frank Julian Warne and regarded "Slavs" and "English-speaking races" as the relevant categories to measure intermarriage, the rates would have been low.[101] Given the pattern of marriage across national but within religious lines, intermarrying couples may have been forging a "Catholic whiteness" that did not actually include all whites.[102]

Moreover, intermarriages among new immigrants did not necessarily signal an amalgamation of cultures. They often included agreements and/or quarrels about what kind of food would be cooked, and in what parish and neighborhood the family would locate. When things went badly or well over the years, the conclusions family members, communities, and sometimes the partners themselves drew were often couched in "race" terms, calibrating the (un)suitability of various groups as relatives. Thus the Italian press might brand a murder as the tragic consequence of Irish–Italian intermarriage, or an intermarried family quarrel might end with a Greek American being slurred as a "half nigger."[103] Though jocular, the spate of films on Irish–Jewish marriages, most notably *Abie's Irish Rose*, illustrated that intermarriage was not only an index of acceptance but also a site for elaborating differences.[104]

In one dramatic way, however, intermarriage taught new immigrants and their children that it mattered that they were white. Marriage across the color line was not only a taboo but also, in a large majority of states, a crime. When new immigrant parents opposed interimmigrant marriages, they could bring the family and community pressure to bear. In opposing interracial dating, they could find juvenile authorities willing to declare such behavior delinquent. When new immigrant men moved against Filipino Americans romancing new immigrant women, they could know that Polish, Italian, and Irish American cops would give them a wide berth. When Virginia forced through the Racial Integrity Act in 1924, that state's new immigrants as Caucasians could claim the right to marry as they pleased with any Europeans, despite the fact that it was Anglo-Saxon Clubs that decisively lobbied for the law.[105] Within a decade, state policy would take a far more proactive role in helping make new immigrants feel at home in the white houses of the United States. The New Deal made the federal government the enforcer of the restrictive covenants through which despised European races avoided becoming antineighbors in an era of immigration restriction.

A New Deal, an Industrial Union, and a White House: What the New Immigrant Got Into

The significance of the new nationalism that had been incubated in the thirties and fanned to a fever pitch by the war mobilization was that it was broadly inclusive of the white working class (Blacks, Mexicans, and Japanese-Americans need not apply) and was propped up by powerful material supports.

MIKE DAVIS, HISTORIAN (1986)

I pity the poor immigrant, when his gladness comes to pass.

BOB DYLAN, FOLKSINGER (1967)

With U.S. entry into World War II looming in the summer of 1941, the African American trade union leader A. Philip Randolph threatened a mass march on the nation's capital if black demands for an executive order to enforce nondiscrimination in defense industries were not met. Anxious to stem the tide of Randolph's March on Washington movement (MOWM), Franklin D. Roosevelt's administration called on one political leader and one trade unionist to mediate matters. The politician was New York City's Fiorello LaGuardia, who publicly identified with his Italian American heritage more than with his mother's Jewishness, and who was sought out for his "great influence with . . . Negroes." The labor leader was Sidney Hillman, born in Lithuania and, as president of the Amalgamated Clothing Workers of America and vice president of the Congress of Industrial Organizations (CIO), the most influential Jewish trade unionist in the United States. That the most urgent question of race and class to that point in the twentieth century could have been mediated, albeit indecisively, by figures from new immigrant communities speaks volumes about the changes that occurred between the end of World War I and the start of World War II.[1] Largely deprived of the right to immigrate to the United States during these years, eastern and southern Europeans nonetheless came to occupy important roles as the mass base and secondary leadership in New Deal political coalitions and industrial unions.

The political mobilizations predated Roosevelt's presidencies. Al Smith's failed 1928 campaign for president had already energized new immigrants as voters, though largely around cultural issues, especially opposition to Prohibition and anti-Catholicism, rather than around what Gary Gerstle has called the "working-class Americanism" on offer during the New Deal. As the crucial 1936 presidential election approached, labor-inspired efforts and trends in naturalization mattered greatly in adding 6 million new voters, 5 million of whom supported Roosevelt. But the national story far understates the empowering aspects of local and state initiatives. The children of new immigrants were not about to enter the White House as president. None ever did. They entered as advisers because of successful coalition building at the local and state level. At a time when Democrats and Republicans vied for the votes of new immigrant communities strenuously, figures like Mayor Anton Cermak, the Czech American Chicago Democrat, and LaGuardia, a liberal Republican, created enduring multinational new immigrant-led coalitions in the nation's most important cities. Cermak, as Lizabeth Cohen writes, connected Chicago's workers "not only to a unified Democratic Party on the city level but also to the national Democratic Party." LaGuardia, whose 1933 election announced the victory of an Italian–Jewish mobilization over Irish American machine politics, had the popularity, reform credentials, and union support necessary to make him more influential in the New Deal than many Democrats. Through the CIO, formed as a separate body after fierce conflicts during the 1935 American Federation of Labor convention, new immigrants and their children could claim unprecedented influence on organized labor's leadership, membership, and political fortunes. As industrial unionism took off in the mid-1930s, it was possible in Pennsylvania to speak of the state's and nation's "New Deal government" and of hunky support for both such governments as decisive. If the inward-looking and reactionary neighborhood improvement association symbolized the fragile inclusion of new immigrants in the 1920s, soaring hopes born of constituting the leading edge of a liberal political realignment did so a decade later. But New Deal liberalism and the CIO never consistently rejected the racial parochialism of the 1920s and ultimately deepened its sway, especially in the area of housing.[2]

The sense of power resulting from new, interimmigrant unities was palpable. When a rival of Cermak's paraded his own "back-to-the-Mayflower" 100 percent American heritage as a qualification for office, the reply exuded a confidence born of knowing that varied constituents would identify with it. Cermak, a second-generation Czech American, marvelously assured voters that his ancestors had come "as fast as they could." The growing political power of new immigrants made differences large and small. By 1936, the anti–new immigrant but pro-labor sociologist Edward A. Ross published an autobiography featuring a significant recantation. Ross disowned a long career of Slavophobia. "I characterized some of our immigrants from Eastern Europe as beaten members of beaten breeds," he wrote, considerably understating matters. He added, "I rue this sneer."[3]

However, the growth of unity in politics concealed significant continuing vulnerabilities among new immigrants. That Hillman could be viciously baited by anti-Semites for his role in the Roosevelt administration and that LaGuardia would dismiss one of his top staffers for calling him a guinea illustrates as much. More broadly, a Hillman or a LaGuardia would have known that entering the White House as president was barred to them, constitutionally in the former case and politically in the latter.[4] However, as Gerstle has argued in a provocative foray into psychohistory rare among U.S. historians, new immigrant New Dealers developed a symbolic solution for securing access to the White House by seeing Roosevelt as a "Nordic father figure." That FDR provided access to acceptance and to the highest reaches of political power and social benefits in a way that would have been hard to even imagine in 1924 goes far to explaining Roosevelt's fatherly appeal. But the deeper psychological processes Gerstle proposes may also apply in different ways to the new immigrant generation and its children. How Roosevelt spoke was one element in his appeal. The journalist Lee Silver remembers New York's Upper West Side as an immigrant place where literally nobody knew what Herbert Hoover "was talking about." But when "Roosevelt came on, with his method of repeating what he had to say [and his] deliberate cadences," people began to understand the language of politics.[5]

If New Deal supporters could deeply identify with a "Nordic" president, the reforms they expected sometimes benefited jobless, poor, and working people broadly. Since these reforms often tended to stop short of challenging the color line, the question of whether the New Deal that new immigrants supported and shaped was also a new departure in terms of racial justice remains a hotly debated one. Whether the New Deal marked a departure toward an interracial politics of the working poor signaled by Hillman, LaGuardia, and Randolph being in the same room, or whether it expanded a white supremacist politics to include eastern and southern Europeans, is not easily determined. The New Deal typically addressed itself directly to neither racial oppression nor discrimination based on national origins. Yet its economic policies were experienced differently across racial lines. In its discussion of race and the New Deal, Edwin Amenta's *Bold Relief* clarifies some of the complications. Amenta asks if the New Deal was "fair" racially and then wonders what "fair" could mean in this context, posing a series of questions about New Deal social policy: "Did African Americans fare better by way of social policy than they would have in the private labor market? Or with the policy system prior to the New Deal? Did African Americans do as well as white Americans under the work and relief policy? Did social policy promote segregation or integration?" As Amenta observes, "The answers to these questions are not all the same."[6] In our era of liberal retreat and fragile interracial coalition politics, it is perhaps unsurprising that historians would focus on questions that allow Roosevelt's achievements to be seen most affirmatively. Thus Amenta makes race a tiny part of his approving discussion of New Deal reforms and one largely confined to how work relief was administered in the South. Patricia Sullivan's *Days of Hope* centers race and democracy in her investigation of the New Deal era but, like Amenta, she trains her focus on the South, casting Roosevelt as in dialogue, and ultimately in confrontation, with conservative Democrats there. She sees him moving slowly, but moving withal, and ultimately mobilizing the hopes of a whole generation of Dixie's reformers across the color line.[7]

Two approaches from recent studies offer provocative and subtly different shorthand characterizations useful for getting beyond a southern framework and thinking about new immigrants, race, and the New Deal. The first approach is typified by Philip Rubio's *A History of Affirmative Action*. Rubio keeps faith with the irony of his title by stressing that the New Deal was of a piece with the longer run of U.S. history, in which whites benefited from racist state policies that amounted to a vast unspoken affirmative action program for the dominant race. Thus Rubio terms Franklin Delano Roosevelt's reform initiatives as the "New (White) Deal." Craig Steven Wilder's fine local study of "race and social power" in Brooklyn provides an alternative characterization of great use for looking at new immigrants and the New Deal. He holds that by "drawing its harshest divisions along white–black racial lines, the New Deal blurred the boundaries of European ethnicity . . . with a potent *whitening* [emphasis original] experience." He thus provides a critical reminder that the white supremacist dimensions of the New Deal extended beyond any simple capitulation to southern segregation. Wilder leaves open the possibility that the New Deal was radically inclusive of new immigrants and that this dynamic was also part of its racial politics.[8] This chapter considers characterizations of the New Deal as (1) "white" and as (2) "whitening." To do the first necessitates some rehearsing of New Deal policy history and race generally in order to show what lessons were being taught to the new immigrant communities championing its reforms. To address the second requires turning to the specific impact of New Deal racial policies on those communities and their impact on the policies.

WELFARE AND THE "WHITE SECURITY STATE"

Political scientist Linda Faye Williams understands the New Deal's racial limitations as born of the need to accommodate itself to the older segregation practiced by Jim Crow southern Democrats, as well as to the restrictive covenants being incorporated by its supporters in northern cities and suburbs. Characterizing this achievement as the creation of a "white security state," Williams focuses the discussion aptly. She sees New Deal reforms as providing a social safety net to those whom it accorded full citizenship and by and large giving only emergency relief to those who were defined as not white. Indeed in many ways—to frame matters in terms of earlier discussions of the state and restrictive covenants—New Deal inclusions and exclusions reunited older nineteenth-century discourses regarding non-Europeans as "anticitizens" with newer twentieth-century ones suspecting them as "antineighbors."[9]

Those who pay tribute to the New Deal's racial progressivism tend to emphasize welfare and work relief and ignore housing subsidies. For example, Nancy Weiss's excellent study of black voters turning away from the Republican "party of Lincoln" and to the Democratic party of Roosevelt during the Depression identifies the availability of benefits and particularly of jobs with the Works Progress Administration (WPA) as a key to that transformation. Amenta counts 11 percent of the workforce in 1939 as nonwhite but finds African Americans holding one WPA job in seven at wages higher than those available to them in private industry. However, he immediately adds that African American poverty and unemployment were so great that black recipients did not draw a disproportionately high share of aid "with respect to need," neatly illustrating the contradictions that vex attempts to declare whether or not New Deal racial policies were progressive.[10]

The question of need cannot be ignored. The 1930s, far from being a decade in which common misery produced interracial unity in a simple way, saw the modern racial disparity in unemployment emerge in northern cities, with African American joblessness roughly doubling that of whites by the decade's end. The crisis most dramatically impacted black women who, as Lois Rita Helmbold has shown, lost jobs in the service sector and made no gains in any other. In the early 1930s, with unemployment reaching 25 percent of the whole workforce and another large cohort getting a tiny number of hours of work per week, such disparities were overwhelmed by a common demand for relief. Unemployed Councils, led by Communists and other radical organizers, built perhaps the most integrated and multinational urban mass movement in U.S. history. However, by the middle and later 1930s partial recovery pulled white urban unemployment rates below crisis levels but left African American communities mired in the Depression.[11]

Thus the slight statistical overrepresentation of African Americans in WPA jobs reflected not only progress but also the reality that the New Deal state did not contest discriminatory hiring and layoff policies. Moreover, "New (White) Deal" policies kept people of color from the forms of work relief best compensated and most connected to securing steady employment. Mexican Americans and Native Americans suffered wholesale exclusions from such programs in the Southwest, and the New Deal's continuation of repatriation policies begun under Herbert Hoover particularly connected the former group, citizens or not, to the charge of being "undeserving" of welfare. In comparison to whites more African Americans were on relief, were on the rolls for a longer period of time, and were more likely to receive general benefits than work relief. With the rate of African Americans on "cash relief" inching above 50 percent in the urban northeastern and north central United States in 1935, quadrupling white rates, the idea that the "dole" was a black thing took quick and firm hold, crowding out the reality that private discriminators and the government were, as Michael Brown writes, "coercively substituting relief for jobs."[12]

More broadly, what Linda Gordon has called the "dual social citizenship" surrounding welfare flowed from the stark racial disparities in coverage under the Social Security Act of 1935. That law, "universal in name only," covered only 53 percent of workers under its standard, holding only the stably employed, relatively high-waged citizen-worker fit for the social right of old-age pensions. Restrictions ensured that even fewer could qualify for unemployment compensation. Premised on the "annuity fiction" that regressive payroll taxes funded the pension program, the law exacted some sacrifices as it conferred benefits. It deliberately fostered a sense of entitlement, based on having paid into the system, answering conservative assaults couched as attacks on the "dependency" created by welfare measures.[13]

Historic and worsening patterns of discrimination guaranteed that Social Security exclusions based on low wages and episodic employment fell most heavily on workers of color. The exclusion of domestic service and agricultural workers, precisely those sectors into which black and Mexican workers had historically been slotted, exacerbated such tendencies. Of 5.5 million African American workers at the time, only 2 million labored outside those excluded sectors. While these exclusions are usually cast as capitulations to southern conservatism, the 1936 formulation of the activist economist Paul Douglas pointed also to "Congressmen from other sections of the country where there were unpopular racial or cultural minorities" as culprits. A solid majority of white workers, and particularly white male workers, literally had their rights to social citizenship insured. Huge majorities of black and Mexican American workers stood "outside the law" where benefits were concerned, sharpening the line between the "dependent" nonwhite recipients of "welfare" and the overwhelmingly white citizen-beneficiaries of entitlements.[14]

The program under the Social Security Act that remained most susceptible to being despised as "welfare," Aid to Dependent Children (ADC), provided an apt illustration of the terms under which the white security state incorporated people of color. Social Security channeled aid to families overwhelmingly through the relationship of wives and children to stably employed (white) male workers. To the extent that male workers of color were left out, their survivors and dependents likewise were. Black and Mexican American women, concentrated in low-wage labor, were excluded as direct participants in almost all social security programs. Aid came significantly through ADC, with single mothers of color having to fight its locally controlled bureaucracies for benefits as little as one-sixth of work relief wages. Those bureaucracies continued to imagine a sharp split between deserving and undeserving homes, between "legitimate" and "illegitimate" children. Against these odds, African American children came to comprise about one ADC recipient in six by 1939, quintupling the rate at which they received mother's pensions. Such a pattern of benefits mirrored that of WPA work, and with the same effect. The success at racially democratizing relief was partial in the extreme, not nearly commensurate with the proportion of children of color in poverty. But the successes were more than enough to spark moral panic regarding black out-of-wedlock births and contributed to a sense that ADC constituted a governmental giveaway rather than a citizen's entitlement, marking the mother as well as the children as dependent.[15]

In much of the 1930s, new immigrant communities looked to work and direct relief programs for the survival of families. However, they did so with less frequency than people of color and with an increasing sense of entitlement based on their power as worker-citizens who had made the New Deal. With the rise of Social Security and, as discussed below, federal housing subsidies, it became possible to accept aid without acknowledging dependence. In fact, certain kinds of aid became the hallmarks of independent citizenship. On the other hand, the second-class benefits that African Americans received reinforced the view that their communities were pathological and the fear that "welfare" went disproportionately to those communities. A writer on the Connecticut Federal Writers Project summarized oral history testimonies in a way that underlines the whitening impact of dual social citizenship.

> The Slovak people as much as the people from other ethnic groups on the block, feel the negro people are treated better, and given more relief by the city welfare, than any other group of people. They say that the negroes are given better dietaries and more milk and that . . . the negroes don't have to go through as much red tape as do white people.

As one white Detroiter put it, "Whites pay taxes; Negroes get housing and relief." Such a misplaced sense of racial grievance regarding welfare benefits survived in the post–World War II period, despite massive housing subsidies to new immigrant families, and structured the continuing casting of blacks and Mexicans as unfit neighbors and suspect citizens.[16]

REGARDLESS OF RACE:
THE CIO, NEW IMMIGRANTS, AND INTERRACIAL WHITE UNIONISM

The pictures of Sidney Hillman and Fiorello LaGuardia meeting with Philip Randolph present double images. These men all represented aggrieved communities on the move. The Roosevelt administration brought them together out of a sense that new immigrant leaders had experience in interracial coalitions. However, those experiences were at best uneven. LaGuardia was capable of both championing the integration of major league baseball and of decrying the ill effects of the changing "complexion" of neighborhoods. Hillman helped lead labor's Non-Partisan League, which cooperated unevenly with the National Negro Congress, led for a time by Randolph, in efforts to reelect Roosevelt to an unprecedented third term in 1940. His own international union typified garment trade patterns of some inclusion but little empowerment of black and Puerto Rican members. Hillman and LaGuardia were perfect choices to confer with and caution Randolph, but not necessarily to express solidarity with him.[17]

Indeed the specific issue of employment discrimination speaks to the question of why new immigrant labor leaders and African Americans might have been tempted toward cooperation and why the former group would have known that alternative strategies were also open to them. When Randolph's agitation forced the creation of a wartime Fair Employment Practices Committee (FEPC), 43 percent of all New York City complaints processed by it came from Jewish workers, who particularly faced discrimination linked, as in the case of blacks, to their alleged unsuitability to work with machines. Discrimination against Jews and other new immigrants took both public and private forms. The New York State Employment Service, for example, honored employers' desires to bar Jews, Italians, and others—desires phrased variously as requirements for "Nordic American," "northern European," or "Anglo-Saxon" workers. In one arresting case Jews were prohibited from entering a wartime workplace in deference to the sensibilities of German American workers.[18] Unions continued to bar noncitizens from membership, with one-third of all U.S. trade unionists at the start of the 1930s belonging to labor organizations holding such a policy. Knowing that employers and unions would be tempted to use appearance, names, language, and accent to dismiss workers as possible "aliens," the war production planners viewed discrimination against "racials," as new immigrants and their children were sometimes revealingly called, with alarm. However, experts came to view such discrimination as not "race" based and therefore as susceptible to solution through campaigns based on naturalization and investigation of loyalty. Richard Steele's excellent work on these matters captures the differences that would have made Hillman know that anti-Jewish discrimination could be addressed on some level without the FEPC. According to Steele, "While the pressure for ending discrimination against blacks came mainly from African Americans themselves, the impetus for taking on the problems of white minorities came from inside the government." Government officials, he added, "seem to have believed that remedying the ethnic employment problems was both easier and more important than similar efforts on behalf of blacks."[19]

State policies worked even more powerfully to blunt the possibility of productive interracial (i.e., largely black–new immigrant) alliances through labor laws that were largely race neutral in their language. In an important essay on color-blind unionism, the legal scholar Marion Crain shows that "labor laws reinforce the fictions that class solidarity is race-neutral, treating occupational identity as the only relevant factor in constituting worker groups." Not surprisingly, Crain starts with the New Deal. The two key pieces of labor legislation in that period closely replicate the patterns seen in its expansion of the welfare state in the 1930s. Both the 1935 National Labor Relations Act (NLRA) and the 1938 Fair Labor Standards Act (FLSA) spoke to the rights of labor, largely without explicitly mentioning race. However, especially in the latter case, New Deal labor legislation effectively excluded from coverage sectors of the labor force, including most workers of color, making the very idea of fairness and economic citizenship a matter of race. Modeled on the 1926 Railway Labor Act, a law that ratified and emboldened the white supremacist unions in that sector, the NLRA provoked great fears among civil rights groups. To prevent the "closed shop" requirement—that workers belong to a union if one was democratically chosen—from becoming in practice what NAACP leader Harry E. Davis called the "white shop," civil rights organizations fought for a clause in the NLRA barring racial discrimination. Indeed under the originally proposed law, the closed shop would have been reserved for unions not practicing discrimination. The AFL declared its willingness to see the whole bill go down to defeat rather than countenance any such clause and prevailed with the backing of the Roosevelt administration. Paul Moreno captures the thrust of reform: "Rather than reduce the discriminatory power of labor unions, the New Deal enhanced union power." It consciously chose not to do both together and tragically portrayed such a stance as "prolabor."[20]

Fear of a great expansion of AFL "white shop" unionism must be counted among the calculations making African American leaders so enthusiastically receptive to the relative egalitarianism of the CIO. Moreover, although historians overwhelmingly write about the relatively liberal CIO and race, the AFL and railway brotherhoods rapidly brought members into "white shop" unions under New Deal labor legislation. At the end of World War II two-thirds of organized labor's 12 million members were outside the CIO, which never grew substantially beyond its 1945 strength. Moreover, two-thirds of black trade unionists were outside of the CIO, either by choice or necessity, continuing to pay dues to organizations that nationally were loath to challenge Jim Crow. When the AFL's racism was challenged at its 1941 convention, top leaders urged black workers to be "grateful" and offered a non sequitur, "human nature cannot be changed," in response. Affiliates repeatedly offered themselves as alternatives to relatively egalitarian CIO racial practices in union jurisdictional disputes.[21] Gunnar Myrdal's classic 1944 study of race in the United States argued that the "white shop" was so ubiquitous as to seem natural and was so powerfully maintained that only massive concerted actions could have broken its hold. Legal challenges and, to a lesser extent, National Labor Relations Board decisions came in limited cases to make it possible to challenge procedurally the most blatant instances of trade union racism as an unfair labor practice.[22]

In 1938 Roosevelt signed the Fair Labor Standards Act, providing a minimum wage, maximum hours, and overtime protections to many U.S. wage workers. Those left out again included domestic workers and farm laborers—overwhelmingly not white and indeed a majority of all black and Mexican American workers. Conservatives demanded that such workers not come under the rubric of fair treatment, and New Dealers acquiesced. Suzanne Mettler's apt summary of the FLSA's limitations with regard to women workers applies even more starkly to workers of color. They too "had the most to gain from the law," and especially from its wage protections, but they were "excluded from the jurisdiction of labor standards."[23]

CIO commitments to racial justice, though real and at times remarkable, were no match for the exclusionary impact of New Deal labor legislation, let alone the long history of racism in management and trade unions. Recent scholarship powerfully accounts for the sense of possibility in the 1930s that a different outcome was possible. Historians generally agree that the early CIO created a distinctly and avowedly nondiscriminatory, and sometimes actively inclusionary, alternative to the AFL's longstanding pattern of winking at Jim Crow. Historians also agree that the CIO produced a wave of black and Mexican American support for industrial unionism, especially among leading intellectuals and civil rights organizations such as the NAACP and even the Urban League in the late 1930s. Industrial workers themselves supported it by the time the war broke out. During its first five years, the CIO saw black trade union membership quintuple. The radical journalist Carey McWilliams, "profoundly stirred" in 1937 by interracial organizing in which Mexican Americans were central, argued more broadly that "most racial minorities" were developing a conviction that "their particular problems can best be addressed through the instrumentality of an organized labor movement."

Finally, a surprising consensus has developed among historians and sociologists of various political orientations that Communist-led unions provided the most vigorous, public, and sustained support for racial equality within the CIO, even during war years, when Communist emphasis on national unity resulted in party directives counseling against direct action on behalf of racial justice.[24] Had things broken a little differently, or had white workers been less backward, historians often implicitly or explicitly conclude, the CIO might have succeeded as an antiracist project. Indeed some historians argue that it might have become the institution around which the civil rights movement organized itself in postwar years.[25]

What is most striking about industrial unionism and white supremacy is the wide variety of seemingly contradictory practices, even in locals from the same city and with similar demographics among the rank and file and analogous left influence among the leadership. Thus Steven Scipes's comparative historical sociology of packinghouse workers and steelworkers in Chicago shows the former insisting on racial equality as a principle on and off the job and including black workers in top local leadership as early as 1939. Chicago's CIO steelworkers union similarly represented many black workers but took a dramatically different course. It left, according to Scipes, no pre–1955 record at the district level of ever addressing discrimination in hiring or upgrading, despite the transformation of racial consciousness in individual locals, most notably among Italian American workers at Republic Steel after the 1937 Memorial Day massacre proved that antilabor terror drew no color line. Indeed the same international union, and even the same leader, might act differently in various contexts. Mine, Mill, the left-led union that championed racial justice in Birmingham, Alabama, and was memorialized for its egalitarianism in the classic film *Salt of the Earth*, tolerated color bars at Butte, Montana, area workplaces and had no effective answer when members there took direct action against wartime plans to integrate. Harry Bridges could provide the leadership that made the International Longshoremen's and Warehousemen's Union (ILWU) significant for its egalitarianism in Hawaii and, with deep contradictions, at times on the West Coast. But he could also countenance, as a Pacific region leader of the CIO, go-slow approaches if a vigorous fight might interfere with ILWU, CIO, or Communist prospects in union organizing, infighting, and elections.[26] Such patterns do not so much erode the generalization that the CIO, and the left within it, had a superior record on race as call into question the premises on which that record was based and the limits of solidarity set by not only rank-and-file racism but also the logic of the CIO project itself.

The hopes of CIO militants and their supporters did not rest on the weak reed of New Deal labor policy but on the strong arms, often graphically depicted in an interracial handshake, of members organized around the celebrated slogan "Black and white/Unite and fight." What might be called nonracial syndicalism—the long-standing belief among some organizers that racially mixed industries *already* gave rise to common workplace experiences that industrial unions could translate into powerful interracial unions—ensured that such hopes existed independently from state policies on race. Nonracial syndicalism drew on long traditions of U.S. unionism, left and right, in centering hopes for change at the point of production. It underwrote what Robert Zieger has aptly called the essentially "economic" CIO response to race, a logic with appeals across the color line.[27] Such logic resonated sufficiently to make W.E.B. Du Bois virtually alone among major national black leaders for a time in warning that, whatever its virtues as a union, the CIO could not bear the weight of functioning as an alternative to social movements organized by communities of color. Du Bois realized that even as nonracial syndicalism announced its principles, it also revealed its limits. Although he called for black workers to "affiliate with such trade unions as welcome them and treat them fairly," Du Bois insisted that the "Negro faces in the current labor movement, especially in the A F of L and also even in the CIO, the current racial patterns of America."[28]

The central vulnerability of the nonracial syndicalist position flowed from the racially patterned way jobs were distributed in U.S. industry. Nonracial syndicalism argued that just as workers labor together across lines of race, they should also unionize, deliberate, struggle, and live together. But workers did not by and large labor together interracially. Indeed the daily patterns that Lizabeth Cohen and others detail as keys to building a "culture of unity" on Chicago's south side—racially mixed work experiences, lunches with people of one's own nationality, and integrated union meetings, perhaps in a Slavic tavern—were anything but typical.[29] When a New Deal agency surveyed 1,500 firms in Philadelphia in 1940, for example, it found that only five had *any* black production workers.

Well into World War II, Cleveland's plants were said to be integrated in only "a few" unskilled positions. At the General Motors factory in that city the bar against black production workers was said by management to stem from the fact that the union "wouldn't stand for it" any other way. A survey of over 2,000 New York City defense firms in 1941 found that a third had a blanket "white required" policy and another third "white preferred." In 1942 African Americans could apply for 18 percent of war-related job openings in Michigan, less than that in Ohio, and just one job in sixteen in Indiana. Southern textiles and railway operations were notorious for their exclusions. Nonracial syndicalism could carry considerable practical grandeur. As one steelworker put it, "You must forget that the man working beside you is a 'Nigger,' Jew or 'Pollock.' The man working beside you, be he negro, Jew or Pollock is a working man like yourself. . . . You work together—FIGHT TOGETHER." But to the very considerable extent that Jim Crow reigned at work, such a position remained an abstraction.[30]

When the labor force was mixed, workers of color tended to be concentrated in a few departments. The idea that certain jobs, usually dirty and/or dangerous ones, were "nigger work" (or, more politely, "Negro jobs") degraded the workers and devalued the work. Conversely, relatively high-paying jobs, designated as skilled but sometimes requiring only brief training, went exclusively to white workers. Workplaces tended to look white to most white workers and material incentives created an interest in seeing a job as "naturally" white. Although progressive union leaders could adduce additional arguments for supporting racial justice—strengthening solidarity, depriving management of a pool of racially aggrieved potential strikebreakers, and nurturing New Deal political coalitions, for example—nonracial syndicalism consistently bumped up against the limits set by the fact that the labor force was already racially divided. When Gunnar Myrdal famously wrote of the "self-perpetuating color bar" in 1942, such realities were painfully obvious. "To give white workers a monopoly on all promotions," he insisted, "is . . . to give them an interest in job segregation."[31]

Nonracial syndicalism also confronted limits set by its own history. The embrace of Jim Crow practices by the AFL had long been accompanied by appeals from its leaders to accept some black members as, in the words of Samuel Gompers, a matter of "self-preservation." This proposition made organizing more effective where black workers were present but certainly did not expand their presence. Indeed the AFL pioneered in using the color-blind language "regardless of race" (or in Gompers's case "irrespective of race"), including such rhetoric in the same documents announcing its strategic capitulations to Jim Crow and color bars. The CIO inherited the socialist tendency to see the "race question" as fully subordinate to issues of class. Eugene V. Debs, the union leader and socialist politician, took the latter view when he proclaimed, ostensibly as an overture to black workers, that socialism had "nothing special to offer the Negro." To simply dismiss CIO race policies as "neo-Debsian" or as recapitulations of Gompers's views misses complexity and change. But it is fair to say that the CIO as a whole never reckoned with labor's past where race was concerned. It put forward the predivision record of the industrial unions that came out of the AFL to form the CIO as evidence that nonracial syndicalism worked, ignoring a long history of complicity in AFL racism by those internationals organized on industrial or semi-industrial lines as well as the abject failures of those unions to fight for promotion and hiring of workers of color. One historian of the International Ladies Garment Workers Union, for example, precisely summarizes that union's failure to address race, before and after the CIO, by going straight to the limits of nonracial syndicalism: "Unionization of the colored Americans neglected a crucial issue: What occupations were open to black Americans?"[32]

The very watchwords of CIO policy on this issue took shape around constant and precise reiterations of the AFL principle that unions organized "regardless of race." CIO leaders could sound like Debs when they boasted that their movement "does not ask questions of race or color." As the historian Robert Zieger put it, from the right to the center-left of the organization's leadership, the CIO "discouraged racial militancy" because "the notions that race played some special, festering role in American industrial life and that black workers had special claims to representation and opportunity were foreign to them." Indeed when race-conscious remedies were proposed, even center-left CIO leaders opposed them as "Jim Crowism in reverse."[33]

To say that the CIO did not "retreat" from egalitarian principles on race but acted more or less in accordance with its founding logic is not to suggest that workers of color were foolish to commit themselves to that organization, especially since they also fought inside it to end discrimination. The white unionists who heard the CIO as saying that battles with the employer always came first, that the majority would settle the issue, or that "regardless of race" organizing was about pragmatic unity far more than antiracist principles were not making things up. White rank-and-file workers could hear the CIO bureaucracy saying that Jim Crow was just another matter up for negotiation and voting. One wartime Philadelphia transit hate striker expressed his sense of betrayal when a CIO affiliate supported hiring a few black motormen. He emphasized that workers had been promised they were joining an "autominous [sic] union, governed in all issues by the rank and file." The union, as one CIO official put it, "is run by the membership," and "the whites outnumber the blacks."[34]

Recent scholarship on the CIO has begun to reflect the ways in which the organization's nonracial syndicalist founding principles on race ensured that it would not transcend the existing arrangements of the labor market, even as advances over AFL practices occurred. Thus Bruce Nelson, the most sophisticated historian of race, the labor process, and the CIO, writes that

> the argument that racial discrimination imposed an economic cost on black and white steelworkers alike contradicted the experience of many steelworkers. In an industry where the income gap between the skilled and unskilled was unusually large, many whites must have known that genuine equality for blacks, based on their ability and seniority, could impose an economic cost on them; it could mean giving up their privileged access to the skilled jobs, higher pay, and better, safer working environment that the wages of whiteness proffered.

Nelson perfectly captures the extent to which nonracial syndicalism could color CIO views when he writes that "many locals noted the absence—even the exclusion—of African Americans from their plants and managed to conclude that this signified the absence of racial discrimination." Michael Honey, much more sanguine than Nelson regarding the CIO's record on race, notes that even the Communist-led National Maritime Union "did not challenge" the color bar. It reserved deckhand work on the Mississippi River to whites, although its members acted as "footsoldiers" on picket lines for integrated CIO unions. Honey finds that the CIO's delay in confronting "occupational segregation" bled over into supporting segregation itself, with the result that "industrial unions played a crucial role in undermining black economic progress."[35]

Stanley Greenberg's important comparative study of race and class in South Africa, Israel, and the United States similarly speaks of CIO policy as unfolding inside a system committed to "reserving white work" and stresses how the nonracial syndicalist position—"we just organized who they hired"—led to a reality in which "most of the industrial unions inherited their 'nigger jobs' [but] later helped forge a labor framework that entrenched them." Robert Zieger writes that under Walter Reuther's leadership the UAW fully respected the existing racial setup of the "lily-white skilled tradesmen, whose crafts remained more heavily segregated than even the notorious AFL building trades." In their actions and inactions unions defined the content of nonracial syndicalism for the white rank and file.[36]

For new immigrants and their descendants, the CIO was important not only as an arena in which the racial order of the United States was learned but also and especially as a site where their own place in that order was defined. New scholarship teaches all too little on the latter score. Zieger's massive and useful recent history of the CIO, for example, ignores the immigrant and immigration in both its index and its text. The fascination with the CIO's sloganeering around its desire to cause "Negro and white" to "unite and fight" has tended to render racial divisions among whites invisible, much as Communist Party "trials" of its allegedly "white chauvinist" members in the 1930s obscured the fact that those famously accused were, as Urgo-Finns and Slavs, themselves positioned outside the security that full white citizenship implied.[37] However, given the vivid memories of how appeals by employers to Nordic nativism against new immigrants had undermined the post–World War I strike wave and the continuing prejudices directed against eastern and southern Europeans, the idea of a unified white working class could not have been assumed by those who lived through the early years of the CIO. Both the union staffers and the CIO's enemies realized as much. Chicago's George Patterson described the diet of an industrial union organizer as similar to that of a machine politician courting new immigrant votes: "Hungarian goulash, minestrone soup, lox and blintzes of creamed cheese, corned beef on . . . rye bread, gelfilte fish, and other exotic dishes." When Texas businessman F. A. Robinett wrote to congratulate Cleveland's mayor for an attack on the CIO, he underlined how industrial unionism could be branded as un-American and less than white on varied fronts. The CIO, according to Robinett, consisted of "Kikes, Wobblies, Sheenies, Flannel-Mouthed-Shanty-Irish, Anarchists, Communists, Hop-Heads, . . . Dagoes, Niggers, and general Under-World elements."[38]

Clearly part of the CIO story lay in the increasing ability of Americanized new immigrants and the second generation to join with the descendants of old immigrants in building a CIO "culture of unity." In many ways the left and the CIO provided both a barometer of the white Americanization of new immigrants and a forum for furthering such a process. Attempts by the Communist Party to emphasize its "Americanism" during the Popular Front period of early CIO organizing, for example, included a hotly debated decision to emphasize baseball over soccer news in the sports pages of the *Daily Worker*. More than a change of line, this decision bespoke the fact that young new immigrant workers already fervidly followed the U.S. national game, whose Jim Crow policies the Communists fought. Thus when the immigrant-based and Communist-connected International Workers Order started a softball league in 1936, Lester Rodney, the sports editor of the *Daily Worker*, could bring out the Italian American New York Yankee superstar Joe DiMaggio to publicize the effort. And he could be assured of new immigrant readers when writing about baseball. Rodney later insisted that neither he nor others joining the communist movement in the 1930s were "foreign-minded kids" in need of "Americanization." Indeed the communist hope after immigration restriction that "the immigrated masses are becoming stabilized and more fully united with native workers" is now part of the reigning wisdom among social historians writing about the 1930s. But in many instances the CIO more fully bespoke new unity among and across new immigrant nationalities than between them and the native-born whites, let alone between new immigrants and workers of color. The mine and clothing workers organizations central in founding the CIO had a long history of cooperation among immigrant nationalities, far more than successful solidarity across the color line. In city after city, especially in auto and steel, the new CIO unions, and industrial unionism generally, were seen and talked about as hunky or "foreign-born" movements, with both terms suggesting new pan-Slavic and even pan–new immigrant cooperation around the New Deal and union organizing. Playwrights influenced by labor militancy and by Marxism portrayed, as Colette Hyman shows, "white working class characters of different European origins creat[ing] a shared culture among themselves [with] full residential integration." Meanwhile the "black and white characters remained largely in their respective cultural and geographical spheres . . . working together toward discrete goals."[39]

In such a situation the CIO could symbolize in the same moment the vulnerabilities and the achievements of new immigrant communities. In Johnstown at the time of the Little Steel strike in 1937, the old immigrant labor force commanded jobs in the "status plants" with new immigrants concentrated in the "foreign plants." The antistrike "back to work" movement enrolled the former group, and the strike loyalists were concentrated among the latter. For new immigrants, the conflict was about traditional workplace demands but they also insisted that "you are not going to call us 'Hunky' no more." Typically, young workers joined the CIO before their immigrant parents did, and the generational dynamics were emotional and complex. "Dad," one steel striker explained, "we don't want to live like Hunkies anymore, like you . . . , treated like trash." First-generation southern and eastern Europeans often came to CIO unions in a second wave, overcoming bitter memories of earlier betrayals by the AFL, committing with fierce loyalty, and making solidarity between new immigrants and their children a founding solidarity of CIO locals. Sometimes the generations and nationalities united around an attempt to rehabilitate "hunky" by making it a badge of honor and masculinity, regardless of nationality. In the Monongahela Valley, where a steel union journal held "we are all hunkies, or foreigners," the so-called hunky was "the man that has the backbone . . . to fight for his just dues."[40]

The same combination of peril and promise animated new immigrant loyalty to the CIO leadership. Louis Adamic's arresting 1942 study of nativism and resistance, *What's Your Name?*, included a long, sad section on immigrants who "promiscuously changed" their "foreign-sounding" names "for the sake of a job." Economically driven name changes contributed to obituaries that included lines like "Mr. Smith is survived by his father Mr. Stanislaw Smyzanski and his older brother Frank Smyzanski." He continued, turning to industrial unionism:

The name of the present secretary of Die Casting Workers, C.I.O., is Edward T. Cheyfitz. Jacob S. Potofsky is acting president of the Amalgamated Clothing Workers. Most of the other big names in the garment trade unions in New York are Jewish and Italian, and many district and local officials in some of the new C.I.O. unions have such tags as Damich and Zwaricz.

The pattern Adamic identified fits with statistical evidence regarding the relative prevalence of new immigrant leaders in the CIO. According to one study, such new immigrants provided 30 percent of the leadership of the industrial unions, compared with only 19 percent of the AFL leadership. Even so, these gains tended to come, except in unions connected to clothing production, largely at the level of secondary leadership.[41]

New immigrant generations and individuals differed regarding what working-class Americanization meant for the fate of national cultures. Yet Thomas Gobel reflected an important truth when he wrote that for them the CIO "did not only promise higher wages, it also included the vision of acceptance by American society." The CIO organized at a time when the *Oxford English Dictionary* accurately defined "American" around the categories of European origins, white racial status, and citizenship.[42] CIO unions could never embody new immigrant "self-confidence" that American rights could be claimed, and fears that they couldn't, without running squarely into assumptions and realities regarding race. At times claiming American status specifically invoked whiteness. In the Philadelphia transit hate strike an Italian American worker, wounded overseas, offered a white and American rationale for exclusion: "I put in my time in the Navy [and] when I came back, this company offered me a job. This is a white man's job, and I for one, don't intend to let any Negro take [it] away."[43] The pro–New Deal, pro-CIO, and tellingly named *American Slav* made a similar connection with far less venom. The journal's front cover regularly appealed—once with Roosevelt beaming at potential readers—to "Bulgarians, Croatians, Czechs, Karpatho-Rus, Poles, Russians, Serbians, Slovaks, Slovenians [and] Ukrainians" by reminding them that they belonged to "the largest family of white people on earth [a] family of over 225,000,000 Slavs." Michael Goldfield's remark on the role of the CIO's "espousal of racial egalitarianism . . . whatever its varying degrees of substance" in imparting "moral authority" to organized labor might thus be partnered with an acknowledgment of the intrawhite inter-racialisms of the CIO and the crusading image it gained specifically from those initiatives.[44]

Reflecting on the 1930s experience of mass unemployment and the fact that workers of color tended to labor in very few places, and often in jobs labeled as "nigger work," new immigrants could fear integration even as they knew (or remembered) the experience of discrimination. Published just after World War II, "Race Relations in Industry," by the sociologist Everett C. Hughes, referred to an industry in which

> Italians, who had been limited to poorer jobs, were annoyed when Negroes were hired to work alongside them, not because they disliked Negroes particularly, but on the ground that—since they knew what people thought of Negroes—the hiring was additional evidence that management had a low opinion of the Italians. Like other actions of management, the hiring of new kinds of workers is regarded as a social gesture, as an expression of management's opinion of the job and of the people already on the job.

Hughes reported that a Polish American woman worker spoke for thousands of others when she pursued such logic and told researchers, "I guess that they [Negroes] have to work somewhere, but I wish it didn't have to be here." The CIO's nonracial syndicalism allowed for the expression of such wishes and avoided the kind of broad assault on color bars that would have assuaged fears that integration implied the degradation of a particular job classification, plant, or nationality.[45]

Within the CIO itself, the unequal positions of new immigrant workers and workers of color ensured that nonracial syndicalist policies could empower new immigrants around the defense of white interests, revealing that, as John S. Heywood argues, "not all dimensions of [union] voice need be appealing." By the late 1930s, the new immigrants in steel had grown, as a CIO publicist aptly put it, "to middle age in the industry." One aspect of such maturation was that gradually the "distinction between 'hunky' and 'English-speaking' began to lose its corrosive force." Another was that new immigrants and their sons increasingly rose to skilled jobs. By 1930, less than half of European-born workers in steel had unskilled jobs, down from two-thirds in 1910. The coming of the CIO both reflected and, through seniority systems, protected such advancements. Pittsburgh-area oral histories of steelworkers show black and new immigrant workers agreeing that the CIO made it possible for Catholics and hunkies to secure and even dominate "high jobs" in the industry and even become "bosses." Seniority removed the threat of arbitrary downgrading and dismissal. Seniority succeeded "in weakening workplace discrimination, particularly against white 'ethnic' workers," John Hinshaw writes. "But," Hinshaw adds, "ironically seniority also institutionalized discrimination" against African American workers.[46]

The job of craneman provides a telling example of how efforts to preserve white skilled and semiskilled positions could hold specific meaning for new immigrants. "Cranes," Judith Stein writes regarding steel, "were essential to move everything [including] 60 ton ladles of molten metal. The safety of men who worked below depended on the skill of elite cranemen who carried the heaviest and hottest material." As the tearful and powerful scenes regarding blacks struggling for crane jobs in a wonderful film by Ray Henderson and Tony Buba, *Struggles in Steel,* demonstrate, status and masculinity as well as income hinged on moving into such positions, which could be learned in two weeks of training on the job. Moreover, black workers were often "hookers," helping on crane work, and were thus poised to learn to operate cranes. The union's unwillingness to challenge discrimination in crane operation is a textbook example of nonracial syndicalism's ability to cohabit with white privilege.[47]

In an important center of steel production like Duquesne Works, foot-dragging on the integration of crane operation was on one level a defense of specifically "hunky work," now skilled, rather than "white work." As early as 1920 southern and eastern Europeans held over half of the crane jobs at Duquesne Works and the second generation another quarter. When the CIO raised issues of seniority-based promotions, it did so to protect and extend new immigrant gains. When management opened a few crane jobs to black workers in the context of war production, the CIO local at Duquesne Works filed a grievance, perfectly illustrating the limits of the nonracial syndicalism and defining the incorporation of new immigrants. The use of black cranemen, it held in defending the interests of white new immigrant members, was "an intolerable condition" because it was one that had "never existed in this plant before."[48]

The CIO's nonracial syndicalist positions also drained urgency from efforts to build black–new immigrant unity outside the factories. Chicago labor organizer Stella Nowicki recalled her time as a packing-house union militant in the early CIO: "We worked in the stockyards with blacks but when we came home, we went to lily-white neighbor-hoods and blacks went to their ghetto. How were we going to bridge that?" Nowicki remembered several activities bringing together Com-munists, Catholics, and communities to attempt to construct a bridge. The United Packinghouse Workers of America (UPWA) pushed uncom-monly hard for antiracist positions in the workplace and beyond, leading some observers to credit the union with cutting down on antiblack epi-thets shouted by children in back of the yards new immigrant packing communities. However, Nowicki does not portray the union as central to bridging efforts off the job. The UPWA far surpassed the pattern of CIO support for fair housing, which consisted of making national pronounce-ments of support for litigation rather than mounting effective local cam-paigns, but even it made only modest strides. A UPWA-commissioned 1956 "self-survey" of racial attitudes and practices in the union by black sociologist John Hope II found much to praise but noted that while the international "officially recognizes its responsibility in eliminating dis-criminatory practices in communities where its members live, efforts in this area have been understandably less intensive, more widely scat-tered, and less productive of demonstrable results than those within the union and its plants." Nowicki's recollections, like the union's record, both challenge and reflect CIO approaches hoping for racial progress through workplace-centered class unity. On the one hand, they allow that a whole realm of life was little touched by solidarity at work. On the other hand, they replicate nonracial syndicalism's tendency to inflate workplace diversity—African Americans held 31 percent of Chicago's packing jobs in 1930 and only 20 percent in 1940—and to separate on-the-job organizing from after-hours racism.[49]

In the 1930s and 1940s white workers, and specifically new immi-grants, developed interracial plant friendships, even as they drew the (color) line at "socializing" after work and bringing black coworkers home. "We only saw the colored," according to one Polish American packinghouse worker, "when we were at work or coming home." As one fair housing advocate summarized the situation in Detroit, white and

African American workers "worked side-by-side without too much trouble, and even joined the same unions. But when they left the factories for their homes there was trouble. Workers had been told that Negroes make bad neighbors." The trouble in Detroit ultimately turned into one of the war's most destructive white racist riots. The conflict was said to be led by new immigrants, either Polish Americans or Italian Americans wearing white headbands. It was sparked by attempts to block the Sojourner Truth Homes, public housing with black residents near white homes. In 1949, a tragic drama in Englewood on Chicago's south side summed up the coexistence of industrial possibilities and community bigotry where race was concerned. A CIO official invited a dozen black workers to a reception at his house, but neighbors assumed he was showing the residence to prospective buyers. Days of white rioting ensued, with such major institutions as parishes and police enabling the terror.[50]

Nonetheless, conceptualizing the residents of new immigrant neighborhoods as learning one lesson about race at work and another at home misses consistent patterns in which the logic of the white house and white neighborhood penetrated the workplace and the union. The CIO unions constantly faced difficult decisions around race and toilets or washrooms at work, around integration of cafeterias, around Jim Crow bowling alleys and leagues in union-sponsored recreational activities, and around the color line at union-sponsored dances and celebrations. One hate strike at a Chevrolet plant in 1944, for example, idled 1,500 UAW members who were protesting the dismissal of seven white women workers who had balked at "working alongside" black women because the new arrangement would necessitate their using "white toilets." Indeed the UAW inherited a work culture in which alarm could result if the coats of African Americans hanging in closets touched those of whites.[51]

Moreover, the line between the fear of black neighbors and the fear of black coworkers was indistinct because access to neighborhoods around factories and docks also often meant access to jobs in those workplaces. Thus the CIO suffered at Wisconsin Steel because white, often "ethnic," workers appreciated management's Jim Crow hiring practices as expressing a "respect for their neighborhood life" by keeping "antineighbors" out of the area. The Philadelphia transit hate strike featured a similar dynamic, with Irish and new immigrant Catholic workers seeing the conflict as a defense of white neighborhoods. Since transit authorities assigned drivers to car barns near their homes, and since several such depots were near areas of growing African American population, motormen were viewed as anchoring threatened white and "ethnic" enclaves. Animosity to the FEPC ruling on African American employment seemed, as James Wolfinger aptly shows, a companion to Philadelphia struggles to keep public housing serving blacks out of white areas. Nor was the FEPC deaf to white appeals that race, jobs, and housing were "intimately con-nected." In Philadelphia a representative of the bureaucracy promised that "non-white workers will not make an invasion of white preserves."[52] Such white and new immigrant preserves were also supported, and at times threatened, by New Deal housing policies.

REDLINES TO WHITENESS: RACE, NEW DEAL HOUSING POLICY, AND THE NEW IMMIGRANT

The CIO's nonracial syndicalism existed in the context of broader union initiatives emphasizing the importance of politics, expressing and en-couraging new immigrant alliances with the New Deal. Moreover, the New Deal itself spoke passionately and acted dramatically on the issue of housing. During the 1936 election campaign, Roosevelt supporters rallied in part around the slogan that the New Deal had "helped us save our homes." The next year his second inaugural address signaled the need for further action, famously proclaiming "one-third of a nation ill-housed." In 1944 Roosevelt included a good house among the provi-sions of the Second Bill of Rights of Americans, presaging new housing initiatives under the GI Bill of Rights. As Thomas Sugrue has argued, the New Deal made home ownership subject to a sense of entitlement. But Sugrue specified further that the entitlement was delimited in New Deal policy terms: It would be a "white entitlement to a home in a racially homogeneous neighborhood."[53] Far from challenging the no-tion that the person of color was an "antineighbor," the New Deal blessed, rationalized, and bankrolled that notion. In doing so it im-parted powerful lessons and expectations to new immigrants and their descendants regarding the extent to which reformers tolerated and for-warded white privilege. It also encouraged—and in some ways re-quired—them to literally invest in whiteness. Insofar as housing policy also discriminated against urban neighborhoods of mixed nationalities, it encouraged the descendants of new immigrants to borrow in order to suburbanize and whiten.

Those who fought for fair housing realized as much with exemplary clarity in the 1930s, 1940s, and 1950s. They understood New Deal housing policy as both racist and whitening. In 1938, the *Los Angeles Sentinel*, a fighting African American newspaper, provoked its readers with a transnational comparison. Under the headline "Ghettoes, American Style," the *Sentinel* editorialized that those who "have been protesting Hitler's despicable plan to herd German Jews into ghettoes will be surprised to learn that their own government has been busily planning ghettoes for American Negroes" through New Deal housing policies. Looking back on the first two decades of the Federal Housing Authority (FHA), which was created in 1934 and quickly became the centerpiece of New Deal reforms in this area, fair housing advocate Charles Abrams found that the agency had "adopted a racial policy that could well have been culled from the [Nazi] Nuremberg laws." Even if we allow that such assessments reflect the heat of battle (Nikhil Singh's comparisons of New Deal/Fair Deal housing policies to the "state-sponsored apartheid" of South Africa, that other pioneering site of state-sponsored white suburbanization, are more sober and compelling), they nonetheless provide an apt reminder of how a New (White) Deal could deepen existing patterns of private and corporate discrimination and create new conditions for white unity and for white violence in defense of privilege.[54]

From its earliest days the New Deal implemented a two-tier housing policy. On the one hand, the initiatives in the realm of public housing provided for mostly low-income workers. These initiatives bowed to segregation but served the poor across the color line. Like direct relief benefits, public housing was quickly typed in many places as "welfare" for African Americans, as a "handout for the feckless." On the other hand, government support for private housing massively and deliberately benefited white home owners and white prospective buyers. It was not seen as welfare at all.[55]

By and large African Americans did not get housing, and they especially did not get integrated and private housing through federal programs. The earliest incarnation of these policies, the Public Works Administration (PWA), made what housing historian Gail Radford has called the "decision not to disrupt preexisting patterns of neighborhoods" and sought to house African Americans "in deteriorated sections of cities where they already lived." Its projects were separate and unequal. Even so, it provided some housing to African Americans, in contrast, for example, to the Federal Subsistence Homesteads Corporation, which so respected the locally "existing economic and social pattern" of the thirty-one communities in which it began work that "not one was racially integrated" and "not one was solely for Negroes."[56]

When the PWA ended in 1937, public housing came largely under the aegis of the United States Housing Authority (USHA). Recognizing that it had a constituency among people of color, the USHA set up an office of race relations. Hopes ran so high that the NAACP journal regarded the early USHA as pursuing a "more fair and equitable racial policy [than] any other branch of the Federal Government." However, conceived in an atmosphere of austerity, USHA initiatives in public housing cut back greatly on PWA standards, putting up structures increasingly easily identified, according to a prominent architect, as "those buildings which the government built to house poor people." Most critically, the agency deferred to local control in site selection and other matters, often guaranteeing Jim Crow. The Detroit riots typified a horrific series of hot and cold wars in the 1940s and early 1950s through which whites, including many of new immigrant background, attempted to "contain" the movement of racialized groups. Reenergized neighborhood improvement associations organized local opinion and hate. Improvised and especially inadequate for urbanizing workers of color, "war housing" made it even easier for white home owners to confirm their fears of the "antineighbor" by looking at ghetto and barrio conditions. Where integrated public housing was built, it was often only nominally so, with the tenants overwhelmingly white or with blacks put on one end of a project. With the top tier of federal housing initiatives reserved for whites, public housing, as the historian Craig Steven Wilder reminds us, became "the only new construction available to black and Puerto Rican people," and it "was normally constructed in segregated areas and therefore only served to reinforce ghettoization."[57]

The two tiers of New Deal housing policy worked together to make white houses even more attractive to new immigrants. If the second-class tier consisting of public housing acknowledged white supremacy by conforming to local Jim Crow practices, the higher private-housing tier ac-

tively and tragically traded on connections between whiteness and property. As one activist acidly put it at the time, "Segregation was not only
practiced but . . . openly extorted." The creation of the Home Owners
Loan Corporation (HOLC) in 1933 set vital precedents in this regard.
With Roosevelt proclaiming that mortgages on single-family homes
formed the "backbone of the American financial system," with half of national mortgage debt in default, and with the situation still worsening,
general aspirations for national recovery coincided with new immigrants'
desire to retain their hard-won homes. HOLC provided loans on more
than a million mortgages in its first year and ultimately saved 10 percent
of owner-occupied nonfarm residences. Conceived at a time when New
Deal strategies turned on bringing business groups into national planning
processes, HOLC eagerly sought the advice of real estate industry leaders and expert appraisers, incorporating their concern with the alleged relationships between racial homogeneity and property values. The agency
produced detailed neighborhood maps as guides to lending priorities.
Tellingly called residential security maps, these documents graded neighborhoods into four categories of desirability. They obsessed, as Kenneth
Jackson has shown, more about the location and movement of African
Americans than any other demographic trend, charting the black presence anxiously. On these maps red lines surrounded neighborhoods rated
the least fit for loans, and almost invariably the "color line was followed"
in limning "redlined" boundaries. "Instituted and institutionalized" by
HOLC, both the term redlining and its practice had long, destructive
lives. Although HOLC itself existed for short-term emergency purposes,
its precedent in giving a reform government's imprimatur to racist lending and planning practices was of enduring importance. Moreover, both
banks and new government policies directed toward the private housing
market, notably those of the FHA and the Veterans Administration (VA),
embraced HOLC patterns of rating, mapping, and discriminating in ways
that would soon apply to loans for new construction.[58]

By 1948 the FHA amply earned the censure of an NAACP official,
who characterized its practices as having done "more than any other single instrumentality to force nonwhite citizens into substandard housing
and neighborhoods." The FHA represented an open incarnation of the
New Deal alliance between white supremacist southern Democrats and
northern segregationist forces, in this case realtors, bankers, and white

urban and suburban home owners. It answered criticisms from the civil rights movement by invoking the necessity of southern conservative votes and cooperation from real estate industry leaders if programs to stimulate the production and marketing of private housing were to succeed. The mechanism through which the FHA massively encouraged home construction and significantly centralized the building industry involved guaranteeing loans made by private lenders to private citizens for "FHA-approved" projects. The agency's requirement for self-amortizing mortgages cut risks to banks and FHA policies made it possible for buyers to purchase homes with a 10 percent down payment, a tiny fraction of the prior norm. FHA standards led to lower monthly payments, cheaper initial housing prices, and some guidelines regarding design. Providing aid, indeed largesse, to the private sector, the FHA helped return housing starts to the 1929 level of 500,000 by 1940. A decade later, the figure reached 2 million. As David Freund's research shows, this stimulation of access to mortgage credit was racially targeted, proceeding by "defining non-whites as incapable of participating" as subsidized citizen home owners.[59]

Myrdal perceptively insisted at the time that all New Deal reforms predicated on "ordinary business principles" tended to leave out racialized communities, which were already lacking resources in addition to being subject to discrimination. With whites having more than twice the income of blacks, pouring federal resources into stimulating means-tested loan programs was bound, in the absence of preferential options for the racially oppressed poor, to increase the value of "whiteness as property." But beyond the racial outcomes dictated by the "raceless" logic of the market in an unequal society, the FHA constructed powerful preferential options for whites. Its guidelines and redlines insistently linked race and class, with the FHA underwriting manuals branding "pigpens and unwelcome races . . . as equally objectionable" and enjoining planners and lenders to engineer occupancy "by the same social and racial classes."[60]

With new developments literally featuring signs of FHA approval as assets, the Roosevelt and Truman governments coerced the extension of policies based on spurious real estate industry perceptions of the tie between racial exclusion and value. Two specific policies undergirded this awful achievement by the white security state. First, the FHA judged neighborhoods not only by their demographics but also by their racist mobilization. Its 1938 underwriting manual, for example, counseled neighborhoods to enhance ratings by taking "fullest advantage . . . of available means to protect the area against adverse influence and to insure that it will develop into a homogeneous racial district." What the agency called "racial occupancy" (occupancy by northern and western Europeans was seen as raceless) stood alongside such pollutants as "smoke" and "odors."[61] Restrictive racial covenants, whose constitutionality had rested on a contrived distinction between the public and the private, now garnered official federal praise. Indeed FHA documents provided a model covenant and trumpeted the device as the "surest possible protection against undesirable encroachment and inharmonious use." Further, the FHA advised that underwriters should consider as a positive good efforts to instill a commitment to segregation among the neighborhood's "younger generation," and should assess the racial character of nearby areas in order to judge the likelihood of racial "infiltration."[62] The agency thus endorsed the idea that racist mobilization, education, and vigilance were neighborhood improvements.

To point to such tragedies is in keeping with some of the best recent scholarship on housing policy, urban history, and race. However, the lines of analysis advanced in this book define new emphases. First, while they glance backward to the New Deal's housing policies, the best accounts of post–World War II segregation and the roots of "white backlash" against civil rights usually begin with the 1940s. To do so underplays the vital racial precedents set at the height of the New Deal—so much so that one interesting recent effort to name periods as dominated by either "civic nationalism" or "racial nationalism" simply enshrines the New Deal in the former category. Such a chronology also separates segregationist campaigns of the 1940s from their roots in restrictive covenant campaigns of the 1920s. Thus even as the new scholarship usefully troubles the timing and even the naming of "white backlash," it may leave open the possibility that racist mobilizations after World War II can be seen as growing mainly out of reactions to changes wrought by civil right gains.[63] The argument here, however, is that what is called white backlash derived importantly from white expectations created by (and even before) the racial nationalism of the New Deal. When white opponents of the Sojourner Truth Homes acted in World War II Detroit, they did so with full awareness that the state could make race. One of them, in the wake of mass deportations of Mexican workers from Detroit, proposed resettling black Detroiters onto farms. A second noted that Uncle Sam's own armed forces practiced Jim Crow. Another pointed out that the FHA would "offer no further loans in Negro neighborhoods."[64]

The most revealing and sustained segregationist rhetoric in the neighborhoods of Detroit and elsewhere simply declared, "We have the right to choose our own neighbors." Variously styled as "the right to racially homogeneous neighborhoods," "white entitlement," and "freedom of choice," this stance connected northern urban segregationism with claims on the state characteristic of the ascendancy of new immigrants during the New Deal, not with a defensive reaction. Linking the pursuit of happiness to the homogeneous neighborhood, such claims often grounded themselves in pro-whiteness and even defense of liberty, not simply racism. The contradictory ways in which new immigrants and their descendants participated in claiming their right to white social citizenship and in mounting violent and nonviolent campaigns to exclude people of color speak to the illusions and investments the New Deal helped create among those whom it tenuously and partially empowered. Of course in no society, least of all a market-based one, does a "right to choose neighbors" exist. In truth, high-sounding pro-segregation rhetoric typically asserted no such broad right, but instead reflected the debasement of language by white supremacy when it assumed that "freedom" inhered in the ability to avoid living near "Negroes . . . Chinese, Mexicans, American Indians, and other minorities."[65]

Meanwhile the FHA, HOLC, and VA actually ensured that new immigrants and their descendants would have less and less ability to choose to develop their own urban neighborhoods. New Deal housing policies empowered and advantaged new immigrants, but as whites, not as new immigrants. Such policies form perhaps the clearest example of the New Deal's "whitening" reforms. They expanded and clarified the ways state policy could favor whites, raising the stakes for the claiming of white identity. They also advertised the coercion that accompanied federal blandishments. HOLC played a pioneering role in this regard as well. On one of its neighborhood evaluation forms, the second question had a series of parts. As Wilder summarizes, "Question 2C asked for the percentage of foreign-born people in a community; 2D the percentage of Negroes; and 2E if one of these was infiltrating." One part of the real es-

tate industry race lore that HOLC sought to embody remained a suspicion that new immigrants menaced property values and bore watching.
Indeed industry publications taught that the entry of new immigrant populations immediately threatened property values and also represented a
stage in the decline of a neighborhood and its slide into becoming an
African American area. After "successively lower classes of native-born
whites" arrive, one primer for appraisers held, "the foreigner then enters . . . followed by the Negro or other colored races."[66] In Brooklyn, the
HOLC systematically downgraded areas with new immigrant "lower-
grade" populations, especially Italian and Polish Americans. Sometimes
these neighborhoods descended into the redlined D category; at others, a
revealingly probationary C minus was the rating. In Chicago, D grades
characterized many Italian American neighborhoods, with their deficiencies being broached in the HOLC survey report section on "racial concentrations." HOLC particularly stigmatized "mixed race" areas, applying
the term to "Scandinavian, Italian, and Irish" blocks, for example. Because
HOLC's rise coincided in some cities with the weakening of nationality-
based savings and loan associations, such discrimination in the provision
of state-sponsored credit was critically timed to substitute the white security state for immigrant institutions as a source of credit.[67]

FHA guidelines took up the attack on "mixed race" neighborhoods
with a vengeance, cautioning against the presence of, or even possible infiltration by, "socially antagonistic" populations or "incompatible racial elements." The FHA (and real estate textbooks that first structured and
later imitated its language) branded mixed neighborhoods as both poor
risks and unhappy places. Sometimes the FHA took care to say that "inharmonious racial and nationality groups" were what sapped value, but
"race" still often stood in for "nationality." Thus expert opinion cast "antipathetic racial groups" as "gnaw[ing] at the edges" of neighborhoods
and threatening their "very core." If Jews and Italians shared space, the
neighborbood suffered from the presence of "antipathetic" races. Since
the urban neighborhoods in which new immigrants and their children
lived were typically such mixed areas, FHA policies threatened urban
communities across lines of nationality.[68]

Thus while helping the descendants of new immigrants get more favorable credit and cheaper homes, the FHA and VA also directed them
away from the mixed urban areas containing immigrant neighborhoods

and ethnic institutions. In the mixed Boyle Heights area of Los Angeles, for example, the FHA withheld its approval for insured loans because it saw the neighborhood as a "melting pot . . . literally honeycombed with . . . subversive racial elements." In St. Louis County, seen as "white" and therefore not affected by the "adverse influence" of race, FHA-approved loans from 1934 to 1960 averaged 6.3 times the per capita levels of the city of St. Louis, seen as racially mixed largely because its large white majority included "inharmonious" groups. Per capita FHA-guaranteed loans in suburban Long Island's Nassau County outpaced those of Brooklyn by an 11 to 1 ratio and of the Bronx by 60 to 1. In the entire history of the FHA, no Newark neighborhood ever received a top rating.[69]

Of course the "white suburb," so overwhelmingly the beneficiary of federal aid for housing and highways in the 1940s and 1950s, could have been termed "mixed" too, if the national heritage of those moving there were traced back far enough. Indeed any serious demographic study would have found many suburban residents descended from stable unions between "inharmonious racial and nationality groups." But suburban developments, new and protected by firm restrictions against non-Europeans, the most threatening potentially "infiltrating" racial groups, seemed not to require such strict scrutiny where the descendants of new immigrants were concerned. Suburban subdivisions could profit from being seen as raceless, as well as planned and stable. With Uncle Sam increasingly promoting the idea that U.S. levels of consumption, born of free enterprise, proved superiority over the Soviet system, the suburban house became an important (white) American symbol and the subsidized suburban home owner the quintessential social citizen. "When you rear children in a good neighborhood," one subdivision promoter told *Time* in 1947, "they will go out and fight Communism."[70] Thus even as liberal anticommunism created new openings to attack Jim Crow as undermining national unity and embarrassing the nation in the Cold War, it simultaneously promoted the white suburb as the apotheosis of free market development, consumer society, and the American Dream. In one dramatic 1946 instance of this contradiction, one face of the liberal Cold War state, the Justice Department, sued the Mortgage Conference of New York for conspiring to violate black and Puerto Rican civil rights by steering loans according to the security maps, as was more or less required by other agencies of the liberal state.[71]

Such policies in the relation of the state to race and housing, however much they spoke in the name of unifying national ideals, created sharp splits among new immigrants even while helping them enter the white house of the nation. The divide between those who suburbanized and those who persisted (even for only a bit longer) in urban new immigrant neighborhoods and parishes was articulated in several ways. "Staying put" could express a loyalty to neighbors, institutions, and the city, since the flip side of industry and state-sponsored apartheid was that when neighborhoods did change they often did so suddenly. Real estate profiteering, "blockbusting," dictated that the timing of flight mattered greatly to a family's profit or loss, and staying put under those conditions seemed to be a measure of loyalty. But persisting in the old neighborhood also could be termed being "left behind," for lack of resources. In many new immigrant families, the second generation (and increasingly the third) was best poised to make the suburbanizing move. They were leaving home and needed new quarters, were qualified for VA-approved mortgages, and sometimes had GI Bill educational benefits to make them surer loan risks. Frequently it was parents who were left behind. "The elderly who were unwilling or unable to flee," as David Hellwig puts it, remained in communities "now increasingly non-white." In an ironic way, such patterns validated the FHA's notion that the city embodied "inharmonious racial groups" while the suburb expressed a whiteness that required little racial concern. Appraisers specifically noted the presence of the "foreign born" as a threat to neighborhood security, while the suburbs constituted an adventure largely undertaken by those born in the United States.[72]

The ethnographer Robert Orsi, reflecting on Italian American migration away from Harlem, notes that what was lived as "staying put" or as "being left behind" was often remembered as being "driven out" of neighborhoods by blacks and Latinos, even though the demography and the chronology of moving often fit such a scenario poorly. Orsi's point is aptly paired with Freund's recent work, which finds that "countless Detroit area whites fashioned their growing enthusiasm for homeownership and for suburban life. . . by painting the 'city' as a place undermined by crowded and deteriorating living conditions. . . , by renters, and—most conspicuously—by the presence of Black people." In fact, African Americans composed less than a tenth of Detroiters in 1940 and far less than a third in 1960, and were still well short of a majority in 1970.[73] But the white suburb's need to imagine a black, antineighborly, and uninhabitable city structured perceptions, even as it added to the allure of the often shoddy and drab suburban working-class subdivision and hastened the forgetting of who—and what—was left behind. Moreover, the impossibility of urban life, as viewed from the white suburb, captured an unfolding tragedy that was real, as housing and planning policies undermined the city for all who stayed there. Given their decimation through immigration restriction, their coerced incorporation as whites within the liberal state, and the internal divisions among those who were left behind and those precariously arrived in suburbs, new immigrant populations were poorly situated to enter multiracial initiatives to remake cities or to resist the bureaucratization of unions. The New Deal brought new immigrants more fully into the hopelessly intertwined traditions of exclusion-based white nationalism and inclusive efforts at reform. As they lived through their last decade as races and their first as ethnic Americans during the presidencies of Roosevelt and Truman, those new immigrants and their descendants were tempted and even compelled to appeal to both traditions. But the rewards were greater and more consistent for appealing to the former tradition.

The Houses We've Lived in and the Workings of Whiteness

The House I Live In, the title of Frank Sinatra's 1945 pro-tolerance short film and song, evoked a warm image dear to new immigrant communities. Sinatra, under fire earlier in the war as an alleged draft dodger, donated his services to the project. Reportedly his habit of giving impromptu talks against bigotry at high schools structured its contents. He begins the short by singing romantically in a studio. Stepping outside for a cigarette, Sinatra encounters a gang of prepubescent white toughs about to commit what would now be called a "hate crime" on a scared schoolboy victim. The singer saves the day, invoking patriotism and the need for unity. His finale is the stirring Earl Robinson and Abel Meeropol song "The House I Live In." The chastened gang understands when he sings of a nation based on an exchange of the "howdy and the handshake" shared by "all races, all religions."[1] The appeals that the film could (and could not) make take us to the heart of the dramas and tragedies described in this book.

Because Meeropol and Robinson participated in Communist causes, with which Sinatra regularly but more indirectly associated himself during these years, and because the film received a special Oscar in 1945, admirers regularly celebrate it as a high point of "cultural front" antiracist radicalism. Even today enemies still trouble themselves to brand the song a "virtual Communist anthem." FBI agents anticipated both views in the 1940s, regarding it as dangerous for its antiracism and its leftism.[2] That the songwriters and the film's screenwriter, Albert Maltz, fell victim to the postwar red scare—and that Sinatra almost did based in significant measure on his association with *The House I Live In*—add to the mystique, though today the short is far more often written or read about than it is seen. The song is connected to the struggle against antiblack racism in that Paul Robeson featured it in postwar concerts, the African American left-wing singer Josh White first recorded it, Sinatra reported being inspired in these years by Gunnar Myrdal's research on race, and Meeropol also wrote the lyrics to "Strange Fruit," Billy Holiday's classic antilynching song. But when Meeropol saw *The House I Live In,* he staged a passionate one-artist protest after he realized the film had cut the line "my neighbors, white and black" from his lyrics, and he was ejected from the theater. Why did the song so easily come to sound like an empty patriotic hymn when the born-again conservative Sinatra reprised it a quarter century later at the Nixon White House, or in 1986 at the rededication of the Statue of Liberty before Nancy Reagan, or in support of the 1991 Gulf War? Why was the film's cast all white?[3]

The answers to such questions lie in large measure in the difficulty with invoking a house as a metaphor for the nation in the production's title. People of color and whites did not live in the same house or in the same neighborhood, in the 1940s any more (indeed less) than in the 1920s. Nor could they feel similarly at home in the United States. Seeking, as Gerald Meyer has written, "to disseminate [a] Popular Front anthem to the widest possible audience," Maltz and director Mervyn LeRoy erased race. In doing so the film more or less conformed to national Communist Party positions subordinating antiracist campaigns to wartime unity. Moreover, they made the cast white but "ethnic," so that the cutting of the lyrics dovetailed with the visual and narrative contexts of the film. The rescued child was to be seen as Jewish and his tormenters appeared as presumably Catholic children of new immigrants. Sinatra evoked his father's immigrant status and forcefully argued that religious intolerance only made sense "to a Nazi or somebody who's stupid." The choice of a Jewish victim was of course apt given the realities of an anti-Nazi war and the significant problem of anti-Semitic street violence in some cities, especially Boston, during the war. Moreover, Hollywood had been anything but eager to take up anti-Semitism or even portray recognizably Jewish characters during the previous decade. But cutting people of color is nevertheless revealing. For example, Irish American street violence caused black and Jewish youth to unite for self-protection in some instances. A film based on that scenario—let alone with White or Robeson or more boldly Holiday in Sinatra's role—would have taught far different lessons. Moreover, as Judith Smith's marvelous *Visions of Belonging* has shown, *The House I Live In* fits squarely into a pattern of early Cold War films that attempted, with mixed results, to make "anti-Semitism stand for all racisms."[4]

A series of significant racist riots—especially those pitting whites against blacks and Mexican Americans in Detroit and Los Angeles—turning on the occupation of urban space by people of color during the war suggested that the neat lesson taught by Sinatra would have been far more controversial with Meeropol's lyrics restored or with African Americans in the film's cityscape. The specifics of Sinatra's appeals to the youths further undercut any connection to an attack on antiblack racism, even as they illustrated the relative ease with which new immigrants could claim a place in the white house of the U.S. nation. At a time when debates over segregation in popular music were maturing, for example, Sinatra begins the film by fronting a white band in the studio. Initially the youths are unconvinced by Sinatra's assertion that he is an "American" and that they are acting like "Nazi werewolves." When an affable ringleader objects that his dad has been wounded and that his family is surely a good American one, Sinatra seizes the opening by asking if the wounded father received a blood transfusion. He then asks the Jewish youth if his parents give blood. The affirmative answers in both cases establish the common bloodline that is America. But "black blood" was segregated, or simply not collected, in World War II blood bank efforts, despite the signal role of the African American doctor Charles Drew in creating the system. This accomplishment, and this affront, weighed on the minds of African Americans, with the National Association for the Advancement of Colored People (NAACP) awarding Drew its Springarn Medal as *The House I Live In* was being produced. Radio soap operas opened minor parts to blacks during World War II. However, when the popular *Lone Journey* series ventured to have a white character say that "Negro blood is the same as ours," a formal reprimand resulted. Even Meeropol's ringing lines "All races, all religions/That's America to me" could be heard in this context as deploying "race" in the time-honored

tradition of referring to Jews and Italians as racial groups. Attacks on antiblack racism could be left for later.[5]

If we follow Sinatra off the set, the reasons artists and organizers might
have been tempted to make African Americans disappear in the interest
of building the "broadest possible" unity become clear. In 1945 the singer
took *The House I Live In* on the road, making thirty "pro-tolerance" public appearances and performing the song in Gary, Indiana, to oppose a
white supremacist student strike and perhaps also at Benjamin Franklin
High School in Harlem, where Italian American students had attacked
black students. In both cases Sinatra defended symbols of intercultural
unity. Gary stood as an exemplary "CIO town" with prominent left-wing
unionists in the plants and the local parent-teacher association. Leonard
Covello, the first Italian American school principal in New York City, led
Franklin High, which enrolled, as Covello proudly pointed out, "forty-
one nationalities, or races." The Communist-supported independent left-
ist U.S. Congressman Vito Marcantonio, leader of a remarkable Italian
American, Puerto Rican, and African American coalition, served the area
as its representative. In neither Gary nor Harlem was it possible to elide
the race issue as *The House I Live In* film had done. Indeed the buildup
to Sinatra's New York City appearance included a splashy intervention in
the Columbus Day parade by five hundred Franklin High students,
flanked by parents, with a float featuring the Statue of Liberty and ban-
ners proclaiming "Americans All—Negro, Jewish, Catholic, and Protestant" and "Unite and Fight Against Race-Hate." Sinatra wore and toyed
with a gold St. Christopher medallion engraved on its reverse with the
Star of David, but he also spoke out against antiblack racism, forcefully
denouncing the idea of "biological differences" among races.[6]

However, the appeal of *The House I Live In*, now repeated and expanded in real life, could not work the same magic offscreen. Sinatra's
expansive campaign for tolerance attracted interest, as he realized, almost entirely in the "Negro weeklies." While a special Oscar rewarded
his film, only the *Daily News* and the Communist Party's *Daily Worker*
among the area's many daily papers covered Sinatra's appearance at
Franklin High. Sharp racial divisions plagued Italian Harlem. Viola Mellone wrote to Covello claiming to represent the views of "thousands of
white mothers in this section of Harlem" who allegedly saw black youth
as too close to "savagery and cannibalism to be inserted into civilization."

A confrontation between Marcantonio and a group of loiterers near the school ended when he wheeled and left after being asked. "If you had a sister, would you want her to marry a n____?" Indeed the events in Harlem underlined the fact that *The House I Live In* had eliminated not only people of color but also women from its street scenes. By making tolerance a matter to be handled by bombardiers and boys, the film elided the messy fact that it was precisely cross-gender relationships that excited white fear and fury.[7]

Gary proved an especially troubling case, as the hate strikes there included many eastern and southern Europeans; both the sense of entitlement and the form of protest animating the strikes were linked to the feeling of empowerment generated by CIO culture. Beginning during the war, the student strikes in Gary brought pressure to bear on not only the schools but also federal officials charged with enforcing antidiscrimination measures in the factories, perfectly illustrating the one-sidedness of the CIO's nonracial syndicalist assumptions that change flowed from factories to communities. The Gary strike found imitators across the Illinois border in at least three Chicago area working-class high schools. A spokesperson for the National Association for the Advancement of Colored People (NAACP) observed that each walkout "broke out in areas where there is a heavy concentration of the foreign-born—Italian, Hungarian, Polish." In Gary the crowd admired Sinatra the star but was so sharply antagonistic to his message that he began with posturing: "I can lick any son of a bitch in this joint." When Sinatra accused right-wing Catholic leaders, including the president of the Hungarian Political Club, of fomenting the strikes, the priest heading Gary's Catholic Youth Organization left the stage "in disgust." Gary's mayor bitterly confronted the singer after the speech. Sinatra got nowhere in changing the behavior of the strikers. They did not accept that white and black students shared common "blood" and they even insisted that the races not share a common swimming pool at the school.[8]

Following Sinatra a little farther allows us to reexamine the racial oppression, confusion, and "progress" experienced by new immigrants and their descendants in the first half of the twentieth century and to see that the acceptance of an "ethnic" star as a symbol and an advocate of national unity had its limits and complications. In 1947 Sinatra punched the reactionary columnist Lee Mortimer when—accounts vary—Mortimer called him a "dago" or Sinatra made a gay-baiting assault on Mortimer. When he explained the incident to Hedda Hopper, a competitor of Mortimer in the business of disseminating Hollywood gossip, Sinatra emphasized that Mortimer had insulted "my race and my ancestry." The Italian American *L'Unitá del Popolo* saw "race"—in more than one of its various meanings—at the bottom of Mortimer's ensuing anti-Communist vendetta against Sinatra. It editorialized under the front-page headline: "We are in Solidarity with Sinatra in the Struggle Against Racism." The editorial held that the singer's treatment, like his message, "recalled the brutal memories of the innumerable humiliations suffered, not so long ago, by our grandparents and parents," and praised Sinatra's outspoken campaign "against Jim Crowism . . . against anti-Semitism and against the denigration of his own people of origin." On the right, the campaign against Sinatra focused on not only ties to Communist artists and activists but also the status of *The House I Live In* as what one FBI informant called "a racial tolerance production." To join left-wing politics with even hints of antiracist agitation threatened to send the increasingly secure world of second- and third-generation immigrants back to the slights and uncertainties suffered earlier in the century. So too did association with organized crime and, ironically enough, with racist mobs, whose postwar activities were sometimes simplistically laid at the door of new immigrant communities.[9]

Such complications remind us that any periodization of when new immigrants and their descendants ceased to be victimized on "racial" grounds—let alone of when they ceased feeling so victimized—is bound to be vexed. But clearly much had changed. That it could seem logical to enlist Jewish and Italian American radical entertainers to provide the words and vision for a patriotic vehicle stood in sharp contrast to treatment the immigrant left received during and after World War I—being spied on and deported. Of course, the nature of the war, and the extent of left-wing support for it, mattered greatly in this connection, as did the strength of the CIO. However, in Sinatra's case early charges of disinterest in the war effort offered a particular opportunity to connect nationality and lack of loyalty, especially since Italy was for a time an enemy. That no such racial/national baggage prevented Sinatra from speaking to and for the United States illustrated the extent to which Italian Americans could now feel at home in the nation and helped account for the ease with which the film baited "Japs"—the only racialized group actually mentioned in *The House I Live In*. The contrast between treatment of the Italian Americans and the Japanese, the other non-Nordic group subject to being linked by ancestry to the fascist war effort, was stark. As 120,000 Japanese Americans—40,000 of them classed as enemy aliens—went to detention camps, Italian American aliens suffered only relatively brief harassment, especially directed against Pacific Coast fishermen and waterfront residents. With a congressional committee holding that evacuation policies for Italian Americans were "out of the question if we intend to win this war," Roosevelt urged caution. In May 1942, almost two-thirds of all enemy aliens were Italian Americans but less than one-seventh of enemy aliens in federal custody were. The following month New York City's Italian American mayor, Fiorello LaGuardia, led the New York at War procession, which banned Japanese Americans. In the context of the 1942 election, Roosevelt rescinded the enemy alien designation against Italian Americans and expedited naturalization processes for them. Japanese aliens, who unlike Italians had never had the any opportunity to naturalize, stayed in custody. Earl Warren, a supporter of Japanese internment who later served as chief justice of the U.S. Supreme Court, explained that Italians were "just like everybody else" and therefore should not be held. A remarkable article published by the NAACP found the Japanese to be victims of "barbarous treatment [as a] result of the color line" and Italians able to escape such treatment because they were "white."[10]

Even the most notorious racist in U.S. politics, Mississippi senator Theodore Bilbo, seemed to reluctantly agree that Italian Americans could not be racially attacked. Bilbo had responded to an Italian American supporter of fair employment practices by addressing her as "My Dear Dago." When Marcantonio rebuked him, the Mississippian additionally called his adversary a "political mongrel." However, as the controversy garnered press attention, Bilbo reined in his tendency to demean "racial" and "ethnic" minorities in the same screeds. He assured all that he acted out of "the respect and love I have for the Caucasian blood that flows not only in my veins but in the veins of Jews, Italians, Poles and other nationalities of the White race [whom] I would not want to see contaminated with Negro blood."[11]

Sinatra and Marcantonio hoped that the political power held by Italian Americans and other new immigrants might be tempered by a memory of racial and national oppression and might undergird broad coalitions. At a community mass meeting just before Sinatra's appearance at Franklin High, Marcantonio held, "We've got to fight the Bilbos . . . all over the world. We, of Italian origin, know the meaning of discrimination because we have been exploited, so we refuse to discriminate against others." Sinatra credited what he learned "going to school in Jersey," including being called a "dirty guinea," with animating his antiracist activism. A decade after Sinatra's visit, a Gary steelworker was still applying a variant of this logic. He led into an argument for tolerance with, "Twenty years ago when I went to school we were called Hunkies. . . . Now there's this talk against colored people."[12] However, the lessons taught by discrimination and by overcoming it could easily be forgotten or even processed into exclusionary narratives. One East Harlem resident enthusiastically supported Bilbo as "our only savior from a complete mongrelization of the human race."[13] In 1953 Cleveland mayor Thomas A. Burke appeared before an angry crowd of white residents united around their "right" to live in a white neighborhood. Some of the children of new immigrants in the audience told of their travails with discrimination and of their triumph in building a "fine neighborhood." The mayor, like Sinatra, tried to turn such arguments slightly, reminding protesters of the bigotry historically directed against their communities and encouraging tolerance. But, came the puzzled reply, "We're all white."[14]

The sprawling stories of *The House I Live In*, of what it achieved and of what it repressed, and of what happened when Sinatra tried to take its drama into the real world, raise the possibility that the short film might exemplify left-liberal initiatives in the New Deal era, even if it was not the high point. To say as much challenges romanticized accounts of the period which suppose, as Michael Denning does at times, that the "Popular Front social movement was . . . as committed to the politics of racial justice as it was to the politics of industrial unionism." Nor do lamentations for the New Deal that see it as a lost age of broadly transcendent unities of class or nation offer a model that helps us understand how race (dis)appeared in *The House I Live In*. Steven Fraser and Gary Gerstle have recently held, for example, that the "fall of the New Deal order" eclipsed the "labor question," and that postwar movements substituted "race for class as the great unsolved problem in American life." David Montgomery has more loosely concluded that the New Deal created a "capacious image of America" by linking "patriotism to the cause of social reform." Indeed for Montgomery, the New Deal was victim of its own success when "representatives of the new white urban voting blocs" came by the late 1940s to be "committed primarily to preserving their earlier gains" in the context of the Cold War and conservative onslaughts. As we have seen, looking closely at New Deal housing policy and more soberly at race and the House of Labor calls into question such contentions where politics and unionism are concerned. The New Deal took in, and coerced, members of new immigrant communities via appeals to *both* race *and* class. Nor are any sweeping generalizations on the antiracism, or the successful appeals to class/national unity, of the left-wing supporters of the New Deal easily sustained in the world of culture. The "intercultural" unity of the late 1930s, and wartime efforts to bring together "Americans All" in audiences and coalitions supporting victory over fascism, often included people of color belatedly and contradictorily.[15]

Instead, the broad story of *The House I Live In* is exemplary because it sums up the persecutions that caused new immigrants to organize for inclusion and exclusion at the same time and to put the house at the center of their worlds. It speaks to the promise that their initiatives would intersect with freedom movements of people of color and the ways in which stark differences between less and less provisionally white new immigrants and their children on the one hand and people of color on the other made it tempting to strategically avoid those intersections and difficult to inhabit them. Sinatra tried to parry right-wing attacks by saying that conservatives were going after him because he stood up for veterans' efforts to gain homes, making a raceless appeal that nonetheless evoked the New Deal heritage of securing the white house. At about the same time, the black magazine *Ebony* published a photo-essay that played off and took on the politics of Sinatra's film. Titled "The House We Live In," it insisted that New Deal rhetoric and wartime unity rang hollow in a nation that functioned as a white house: "The tenth man of America has always been part of the third of the nation ill-housed. . . . Never will a white man in America have to live in a ghetto hemmed in by court-approved legal documents, trapped by an invisible wall of hate much more formidable than the Siegfried line." *Ebony's* military metaphor referred to the Nazi Siegfried lines, one variant of defensive fortifications between France and Germany built in the 1930s, but the original Siegfried line was a World War I construction. The tortured and tortuous relationship of new immigrants to immigration restriction and state repression in the wake of the first war was not repeated at the end of the second. The ghetto had unequivocally become black, and eastern and southern Europeans far more securely a part of the master race. The ambiguities through which the latter groups lived, and ways that they were resolved by new immigrant self-activity, by state policy, and by economic changes, structured much of the story of politics as well as race in the long early twentieth century in the United States.[16]

ACKNOWLEDGMENTS

This book was twelve years in the making, with several books, edited and authored, intervening. Its long maturation has afforded many opportunities to accumulate debts. I am thankful, for example, for the many forums that gave me the opportunity to speak about issues related to this study, including the Kyoto American Studies Seminar, the University of Sydney, Otago University (New Zealand), Victoria University (New Zealand), Grinnell College, Loyola University (Chicago), the Kaplan Distinguished Lecture at the University of Pennsylvania, Solidarity Summer School, the United Auto Workers New Directions Movement's Summer School, the United Steelworkers Summer School, the Labor History Group at the University of Pittsburgh, the Thomas Merton Center, the Black Student Union at the University of Binghamton, the Atlanta Seminar in the Comparative History of Labor, Industry, and Technology, the University of Virginia Museum of Art, Princeton University, Northern Illinois University, the Bluegrass Symposium at the University of Kentucky, the Ethnic Studies Lecture Series at the University of California–San Diego, the David Noble Lecture Series at the University of Minnesota, the Black History Month Lecture Series at Spelman College, the Lefler Lecture Series at Carleton College, the Sidore Lecture Series at the University of New Hampshire, the University of California Conference on Whiteness (Berkeley), the "Then What Is White?" Conference at the University of California–Riverside, Dartmouth College, the Theorizing Whiteness Conference at Williams College, Northern Kentucky University, the Hewlett Lecture Series at Linfield College, the Commonwealth Fund Conference at the University of London, the Provost's Lecture Series at

Bowling Green State University, the Sprinker Memorial Conference at the State University of New York at Stony Brook, Southern Illinois University at Edwardsville, Southern Illinois University at Carbondale, Washington University, St. Louis University, the University of Michigan, Ripon College, Macalester College, Zion Baptist Church Summer School in Minneapolis, the University of Wisconsin at Madison, the Dane County Labor Council Lecture Series, the University of Toronto, and the *New Left Review* Lecture Series. In addition, the ongoing stimulation of the Race, Ethnicity, and Migration Group at the University of Minnesota, the Migration Study Group and the Critical Study of Whiteness Group at the University of Illinois, the Southern Educational Fund's initiative on the comparative history of race, and the Social Science Research Council Migration Group have stimulated research and thought.

Research assistance from Tom Mackaman, Anna Kurhajec, Michael Rosenow, Anthony Sigismondi, Tiya Miles, Josie Fowler, Rebecca Hill, Deirdre Murphy, Rachel Murphy, Jacquetta Amdahl, Steve Garabedian, and Robert Frame has sped progress and deepened insights. Ann Conry, Ana Chavier, Aprel Orweck, Colleen Hennen, and others expertly prepared the manuscript for submission. The McKnight Research Award and the Scholar of the College Award at the University of Minnesota, and the Babcock Chair and Mellon Fellowship Funds at the University of Illinois, provided financial support and time to do research and write. Apt editing by Chip Rossetti at Basic Books, as well as editorial advice and encouragement from Bruce Nichols and the late Michael Sprinker, improved organization and argument.

A long period of writing ensures that some who contributed suggestions will go unmentioned and I have chosen to acknowledge debts largely in footnotes. However, the forbearance and encouragement of colleagues with far greater expertise than I in race studies and immigration history surely deserve mention. I am thinking especially and fondly of Jean Allman, Pedro Cabán, Sundiata Cha-Jua, Kent Ono, Kerby Miller, Erika Lee, Jean O'Brien, Hyman Berman, Susan Porter Benson, Josephine Lee, Catherine Choy, Adrian Burgos, Elizabeth Esch, Rudy Vecoli, and James Barrett in this regard. Indeed collaboration with Barrett on a series of articles taught me a great deal and encouraged greater boldness.

My other teachers, who were also sometimes my students, on the subjects treated in this book include George Lipsitz, Matthew Jacobson, George Fredrickson, Tom Guglielmo, Sal Salerno, Nancy Foner, Noel Ignatiev, Jennifer Guglielmo, Wendy Mink, Linda Gordon, Bruce Nelson, Linda Gordon, Donna Gabaccia, Yuichiro Onishi, Josie Fowler, Todd Michney, Peter Rachleff, Tom Sabatini, Franklin Rosemont, Nell Irvin Painter, Matt Basso, Karen Brodkin, the late Michael Rogin, and Sterling Stuckey, among many others.

NOTES

CHAPTER 1

1. *Daily Tribune* (Columbia, Mo.), May 29, 1993; *New York Times,* June 24, 1993; on Rocker, see Douglas A. Blackmon, "How Atlanta Braves and Unlikely Allies Saved John Rocker," *Wall Street Journal,* April 18, 2000, A1. The epigraphs are from James Baldwin and Margaret Mead, *A Rap on Race* (New York, 1971), 67–68; and di Prima in Fred Gardaphe, "Presidential Address," in Dan Ashyk Gardaphe, and Anthony Julian Tamburri, eds., *Shades of Black and White: Conflict and Collaboration Between Two Communities* (Staten Island, 1999), x.

2. On exclusion in tennis, see E. Digby Baltzell, *Sporting Gentlemen: Men's Tennis from the Age of Honor to the Cult of the Superstar* (New York, 1995), 147–162. On the ancestry of the stars, see Peter Bodo, *The Courts of Babylon* (New York, 1995), 420–426; *Current Biography Yearbook* (New York, 1989), 10; on naturalization and race, see Chapter 3; for James's amusement/unsettledness at encountering an Armenian American, see Henry James, *The American Scene* (1907; New York, 1987), 85–86. On the court cases, see *In re Halladjian et al.*, C.C.D. Mass., 174 Fed. 834 (1909) and *U.S. v. Cartozian*, 6 Fed. 919 (2nd Cir. 1925); Report of the Immigration Commission, *Dictionary of Races of Peoples*, Senate Document 662 (Washington, D.C., 1911), 16; on immigration trends, see Silvia Predaza, "Origins and Destinies: Immigration, Race, and Ethnicity in American History," in Pedraza and Ruben G. Rumbaut, eds., *Origins and Destinies: Immigration, Race, and Ethnicity in America* (Belmont, Calif., 1996), 4–9.

3. James, *American Scene*, 61–62, 86 ("racial ingredients"), 93–94 ("Jewry"), 91–92 ("Italians"), 88 ("mitigation"), 61 ("sensitive citizen"), 99 (language and accent), and 91–92 ("colour" and "white-washing"); Alan Trachtenberg, "Conceivable Aliens," *Yale Review* 82 (October 1994): 62, 42–64.

4. Frank Julian Warne, *The Immigrant Invasion* (New York, 1913), title page, 22, 24, 195–196.

5. Lewis, *The Militant Proletariat* (Chicago, 1911), 28–29.

6. On race suicide, Roosevelt, and Ross, see Edward A. Ross, "The Causes of Race Superiority," *Annals of the American Academy of Political and Social Science* 17 (1901): 85–88; John Higham, *Strangers in the Land: Patterns of American Nativism, 1860–1925* (New York, 1974), 147; Thomas G. Dyer, *Theodore Roosevelt and the Idea of Race* (Baton Rouge, 1980), 14–16, 142–167; Thomas F. Gossett, *Race: The History of an Idea in America* (Oxford, 1997), 168–172; Louise Michele Newman, *White Women's Rights: The Racial Origins of Feminism in the United States* (New York, 1999), 144–145.

7. For recent work on race and the new immigration, see James R. Barrett and David Roediger, "Inbetween Peoples: Race, Nationality, and the 'New Immigrant' Working Class," *Journal of American Ethnic History* 16 (Spring 1997): 3–44; David A. J. Richards, *Italian American: The Racializing of an Ethnic Identity* (New York, 1999). The most fully realized study is Karen Brodkin, *How Jews Became White Folks and What That Says About Race in America* (New Brunswick, N.J., 1994); James Baldwin, "On Being 'White' . . . and Other Lies," *Essence*, April 1984, 90–92. The following are noteworthy efforts to grapple with past and present in this regard: Jonathan W. Warren and F. Winddance Twine, "White Americans: The New Majority? Non-Blacks and the Ever Expanding Boundaries of Whiteness," *Journal of Black Studies*, November 1997, 200–218; and Nancy Foner and George M. Fredrickson, eds., *Not Just Black and White: Historical and Contemporary Perspectives on Immigration, Race, and Ethnicity in the United States* (New York, 2004).

8. Matthew Frye Jacobson, *Whiteness of a Different Color: European Immigrants and the Alchemy of Race* (Cambridge, Mass., 1998), esp. 39–136.

9. Oscar Handlin, *The Uprooted* (Boston, 1951), 3. Compare Jacobson, *Whiteness of a Different Color*, 11; Pedraza, "Origins and Destinies," 7; Herbert Gutman, "Class Composition and the Development of the American Working Class," in Gutman, *Power and Culture: Essays on the American Working Class*, ed. Ira Berlin (New York, 1987), 380–394.

10. Sinclair Lewis, *Babbitt* (1922; New York, 1942), 145.

11. Sinclair Lewis, *Kingsblood Royal* (1947; New York, 2001), 9, 11, and back cover ("resigns from the white race"). Compare Sinclair Lewis, *Cass Timberlaine* (New York, 1945), 44–45, for a Lewis character embracing a new United States inclusive of "Italians and Poles and Icelanders and Finns and Hungarians and Slovaks."

12. Computed from tables 5–6 (unpaginated) in Joel Perlmann, *Toward a Population History of the Second Generation: Birth Cohorts of Southern-, Central-, and Eastern-European Origins, 1871–1970*, Working Paper no. 333 (Jerome Levy Economics Institute of Bard College, June 2001); Lewis, *Kingsblood Royal*, 11.

13. Reynolds Scott-Childress, "Race, Nation, and the Rhetoric of Color: Locating Japan and China, 1870–1907," in Scott-Childress, ed., *Race and the Production of Modern American Nationalism* (New York, 1999), 4. *U.S. v. Bhagat Singh Thind*, 261 U.S. 204 (1923).

14. Scott-Childress, "Race, Nation, and the Rhetoric of Color," 6; Thomas Gossett, *Race: The History of an Idea in America* (Dallas, 1963); Jacobson, *Whiteness of a Different Color*, 39–135.

15. Brodkin, *How Jews Became White Folks*, 60; Baldwin, "On Being 'White' . . . and Other Lies," 90, 92.

16. John Higham, *Strangers in the Land: Patterns of American Nativism, 1860–1925* (New York, 1974), 169; Robert Orsi, "The Religious Boundaries of an In-between People: Street *Feste* and the Problem of the Dark-Skinned 'Other' in Italian Harlem, 1920–1990," *American Quarterly* 44 (September 1992); Patrick Wolfe, "Land, Labor, and Difference: Elementary Structures of Race," *American Historical Review*, June 2001, 893 n. 100; Thomas A. Guglielmo, *White on Arrival: Italians, Race, Color, and Power in Chicago, 1890–1945* (New York, 2003); and Guglielmo, "'No Color Barrier': Italians, Race, and Power in the United States," in Jennifer Guglielmo and Salvatore Salerno, eds., *Are Italians White? How Race Is Made in America* (New York, 2003), 29–43.

17. John Dollard, *Caste and Class in a Southern Town* (Garden City, N.Y., 1949), 93; Barry Goldberg, "Historical Reflections on Transnationalism, Race, and the American Immigrant Saga" (paper delivered at the Rethinking Migration Conference, New York Academy of the Sciences, May 1990).

18. Brodkin, *How Jews Became White Folks*, 60, 103; David Scobey, "Commercial Culture, Urban Modernism, and the Intellectual *Flaneur*," *American Quarterly* 47 (June 1995): 330–342; P. Cancilla Martenelli, "Italian Workers at Theodore Roosevelt Dam: An Intermediate Ethnic Group in a Diverse Work Force," in Paola Alessandra Sensi-Isolani and Anthony Julian Tamburri, eds., *Italian Americans: A Retrospective on the Twentieth Century* (Chicago Heights, Ill., 2001), 127–145; Orsi, "Religious Boundaries," 313–347; and Higham, *Strangers in the Land*, 169, where "inbetween-ness" is used in a discussion of racialization of immigrants in the South.

19. Terence V. Powderly, "A Menacing Irruption," *North American Review* 147 (August 1888): 166; see also Gwendolyn Mink, *Old Labor and New Immigrants in American Political Development* (Ithaca, N.Y., 1986), 109; on Powderly and the Knights, see Craig Phelan, "Terence Powderly," in Melvyn Dubofsky and Warren Van Tine, eds., *Labor Leaders in America* (Urbana Ill., 1987), 30–61; Alexander Saxton, *The Indispensable Enemy: Labor and the Anti-Chinese Movement in California* (1971; Berkeley, 1995), 169, 175, 189–192, 221–234.

20. Henry Cabot Lodge, "The Distribution of Ability in the United States," *Century: A Popular Quarterly*, 42 (September 1891): 689; on Lodge, see Higham, *Strangers in the Land*, 96, 141–142, 323.

21. See notes 4–5 above; William Z. Ripley, *The Races of Europe* (London, 1899); Ripley, "The Three European Races," in Earl Court, ed., *This Is Race: An Anthology Selected from the International Literature on the Races of Men* (New York, 1950), 194–206; Ripley, "Races in the United States," *Atlantic Monthly* 102 (December 1908): 745–759; Jacobson, *Whiteness of a Different Color*, 75–76; Gossett, *Race: The History of an Idea in America*, 37–39; Bruce Baum, *The Rise and Fall of the "Caucasian Race"* (forthcoming).

22. Quoted in Joel Perlmann's superb *"Race or People": Federal Race Classifications for Europeans in America, 1898–1913,* Working Paper no. 230 (Jerome Levy

Economics Institute of Bard College, January 2001), 4–13. See also Marian L. Smith, "Race, Nationality, and Reality: INS Administration of Racial Provisions in U.S. Immigration and Naturalization Law Since 1898, Part 1," www.archives.gov/publications/prologue/summer_2002_immigration_law_1.html.

23. See Perlmann, *"Race or People,"* 5–14; Marion T. Bennett, *American Immigration Policies* (New York, 1963), 78.

24. Perlmann, 6–17, 27–40.

25. Perlmann, 43 (quoting Lodge), 40–48.

26. Higham, *Strangers in the Land*, 142, quotes Lodge.

27. Jacobson, *Whiteness of a Different Color*, 42, quotes Lodge; Perlmann, "Race or People," 19–20.

28. Perlmann, *"Race or People,"* 12–50.

29. Perlmann, *"Race or People,"* 51–57; Higham, *Strangers in the Land*, 126–128; Russell A. Kazal, "Irish 'Race' and German 'Nationality': Catholic Languages of Ethnic Differences in Turn-of-the-Century Philadelphia," in Scott-Childress, ed., *Race and the Production of Modern Nationalism*, 149–168; Matthew Frye Jacobson, *Special Sorrows: The Diasporic Imagination of Irish, Polish, and Jewish Immigrants in the United States* (Cambridge, Mass., 1995), 25, 187.

30. Richard Sennett, "Pure as the Driven Slush," in David R. Colburn and George E. Pozzetta, eds., *America and the New Ethnicity* (Port Washington, N.Y., 1979), 198.

31. The Cornell website consulted in 2002 is http://ed1.library.cornell.edu/moa/moa-search.html; the term "ethnic groups" appears once in an article warning against glib use of the term. See J. H. Wright, "The Indo-European Family: Its Subdivisions," *New Englander and Yale Review*, July 1881, 480; Sir William Craigie and James R. Hulbert, *A Dictionary of American English on Historical Principles* (Chicago, 1940), 2:901.

32. Micaela di Leonardo, "Habits of the Cumbered Heart: Ethnic Community and Women's Culture as American Invented Traditions," in Jay O'Brien and William Roseberry, eds., *Golden Ages, Dark Ages: Imagining the Past in Anthropology and History* (Berkeley, 1991), 237; *Oxford English Dictionary* [*OED*] (Oxford, 1989), 5:424.

33. Ellwood Cubberley, *Changing Conceptions of Education* (New York, 1909), 14–15; Higham, *Strangers in the Land*, 64–67; Chapter 3 in this book.

34. Cubberley, *Changing Conceptions of Education*, 14–15; for a superb recent account of the new/old immigrant distinction, see King, *Making Americans*, 59–64.

35. Husband quoted in Perlmann, *"Race or People,"* 25. See also, for example, U.S. Bureau of the Census, *Fourteenth United States Census* (Washington, D.C., 1922), vol. 2, table 1, 897; Young, *American Minority Peoples*, 421 and title page. For a strong account arguing that the census regarded all whites, including immigrants, as categorically separate from people of color, see Melissa Nobles, *Shades of Citizenship: Race and the Census in Modern Politics* (Stanford, Calif., 2000), esp. 48–72.

36. Carpenter, *Immigrants and Their Children*, 92.

37. *OED*, 5:424; for older *OED* entries, see Werner Sollors, ed., *Theories of Ethnicity: A Classical Reader* (Washington Square, N.Y., 1996), 10, 2–12; *Oxford American Dictionary* (New York, 1980), 219. See also Raymond Williams, *Keywords: A Vocabulary of Culture and Society* (New York, 1985), 119; "The Evolution of Language," *North American Review*, 97 (October 1863): 414; John Fiske, "Who Are the Aryans?" *Atlantic Monthly* 47 (February 1881): 224–234, in which Aryan is an "ethnic name" (226).

38. Henry James, "Spiritualism: New and Old," *Atlantic Monthly* 29 (March 1872): 361; Washington Gladden, "Response of Dr. Gladden," *American Missionary* 49 (December 1895): 392; Gladden, "Congregationalism and the Poor," *American Missionary* 45 (December 1981): 466; Sollors, *Theories of Ethnicity*, 3 ("heresies").

39. James, *The American Scene* (1907; New York, 1987), 93, places it in quotes as an odd usage; Sollors, *Theories of Ethnicity*, x–xi, 2–11; Theodore Roosevelt, "The Roll of Honor of the New York Police," *Century: A Popular Quarterly* 54 (October 1897): 811; *Atlantic Monthly*, editorial, 44 (November 1879): 675; 49; Lodge, "Distribution of Ability," 689; United States Immigration Commission, "Dictionary of Races and Peoples," *Reports of the Immigration Commission* (Washington, D.C., 1911), 5:1–8; Alain LeRoy Locke, *Race Conflicts and Interracial Relations: Lectures on the Theory and Practice of Race*, ed. Jeffrey C. Stewart (Washington, D.C., 1992), esp. 12–14; for a revealing military usage of the title *Ethnic Bulletin*, see Nancy Gentile Ford, *Americans All! Foreign-Born Soldiers in World War I* (College Station, Tex., 2001), 61.

40. On Deniker, see Baum, *Rise and Fall*; Victoria Hattam, "Ethnicity: An American Genealogy," in Foner and Fredrickson, *Not Just Black and White*, 42–61, with the quotes at 49, 50, 51; Horace Kallen, *Culture and Democracy in the United States* (1924; New York, 1998), 218 n. 1; Isaac Berkson, "A Community Theory of American Life," *Menorah Journal* 6 (December 1920): 311–313; Julius Drachsler, *Intermarriage in New York City* (New York, 1921), 14–16, 51 n. 32, 72–76; see also Berkson, *Theories of Americanization: A Critical Study with Special Reference to the Jewish Group* (New York, 1920), 61, 79, 81–82; Hattam, *Shadows of Pluralism: The Racial Politics of American Ethnicity* (forthcoming).

41. Hattam, "Ethnicity," 42–61; Fiske, "Who Are the Aryans?" 224–234; Fiske, "The Laws of History," *North American Review*, July 1869, 217, 226; *Living Age*, December 15, 1900, 704; George P. Murdock, "Ethnocentrism," in Edwin R. A. Seligman, ed., *Encyclopaedia of the Social Sciences* (New York, 1931), 5:614.

42. Nathaniel S. Shaler, "The Negro Problem," *Atlantic Monthly* 54 (November 1884): 708; Lodge, "Distribution of Ability," 689; Lafcadio Hearn, "A Midsummer Trip to the West Indies," *Harper's New Monthly Magazine* 77 (September 1888): 623. See also Francis Parkman, "The Native Races," *North American Review* 120 (January 1875): 37.

43. Albert Ernest Jenks, "The Relation of Anthropology to Americanization," *Scientific Monthly* 12 (March 1921): 242–243 (with thanks to Mark Soderstrom); cf.

Niles Carpenter, *Immigrants and Their Children* (1937; New York, 1969), 94–95, 190; St. Clair Drake and Horace R. Cayton, *Black Metropolis: A Study of Negro Life in a Northern City* (New York, 1945), 8. See also Niles Carpenter, *Nationality, Color, and Economic Opportunity in the City of Buffalo* (1927; Westport, 1970), 97.

44. T. J. Woofter Jr., *Races and Ethnic Groups in American Life* (New York, 1933), 142, 4–6; James B. McKee, *Sociology and the Race Problem: The Failure of a Perspective* (Urbana, Ill., 1993), 131–132; cf. Bessie Bloom Wessel, *An Ethnic Survey of Woonsocket, Rhode Island* (Chicago, 1931), 4, 13, 22, 23–26.

45. Caroline F. Ware, "Ethnic Communities," in *Encyclopaedia of the Social Sciences*, 5:607, 611, 608, 607–613 passim; Ware, "Cultural Groups in the United States," in *The Cultural Approach to History* (New York, 1940), 61–89; on Ware's importance, see Rudolph J. Vecoli, "Ethnicity: A Neglected Dimension of American History," in Herbert J. Bass, ed., *The State of American History* (Chicago, 1970), 79; Donald Young, *American Minority Peoples: A Study in Racial and Cultural Conflicts in the United States* (New York, 1932), 421; Robert Ezra Park, "The Nature of Race Relations," in Edgar T. Thompson, ed., *Race Relations and the Race Problem* (Durham, 1939), 3, 3–45 passim; Irvin L. Child, *Italian or American? The Second Generation in Conflict* (New York, 1943), 38, 88, 139.

46. W. Lloyd Warner and Paul S. Lunt, *The Social Life of a Modern Community* (New Haven, 1941), 212, 220; Warner and Lunt, *The Status System of a Modern Community* (New Haven, 1942), 72–73. Compare John T. Zadrozny, *Dictionary of Social Science* (Washington, D.C., 1959), 111.

47. Gary Gerstle, *Working-Class Americanism: The Politics of Labor in a Textile City, 1914–1960* (Cambridge, 1989), 289–290; Philip Gleason, *Speaking of Diversity: Language and Ethnicity in Twentieth-Century America* (Baltimore, 1992), 153–187; Gerstle, *American Crucible: Race and Nation in the Twentieth Century* (Princeton, 2001), esp. 201–209.

48. Sollors, *Theories of Ethnicity*, x; Jacobson, *Whiteness of a Different Color*, 100–102 (for Benedict and Montagu); John Morton Blum, *V Was for Victory: Politics and American Culture During World War II* (New York, 1976), 220; Jennifer A. Delton, *Making Minnesota Liberal: Civil Rights and the Transformation of the Democratic Party* (Minneapolis, 2002), 52; Michael Denning, *The Cultural Front: The Laboring of American Culture in the Twentieth Century* (London, 1997), 9, 130–132; esp. 448.

49. Sollors, *Theories of Ethnicity*, xxxvii n. 2; David Riesman, "Some Observations on Intellectual Freedom," *American Scholar*, 23 (Winter 1953–1954): 15; Oscar Handlin, *Race and Nationality in American Life* (Boston, 1957); Everett C. Hughes and Helen M. Hughes, *Where People Meet: Racial and Ethnic Frontiers* (Glencoe, Ill., 1952), 7, 137–138; Henry Pratt Fairchild, *Dictionary of Sociology* (New York, 1944), 109; Jacobson, *Whiteness of a Different Color*, 109 (Warner). On anthropology, see Richard Jenkins, *Rethinking Ethnicity: Arguments and Explorations* (London, 1997), 11. See also Andrew Greeley, *Why Can't They Be Like Us? Facts and*

Fallacies About Ethnic Differences and Group Conflicts in America (New York, 1969), 22.

50. Sollors, *Theories of Ethnicity*, xxxvii n. 2 for MacIver; *OED*, 5:424–426; Williams, *Keywords*, 119; William Petersen, "Concepts of Ethnicity," in *HEAEG*, 234–242.

51. *OED*, 5:424; Petersen, "Concepts of Ethnicity," 235–236; Michael Novak, *The Rise of the Unmeltable Ethnics* (New York, 1973), 55.

52. Scott-Childress, "Race, Nation, and the Rhetoric of Color," 5; Philip Gleason, "American Identity and Americanization," in *HEAEG*, 46; see also Gossett, *Race*, 442–444. See also Wernor Sollors, *Beyond Ethnicity: Consent and Descent in American Culture* (New York, 1986), 38–39; Mary C. Waters, *Ethnic Options: Choosing Identities in America* (Berkeley, 1990), 1–9, for similar examples of scholars conversant with the history of ethnicity as a concept nonetheless retrofitting it to apply to earlier periods.

53. Thomas A. Guglielmo, "White on Arrival: Italians, Race, Color, and Power in Chicago, 1890–1945" (Ph.D. diss., University of Michigan, 2000), 9–10.

54. Carrie Tirado Bramen, *The Uses of Variety: Modern Americanism and the Quest for National Distinctiveness* (Cambridge, Mass., 2000), 162–163. On Ross and Fairchild, see Gleason, *Speaking of Diversity*, 14, 33, 51–53; Steven Selden, *Inheriting Shame: The Story of Eugenics and Racism in America* (New York, 1999), 27, 40, 43; Higham, *Strangers in the Land*, 109–110, 117, 147, 273, 327; Gossett, *Race*, 168–172, 384–387, 428–429.

55. Stow Persons, *Ethnic Studies at Chicago, 1905–45* (Urbana, Ill., 1987), 60 n. 1 and passim; Jacobson, *Whiteness of a Different Color*, 6. Compare Jacobson, *Special Sorrows*, 19, 185. Park did use "ethnic group" in print, however. See also Robert Ezra Park, *Race and Culture* (Glencoe, Ill., 1950), 20, 92. For for a vigorous critique of such substitutions, Davarian L. Baldwin, "Black Belts and Ivory Towers: The Place of Race in U.S. Social Thought, 1892–1948," *Critical Sociology* 30 (2004): 404.

56. Denning, *Cultural Front*, 448–449 (for Adamic); Gunnar Myrdal with Richard Sterner and Arnold Rose, *An American Dilemma: The Negro Problem and Modern Democracy* (1944; New York, 1962), 927–928; David Gerber, review of *Whiteness of a Different Color*, *Reviews in American History*, September 1999, 442. See also Sollors, *Theories of Ethnicity*, xii; and Desmond King, *Making Americans: Immigration, Race, and the Origins of the Diverse Democracy* (Cambridge, Mass., 2000), 34.

57. Milton Gordon, *Assimilation in American Life: The Role of Race, Religion, and National Origins* (New York, 1964), 24, 26–29.

58. Russell A. Kazal, "Revisiting Assimilation: The Rise, Fall, and Reappraisal of a Concept in American Ethnic History," *American Historical Review* 100 (April 1995): 439; Greeley, *Why Can't They Be Like Us?* 39; Novak, *Unmeltable Ethnics*, 16, 85; Gleason, "American Identity and Americanization," 55. Compare Herbert Gans, *The Urban Villagers: Group and Class in the Life of Italian Americans* (New York, 1962), 32–33.

59. Sylvia R. Lazos Vargas, "Deconstructing Homo[geneous] Americanus: The White Ethnic Immigrant Narrative and Its Exclusionary Effect," *Tulane Law Review* 72 (May 1998): esp. 1529, 1533.

60. Nathan Glazer, "Ethnicity and the Schools," reprinted in *America and the New Ethnicity*, 206; Alexander Saxton, review of Nathan Glazer, *Affirmative Discrimination, Amerasia Journal* 4 (1977): 141–150; Nathan Glazer and Daniel Patrick Moynihan, *Beyond the Melting Pot: The Negroes, Puerto Ricans, Jews, Italians, and Irish of New York City* (Cambridge, Mass., 1963). For the political context, see David Colburn and George Pozzetta, "Race, Ethnicity, and the Evolution of Political Legitimacy," in David Farber, ed., *The Sixties: From Memory to History* (Chapel Hill, N.C., 1994), 119–148.

61. Ben Wattenberg, "Celebrate America's Ethnic Stew," *News-Gazette* (Champaign, Ill.), March 18, 2001.

62. Michael Omi and Howard Winant, *Racial Formation in the United States* (New York, 1986), 15–17; Blauner, as cited in Rodolfo Torres and Robert Miles, "Does 'Race' Matter? Transatlantic Perspectives on Racism after 'Race Relations,'" in Rodolfo D. Torres, Louis F. Mirón, and Jonathan X. Inda, eds., *Race, Identity, and Citizenship: A Reader* (Malden, Mass., 2000), 28; Ronald Takaki, *A Different Mirror: A History of Multicultural America* (Boston, 1993), 9–10.

63. Saxton, review of Glazer, 146.

64. Mink, *Old Labor and New Immigrants*, 46 n. 1; Jacobson, *Whiteness of a Different Color*, esp. 7.

65. Micaela di Leonardo, *The Varieties of Ethnic Experience: Kinship, Class, and Gender Among California Italian Americans* (Ithaca, N.Y., 1984), 24 n. 16.

66. Mary C. Waters, *Ethnic Options: Choosing Identities in America* (Berkeley, 1990), 157.

67. Powderly as quoted in Perlmann, *"Race or People,"* 6; for Ripley and Cohen, see Louis Wirth, *The Ghetto* (1928; Chicago, 1958), 66–67. Cohen's work appeared in 1914 and Ripley's in 1899.

68. David Hollinger, *Postethnic America: Beyond Multiculturalism* (New York, 1995). Cf. Nikhil Pal Singh, *Black Is a Country: Race and the Unfinished Struggle for Democracy* (Cambridge, Mass., 2004).

69. Toni Morrison, "On the Backs of Blacks," *Time*, Fall 1993, special issue, 57.

CHAPTER 2

1. Compare Eric Arnesen, "Whiteness and the Historians' Imagination," *International Labor and Working Class History*, 60 (Fall 2001): 17–18; Matthew Frye Jacobson, *Whiteness of a Different Color: European Immigrants and the Alchemy of Race* (Cambridge, Mass., 1998).

2. Here and below, see *Oxford English Dictionary (OED)*, 1986 ed., 6:937–38; Frederick G. Cassidy and Joan Houston Hall, eds., *Dictionary of American Regional*

English (*DARE*) (Cambridge, Mass., 1991), 2:838; Harold Wentworth and Stuart Berg Flexner, eds., *Dictionary of American Slang* (New York, 1975), 234. See also Sarah Deutsch, "The Elusive Guineamen: Newport Slavers, 1735–1774," *New England Quarterly* 55 (1982); on the imprecision of nineteenth-century usage, see Michael A. Gomez, *Exchanging Our Country Marks: The Transformation of African Identities in the Colonial and Antebellum South* (Chapel Hill, 1998), 103. On Boston, see Stephen Grant Meyer, *As Long As They Don't Move Next Door: Segregation and Racial Conflict in American Neighborhoods* (Lanham, Md., 2000), 14.

3. Carolyn Karcher, *Shadow over the Promised Land* (Baton Rouge, 1980), esp. 256–257; Herman Melville, *The Confidence Man: His Masquerade*, ed. H. Bruce Franklin (1857; Indianapolis, 1967), 15–26; Michael O'Malley, "Specie and Species: Race and the Money Question in Nineteenth-Century America," *American Historical Review* 99 (April 1994): 369–395, esp. 386.

4. Frances E.W. Harper, *Trial and Triumph*, reprinted in Frances Smith Foster, ed., *Minnie's Sacrifice: Sowing and Reaping, Trial and Triumph* (1888–1889; Boston, 1994), 215–221; Tiya Miles, "Only a Negro Turned Wrong Side Out: Blackness and Whiteness in Frances Harper's *Trial and Triumph*" (seminar paper, University of Minnesota, 1996), searchingly raises these issues; see also Robert L. Chapman, ed., *New Dictionary of American Slang* (New York, 1986), 160.

5. William S. Pollitizer, "The Physical Anthropology and Genetics of Marginal People in the Southeastern United States," *American Anthropologist* 74 (June 1972): 722; William Harlen Gilbert Jr., "Memorandum Concerning the Characteristics of the Larger Mixed-Blood Racial Islands of the United States," *Social Forces* 24 (March 1946): 442 passim; Gilbert, "Mixed Bloods of the Upper Monogahela Valley, West Virginia," *Journal of the Washington Academy of Sciences* 36 (January 1946): 1–13; J. K. Dane and B. Eugene Griessman, "The Collective Identity of Marginal Peoples: The North Carolina Experience," *American Anthropologist* 74 (June 1972): 702.

6. Gilbert, memorandum, 442; Higham, *Strangers in the Land: Patterns of American Nativism, 1860–1925* (New York, 1963), 173; David R. Roediger, *The Wages of Whiteness: Race and the Making of the United States Working Class* (London, 1991), 144–145, 180; Robert F. Foerster, *The Italian Emigration of Our Times* (Cambridge, Mass., 1924), 407–408; Charles B. Barnes, *The Longshoremen* (New York, 1915), 8.

7. See the Peter Tamony Papers at Western Historical Manuscripts Collections, University of Missouri–Columbia, notes on "guinea," which include clippings from Fox. On World War II, see Robert L. Chapman, ed., *New Dictionary of American Slang* (New York, 1986), 185. See also O'Neill, *The Hairy Ape, Anna Christie, The First Man* (New York, 1922), 75, for "black guinea." See Richard Gambino, *Blood of My Blood* (1973; Toronto, 1996), 107; and Mario Puzo, *The Fortunate Pilgrim* (Greenwich, Conn., 1964), 52.

8. William Attaway, *Blood on the Forge* (1941; New York, 1987), 122–123; Jeff Kisseloff, ed., *You Must Remember This: An Oral History of Manhattan from the 1890s to World War II* (San Diego, 1989), 345.

9. The poem is reproduced in its entirety in Michael La Sorte, *La Merica: Images of Italian Greenhorn Experience* (Philadelphia, 1985), 95; Irvin L. Child, *Italian or American? The Second Generation in Conflict* (New Haven, 1943), 81, 154–158.

10. Chapman, *Dictionary of American Slang*, 185; Shulman (1948) in Tamony Papers; Piri Thomas, *Down These Mean Streets* (New York, 1967), 39; on Italian Americans and Puerto Ricans, see Robert Orsi, "The Religious Boundaries of an Inbetween People: Street *Feste* and the Problem of the Dark-Skinned 'Other' in Italian Harlem, 1920–1990," *American Quarterly* 44 (September 1992): 313–347.

11. Donald Tricarico, "Guido: Fashioning an Italian-American Youth Style," *Journal of Ethnic Studies* 19 (Spring 1991): esp. 56–57. On place-names, Tamony provides notes on Harry Reasoner's November 10, 1967, broadcast comments on the controversy over changing the name of Guinea Wood Road.

12. On the origins of "greaser" and its application to Mexican Americans, see *OED*, 6:794; Chapman, *American Slang*, 181; R. H. Thornton, ed., *An American Glossary* (London, 1912); Arnoldo DeLeon, *They Called Them Greasers* (Austin, 1982), 14–23; Lewis Garrard, *Wah-to-yah, or The Taos Trail* (Cincinnati, 1850), as clipped in the Tamony Papers. The Joyce and Zola citations are handily accessible at www.concordance.com. See also the Tamony Papers on "greaser" and "greaseball" generally and Duncan Emrich, *It's an Old Wild West Custom* (Kingswood, U.K., 1913), 133–141; Tomás Almaguer, *Racial Fault Lines: The Historical Origins of White Supremacy in California* (Berkeley, 1994), 55–57; Rosaura Sanchez, *Telling Identities: The Californio Testamonios* (Minneapolis, 1995), 1285; John S. Drager, *Shams or Uncle Ben's Experience with Hypocrites* (Chicago, 1899), as clipped in the Tamony Papers; Carlos E. Cortés, "Mexicans," in Stephan Thernstrom, ed., *Harvard Encyclopedia of American Ethnic Groups* (Cambridge, Mass., 1980), 705; Américo Paredes, "The Problem of Identity in a Changing Culture," in Stanley R. Ross, ed., *Views Across the Border: The United States and Mexico* (Albuquerque, 1978), 69; and "On *Gringo, Greaser,* and Other Neighborly Names," in Mody C. Boatright, ed., *Singers and Storytellers* (Dallas, 1961), 285–290; William R. Lighton, "The Greaser," *Atlantic Monthly* 83 (June 1899): 750, 752, 753; J. W. DeForest, "Overland," *Galaxy,* 10 (September 1870): 307; Bret Harte, "Gabriel Conroy," *Scribner's Monthly* 11 (March 1876): 670; Harte as clipped by Tamony from a glossary of Harte terms, *Trent's Trust and Other Stories* (Boston, 1896), 271; Mark Twain, "Memoranda," *Galaxy* 10 (November 1870): 728.

13. Lighton, "Greaser," 760; and Jacob Riis, "The Tenement House Blight," *Atlantic Monthly* 83 (June 1899): 760. For Ross, see Riv-Ellen Prell, *Fighting to Become Americans: Jews, Gender, and the Anxiety of Assimilation* (Boston, 1999), 27. See the dictionary entries above plus *DARE*, 4:789–790; John Fante, *Ask the Dust* (1939; Santa Barbara, Calif., 1980), 44–47; William Foote Whyte, *Street Corner Society: The Social Structure of an Italian Slum* (Chicago, 1955), 140. Tamony's notes on greaseball, greaser, and grease monkey; on "greasy Wops," see Caroline F. Ware, *Greenwich Village, 1920–1930: A Comment on American Civilization in the Postwar*

Years (1963; Berkeley, 1994), 131; on London, see Micaela di Leonardo's introduction to the reprint of *The People of the Abyss* (1903; Chicago, 1995), xv; John Bodnar, Roger Simon, and Michael P. Weber, *Lives of Their Own: Blacks, Italians, and Poles in Pittsburgh, 1900–1960* (Urbana, Ill., 1992), 70; on "greaser," "guinea," and "hunky" as fighting words, see C. Barnhart, "Problems in Editing Commercial Monolingual Dictionaries," in F. W. Household and Sol Saporta, eds., *Problems in Lexicography* (Bloomington, Ind., 1962), 179; and "Tamony to R. W. Burchfield" (c. 1971) in Tamony Papers under "greaser"; Maria Laurino, "Scents: A Selection from a Memoir of Italian American Life," in A. Kenneth Ciongoli and Jay Parini, eds., *Beyond the Godfather: Italian American Writers on the Italian American Experience* (Hanover, N.H., 1997), 102; Stephen A. Buff, "Greasers, Dupers, and Hippies: Three Responses to the Adult World," in Louise Kapp Howe, ed., *The White Majority: Between Poverty and Affluence* (New York, 1970), 60–77, esp. 62–63; Herbert G. Ellis and Stanley M. Newman, "The 'Greaser' Is a 'Bad Ass'; The 'Gowster' Is a 'Muthah': An Analysis of Two Urban Youth Roles," in Thomas Kochman, ed., *Rappin' and Stylin' Out: Communication in Urban Black America* (Urbana, 1972), 370.

14. The Tamony Papers contain extensive notes on "hunky," including the clippings from *Criminal Slang* and *American Speech*; Josephine Wtulich, *American Xenophobia and the Slav Immigrant: A Living Legacy of Mind and Spirit* (New York, 1994), 14–16. The planter is quoted in Gunther Peck, *Reinventing Free Labor: Padrones and Immigrant Workers in the North American West, 1880–1930* (Cambridge, U.K., 2000), 168.

15. By no means did "hun" refer unambiguously to Germans before World War I. See, e.g., Henry White, "Immigration Restriction as a Necessity," *American Federationist* 4 (June 1897): 67; Anne Classen Knutson, "The Enemy Imaged: Visual Configurations of Race and Ethnicity in World War I Propaganda Posters," in Reynolds Scott-Childress, ed., *Race and the Production of Modern American Nationalism* (New York, 1999), 202–208; esp. 216 n. 33; Richard Schneirov, *Labor and Urban Politics: Class Conflict and the Origins of Modern Liberalism in Chicago, 1864–97* (Urbana, Ill., 1998), 300. For more on the expansive usages of "hun" and "hunky," see the Tamony Papers and Paul Krause, *The Battle for Homestead, 1880–1892: Politics, Culture, and Steel* (Pittsburgh, 1992), 216–217; Higham, *Strangers in the Land*, 51; U.S. Immigration Commission, *Dictionary of Races or Peoples*, 92, 128. See also Wtulich, *American Xenophobia*, 15–16; Nelson Algren, *Somebody in Boots* (New York, 1935), 129–130, with thanks to Todd Michney for the reference; John Bodnar, *Workers World: Kinship, Community, and Protest in an Industrial Society, 1900–1940* (Baltimore, 1982), 139 (on "hunky union"); for Sinclair, see *Plays of Protest: The Naturewoman, The Machine, The Second-Story Man, Prince Hagen* (New York, 1912), 145; Alois Koukol, "A Slav's a Man for All That," in Paul Underwood Kellogg, ed., *Wage-Earning Pittsburgh* (1914; New York, 1974), 73–76; John O'Hara, *Appointment at Samarra* (New York, 1945), 66; Herman Feldman, *Racial Factors in American Industry* (New York, 1931), 148, records the foreman's remark.

Margaret F. Byington, *Homestead: Households of a Mill Town* (1910; Pittsburgh, 1974), 132; Niles Carpenter, *Nationality, Color, and Economic Opportunity in the City of Buffalo* (1927; Westport, Conn., 1970), 105. On immigrants and industrial accidents, see William Leiserson, *Adjusting Immigrant and Industry* (New York, 1924), 134; Herbert Gutman, *Work, Culture, and Society in Industrializing America: Essays in American Working-Class and Social History* (New York, 1977), 30; for cautions on the data, see Isaac Hourwich, *Immigration and Labor* (New York, 1912), 458–488.

16. Josef Barton, *Peasants and Strangers: Italians, Rumanians, and Slovaks in an American City, 1890–1950* (Cambridge, Mass., 1975), 20, on pan-hunky identity in Cleveland; Loren Baritz, *The Good Life: The Meaning of Success for the American Middle Class* (New York, 1982); Thomas Bell, *Out of This Furnace* (1941; Pittsburgh, 1976), 124–125, 327–130.

17. Upton Sinclair, *Singing Jailbirds* (Pasadena, 1924), 10; Oswaldo M.S. Truzzi, "The Right Place at the Right Time: Syrians and Lebanese in Brazil and the United States, A Comparative Approach," *Journal of American Ethnic History* 16 (Winter 1997): 20. Albert S. Broussard, "George Albert Flippin and Race Relations in a Western Rural Community," *Midwest Review* 12 (1990): 15 n. 42; J. Alexander Karlin, "The Italo-American Incident of 1891 and the Road to Reunion," *Journal of Southern History* 8 (1942); Edward Haas, "Guns, Goats, and Italians: The Tallulah Lynching of 1899," *North Louisiana Historical Association* 13 (1982): 50; Gunther Peck, "Padrones and Protest: 'Old' Radicals and 'New' Immigrants in Bingham, Utah, 1905–1912," *Western Historical Quarterly*, May 1993, 177; Elizabeth Jameson, *All That Glitters: Class, Conflict, and Community in Cripple Creek* (Urbana, Ill., 1998), 140–160; Richard Gambino, *Vendetta: The True Story of the Worst Lynching in America* (New York, 1977); Georgakas, *Greek Americans at Work* (New York, 1992), 12, 16–17. Philip Mellinger, *Race and Labor in Western Copper: The Fight for Equality, 1896–1916* (Tucson, 1995), 8–16, notes residential segregation among non-Anglo groups, however. Ruth Shonle Cavan and Katherine Howland Ranck, *The Family and the Depression: A Study of One Hundred Chicago Families* (Chicago, 1938), 38–39; Henry Pratt Fairchild, *Greek Immigration to the United States* (New Haven, 1911), 15, 22; for Rowell, see Frank Van Nuys, *Americanizing the West: Race, Immigrants, and Citizenship, 1890–1930* (Lawrence, 2002), 34; Isaiah McCaffery, "An Esteemed Minority? Greek Americans and Interethnic Relations in the Plains Region" (paper, University of Kansas, 1993); Helen Papnikolas, *A Greek Odyssey in the American West* (Lincoln, 1997); see also Donna Misner Collins, *Ethnic Identification: The Greek Americans of Houston, Texas* (New York, 1991), 201–211. Clarence Major, ed., *From Juba to Jive: A Dictionary of African-American Slang* (New York, 1994), 213; Ware, *Greenwich Village*, 141. On Salt Lake City, see Gunther Peck, *Reinventing Free Labor: Padrones and Immigrant Workers in the North American West, 1880–1930* (Cambridge, U.K., 2000), 167, 166–169. See also Paul S. Taylor, *Mexican Labor in the United States* (1930; New York, 1970), 1:355–356.

18. Donna Gabaccia, "The 'Yellow Peril' and the 'Chinese of Europe': Global Perspectives on Race and Labor, 1815–1930," in Jan and Leo Lucassen, eds., *Migrations, Migration History: Old Paradigms and New Perspectives* (New York, 1997); for Chicago, see Marco d'Eramo, *The Pig and the Skyscraper: Chicago, A History of Our Future*, trans. Graeme Thomson (London, 2002), 159; La Sorte, *La Merica*, 139 (Detroit quotation) and 143; Clemente in Dominic Candeloro, ed., *Voices of America: Italians in Chicago* (Chicago, 2001), 109; for London, see Alexander Saxton, *The Indispensable Enemy: Labor and the Anti-Chinese Movement in California* (1971; Berkeley, 1995), 281; Irvine, as quoted in Kathryn J. Oberdeck, "Popular Narrative and Working-Class Identity: Alexander Irving's Early Twentieth-Century Literary Adventures," in *Labor Histories: Class Politics and the Working Class Experience*, ed. Eric Arnesen, Julie Greene, and Bruce Laurie (Urbana, Ill., 1998), 215. George E. Cunningham, "The Italian: A Hindrance to White Solidarity in Louisiana, 1890–1898," *Journal of Negro History* 50 (January 1965): 34, includes the quotes on 1898. On "dago," see Thomas A. Guglielmo, "White on Arrival: Italians, Race, Color, and Power in Chicago, 1890–1945" (Ph.D. diss., University of Michigan, 2000), 3; on New Orleans, see Michael Mizell-Nelson, "Challenging and Reinforcing White Control of Public Space: Race Relations on New Orleans Streetcars, 1861–1965" (Ph.D. diss., Tulane University, 2001); on Ponchatoula, see Vincenza Scarpaci, "Walking the Color Line: Italian Immigrants in Rural Louisiana, 1880–1910," in Jennifer Guglielmo and Salvatore Salerno, eds., *Are Italians White? How Race Is Made in America* (New York, 2003), 73.

19. Higham, *Strangers in the Land*, 66; Rudolph Vecoli, "Are Italian Americans Just White Folks?" *Italian Americana*, Summer 1995, 156. For the 1926 survey, see Gunnar Myrdal, *An American Dilemma: The Negro Problem and Modern Democracy* (New York, 1944), 393; Panunzio as quoted in Steven J. Belluscio, "Self-Mutilation or Self-Empowerment: Passing in the Modern African/American and Italian/American Novels," in Dan Ashyk, Fred L. Gardaphe, and Anthony Julian Taburri, eds., *Shades of Black and White: Conflict and Collaboration Between Two Communities* (Staten Island, 1999), 318; and Constantine M. Panunzio, *The Soul of an Immigrant* (New York, 1921), 81–82. For the 1926 survey, see Gunnar Myrdal, *An American Dilemma: The Negro Problem and Modern Democracy* (New York, 1944), 393; Arnold Shankman, *Ambivalent Friends: Afro-Americans View the Immigrant* (Westport, Conn., 1982), 100; Guglielmo, "White on Arrival," 56; Gary W. McDonogh, ed., *The Florida Negro: A Federal Writers' Project Legacy* (Jackson, Miss., 1993), xii; Zondra Hughes, "What Happened to the Only Black Family on the *Titanic*?" *Ebony* 55 (June 2000): 154; Leonard Dinnerstein and David M. Reimers, *Ethnic Americans* (New York, 1988), 85; Virginia Yans-McLaughlin, *Family and Community: Italian Immigrants in Buffalo, 1880–1930* (1971; Urbana, Ill., 1982), 116; Paola Sensi-Isolani, "Company Policies and Ethnic Relations: Italian and African American Workers in California's Lumber Industry" (paper, c. 2000) on Siskiyou County; William Dean Howells, *An Imperative Duty* (New York, 1893), 149; Arnold Shankman, *Ambivalent*

Friends: Afro-Americans View the Immigrant (Westport, 1982), 87; La Sorte, *La Merica*, 90 (on "wops"). On the Alabama case, see Jacobson, *Whiteness of a Different Color*, 4. For Roosevelt, see J. Anthony Lukas, *Big Trouble: A Murder in a Small Western Town Sets Off a Struggle for the Soul of America* (New York, 1997), 395; Bunche, *World View of Race*, 69, 73.

20. Jim Seymour, "They're Only a Couple of God-damn Dagoes," *Industrial Pioneer*, December 1921, 21; Eugene Lyons, *The Life and Death of Sacco and Vanzetti* (1927; New York, 1970), 25–26. Thanks to Rebecca Hill for these references.

21. On the eyewitness testimony, race, and color, see John Dos Passos, *Facing the Chair: Sacco and Vanzetti* (1927; New York, n.d.), 86–87, 99; Elizabeth Gurley Flynn, *The Rebel Girl: An Autobiography, My First Life (1906–1926)* (1955; New York, 1973), 302. On Lawrence, see Michael Miller Topp, "'It Is Providential that There Are Foreigners Here': Whiteness and Masculinity in the Making of Italian American Syndicalist Identity," in Jennifer Guglielmo and Salvatore Salerno, eds., *Are Italians White?* (New York, 2003), 105.

22. Brody, *Steelworkers*, 120; Davis, as quoted in Herbert G. Gutman, "The Negro and the United Mine Workers of America: The Career and Letters of Richard L. Davis and Something of Their Meaning, 1890–1900," in Julius Jacobson, ed., *The Negro and the American Labor Movement* (Garden City, N.Y., 1968), 78, 75 n.; Isaac B. Berkson, *Theories of Americanization: A Critical Study with Special Reference to the Jewish Group* (New York, 1920), 56; W. Lloyd Warner and J. O. Low, *The Social System of the Modern Factory: The Strike* (New Haven, 1947), 140; Gershon Legman, *The Horn Book* (New York, 1964), 486–487; *Anecdota Americana: Five Hundred Stories for the Amusement of Five Hundred Nations That Comprise America* (New York, 1933), 98; Nathan Hurvitz, "Blacks and Jews in American Folklore," *Western Folklore*, October 1974, 304–307; John Fitch, *The Steel Workers* (New York, 1911), 147; on Butte, see David, *The Butte Irish: Class and Ethnicity in an American Mining Town, 1875–1925* (Urbana, Ill., 1989), 258, 286 n. 7; F. James Davis, *Who Is Black? One Nation's Definition* (University Park, Pa., 1991), 161; George Eaton Simpson and J. Milton Yinger, *Racial and Cultural Minorities* (New York, 1958), 113–114. On Bayonne, see John Bukowczyk, "The Transformation of Working-Class Ethnicity: Corporate Control, Americanization, and the Polish Immigrant Middle Class in Bayonne, New Jersey, 1915–1925," in Robert Asher and Charles Stephenson, eds., *Labor Divided: Race and Ethnicity in United States Labor Struggles, 1835–1960* (Albany, 1990), 291; and Bukowczyk, "Migration and Capitalism," *International Labor and Working Class History*, Fall 1989, 72; for Ford, see *The International Jew*, vol. 3, *Jewish Influences in American Life* (Dearborn, Mich., 1921), 8, 66. The best recent account of Jews and race in the South is Leonard Rogoff, "Is the Jew White? The Racial Place of the Southern Jew," *American Jewish History* 85 (September 1997): 195–230. On Jews being seen as "black Orientals," see Sander L. Gilman, *Making the Body Beautiful: A Cultural History of Aesthetic Surgery* (Princeton, 1999), 89–90; on the Iron Range, see Jennifer A. Delton, *Making Minnesota Lib-*

eral: Civil Rights and the Transformation of the Democratic Party (Minneapolis, 2002), 47; Daniel Trees, *How Columbus and I Discovered America: The Life and Adventures of an Immigrant* (Ann Arbor, 1965), 13, 22, 26, 64–66, 102; Emory S. Borgardus, "Comparing Racial Distance in Ethiopia, South Africa, and the United States," *Sociology and Social Research* 52 (January 1968): 149–156; Bogardus, *Immigration and Race Attitudes* (Boston, 1928), 23–25.

23. Jacobson, *Whiteness of a Different Color*, 90; for the 1911 report, 69.

24. On Blumenbach and his influence, see Gossett, *Race*, 37–39; *U.S. v. Bhagat Singh Thind*, 261 U.S. 204 (1923). On whiteness and naturalization, see Ian F. Haney-Lopez, *White by Law: The Legal Construction of Race* (New York, 1996).

25. Richards, *Italian American*, 72–73; James West Davidson, Mark H. Lytle, Christine Leigh Heyrman, William E. Gienapp, and Michael B. Stoff, *Nation of Nations: A Narrative History of the American Republic* (Boston, 1998), 2:638; A. William Hoglund, *Finnish Immigrants in America, 1908–1920* (Madison, 1960), 112–114; Nancy Faires Conklin and Nora Faires, "'Colored' and Catholic: The Lebanese in Birmingham, Alabama," in Eric J. Hooglund, ed., *Crossing the Waters: Arabic-Speaking Immigrants to the United States Before 1940* (Washington, D.C., 1987), 75–76, for the southern quotations; Fairchild, as quoted in Stanley Fish, "Bad Company," *Transition* 56 (n.d.): 61. Allan Bérubé, "Intellectual Desire," *GLQ: A Journal of Lesbian and Gay Studies* 3 (1999): 143; Sarah Gualtieri, "Becoming 'White': Race, Religion, and the Foundations of Syrian/Lebanese Ethnicity in the United States," *Journal of American Ethnic History* 26 (Summer 2001): 29–58; Alixa Naff, *Becoming American: The Early Arab Immigrant Experience* (Carbondale, Ill., 1985), 255–259; Warne, *Immigrant Invasion*, 138–139; Niles Carpenter, *Immigrants and Their Children* (1927; New York, 1969), 62; Rogoff, "Is the Jew White?" 207–210; Lawrence Glickman, "Inventing the 'American Standard of Living': Gender, Race, and Working-Class Identity, 1880–1925," *Labor History* 34 (Spring-Summer 1993): 232–233; Matthew Frye Jacobson, *Barbarian Virtues: The United States Encounters Foreign Peoples at Home and Abroad, 1876–1917* (New York, 2000), 81; Emmons, *Butte Irish*, 256; on the looks of Russians, see Alexis Sokoloff, "Mediaeval Russia in the Pittsburgh District," in Kellogg, *Wage-Earning Pittsburgh*, 81–82; J. Walter Thompson Company, "Facts About the Foreign Population in America," *Newsletter*, July 10, 1924, in Thompson Collection at Duke University Library (thanks to Maurice Manring for this citation). Erika Lee, *At America's Gates: Chinese Immigration during the Exclusion Era* (Chapel Hill, 2003), 31, 35, 36; cf. Eric Goldstein, "The Unstable Other: Locating the Jew in Progressive-Era American Discourse," *American Jewish History* 89 (December 2001): 384; for the medical dimensions, see Alan M. Kraut, *Silent Travelers: Germs, Genes, and the Immigrant Menace* (New York, 1994).

26. The reaction to the lynching is as quoted in Jerre Mangione and Ben Morreale, *La Storia: Five Centuries of the Italian American Experience* (New York: HarperCollins, 1992), 205–206; Richard Weiss, "Racism in the Era of Industrialization," in

Gary Nash and Richard Weiss, eds., *The Great Fear: Race in the Mind of America* (New York, 1970), 134–135.

27. Dyer, *Roosevelt and Race*, 20–61, 28, 144 for "English-speaking race"; Fitch, *Steel Workers*, 147; Chapter 3 in this book.

28. Warne, *Immigrant Invasion*, 58–60; Hourwich, *Immigration and Labor*, 78; Peter Roberts, *English for Coming Americans* (New York, 1918), 99–100; Jacob Riis, *How the Other Half Lives* (1901; New York, 1971), 49–59; Dyer, *Roosevelt and Race*, 144.

29. Wtulich, *American Xenophobia*, 15–18; Conklin and Faires, "'Colored' and Catholic," 78; Trees, *Columbus and I*, 64–65, 113–114.

30. Warne, *Immigrant Invasion*, 253; John R. Commons, *Races and Immigrants in the United States* (New York, 1907), 10–11; Oscar Handlin, *The Uprooted: The Epic Story of the Great Migration That Made the American People* (1951; Boston, 1973), 8 (on Italy and Greece); Bruce Stave and John F. Sutherland with Aldo Salerno, *From the Old Country: An Oral History of European Migration to America* (New York, 1994), 206–212; Higham, *Strangers in the Land*, 109, quoting Ross; for Ross on heredity and environment, see Julius Weinberg, *Edward Alsworth Ross and the Sociology of Progressivism* (Madison, Wis., 1972), 156–157.

31. Jacobson, *Barbarian Virtues*, 82, 162, 186; Higham, *Strangers in the Land*, 309; the Statue of Liberty's inscription is Emma Lazurus, "The New Colossus" (1883); Eugene E. Leach, "The Literature of Riot Duty: Managing Class Conflict in the Streets, 1877–1927," *Radical History Review* 56 (1993): 34; Edward Alsworth Ross, *The Old World in the New* (New York, 1914), 291; Riis, *Other Half Lives*, photos, unpaginated.

CHAPTER 3

1. Horace M. Kallen, *Culture and Democracy in the United States* (New York, 1924), 129; Niles Carpenter, *Nationality, Color, and Economic Opportunity in the City of Buffalo* (1927; Westport, Conn., 1970), 105; Gads Hill Center, *May Report* (1915) and concert leaflet, as provided by Professor Steven Rosswurm (Lake Forest College).

2. Joseph Loguidice, interview by Joe Sauris, July 25, 1980, Italians in Chicago Project, Box 6, Immigration History Research Center, University of Minnesota; for a similar case in New Orleans, see William Ivy Hair, *Carnival of Fury: Robert Charles and the New Orleans Race Riot of 1900* (Baton Rouge, 1976), 152.

3. Henry James, *The American Scene* (1907; New York, 1987), 61–62; Henry Pratt Fairchild, *Greek Immigration to the United States* (New Haven, 1911), 236–237; Jacob Riis, *How the Other Half Lives* (1901; New York, 1971) and below.

4. *U.S. v. Bhagat Singh Thind*, 261 U.S. 204 (1923); *Thind* and related cases are expertly treated in Ian Haney-Lopez, *White by Law: The Legal Construction of Race* (New York, 1996), 37–110. For the survey data, see Emory S. Borgardus, *Immigra-*

tion and Race Attitudes (Boston, 1928), 23–25. For Toomer, see "Race Problems and Modern Society," in Werner Sollors, ed., *Theories of Ethnicity: A Classical Reader* (New York, 1996), 173.

5. See Chapter 2 above.

6. Joan Jensen, *Passage from India: Asian Indian Immigrants in North America* (New Haven, 1988), 258, 283.

7. Ralph Bunche, *A World View of Race* (Washington, D.C., 1936), 69.

8. Thomas G. Dyer, *Theodore Roosevelt and the Idea of Race* (Baton Rouge, 1980), 131, 143–144; Miriam King and Steven Ruggles, "American Immigration, Fertility and Race Suicide at the Turn of the Century," *Journal of Interdisciplinary History* 20 (Winter 1990): 347–369. On "stock," see M. G. Smith's wonderful "Ethnicity and Ethnic Groups in America: The View from Harvard," *Ethnic and Racial Studies* 5 (January 1982): 17–18.

9. Rogers M. Smith, *Civic Ideals: Conflicting Visions of Citizenship in U.S. History* (New Haven, 1997), 30–31. Buff, in a draft chapter to her dissertation, "Foundational Fictions and Racial Ideologies: Immigration and Indian Policies in the 1950s and '60s" (University of Minnesota, 1994). On race and naturalization law, see also D. O. McGovney, "Race Discrimination in Naturalization, Parts I–III," *Iowa Law Bulletin* 8 (March 1923); and McGoveney, "Race Discrimination in Naturalization, Part IV," *Iowa Law Bulletin* 8 (May 1923): 211–244; Charles Gordon, "The Race Barrier to American Citizenship," *University of Pennsylvania Law Review* 93 (March 1945): 237–258; Stanford Lyman, "The Race Question and Liberalism," *International Journal of Politics, Culture, and Society* 5 (Winter 1991): 203–225.

10. *In re Dow*, C.C.A., 222 Fed. 145 (4th Cir. 1915); *Ex parte Dow*, D.C.E.D., S.C., 211 Fed. 486 (1913); *U.S. v. Bhagat Singh Thind*, 261 U.S. 204 (1923).

11. See notes 4 and 9 above and A. William Hoglund, *Finnish Immigrants in America, 1908–1920* (Madison, Wis., 1960), 112–114; Peter Kivisto, *Immigrant Socialists in the United States: The Case of Finns and the Left* (Rutherford, N.J., 1984), 127–128; Carl Ross, *The Finn Factor in American Labor, Culture, and Society* (New York, 1978), 115. The whiteness of Armenians was sometimes at issue, even if they lived on "the west side of the Bosphorus." See *In re Halladjian et al.*, C.C.D. Mass., 174 Fed. 834 (1909); and *U.S. v. Cartozian*, 6 F.2d, 919 (1925).

12. *In re Dow*, C.C.A., 226 Fed. 145 (4th Cir. 1915); Kiyoshi Karl Kawakami, *Asia at the Door: A Study of the Japanese Question in the Continental United States, Hawaii, and Canada* (New York, 1914), 15 (thanks to Taro Iwata for the citation).

13. *Ex parte Shahid*, D.C.D. Ore., 179 Fed. 1002 (1910); *In re Dow*, C.C.A., 226 Fed. 145 (4th Cir. 1915); *In re Najour*, C.C., N.D., Ga., 174 Fed. 735 (1909).

14. Haney-Lopez, *White by Law*, 106; Oscar Handlin, *Race and Nationality in American Life* (Boston, 1957), 205; George Cunningham, "The Italian: A Hindrance to White Solidarity in Louisiana, 1890–1898," *Journal of Negro History* 50 (January 1965): 33–35. Jean Scarpaci, "A Tale of Selective Accommodation: Sicilians and Native Whites in Louisiana," *Journal of Ethnic Studies* 5 (1977): 44–45,

notes the use of "dago clause" to describe the provision. On Maryland, see Gordon H. Shufelt, "Jim Crow Among Strangers: The Growth of Baltimore's Little Italy and Maryland's Disfranchisement Campaigns," *Journal of American Ethnic History* 19 (Summer 2000): 48–78; quotation from 54. For the Irish, see David Roediger, *The Wages of Whiteness: Race and the Making of the American Working Class* (New York, 1991), 140–143; and Steven P. Erie, *Rainbow's End: Irish-Americans and the Dilemmas of Urban Machine Politics, 1840–1985* (Berkeley, 1988), 25–66, 96, table 10.

15. *L'Italia,* October 12, 1912, as quoted in Anthony J. Sigismondi, "White or In-between: The Racial Identity of Italians in Chicago from 1890–1940" (seminar paper, Northern Illinois University, 2002); Reginald Horsman, *Race and Manifest Destiny: The Origins of American Racial Anglo-Saxonism* (Cambridge, Mass., 1981), 250–253; Dyer, *Roosevelt and the Idea of Race*, 131; Mink, *Old Labor and New Immigrants in American Political Development: Union, Party, and State, 1875–1920* (Ithaca, N.Y., 1986), 224–227. These advantages in political participation set new immigrants apart from the majority of the African American population. See Eugene J. Cornacchia and Dale C. Nelson, "Historical Differences in the Political Experiences of American Blacks and White Ethnics," *Ethnic and Racial Studies* 15 (January 1992): 102–124; Liette Gidlow, "Delegitimating Democracy: 'Civic Slackers,' the Cultural Turn, and the Possibilities of Politics," *Journal of American History* 89 (December 2002): 939, reports voting by noncitizens in the 1920s in many states; but see Alexander Keyssar, *The Right to Vote: The Contested History of Democracy in the United States* (New York, 2000), 136–140 and table A-12 for the ending of "alien suffrage" laws by 1926.

16. On labor/Indian comparisons, see Richard Slotkin, *The Fatal Environment: The Myth of the Frontier in the Age of Industrialization* (New York, 1985), 226–268; and Richard Drinnon, "'My Men Shoot Well': Theodore Roosevelt and the Urban Frontier," in David Roediger and Franklin Rosemont, eds., *Haymarket Scrapbook* (Chicago, 1986), 129–130. On "Finno-Tartars" as Mongolians, see Edward A. Ross, *The Old World in the New* (New York, 1914), 168–169. On the Minnesota Finns, in addition to the citations in the note above, see Gerald Ronning, "'I Belong in This World': Native Americanisms and the Western Industrial Workers of the World, 1905–17" (Ph.D. diss., University of Colorado, 2002), 170–227, esp. 203; Loree Miltich, "Social Silence, Heartbreak, and the Dream of Safety: New Immigrants, Race, and Class on Minnesota's Iron Range, 1890–1930" (Ph.D. diss., Union Institute and University, 2002).

17. Dyer, *Idea of Race*, 132.

18. On Walker, see Margo J. Anderson, *The American Census: A Social History* (New Haven, 1988); John Higham, *Strangers in the Land: Patterns of American Nativism, 1860–1925* (New York, 1974), 142–143, 147, 149; Walker, "Restriction of Immigration," *Atlantic Monthly,* June 1896, 822–829; Barbara Solomon, *Ancestors and Immigrants: A Changing New England Tradition* (Cambridge, Mass., 1956), 71–76.

19. Anderson, *American Census;* Solomon, *Ancestors and Immigrants,* 71–76; for the quotations, Mink, *Old Labor and New Immigrants,* 126.

20. Anderson, *American Census,* 133–134. Higham, *Strangers in the Land,* 142, rightly observes, however, that Walker was not much given to "comprehensive racial theorizing."

21. Walter Benn Michaels, "The Vanishing American," *American Literary History* 2 (Summer 1990): 231.

22. Mink, *Old Labor and New Immigrants,* 125; Walker, "The Tide of Economic Thought," *Publications of the American Economic Association* 6 (January–March 1891): 37; Robert Asher, "Union Nativism and the Immigrant Response," *Labor History* 23 (1982): 328; Alan Kraut, *Silent Travelers: Germs, Genes, and the "Immigrant Menace"* (New York, 1994); on "hookworm," see Ross as quoted in Katrina Irving, *Immigrant Mothers: Narratives of Race and Maternity, 1890–1925* (Urbana, Ill., 2000), 52.

23. Stephen Jay Gould, *The Mismeasure of Man* (New York, 1981), 115, quotes Cope.

24. Quoted in Mink, *Old Labor and New Immigrants,* 109–110.

25. Grant, *The Passing of the Great Race* (1916; New York, 1921), esp. xxviii–xxxii; Higham, *Strangers in the Land,* 106–233. Ross as quoted in Barbara Foley, *Spectres of 1919: Class and Nation in the Making of the New Negro* (Urbana, Ill., 2003), 125. On the 1912 hearings, see Thomas A. Guglielmo, "White on Arrival: Italians, Race, Color, and Power in Chicago, 1890–1945" (Ph.D. diss., University of Michigan, 2000), 3.

26. Mark Pittenger, "A World of Difference: Constructing the 'Underclass' in Progressive America," *American Quarterly* 49 (March 1997): 49, 52–55. Stephen A. Thernstrom et al., eds., *Harvard Encyclopedia of Ethnic Groups* (Cambridge, Mass., 1980), 379; the quotations are from Dyer, *Idea of Race,* 55, 66, 132. See also 29–30 and 110–144 passim in Dyer. On Roosevelt and race, see also Gary Gerstle, *American Crucible: Race and Nation in the Twentieth Century* (Princeton, 2001), 14–43. On Fiske, see Michael D. Clark, "The Empire of the Dead and the Empire of the Living: John Fiske and the Spatialization of Tradition," *American Studies* 38 (Fall 1997): 92, 102. For Ross, see Julius Weinberg, *Edward Alsworth Ross and the Sociology of Progressivism* (Madison, Wis., 1972), 156–157.

27. Dyer, *Idea of Race,* 130, 150–154; Karen Brodkin, *How Jews Became White Folks and What That Says About Race in America* (New Brunswick, N.J., 1998), 60; Pittenger, "A World of Difference," 48–55; W. W. Husband as quoted in Joel Perlmann, *"Race or People": Federal Race Classifications for Europeans in America, 1898–1913,* Working Paper no. 320 (Jerome Levy Economics Institute of Bard College, 2001), 25.

28. Gilman, "Dangerous Liaisons: Black Jews, Jewish Blacks, and the Vagaries of Racial Definition," *Transition* 64 (1994): 46–47; James R. Barrett, "Americanization from the Bottom Up: Immigration and the Remaking of the Working Class in the United States, 1880–1930," *Journal of American History* 79 (December 1992): 996.

29. Wilson, as quoted in Mink, *Old Labor and New Immigrants*, 223, 226; Pedro Cabán, "Subjects and Immigrants During the Progressive Era," *Discourse* 23 (Fall 2001): 28.

30. James Weinstein, *The Corporate Ideal in the Liberal State* (Boston, 1968).

31. Dyer, *Idea of Race*, 8, 129; Philip Gleason, *Speaking of Diversity: Language and Ethnicity in Twentieth-Century America* (Baltimore, 1992), 13–15; Higham, *Strangers in the Land*, 205.

32. See Elaine Tyler May, *Barren in the Promised Land: Childless Americans and the Pursuit of Happiness* (New York, 1995), 61, 72–75, which includes the quotations from Roosevelt on "outshading"; see also Dyer, *Idea of Race*, 66–68, 132–135; and Linda Gordon, *Woman's Body, Woman's Right: Birth Control in America* (New York, 1990).

33. Mink, as quoted in Linda Gordon, *Pitied But Not Entitled: Single Mothers and the History of Welfare* (New York, 1994), 48–49; Higham, *Strangers in the Land*, 121, 304.

34. Lasch-Quinn, *Black Neighbors: Race and the Limits of Reform in the American Settlement House Movement, 1890–1945* (Chapel Hill, 1993), 22, 14–30 passim; May, *Promised Land*, 70–71, 109–110; Valerie Babb, *Whiteness Visible: The Meaning of Whiteness in American Literature and Culture* (New York, 1998), 140–141.

35. Kraditor, *Ideas of the Woman Suffrage Movement, 1890–1920* (New York, 1965), 139, 123–162; for Kelley, see also Gordon, *Pitied But Not Entitled*, 86.

36. John R. Commons, *Races and Immigrants in America* (New York, 1907), 150; James R. Barrett, "Unity and Fragmentation: Class, Race, and Ethnicity on Chicago's South Side, 1900–1922," in Dirk Hoerder, ed., *"Struggle a Hard Battle": Essays on the Working Class Immigrants* (Dekalb, Ill., 1986), 235; Niles Carpenter, *Immigrants and Their Children* (New York, 1969), 286; for the steel strike quote, see Foley, *Spectres of 1919*, 3–14; Charles Guliet, *Labor Policy of the U.S. Steel Corporation* (New York, 1924), 129; Harold M. Baron, *The Demand for Black Labor* (Cambridge, Mass., n.d.), 21–23; Sterling Spero and Abram Harris, *The Black Worker* (New York, 1969), 174–177; Edward Greer, "Racism and U.S. Steel," *Radical America* 10 (September–October 1976): 45–68; Paul F. McGouldrick and Michael Tannen, "Did American Manufacturers Discriminate Against Immigrants Before 1914?" *Journal of Economic History* 37 (September 1977): 723–746; John R. Commons, "Introduction to Volumes III and IV," in Commons et al., *History of Labour in the United States* (1935; New York, 1966), 3:xxv; John Bodnar, Roger Simon, and Michael Weber, *Lives of Their Own: Blacks, Italians, and Poles in Pittsburgh, 1900–1960* (Urbana, Ill., 1992), 5. A cartoon from Ernest Riebe, *Mr. Block* (1913; Chicago, 1984), unpaginated, graphically shows divided, competing work gangs. See also Gordon, Edwards, and Reich, *Segmented Work, Divided Workers: The Historical Transformation of Labor in the United States* (Cambridge, U.K., 1982), 141–143; and William Leiserson, *Adjusting Immigrant and Industry* (New York, 1924), 92–93. On the compatibility of scientific management and the crude playing off of national groups, see

David Montgomery, *The Fall of the House of Labor: The Workplace, the State, and American Labor Activism, 1865–1925* (Cambridge, U.K., 1987), 242–244. See also Allan Kent Powell, *The Next Time We Strike: Labor in Utah's Coal Fields, 1900–1933* (Logan, 1985), 92, for quotes on the 1911 strike; Matthew Frye Jacobson, *Barbarian Virtues: The United States Encounters Foreign Peoples at Home and Abroad, 1876–1917* (New York, 2000), 86, for the Dillingham Commission's figures; and Grace Abbott, *The Immigrant and the Community* (1917; New York, 1921), 211, for the Industrial Commission quotations. See, however, Isaac A. Hourwich, *Immigration and Labor: The Economic Aspects of European Immigration to the United States* (New York, 1912), 53–55, which tellingly criticizes government statistics on unionization rates among immigrants.

37. David Brody, *Steelworkers in America: The Nonunion Era* (New York, 1960), 120; Peter Speek, "Report on Psychological Aspect of the Problem of Floating Laborers," United States Commission on Industrial Relations Papers, June 25, 1915, 31 (thanks to Tobias Higbie for this citation). For the Brooklyn example, Bruce Nelson, *Divided We Stand: American Workers and the Struggle for Black Equality* (Princeton, 2001), 158–170; Huginnie, *Strikitos* (forthcoming); on track laborers, see Abbott, *The Immigrant and the Community*, 33–34; Dan Georgakas, *Greek Americans at Work* (New York, 1992), 17; Leiserson, *Adjusting Immigrant and Industry*, 71–72. Antonio Ríos Bustamante, "As Guilty as Hell: Mexican Copper Miners and Their Communities in Arizona, 1920–1950," in John Mason Hart, ed., *Border Crossings: Mexican and Mexican-American Workers* (Wilmington, Del., 1998), 170; Linda Gordon, *The Great Arizona Orphan Abduction* (Cambridge, Mass., 1999), 104; Phylis Cancilla Martinelli, "Racial Formation and Italians in Arizona History: Italians as a Semi-Racialized Group" (paper presented at the Race, Ethnicity, and Migration Conference at University of Minnesota, November 2000). On Montana, see Matthew L. Basso, "Metal of Honor: Montana's World War Two Homefront, Movies, and the Social Politics of White Male Anxiety" (Ph.D. diss., University of Minnesota, 2001), 186–187. On "kikes," see W. Lloyd Warner and J. O. Low, *The Social System of the Modern Factory* (New Haven, 1947), 140. For the shipping executive's remarks, see Montgomery, *Fall of the House of Labor*, 81. On Kansas City, see Roger Horowitz, *"Negro and White, Unite and Fight": A Social History of Industrial Unionism in Meatpacking, 1930–1990* (Urbana, Ill., 1997), 90. On Buffalo, see Carpenter, *Nationality, Color, and Economic Opportunity*, 126, 130. On Monessen, see John Bodnar, *Workers' World: Kinship, Community, and Protest in an Industrial Society, 1900–1940* (Baltimore, 1982), 93.

38. Carpenter, *Nationality, Color, and Economic Opportunity*, 118–126; Herman Feldman, *Racial Factors in American Industry* (New York, 1931), 147; for Johnstown, as quoted in Ewa Morawska, *For Bread with Butter: The Life-Worlds of East Central Europeans in Johnstown, Pennsylvania, 1890–1940* (Cambridge, U.K., 1985), 168; Gabriela F. Arredondo, *Mexican Chicago: Negotiating Race, Ethnicity, and Identity, 1916–1939* (forthcoming).

39. Richard W. Steele, "No Racials: Discrimination Against Ethnics in American Defense Industry," *Labor History* 32 (Winter 1991): 66–90; Sigismondi, "White or Inbetween," 5–6, 10; quotes from the Chicago oral histories; "Notes on WASP," Tamony Papers, Western Historical Manuscripts Collection, University of Missouri, which include "Lil Abner: Broadway and Dogpatch," *Life,* January 14, 1957, 74–83. For the standard explanation of the meaning and trajectory of the term, see Howard G. Schneiderman, "The Protestant Establishment: Its History, Its Legacy, Its Future?" in Silvia Pedraza and Ruben Rumbaut, eds., *Origins and Destinations: Immigrations, Race, and Ethnicity in America* (Belmont, Calif., 1996), 141–142.

40. Herbert Gutman, *Work, Culture, and Society in Industrializing America* (New York, 1976), 3–78; Jean Scarpaci, "Immigrants in the New South: Italians in Louisiana's Sugar Parishes, 1880–1910," *Labor History* 16 (Spring 1975): 175; Stanley Lieberson, *A Piece of the Pie: Black and White Immigrants Since 1880* (Berkeley, 1980), 346–350; Carpenter, *Nationality, Color, and Economic Opportunity*, 107–111. Management's judgment also changed briefly in favor of African Americans in the early 1920s. See Peter Gottlieb, *Making Their Own Way: Southern Blacks' Migration to Pittsburgh, 1916–1930* (Urbana, Ill., 1987), 126, 162; Baron, *Demand for Black Labor*, 22.

41. Quotes from Lieberson, *Piece of the Pie*, 348; Thaddeus Radzialowski, "The Competition for Jobs and Racial Stereotypes: Poles and Blacks in Chicago," *Polish American Studies* 33 (Autumn 1976): 16; John R.Commons et al., *History of the Labour Movement in the United States* (New York, 1918–1935), 3:xxv; Sundiata Keita Cha-Jua, *America's First Black Town: Brooklyn, Illinois, 1830–1915* (Urbana, Ill., 2000), 16; Nelson, *Divided We Stand*, 159 (including the Alabama quotation); Everett Cherrington Hughes and Helen MacGill Hughes, *Where Peoples Meet: Racial and Ethnic Frontiers* (Glencoe, Ill., 1952), 67; T. J. Woofter Jr., *Races and Ethnic Groups in American Life* (New York, 1933), 144, citing Feldman favorably.

42. Melvyn Dubofsky, *We Shall Be All: A History of the Industrial Workers of the World* (Urbana, Ill., 1988), 8; Stewart E. Tolnay, "African Americans and Immigrants in Northern Cities: The Effect of Relative Group Size on Occupational Standing in 1920," *Social Forces* 80 (December 2001): 595–597; Carpenter, *Nationality, Color, and Economic Opportunity*, 146; Margaret F. Byington, *Homestead: The Households of a Mill Town* (1910; Pittsburgh, 1974), 132; Lieberson, *Piece of the Pie*, 299–354; Feldman, *Racial Factors*, 40–41; Jennifer L. Hochschild, *Facing Up to the American Dream: Race, Class, and the Soul of the Nation* (Princeton, 1995), 228; Robert F. Foerster, *The Italian Emigration of Our Times* (Cambridge, Mass., 1919), 408, 356–400; Phylis Cancilla Martinelli, "Comparing the Status of Latins in a 'Mexican Camp' and a 'White Man's' Camp" (forthcoming); Philip Mellinger, *Race and Labor in Western Copper: The Fight for Equality, 1896–1918* (Tucson, 1992), 42; for comparisons with Irish American wages, see Michael La Sorte, *La Merica: Images of Italian Greenhorn Experience* (Philadelphia, 1985), 65; Richard Gambino, *Blood of My Blood: The Dilemma of Italian Americans* (New York, 1996), 77; *Divided We Stand*, 167–169;

McGouldrick and Tannen, "American Manufacturers," 724, 725–736 passim; Woofter, *Races and Ethnic Groups*, 143–144; John R. Commons and William Leiserson, "Wage-Earners of Pittsburgh," in Paul Underwood Kellogg, ed., *Wage-Earning Pittsburgh* (1914; New York, 1974), 100–101; John Bodnar, "The Impact of Emigration on the Black Worker: Steelton, Pennsylvania, 1880–1929," *Labor History* 17 (Spring 1976): 214–229. On "dead lines," see Chapter 6 in this book. On Gary, see Raymond A. Mohl and Neil Betten, *Steel City: Urban and Ethnic Patterns in Gary, Indiana, 1906–1950* (New York, 1986), 87.

43. Barrett, "From the Bottom Up," 1002. The finest analyses of this reality are found in Alexander Saxton, *The Indispensable Enemy: Labor and the Anti-Chinese Movement in California* (1971; Berkeley, 1995), 268–284; and in Hourwich, *Immigration and Labor*, 346–349.

44. Higham, *Strangers in the Land*, 305, 321–322.

45. Andrew Neather, "Popular Republicanism, Americanism and the Roots of Anti-Communism, 1890–1925" (Ph.D. diss., Duke University, 1993), 242, 235–240; Robert G. Lee, *Orientals: Asian Americans in Popular Culture* (Philadelphia, 1999), 51–82, provocatively and convincingly argues for the centrality of Chinese exclusion in making the "white worker" after the Civil War. Mink, *Old Labor and New Immigrants*, 71–112. The classic expression of biological and cultural racism is Samuel Gompers and Herman Guttstadt, *Meat vs. Rice: American Manhood Against Asiatic Coolieism: Which Shall Service?* (San Francisco, 1902). For the view that many unionists were able to sustain a distinction between "coolies" and the Chinese "race," see Andrew Gyory, *Closing the Gate: Race, Politics, and the Chinese Exclusion Act* (Chapel Hill, 1998).

46. Mink, *Old Labor and New Immigrants*, 45–112; Lawrence Glickman, "Inventing the 'American Standard of Living': Gender, Race, and Working-Class Identity, 1880–1925," *Labor History* 34 (Spring–Summer 1993): 221–235.

47. Mink, *Old Labor and New Immigrants*, 71, 109; Paul Krause, *The Battle for Homestead, 1880–1892* (Pittsburgh, 1992), 216; Du Bois, as quoted in Jacalyn D. Harden, "Double-Crossing the Color Line: Japanese Americans in Black and White Chicago, 1945–1996" (Ph.D. diss., Northwestern University, 1999), 28. On the close policy ties between Chinese exclusion and immigration exclusion generally, see Lucy Sayler, *Laws Harsh as Tigers: Chinese Immigrants and the Shaping of Modern Immigration Law* (Chapel Hill, 1995); Alexander Saxton, *The Indispensable Enemy*, 273–278. Debs, as quoted in Jacobson, *Barbarian Virtues*, 86.

48. Catherine Collomp, "Unions, Civics, and National Identity: Organized Labor's Reaction to Immigration, 1881–1897," in Marianne Debouzy, ed., *In the Shadow of the Statue of Liberty: Immigrants, Workers, and Citizens in the American Republic, 1880–1920* (Urbana, Ill., 1992), 240, 242, 246.

49. Neather, "Roots of Anti-Communism," 242; Henry White, "Immigration Restriction as a Necessity," *American Federationist* 17 (April 1910): 302–304.

50. Asher, "Union Nativism," 328.

51. Neather, "Roots of Anti-Communism," 242, 267; Gompers, as in Arthur Mann, "Gompers and the Irony of Racism," *Antioch Review* 13 (1953): 212; in Mink, *Old Labor and New Immigrants*, 97; and David Brody, *In Labor's Cause: Main Themes on the History of the American Worker* (New York, 1993), 117. Compare Prescott F. Hall, "Immigration and the Education Test," *North American Review* 165 (1897): 395. For Gompers's affinities to a leading racial nativist, see Lydia Kingsmill Commander, see "Evil Effects of Immigration," *American Federationist* 12 (October 1905).

52. McGovern, in Montgomery, *Fall of the House of Labor*, 25; Asher, "Union Nativism," 339, 338–342; Mink, *Old Labor and New Immigrants*, 203; Lieberson, *Piece of the Pie*, 341–344. Compare the explicit Anglo-Saxonism of *Railroad Trainmen's Journal*, discussed in Neather, "Roots of Anti-Communism," 267–268. See Alexander Saxton, "Race and the House of Labor," in Gary B. Nash and Richard Weiss, eds., *The Great Fear: Race in the Mind of America* (New York, 1970), 115, for the intriguing view that Gompers could be studiously vague in his language of excluding and including immigrants. On union density, race, and immigration, see Hourwich, *Immigration and Labor*, 327, 324–352, 524–527. For Mitchell, see U.S. Industrial Commission, *Report on the Relations and Conditions of Capital and Labor Employed in the Mining Industry* (Washington, D.C., 1901), 12:38, 50–51, 120–121. Thanks to Caroline Waldron for the last reference.

53. Lieberson, *Piece of the Pie*, 342–347; Donna Gabaccia, "The Yellow Peril and the Chinese of Europe" (paper, 1993), 17–19; Mink, *Old Labor and New Immigrants*, 108; Donald Young, *American Minority Peoples* (New York, 1932), 141. On Philadelphia, see Howard Kimeldorf, *Battling for American Labor: Wobblies, Craft Workers, and the Making of the Union Movement* (Berkeley, 1999), 25.

54. Graham, "The Un-Americanizing of America," 302–304, runs the same 1910 issue of the *American Federationist* as "Where Yanks Meet Orientals" and "The International Fraternity of Labor." J. A. Edgerton, "Brotherhood of Man," *American Federationist* 12 (April 1905): 213, runs an issue before Augusta H. Pio, "Exclude Japanese Labor," which appeals to anything but a sense of brotherhood. On race suicide, see Lizzie M. Holmes, review of *The American Idea*, *American Federationist* 14 (December 1907): 1998; A. T. Lane, *Solidarity or Survival? American Labor and European Immigrants, 1830–1924* (Westport, Conn., 1987), 176–177, 200–201.

55. Asher, "Union Nativism," brilliantly develops this point; see also Mink, *Old Labor and New Immigrants*, 198–203; Karen Brodkin, *How Jews Became White Folks*, 56.

56. Asher, "Union Nativism," 345, for the quote. See also Philip S. Foner, *History of the Labor Movement in the United States* (New York, 1964), 3:256–281; Stanley Feldstein and Lawrence Costello, eds., *The Ordeal of Assimilation: A Documentary History of the White Working Class* (Garden City, N.Y., 1974), 345; Hourwich, *Immigration and Labor*, 351–352.

57. Barrett, "From the Bottom Up," 1010 passim; cf. Brody, *In Labor's Cause*, 128; Montgomery, *House of Labor*, 172–173; Frank Julian Warne, *The Slav Invasion and the Mine Worker* (Philadelphia, 1904), 43–57, and (for the quotations) 88, 120, 121, 117; Leiserson, *Adjusting Immigrant and Industry*, 245, 235, 169–245 passim. For Warne's second thoughts, see *The Immigrant Invasion* (New York, 1913), esp. 190. On the English-speaking worker and his suspicions of the foreigner, see Peter Roberts, *The Problem of Americanization* (New York, 1920), 42. The fullest of Ripley's writings on race is his *Races of Europe: A Sociological Study* (New York, 1899).

58. Asher, "Union Nativism," 330; Covington Hall, "Labor Struggles in the Deep South," Labadie Collection, University of Michigan, 1951, 122, 138, 147–148, 183; *Voice of the People*, March 5, 1914; David Roediger, *Towards the Abolition of Whiteness* (London, 1994), n. 75. See also Peck, "Padrones and Protest," 172. On Arizona, see esp. Martinelli, "Comparing the Status of Latins" (forthcoming); Gordon, *Great Arizona Orphan Abduction*, 209–245; Mellinger, *Race and Labor*, 36–43. Martinelli draws "honorary Mexican" from Katherine A. Benton, "What About Women in a 'White Man's Camp'? Gender, Nation, and the Redefinition of Race in Cochise County, 1853–1941" (Ph.D. diss., University of Wisconsin, 2002), 19.

59. Speek, "Floating Laborers," 31, 34, 36; Asher, "Union Nativism," 330; Carl Weinberg, "The Battle of Virden, the UMWA, and the Culture of Solidarity," in Rosemary Feurer, ed., *Remember Virden, 1898* (Chicago, 1998), 7.

60. See John Howard Keiser, "John Fitzpatrick and Progressive Unionism, 1915–1925" (Ph.D. diss., Northwestern University, 1965), 38–41.

61. *New Majority* (Chicago), November 22, 1919, 11; William D. Haywood, *Bill Haywood's Book* (New York, 1929), 241–242.

62. Du Bois, as quoted in Thomas Holt, "The Political Uses of Alienation: W.E.B. Du Bois on Politics, Race, and Culture," *American Quarterly* 42 (June 1990): 313; Peck, "Padrones and Protest," 173; Elizabeth Jameson, *All That Glitters: Class, Conflict, and Community in Cripple Creek* (Urbana, Ill., 1998), 153, 159.

63. Dominic A. Pacyga, *Polish Immigrants and Industrial Chicago: Workers on the South Side, 1880–1930* (Columbus, 1991), 172. James R. Barrett, *Work and Community in the Jungle* (Urbana, Ill., 1987), 172–174. On Boston, see Kimeldorf, *Battling for American Labor*, 25–26; for McDowell, Philip S. Foner and Ronald L. Lewis, eds., *Black Workers: A Documentary History from Colonial Times to the Present* (Philadelphia, 1989), 301–302. If newly organized Poles read John Roach's "Packingtown Conditions," *American Federationist* 13 (August 1906): 534, they would have seen strikebreaking described as an activity in which "the illiterate southern negro has held high carnival" and have wrongly learned that the stockyards was broken simply by black strikebreakers, "ignorant and vicious, whose predominating trait was animalism."

64. Gompers, "Talks on Labor," *American Federationist* 12 (September 1905): 636–637. Cf. Saxton, "House of Labor," 115; Michael Kazin, *Barons of Labor: The*

San Francisco Building Trades and Union Power in the Progressive Era (Urbana, Ill., 1987), 166.

65. Virginia Yans-McLaughlin, *Family and Community: Italian Immigrants in Buffalo, 1880–1930* (1971; Urbana, Ill., 1982), 113–116. More generally, see Gerald Rosenblum, *Immigrant Workers and Their Impact on American Labor* (New York, 1978).

66. David Saposs, "The Mind of Immigrant Communities in the Pittsburgh District," in Interchurch World Movement, *Public Opinion and the Steel Strike* (New York, 1921), 239 passim; Saposs, "Popular Misconceptions" in Box 27, Folder 1 of the David Saposs Papers at State Historical Society of Wisconsin (with thanks to Michael Rosenow for the citation and for insights gained from his 2002 University of Illinois seminar paper "Radicals in the Public Imagination: The Making of American Identity and the Great Steel Strike of 1919"); Interchurch World Movement Commission of Inquiry, *Report on the Steel Strike of 1919* ((New York, 1920), 30–31; Byington, *Homestead*, 15. David Brody, *Labor in Crisis: The Steel Strike of 1919* (Philadelphia, 1965), 136–159; Brody, *Steelworkers*, 121 (for the quotation), 231–262; Philip D. Dreyfus, "The IWW and the Limits of Inter-Ethnic Organizing: Reds, Whites, and Greeks in Grays Harbor, Washington, 1912," *Labor History* 38 (1997): 454–469. For the quotations in Saposs interviews, see Saposs, "Interview with Tom Manseel, 11th Ave., Homestead, July 18," and "Interview with Mr. Lane, 2431 Arlington Ave., South Side, August 5th, 1920," both in the 1920 section of the David Saposs Papers at State Historical Society of Wisconsin in Madison. Thanks to Tom Mackaman for the last two citations.

67. Turner, as quoted in Jacobson, *Barbarian Virtues*, 75.

68. On the ex-unionist as immigration official, see Collomp, "Race of Free Men," 19; and, for the quotation, Delber McKee, *Chinese Exclusion Versus the Open Door Policy, 1900–1906* (Detroit, 1977), 30. On immigrants, labor, and repression, see William Preston Jr., *Aliens and Dissenters: Federal Suppression of Radicals, 1903–1933* (New York, 1966). On nativism, the AFL, and national politics, see Mink, *Old Labor and New Immigrants*, 15–44, 236–260. For Hoerder, see his review of Catherine Collomp's *Entre classe et nation: Mouvement ouvrier et immigration aux Etats-Unis, 1880–1920* in *American Historical Review* 107 (September 2002): 668.

69. On Engels and Leninist traditions of arguing that, especially in the imperial powers, a layer of skilled "labor aristocrats" function to keep class rule intact, see Eric Hobsbawm, "Lenin and the Aristocracy of Labor," in *Revolutionaries: Contemporary Essays* (New York, 1973). For an attempt to analyze U.S. labor history in terms of the evolution of "Euro-Amerikan" workers generally as a labor aristocracy, see J. Sakai, *The Mythology of the White Proletariat* (Chicago, 1983). Sakai acknowledges that the new immigration complicated this story and discusses the complications in chapters 4–6.

70. Abbott, *The Immigrant and the Community*, 201–202; Wells as quoted (and then contradicted) in Warne, *The Immigrant Invasion*, 24; John Fitch, *The Steel*

Workers (New York, 1910), 11–12 (quoting Griswold), 142–147; Hourwich, *Immigration and Labor*, 395.

71. Brody, *Steelworkers*, 120.

72. Quoted in Robert Allen with Pamela Allen, *Reluctant Reformers: Racism and Social Reform Movements in the United States* (Washington, D.C., 1974). Mark Pittenger, *American Socialists and Evolutionary Thought, 1870–1920* (Madison, Wis., 1993); Higham, *Strangers in the Land*, 172; London's aminus was characteristically directed against both "racial" and "semiracial" groups, against "Dagoes and Japs." See London, *The Valley of the Moon* (New York, 1913), 21–22; on the native-born socialist majority views, see Charles Leinenweber, "The Socialist Part and the New Immigrant," *Science and Society*, Winter 1968, 1–25.

73. Carpenter, *Nationality, Color, and Economic Opportunity*, 113; Roediger, *Towards the Abolition of Whiteness*, 158–169; Powell, *Next Time We Strike*, 236 n. 11; Barry Goldberg, "'Wage Slaves' and 'White Niggers,'" *New Politics*, Summer 1991, 64–83.

74. Allen with Allen, *Reluctant Reformers*, 183; Roach, "Packingtown Conditions," 534; Radzialowski, "Competition for Jobs," 8 n. 7 passim; Leslie Fishel, "The North and the Negro, 1865–1900: A Study in Race Discrimination" (Ph.D. diss., Harvard University, 1953), 454–471; Ray Ginger, "Were Negroes Strikebreakers?" *Negro History Bulletin*, January 1952, 73–74; on the "niggerscab" image, see Roediger, *Towards the Abolition of Whiteness*, 150–153.

CHAPTER 4

1. Patricia J. Williams, "*Metro Broadcasting, Inc. v. FCC*," *Harvard Law Review* 104 (1990): 525; The *Crusader* epigraph is from Matthew Pratt Guterl, *The Color of Race in America, 1900–1940* (Cambridge, Mass., 2001), 68; Gellert, in an interview with folklore scholar Richard A. Reuss (August 31, 1966), as quoted in Steven Garabedian, "Blues Music, White Scholarship, and American Cultural Politics" (Ph.D. diss., University of Minnesota, 2004), 140.

2. Jane Addams, *Twenty Years at Hull House* (1909; New York, 1960), 183.

3. On settlement houses and segregation, see Valerie Babb, *Whiteness Visible: The Meaning of Whiteness in American Literature and Culture* (New York, 1998), 140, 138–149; Elizabeth Lasch-Quinn, *Black Neighbors: Race and the Limits of Reform in the American Settlement House Movement, 1890–1945* (Chapel Hill, 1993), esp. 22, 14–30.

4. Du Bois, as quoted in Herbert Aptheker's fine introduction to a reprint of *The Gift of Black Folk* (1924; Millwood, N.Y., 1975), 5.

5. See Aptheker's introduction, as cited in note 2 above; Edw. F. McSweeney, "The Racial Contributions to the United States," in *Gift of Black Folk*, 1–29; for Du Bois in the *Forward*, see Nancy J. Weiss, "Long-Distance Runners of the Civil Rights Movement: The Contribution of Jews to the NAACP and the National Urban League

in the Early Twentieth Century," in Jack Salzman and Cornel West, eds., *Struggles in the Promised Land: Toward a History of Black–Jewish Relations in the United States* (New York, 1997), 143–144; Julius Lester, ed., *The Seventh Son: The Thought and Writings of W. E. B. Du Bois* (New York, 1970), 2:82; Du Bois, "The Negro Mind Reaches Out," in Alain Locke, ed., *The New Negro: An Interpretation* (New York, 1925), 412.

6. Finley Peter Dunne, *Mr. Dooley in Peace and in War* (Urbana, Ill., 1988), 33–35; *Dziennik Zwiazkowy,* May 26, 1920; Donna Misner Collins, *Ethnic Identification: The Greek Americans of Houston, Texas* (New York, 1991), 210–211; Dominic A. Pacyga, *Polish Immigrants and Industrial Chicago: Workers on the South Side, 1880–1922* (Columbus, 1991), 221; Anne Sutherland, *Gypsies: The Hidden Americans* (New York, 1975), 248–252; Gunnar Myrdal, *An American Dilemma: The Negro Problem and Modern Democracy* (New York, 1944), 2:603. Dan Georgakas, *Greek Americans at Work* (New York, 1992), 9–12; Louis Adamic, *From Many Lands* (New York, 1940), 113, 121–123, 127, marvelously evokes Tarpon Springs.

7. Hodding Carter, *Southern Legacy* (Baton Rouge, 1950), 106; Arnold Shankman, *Ambivalent Friends: Afro-Americans View the Immigrant* (Westport, Conn., 1982), 100; Joseph P. Cosco, "Lynching Those Magnificently Miserable Italians: Mark Twain Revisits an American Tragedy," *Columbia Journal of American Studies* 5 (2002): 117–118 n. 21; Paola Sensi Isolani, "La Pelle in California, I Soldi in Italia: The Italian Strike in McCloud, California, 1909," *Studi Emigrazione* 27 (Spring 1990): 108–119; Rudolph J. Vecoli, "'Free Country': The American Republic Viewed by the Italian Left, 1880–1920," in Marianne Debouzy, ed., *In the Shadow of the Statue of Liberty: Immigrants, Workers, and Citizens in the American Republic, 1880–1920* (Urbana, Ill., 1992), 38, 33–34 for quotations; Jennifer Guglielmo, "Negotiating Gender, Race, and Coalition: Italian Women and Working-Class Politics in New York City, 1880–1945" (Ph.D. diss., University of Minnesota, 2003), 201–268; Michael Miller Topp, "'It Is Providential That There Are Foreigners Here': Whiteness and Masculinity in the Making of Italian American Syndicalist Identity" (paper presented at the Race, Ethnicity, and Migration in a Global Context Conference, University of Minnesota, November 2000); and Vincenza Scarpaci, "Walking the Color Line: Italian Immigrants in Rural Louisiana," in Jennifer Guglielmo and Salvatore Salerno, eds., *Are Italians White?* (New York, 2003), 98–110, 60–76; on the anti-imperialism and race thinking of *Il Proletario*, see Topp, "It Is Providential"; on the Paterson group, see Salvatore Salerno, "'Odio di Razza?': The Beginnings of Racial Discourse in the Italian American Anarchist Community" (paper presented to the American Italian Historical Association, New York, 1998); on The Bandits of All Laws, see Robert E. Park, *The Immigrant Press and Its Control* (New York, 1922), 226–228; Arturo Labriola, "*Le Razza di Colore e il Socialismo*" (New York, 1934); on Speranza, see Thomas Guglielmo, "The Triumph of Difference: Gino Speranza and the Conceptions of Race and Italian Racial Identity, 1900–1927" (paper, University of Michigan, 1997), 6. Thanks to

Jennifer Guglielmo for a translation of Labriola. For the final two quotations, see Michael La Sorte, *La Merica: Images of Italian Greenhorn Experience* (Philadelphia, 1985), 146–147; for Zappa, see Philip Rubio, *A History of Affirmative Action, 1619–2000* (Jackson, Miss., 2001), 77.

8. The quotation from *Dziennik Ludowy,* November 14, 1907, was provided by Mary Cygan; see *Dziennik Chicagoski,* January 7, 1928; on the Lithuanian example, the quotations are from Kotaro Nakano, "Preserving Distinctiveness: Language Loyalty and Americanization in Early Twentieth Century Chicago" (paper presented at the Kyoto American Studies Seminar, 2000), 3. Thaddeus Radzialowski, "The Competition for Jobs and Racial Stereotypes: Poles and Blacks in Chicago," *Polish American Studies* 33 (Autumn 1976): 17; Robert M. Zecker, *"Negrov Lyncovanie* and the Unbearable Whiteness of Slovaks: The Slavic Press Covers Race" (paper presented to the American Studies Association, Detroit, October 2000).

9. *Jewish Daily Courier,* August 5, 1912. Except where otherwise noted, all citations to Chicago foreign-language newspapers are to the Chicago Foreign Language Press Survey compilations. The survey was undertaken between 1936 and 1941 and is deposited at the Chicago Historical Society; *Jewish Daily Courier,* April 22, 1914; for the *Forward,* Weiss, "Long-Distance Runners," 128; for the rabbi, Matthew Frye Jacobson, *Whiteness of a Different Color: European Immigrants and the Alchemy of Race* (Cambridge, Mass., 1998), 256; for the *Call,* see Philip S. Foner, *American Socialism and Black Americans: From the Age of Jackson to World War II* (Westport, Conn., 1977), 285; Hasia Diner, *In the Almost Promised Land: American Jews and Blacks, 1915–1935* (Westport, Conn., 1977), 226; for *Freie Arbeiter Stimme,* see Park, *Immigrant Press,* 221; Louis Wirth, *The Ghetto* (Chicago, 1928), 230; on *Lincherei* and Opatoshu, see Paul Buhle, "Radical Novel, 1870–1930," in Mari Jo Buhle, Paul Buhle, and Dan Georgakas, eds., *Encyclopedia of the American Left* (New York, 1998), 671; for Gellert, see Garabedian, "Reds, Whites, and the Blues," 152, 175–177; Albert Jenks, "The Practical Value of Anthropology to Our Nation," *Science,* February 18, 1921, 155; Mamie Garvin Fields with Karen Fields, *Lemon Swamp and Other Places: A Carolina Memoir* (New York, 1983), 149–150. I thank Mark Soderstrom for the Jenks reference.

10. Weiss, "Long-Distance Runners," 123–152; Jonathan Zimmerman, "'Each Race Could Have Its Heroes Sung': Ethnicity and the History Wars in the 1920s," *Journal of American History* 87 (June 2000): 94–103; Diner, *Almost Promised Land,* 219, 199–230; Herman Feldman, *Racial Factors in American Identity* (New York, 1931), 184; Lisa McGirr, "Black and White Longshoremen in the IWW: A History of the Philadelphia Marine Transport Workers Industrial Union Local 8," *Labor History* 37 (Summer 1995): 380; Howard Kimeldorf, *Battling for American Labor: Wobblies, Craft Workers, and the Making of the Union Movement* (Berkeley, 1999), 59–60. The ILGWU's overall record on race was mixed, however. See Herman D. Bloch, *The Circle of Discrimination* (New York, 1969), 97–115. For Woodbey, see Sally M. Miller, "For White Men Only: The Socialist Party of America and Issues of

Gender, Ethnicity, and Race," *Journal of the Gilded Age and Progressive Era* 2 (July 2003): 19.

11. Ronald L. Lewis, *Black Coal Miners in America: Race, Class, and Community Conflict, 1780–1980* (Lexington, 1987), 110.

12. James Barrett, *Work and Community in the Jungle: Chicago's Packinghouse Workers, 1894–1922* (Urbana, 1987).

13. C. L. R. James, *C. L. R. James on the "Negro Question,"* ed. Scott McLemee (Jackson, Miss., 1996), 113.

14. On New York City, see Bruce Nelson, *Divided We Stand: American Workers and the Struggle for Black Equality* (Princeton, 2000); Cal Winslow, "On the Waterfront: Black, Italian, and Irish Longshoremen in the New York Harbour Strike of 1919," in John Rule and Robert Malcolmson, eds., *Protest and Survival: Essays for E. P. Thompson* (London, 1993), 355–393; *The Irish People Monthly* 3 (May 1933): 5 (in a series of short items); Goodman as quoted in Jacobson, *Whiteness of a Different Color,* 251; on Irish freedom as a "race" issue, see William M. Tuttle, *Race Riot: Chicago in the Red Summer of 1919* (New York, 1984), 135.

15. William Attaway, *Blood on the Forge* (1941; New York, 1987), 130; Frederick Douglass, *My Bondage and My Freedom* (1855; Chicago, 1970), 76; Eric Lott, *Love and Theft: Blackface Minstrelsy and the American Working Class* (New York, 1993), 95.

16. See Patti Jones's superb liner notes to *Allison Wonderland: The Mose Allison Anthology* (Rhino Records, 1994).

17. Mezz Mezzrow and Bernard Wolfe, *Really the Blues* (New York, 1946), 18, 315–316; and as quoted in Maria Damon, "Jazz-Jews, Jive, and Gender: The Ethnic Politics of Popular Music Argot," in Jonathan Boyarin and Daniel Boyarin, eds., *Jews and Other Differences: The New Jewish Cultural Studies* (Minneapolis, 1997), 156; Robeson, in Jeffrey Melnick, *A Right to Sing the Blues: African Americans, Jews, and American Popular Song* (Cambridge, Mass., 1999), 180.

18. Melnick, *Right to Sing the Blues,* 174–175 (Hecht) and 95–196; Diner, *Almost Promised Land,* 69, quotes the *Forward.*

19. O'Connell, as quoted in George Potter, *To the Golden Door: The Story of the Irish in Ireland and America* (Boston, 1960), 372; Morrison in conversation with David Roediger, February 1, 1996; Charley Pride with Jim Henderson, *PRIDE: The Charley Pride Story* (New York, 1994), 46–47. Even so, Pride admired the Latvians and learned some of their language.

20. James Baldwin, "On Being 'White' . . . and Other Lies," *Essence,* April 1984, 90, 92; Baldwin, "White Man's Guilt," in *The Price of the Ticket* (New York, 1985), 413–414.

21. Malcolm X, with Alex Haley, *The Autobiography of Malcolm X* (New York, 1984), 399; Pryor, as in John A. Williams and Dennis A. Williams, *If I Stop I'll Die: The Comedy and Tragedy of Richard Pryor* (New York, 1991), 94; St. Clair Drake and Horace R. Cayton, *Black Metropolis: A Study of Negro Life in a Northern City*

(New York, 1945), 57. John Oliver Killens, in his foreword to Attaway, *Blood on the Forge*; Toni Morrison, as cited in Derrick Bell, "Racial Libel as Ritual," *Village Voice*, November 21, 1995, 53.

22. See Peter J. Tamony's intriguing notes on "hunky" (or hunkie) and "honky" (or honkie) in the Tamony Papers, Western Historical Manuscripts Collection; and Ken Johnson, "The Vocabulary of Race," in Thomas Kochman, ed., *Rappin' and Stylin' Out: Communication in Urban Black America* (Urbana, 1972), 143.

23. Baldwin, "On Being 'White,'" 90–92; and in the film *The Price of the Ticket* (1985); Williams, *If I Stop*, 94.

24. Quoted in Gilbert Osofsky, *Harlem: The Making of a Ghetto: Negro New York, 1890–1930* (New York, 1966), 45–46.

25. Robert C. Weisbord and Arthur Stein, *Bittersweet Encounter: The Afro-American and the American Jew* (Westport, Conn., 1970), 32–33.

26. Paul Berman, ed., *Blacks and Jews: Alliances and Arguments* (New York, 1994), 6–7, 8–10; Michael Lerner and Cornel West, *Jews and Blacks: Let the Healing Begin* (New York, 1995), 66–79; on Chafets, Lawrence Joseph, "Can't Forget the Motor City," *The Nation*, December 17, 1990, 775–776; Herbert Hill, "Race, Ethnicity, and Organized Labor," *New Politics* 2nd ser., Winter 1987, 31–82. Stephen Steinberg, *The Ethnic Myth: Race, Ethnicity, and Class in America* (Boston, 1989), 201, uses a 1916 *New Republic* editorial on blacks and immigrants as "deadly foes." A good recent example of the common enemies argument is Murray Friedman, *What Went Wrong? The Creation and Collapse of the Black-Jewish Alliance* (New York, 1994).

27. Thaddeus Radzialowski, "The View from a Polish Ghetto: Some Observations on the First One Hundred Years in Detroit," *Ethnicity* 1 (July 1974): 125–150; Lerner and West, *Jews and Blacks*, 66–67, 69, 79; James Baldwin, "Negroes Are Anti-Semitic Because They're Anti-White," in Nat Hentoff, ed., *Black Anti-Semitism and Jewish Racism* (New York, 1969), 6–7; Ralph Ellison, "The World and the Jug," in *Shadow and Act* (New York, 1972), 126; Charles Mills, *Blackness Visible: Essays on Philosophy and Race* (Ithaca, N.Y., 1998), 80–88; and Lerner, "Jews Are Not White," *Village Voice*, May 18, 1993, 33–34.

28. Joyce Antler, "Between Culture and Politics: The Emma Lazarus Federation of Jewish Women's Clubs and the Promulgation of Women's History, 1944–1989," in Linda A. Kerber, Alice Kessler-Harris, and Kathryn Kish Sklar, eds., *U.S. History as Women's History: New Feminist Essays* (Chapel Hill, 1995), 276, 282; Weisbord and Stein, *Bittersweet Encounter*, 12; Donald Young, *American Minority Peoples* (New York, 1932), 248–253. The 1971 interview is quoted from Steven Hertzberg, "Jews and Blacks," in Maurianne Adams and John Bracey, eds., *Strangers and Neighbors: Relations Between Blacks and Jews in the United States* (Amherst, 1999), 251.

29. Young, *Minority Peoples*, 252; Richard Gambino, *Vendetta* (Garden City, N.Y., 1977), 135; Jack Salzman, "Struggles in the Promised Land," in Salzman and West, *Struggles in the Promised Land*, 1; Eugene Levy, "Is the Jew a White Man? Press

Reaction to the Leo Frank Case, 1913–1915," in Adams and Bracey, *Strangers and Neighbors*, 261–280.

30. On Rock Springs, see Craig Storti, *Incident at Bitter Creek: The Story of the Rock Springs Chinese Massacre* (Ames, Iowa, 1991); on the scope of antiblack racial terror, see Herbert Shapiro, *White Violence and Black Response from Reconstruction to Montgomery* (Amherst, 1988), esp. 115 (Leonard), 114–201; and William M. Tuttle, *Race Riot: Chicago in the Red Summer of 1919* (1970; New York, 1984), 242–247.

31. C. Fred Alford, "If I Am You, Then You Are . . . Fake," in Alan Helmreich and Paul Marcus, eds., *Blacks and Jews on the Couch: Psychoanalytic Reflections on Black–Jewish Conflict* (Westport, Conn., 1998), 58. In the same volume, see Lee Jenkins, "Black-Jewish Relations: A Social and Mythic Alliance," 190 (quoting Baldwin), 189–204.

32. Louis Schmier, "'For Him the *Schwartzers* Couldn't Do Enough': A Jewish Peddler and His Black Customers Look at Each Other," in Adams and Bracey, *Strangers and Neighbors*, 224, 228, 229, 223–244.

33. Philip S. Foner, "Black–Jewish Relations in the Opening Years of the Twentieth Century," in Adams and Bracey, *Strangers and Neighbors*, 240; Diner, *Almost Promised Land*, 72–73; and Micol Seigel's excellent "The Kishineff Pogrom in a Lynch Mob World" (paper, New York University, 1997).

34. Gunther Peck, "Padrones and Protest: 'Old' Radicals and 'New' Immigrants in Bingham, Utah, 1905–1912," *Western Historical Quarterly* 24 (May 1993): 172–173; Peck, "The Greatness of the Greek Spirit," *Saloniki,* February 15, 1919; Georgakas, *Greek America at Work* (New York, 1992), 17; Paul S. Taylor, *Mexican Labor in the United States* (1930; New York, 1970), 1:222; cf. Sarah Gualtieri, "Becoming 'White': Race, Religion, and the Foundations of Syrian Lebanese Ethnicity in the United States," *Journal of American Ethnic History*, Summer 2001, 29–58. Giovanni Schiavo, *The Italians in Chicago: A Study in Americanization* (Chicago, 1928), 15, 105. Thanks to Anthony Sigismondi for the last reference.

35. Robert Orsi, "The Religious Boundaries of an Inbetween People: Street *Feste* and the Problem of the Dark-Skinned 'Other' in Italian Harlem, 1920–1940," *American Quarterly* 44 (September 1992): 316–317, 326–335; Lou De Caro Jr., "Mixed Relations: The Italian American–African American *Dis*-Connection," *Interrace* 3 (May–June 1992): 18–19; Gerald D. Suttles, *The Social Order of the Slum: Ethnicity and Territory in the Inner City* (Chicago, 1968), 34; Steve Nelson, James R. Barrett, and Rob Ruck, *Steve Nelson: American Radical* (Pittsburgh, 1981), 16; Zecker, "Negrov Lyncovanie."

36. Harold David Brackman, "The Ebb and Flow of Race Relations: A History of Black–Jewish Relations" (Ph.D. diss., University of California, 1977), 461–464; Matthew Frye Jacobson, *Special Sorrows: The Diasporic Imagination of Irish, Polish, and Jewish Immigrants in the United States* (Cambridge, Mass., 1995), 197–200; Marilyn Halter, *Between Race and Ethnicity: Cape Verdean American Immigrants, 1860–1965* (Urbana, Ill., 1993), 146–149. See also Gary Mormino and George

Pozzetta, *The Immigrant World of Ybor City: Italians and Their Latin Neighbors in Tampa, 1885–1985* (Urbana, Ill., 1987), 241; and Thomas F. Gossett, *Race: The History of an Idea in America* (New York, 1997), 377.

37. Stan Weir in Alice and Staughton Lynd, eds., *Rank and File: Personal Histories of Working Class Organizers* (Boston, 1973), 191; Florence Mae Waldron, "Quebecois Migrants and the French Canadian 'Nation': Redefining Manhood Through Americanization" (paper delivered to Canadian Historical Association, Toronto, May 2002); Moon-Kie Jung, "Interracialism as Affirmative Action: The Transformation of Hawaii's Working Class" (forthcoming).

38. Radzialowski, "Competition for Jobs and Racial Stereotypes," 14 n. 20.

39. Thomas Guglielmo, *White on Arrival: Italians, Race, Color, and Power in Chicago, 1890–1945* (Oxford, 2003).

40. Loren Baritz, *The Good Life: The Meaning of Success for the American Middle Class* (New York, 1982), 53; Israel Zangwill, *The Melting-Pot* (New York, 1922), 204. The U.S.-centeredness of recent scholarship on white identity complicates study of the forms of race thinking immigrants carried with them. For a critique, see Alastair Bonnett, *White Identities: Historical and International Perspectives* (Harlow, U.K., 2000).

41. Daniel Trees, *How Columbus and I Discovered America: The Life and Adventures of an Immigrant Boy* (Grosse Point, Mich., 1965), 4, 6, 18.

42. Catherine Eagan, "'I Did Imagine . . . We Had Ceased to Be Whitewashed Negroes': The Racial Formation of Irish Identity in Nineteenth-Century Ireland and America" (Ph.D. diss., Boston College, 2000).

43. On the mass wedding and contribution of gold wedding bands, see Joseph S. Roucek and Francis J. Brown, "The Problem of Negro and European Immigrant Minorities: Some Comparisons and Contrasts," *Journal of Negro Education* 8 (January 1939): 307; Guglielmo, *White on Arrival*, 113–128, esp. 118; and Fiorello B. Ventresco, "Italian Americans and the Ethiopian Crisis," *Italian Americana* 6 (Fall–Winter 1980): 18–19; Nelson Peery, *Black Fire: The Making of a Black Revolutionary* (New York, 1994), 72–73; Baldwin, *Price of a Ticket*, 660; Stefano Luconi, "The Influence of the Italo-Ethiopian Conflict on Italian-American Voters: The Case of Philadelphia," *Immigrants and Minorities* 16 (November 1997): 3–7; Leonard Covello, *The Social Background of the Italo-American Child: A Study of Southern Italian Family Mores and Their Effect on the School System in Italy and America* (Leiden, 1967), 121–127. Covello, *The Heart Is the Teacher* (New York, 1958), 188–189, provides evidence on lack of post-Ethiopian invasion black–Italian tensions in one New York school. For a consideration of the impact of Italian fascism on Italian American relations with other immigrant groups in the United States, see Ronald H. Bayor, *Neighbors in Conflict: The Irish, Germans, Jews, and Italians in New York City, 1929–1941* (Baltimore, 1978), 76–81. See also Salvatore J. LaGumina, "African–American and Italian–American Relations in the Light of the Harlem Riots of 1935," in Dan Ashyk, Fred L. Gardaphe, and Anthony Julian Tamburri, eds.,

Shades of Black and White: Conflict and Collaboration Between Two Communities (Staten Island, 1999), esp. 129–131; John Diggins, *Mussolini and Fascism* (Princeton, 1972); and Philip V. Cannistraro, *Blackshirts in Little Italy: Italian Americans and Fascism, 1921–1929* (West Lafayette, Ind., 1999). On *bravi*, and for Jennifer Guglielmo's broader analysis, see her remarkable dissertation on Italian American immigrant women in the United States, "Negotiating Gender, Race, and Coalition: Italian Women and Working-Class Politics in New York City, 1880–1945" (Ph.D. diss., University of Minnesota, 2003), chap. 1. See also Nadia Venturini, "'Over the Years People Don't Know': Italian Americans and African Americans in Harlem in the 1930s," trans. Michael Rocke, in Donna R. Gabaccia and Fraser Ottanelli, eds., *Italian Workers of the World: Labor Migration and the Formation of Multiethnic States* (Urbana, Ill., 2001), 196–213, esp. 202–203 (rings and "progress") and 209 (quoting Du Bois) and, for a series of useful provocations, E. Tani and Kae Sera, *False Nationalism, False Internationalism* (n.p., 1985), 48–91. For Addams, see Chicago Commission on Race Relations, *The Negro in Chicago: A Study of Race Relations and a Race Riot* (Chicago, 1922), 19; Andrew Greeley, *Why Can't They Be Like Us? Facts and Fallacies About Ethnic Differences and Group Conflicts in America* (New York, 1969), 10. For Dattolo, see Bruce Stave and John Sutherland with Aldo Salerno, eds., *From the Old Country: An Oral History of European Migration to America* (New York, 1994), 221–222; on black Madonnas, see especially Joseph Sciorra, "The Black Madonna of East Thirteenth Street," *Voices: The Journal of the New York Folklore Society* 30 (Spring–Summer, 2004), http://www.nyfolklore.org/pubs/voic30-1-2/madonna.html.

44. Orsi, "Inbetween People," 315; Gary Mormino, *Immigrants on the Hill: Italian Americans in St. Louis, 1887–1982* (Urbana, Ill., 1986), 74–75; Report of the U.S. Senate Immigration Commission, *Dictionary of Races or Peoples* (Washington, D.C., 1911), 81–85; Alessandro Triulzi, *L'Africa dall'imaginario alle imagini* (Torino, 1989); Donna Gabaccia, *From the Other Side: Women, Gender, and Immigrant Life in the U.S., 1820–1990* (Bloomington, Ind., 1994), 8; David A. J. Richards, *Italian American: The Racializing of an Ethnic Identity* (New York, 1999), 105–111.

45. Albert Murray, as quoted in John Gennari, "Passing for Italian: Crooners and Gangsters in Crossover Culture," *Transition* 72 (1997): 42–43; Antonio Gramsci, *Selections from the Prison Notebooks*, ed. and trans. Quintin Hoare and Geoffrey Nowell Smith (New York, 1971), 71; Richards, *Italian American*, 107 (Niceforo), 105–115. See also Guglielmo, "White on Arrival," 44–47; Rudolph J. Vecoli, "Racializing Italian Americans: Sources and Resources," *Voices in Italian Americana* 5 (2001): 5. For the Naples line, see Gabriella Gribaudi, "Images of the South: The *Mezzogiorno* as Seen by Insiders and Outsiders," in Robert Lumley and Jonathan Morris, eds., *The New History of the Italian South: The* Mezzogiorno *Revisited* (Devon, U.K., 1997), 87; for Lombroso, see Jennifer Guglielmo, "Negotiating Gender, Race, and Coalition: Italian Women and Working Class Politics in New York City, 1880–1945" (Ph.D. diss., University of Minnesota, 2003), 59–61.

46. Edvige Giunta, "Figuring Race: Kym Ragusa's *fuori/outside*," in Ashyk, Gardaphe, and Tamburri, *Shades of Black and White*, 265; Niles Carpenter, *Nationality, Color, and Economic Opportunity in the City of Buffalo* (1927; Westport, Conn., 1970), 107, 119.

47. Margot Fortunato Galt, "Beyond the Footlights of Immigrant Performing Arts, Or How to Grow Up Ethnic and Not Know It" (paper prepared for the Immigration History Research Center, St. Paul, n.d.), 2; De Caro, "Mixed Relations," 18; "A. J. Tamburri to H-NET List on Italian-American History and Culture [H-ITAM]," February 24, 1997; "Andrea di Tommaso to H-ITAM," February 24, 1997.

48. Mormino, *Immigrants on the Hill*, 20, for all quotations save that of Rossi in La Sorte, *La Merica*, 38, 112. See also Guglielmo, *White on Arrival*, 22–23, 38. On darkness and labor in Italy, see Guglielmo, "Negotiating Gender, Race, and Coalition," 103; and Gabriela F. Arredondo, *Mexican Chicago: Negotiating Race, Ethnicity, and Identity, 1916–1939* (forthcoming).

49. Norman Podhoretz, "My Negro Problem—and Ours," *Commentary* 2 (February 1963): 94; Hugh Rawson, ed., *Wicked Words: A Treasury of Curses, Insults, Put-Downs, and Other Formerly Unprintable Terms from Anglo-Saxon Times to the Present* (New York, 1989), 338–339; Peter Martin, *Schwarze Teufel, edle Mohren* (Hamburg, 1993); Jacob and Wilhelm Grimm, *Deutsches Wörterbuch* (1889; Munich, 1984), 533–535; Russell Andrew Kazal, "Becoming 'Old Stock': The Waning of German-American Identity in Philadelphia, 1900–1930" (Ph.D. diss., University of Pennsylvania, 1998), 534–535; Jonathan Kaufman, *Broken Alliance: The Turbulent Times Between Blacks and Jews in America* (New York, 1988), 109.

50. Jan Nederveen Pieterse, *White on Black: Images of Blacks in Western Popular Culture* (New Haven, 1992); Sander Gilman, *On Blackness Without Blacks* (Boston, 1982), 119–128; 149–150 n. 58; Coco Fusco, *English Is Broken Here* (New York, 1995), 37–63; Franz Kafka, "A Report to the Academy," in *The Basic Kafka* (New York, 1979); Joseph Conrad, *Heart of Darkness and the Secret Sharer* (1899; New York, 1950); Laura Doyle, "The Folk, the Nobles and the Novel: The Racial Subtext of Sentimentality," *Narrative* 3 (May 1995): 162 passim; Allison Blakely, *Russia and the Negro: Blacks in Russian History and Thought* (Washington, D.C., 1986), 35; Jacobson, *Special Sorrows*, 216–217. On the Gellerts, see Garabedian, "Reds, Whites and the Blues," 161–162.

51. Anne McClintock, *Imperial Leather: Race, Gender, and Sexual Conquest* (New York, 1995), 31–36, 207–231; Elizabeth Ewen, *Immigrant Women in a Land of Dollars: Life and Culture on the Lower East Side, 1890–1925* (New York, 1985), 74.

52. L. Perry Curtis, *Apes and Angels: The Irishman in Victorian Caricature* (Washington, D.C., 1971), 13–14; McClintock, *Imperial Leather*, 53; Roger Parham-Brown, "In Romania, the Devil Is Beating His Wife," *Transition* 77 (1999): 34; Lerner and West, *Jews and Blacks*, 66–67; William I. Thomas and Florian Znaniecki, *The Polish Peasant in Europe and America* (New York, 1927), 5:84–85. See also Sander Gilman, "Dangerous Liaisons: Black Jews, Jewish Blacks, and the Vagaries of

Racial Definition," *Transition* 64 (1994): 41–50. On anti-Semitic race theory, see Robert Singerman, "The Jew as Racial Alien," in David A. Gerber, ed., *Anti-Semitism in American History* (Urbana, Ill., 1986), 103–128; Emma Lazarus, "Heine: The Poet," *The Century* 29 (December 1884): 217; Lazarus, editorial remarks, *Harper's New Monthly Magazine*, 96 (March 1898): 576. On "cierna," see Zecker, *"Negrov Lyncovanie."* On Du Bois, see Axel R. Schafer, " W.E.B. Du Bois, German Social Thought, and the Racial Divide in American Progressivism, 1892–1909," *Journal of American History* 88 (December 2001): 932.

53. Gabaccia, *From the Other Side*, 8–9; Melvin G. Holli, "Teuton vs. Slav: The Great War Sinks Chicago's German *Kultur*," *Ethnicity* 8 (December 1981): 411, 413; Larry Wolff, *Inventing Eastern Europe: The Map of Civilization on the Mind of the Enlightenment* (Stanford, 1994), 278–282; Maria Todorova, *Imagining the Balkans* (New York, 1997), esp. 12, 121–127.

54. Celia Stopnicka Heller, *On the Edge of Destruction: Jews of Poland Between the Two World Wars* (New York, 1977), esp. 38–76; Joseph M. Papo, *Sephardim in Twentieth Century America: In Search of Unity* (San José, 1987); 40; Ella Shohat, "Staging the Quincentenary: The Middle East and the Americas," *Third Text* 21 (Winter 1992–1993): 95–105. Cf. Robbie McVeigh, "The Specificity of Irish Racism," *Race and Class* 33 (April–June 1992): 40–43; Jane Helleiner, "Gypsies, Celts, and Tinkers: Colonial Antecedents of Anti-Traveller Racism in Ireland," *Ethnic and Racial Studies* 18 (July 1995): 532–554; Ann Laura Stoler, *Race and the Education of Desire: Foucault's History of Sexuality and the Colonial Order of Things* (Durham, 1995), esp. 69–85; and Lorraine Johnson-Riordan, *Race Wars* (forthcoming).

55. Claude McKay, *A Long Way from Home* (1937; New York, 1969), 274–275; Du Bois, *Darkwater: Voices from Within the Veil* (1920; New York, 1969), 51; Du Bois, *The Autobiography of W.E.B. Du Bois* (New York, 1968), 122; E. Franklin Frazier, "A Negro Industrial Group," *Howard Review* 1 (June 1924): 220. The source for Addams is her typewritten "Digest of the Report of the Seminar on The Church and Race Relations," which was held in Chicago in April 1928 under National Council of Congregational Churches auspices, as paraphrased and (in the doctor's case) quoted in Feldman, *Racial Factors in American Industry*, 194; Myrdal, *American Dilemma*, 2:603; Katayama Sen, as quoted in Josie Fowler, "To Be Red and 'Oriental': The Experiences of Japanese and Chinese Immigrant Communists in the American and International Communist Movements, 1919–1933" (Ph.D. diss., University of Minnesota, 2003), 59.

56. William I. Thomas and Florian Znaniecki, *The Polish Peasant in Europe and America* (Chicago, 1918), 2:284, reprints the letter. For this citation and general help with this chapter I am indebted to Professor Robert Slayton. Compare Josephine Wtulich, *American Xenophobia and the Slav Immigrant: A Living Legacy of Mind and Spirit* (New York, 1994), 97.

57. Robert Zecker to David Roediger, November 4, 1996. Cf. Trees, *Columbus and I*, 11, for a flat description of a first encounter with a black person and 38–39 for a sympathetic view of gypsies.

58. "Little Italy, Cleveland, Ohio" in Clara Grillo Papers (Box 1), Immigration History Research Center, University of Minnesota, Minneapolis. See also Stave and Sutherland with Salerno, *From the Old Country*, 43, for a similar story.

59. Orsi, "Religious Boundaries of an Inbetween People," 341 n. 1; Kerby Miller, *Emigrants and Exiles: Ireland and the Irish Exodus to North America* (New York, 1985), 235, 248, 305; Miller, "Green Over Black: The Origins of Irish-American Racism" (paper in possession of the author, 1969), 10, 90 n. 24; Jo Ellen McNergney Vinyard, "The Irish on the Urban Frontier: Detroit, 1850–1880" (Ph.D. diss., University of Michigan, 1972), 220; cf. Nathan Hurvitz, "Blacks and Jews in American Folklore," *Western Folklore* 33 (October 1974): 304–307.

60. Orsi, "Religious Boundaries of an Inbetween People," 313, 339–341. See also Micaela di Leonardo, *The Varieties of Ethnic Experience* (Ithaca, N.Y., 1984), 174.

61. "Apt students of segregation" is the characterization offered by the Chicago black newspaper, the *Defender*, and quoted in Thomas Lee Philpott, *The Slum and the Ghetto: Neighborhood Deterioration and Middle-Class Reform, Chicago, 1880–1930* (New York, 1978), 194; for "trained," see Du Bois at note 56 above.

62. Kathleen Neils Conzen, David A. Gerber, Ewa Morawska, George E. Pozzetta, and Rudolph J. Vecoli, "The Invention of Ethnicity: A Perspective from the U.S.A.," *Journal of American Ethnic History* 12 (Fall 1992): 27.

63. Lewis, *Black Coal Miners*, 109–110; Irvine as quoted in Kathryn J. Oberdeck, "Popular Narrative and Working-Class Identity: Alexander Irvine's Early Twentieth-Century Literary Adventures," in Eric Arnesen, Julie Greene, and Bruce Laurie, eds., *Labor Histories: Class, Politics, and the Working-Class Experience* (Urbana, Ill., 1998), 210; Mary White Ovington, *The Walls Came Tumbling Down* (New York, 1947), 11, 36; see also Zecker, "*Negrov Lyncovanie*," passim. I also thank Zecker for the amazing Kikta story, found in the Ellis Island Oral History Project.

64. Jennifer L. Hochschild, *Facing Up to the American Dream: Race, Class, and the Soul of the Nation* (Princeton, 1995), 227; Irvin L. Child, *Italian or American? The Second Generation in Conflict* (London, 1943), 35–36; James T. Farrell, *Studs Lonigan: A Trilogy Comprising Young Lonigan, The Young Manhood of Studs Lonigan, and Judgment Day* (Urbana, Ill., 1993), 402.

65. Osofsky, *Harlem*, 45, quotes the educator. On fitness for citizenship, see Matthew Frye Jacobson, *Barbarian Virtues: The United States Encounters Foreign Peoples at Home and Abroad, 1876–1917* (New York, 2000), 93–97.

66. William D. Haywood, *Bill Haywood's Book: The Autobiography of William D. Haywood* (New York, 1929), 181.

67. Clarence Major, *Juba to Jive: A Dictionary of African-American Slang* (New York, 1994), 97.

68. Gabriela F. Arredondo, "'Our Looks Cannot Be Changed by Our Nationality': Negotiating Race and Ethnicity, Mexicans in Chicago, 1916–1939" (paper delivered at the annual meeting of the Organization of American Historians, Toronto, April 1999).

69. Desmond King, *Making Americans: Immigration, Race, and the Origins of the Diverse Democracy* (Cambridge, Mass., 2000), 102. Stanley Lieberson, *Ethnic Patterns in American Cities* (New York, 1963), 206–218; Richard Alba, *Italian Americans: Into the Twilight of Ethnicity* (Englewood Cliffs, N.J., 1985), 54; Shankman, *Ambivalent Friends*, 154; Julius Lester, ed., *The Seventh Son: The Thought and Writings of W.E.B. Du Bois* (New York, 1971), 2:4, reprints Du Bois. Robert K. Murray, *Red Scare: A Study in National Hysteria* (Minneapolis, 1955); Brody, *Steelworkers in America*, 121.

70. See Noel Ignatiev, *How the Irish Became White* (New York, 1995); David R. Roediger, *The Wages of Whiteness: Race and the Making of the American Working Class* (New York, 1999), 133–163.

71. Barrett, *Work and Community*, 224 ("conscious"); Stanley Lieberson, *A Piece of the Pie: Black and White Immigrants Since 1880* (Berkeley, 1980), 301–359; Suzanne Model, "The Effects of Ethnicity in the Workplace on Blacks, Italians, and Jews in 1910 New York," *Journal of Urban History* 16 (November 1989): 33–42; John Bodnar, Roger Simon, and Michael Weber, *Lives of their Own: Blacks, Italians, and Poles in Pittsburgh, 1900–1960* (Urbana, Ill., 1982), 141.

72. Thomas Bell, *Out of This Furnace* (1941; Pittsburgh, 1976), 124; Attaway, *Blood on the Forge*, 122–123; La Sorte, *La Merica*, 81; Roger Horowitz, *"Negro and White, Unite and Fight": A Social History of Industrial Unionism in Meatpacking, 1930–90* (Urbana, Ill., 1997), 90. On mixing in gangs and politics, see Christopher Adamson, "Defensive Localism in White and Black: A Comparative History of European-American and African-American Youth Gangs," *Ethnic and Racial Studies* 23 (March 2000): 278–279.

73. George Lipsitz, "Creating Dangerously: The Blues Life of Johnny Otis," introducing Otis, *Upside Your Head: Rhythm and Blues on Central Avenue* (Hanover, N.H., 1993), xviii–xix; on "middlemen minorities," see Edna Bonacich, "A Theory of Middlemen Minorities," *American Sociological Review* 38 (October 1973): 583–594; Walter Zenner, *Minorities in the Middle: A Cross Cultural Analysis* (Albany, 1991).

74. In Brackman, "Ebb and Flow," 450; Stave and Sutherland with Salerno, *From the Old Country*, 227.

75. Michael Rogin, "Making America Home: Racial Masquerade and Ethnic Assimilation in the Transition to Talking Pictures," *Journal of American History* 79 (December 1992): 1053; Michael Rogin, "Blackface, White Noise: The Jewish Jazz Singer Finds His Voice," *Critical Inquiry* 18 (Spring 1992): 420, 437–438; Robert W. Snyder, *The Voice of the City: Vaudeville and Popular Culture in New York* (Oxford, 1989), 120; Lewis Erenberg, *Steppin' Out: New York Nightlife and the Transformation of American Culture, 1890–1930* (Chicago, 1981), 195. See Brackman, "Ebb and Flow of Conflict," 486, for Tucker's practice of removing a glove at the end of a black-face performance to "show I was a white girl." On the ubiquity of minstrel shows, see Kazal, "Becoming 'Old Stock,'" 546–547; Gads Hill Center (Chicago), *May Report* (1915); *Integrato Metropolitano: New York, Chicago, Torino tre volti dell'emigrazione*

italiana, Un programma della Fondazione Giovanni Agnelli (Torino, March–April 1982), unpaginated, for a minstrel pageant with "America" spelled out by participants. Jane Davis, "'Give 'em the Flash': Gender, Performance, and Mass Culture in the Early Career of Tiny Kline, 1905–1920" (paper presented to the Berkshire Conference on the History of Women, University of Connecticut, June 2002) has material on Kline's transformations and on the minstrel shows at the Jewish settlement house where she stayed for a time.

76. Melnick, *Right to Sing the Blues*, 112–113, 1–196; Burton Peretti, *The Creation of Jazz: Music, Race, and Culture in Urban America* (Urbana, 1992), 205–206; Werner Sollors, *Beyond Ethnicity: Consent and Descent in American Culture* (New York, 1986), 17. Nick Evans's provocative "Racial Discourse in Ethnic Autobiography: 'Black' Self-Fashioning in Mezz Mezzrow's *Really the Blues*" (paper presented to the American Studies Association, Pittsburgh, 1995) sent me back to Sollors's work. On Valentino, see Miriam Hansen, *Babel and Babylon: Spectatorship in American Silent Film* (Chicago, 1991), 245–294; and Siobhan Somerville, *Queering the Color Line: Race and the Invention of Homosexuality in American Culture* (Durham, N.C., 2000), 153–155. "On chameleonic blood," see Daniel Itzkovitz, "Passing Like Me," *South Atlantic Quarterly* 98 (Winter–Spring 1999): 36–57.

77. Allan Kent Powell, *The Next Time We Strike: Labor in Utah's Coal Fields* (Logan, Utah, 1985), 89–92; Josef J. Barton, *Peasants and Strangers: Italians, Rumanians, and Slovaks in an American City, 1890–1950* (Cambridge, Mass., 1975), 20; Barrett, *Work and Community*, 220–221; Pacyga, *Polish Immigrants*, 219–220; Tuttle, *Race Riot*, 54–55, 197–200; Steven P. Erie, *Rainbow's End: Irish Americans and the Dilemma of Urban Machine Politics, 1840–1985* (Berkeley, 1988), esp. 25–66. On the Manasseh Clubs, see Harry Haywood, *Black Bolshevik* (Chicago, 1978), 37; St. Clair Drake and Horace R. Cayton, *Black Metropolis: A Study of Negro Life in a Northern City* (New York, 1945), 54, 145–146; on the Irish, see Leonard Dinnerstein, "The Funeral of Rabbi Jacob Joseph," in David A. Gerber, ed., *Anti-Semitism in American History* (Urbana, Ill., 1986), 275–277; Kazal, "Becoming 'Old Stock,'" 536–537; James R. Barrett, "Americanization from the Bottom Up: Immigration and the Remaking of the Working Class in the United States, 1880–1930," *Journal of American History* 79 (December 1992): 1006; Eithne Luibheid, "Irish Immigrants in the United States," in Jim MacLaughlin, ed., *Location and Dislocation in Contemporary Irish Society* (Cork, Ireland, 1997), 254–261; and the material on "Catholic whiteness" in Chapter 6 in this book. On "hunkies," see Bruce M. Stave and John F. Sutherland with Aldo Salerno, eds., *From the Old Country: An Oral History of European Migration* (New York, 1994), 181; on "greasy wop" and "guinea bastard," see Caroline Ware, *Greenwich Village, 1920–1930: A Comment on American Civilization in the Post-War Years* (1963; Berkeley, 1994), 131; on Buffalo, see Carpenter, *Nationality, Color, and Economic Opportunity*, 119, 121; La Sorte, *La Merica*, 51, 139 (quoting Margariti), 148–152; Harry Golden, preface to Hutchins Hapgood, *The Spirit*

of the Ghetto: Studies of the Jewish Quarters of New York (New York, 1966), ix (face); Rudolf Glanz, *Jew and Irish: Historic Group Relations and Immigration* (New York, 1976), 92.

78. Rick Halpern, "Race, Ethnicity, and Union in the Chicago Stockyards, 1917–1922," *International Review of Social History* 37 (1992): 52–57; Barrett, *Work and Community*, 219–223; Pacyga, *Polish Immigrants*, 221–227; cf. Paul Street, "The Logic and Limits of 'Plant Loyalty': Black Workers, White Labor, and Corporate Racial Paternalism in Chicago's Stockyards, 1916–1940," *Journal of Social History*, Spring 1996, 665; James Grossman, *Land of Hope: Chicago, Black Southerners, and the Great Migration* (Chicago, 1989), 163; on Polish and Lithuanian nationalism, see Victor Greene, *For God and Country: The Rise of Polish and Lithuanian Ethnic Consciousness in America, 1860–1910* (Madison, Wis., 1975), chaps. 7–9; on Italian Americans in the riot, see Guglielmo, "White on Arrival," 86–94; and Addams's remarks in Chicago Commission on Race Relations, *The Negro in Chicago: A Study of Race Relations and a Race Riot* (Chicago, 1922), 19. Thanks to Anthony Sigismondi for the last of the references.

79. Radzialowski, "Competition for Jobs," 16; *Glos Polek,* July 31, 1919; *Daily Jewish Courier,* April 22, 1914; *Narod Polski,* August 6, 1919. For Park, see "Racial Assimilation in Secondary Groups," *American Journal of Sociology* 19 (March 1914): 620, 606–623, as cited in Barbara Foley, *Spectres of 1919: Class and Nation in the Making of the New Negro* (Urbana, Ill., 2003), 289, n. 15. For evidence that violence against African migrant workers in Poland framed part of the reaction of the Polish press in 1919, see Elizabeth McKillen, *Chicago Labor and the Quest for a Democratic Dipomacy, 1914–1924* (Ithaca, N.Y., 1995), 188.

80. Philadelphia *Tageblatt,* June 29, 1924, as reprinted in Kazal, "Becoming 'Old Stock,'" 551, and discussed at 533–534; "Ranen? Afičan," *Obrana,* October 27, 1916; *Sunday Jewish Courier* (Chicago), June 8 and July 27, 1919, in Chicago Foreign Language Press Survey at Chicago Historical Society. Thanks to Robert Zecker for the second citation.

81. *Dziennik Zwiazkowy,* December 5, 1911, as cited in Nakano, "Preserving Distinctiveness," 4–5; on Italian pride as an alternative to whiteness, see Guglielmo, *White on Arrival*, 6; Michael M. Topp, "'It Is Providential That There Are Foreigners Here': Whiteness and Masculinity in the Making of Italian American Syndicalist Identity" (paper presented to the Race, Ethnicity, and Migration Conference, University of Minnesota, November 2000), 13; Luigi Villari, "Relazione dell dott. Luigi Villari gugli Italiani nel Distretto Consolare di New Orleans," *Bolletino dell' Emigrazione* (Italian Ministry of Foreign Affairs, Royal Commission on Emigration, 1907), 2439, 2499, 2532. Thanks to Louise Edwards for the source and the translations. On South Philadelphia, see Stefano Luconi, "A Troubled Partnership: Italian Americans and African Americans in the New Deal Democratic Coalition," in Ashyk, Gardephe, and Tamburri, *Shades of Black and White*, 144. On the postimmigration vitality (and sometimes the forging in the

United States) of European national identities, see Jacobson, *Special Sorrows;* and McKillen, *Chicago Labor and the Quest for a Democratic Diplomacy.*

82. Barrett, "Americanization from the Bottom Up," 1010–1020; John McClymer, "Gender and the 'American Way of Life': Women in the Americanization Movement," *Journal of American Ethnic History* 11 (Spring 1991): 5–6.

83. Niles Carpenter with Daniel Katz, "The Cultural Adjustment of the Polish Group in the City of Buffalo: An Experiment in the Technique of Social Investigation," *Social Forces* 6 (September 1927): 80–82. For similar evidence of an inbetween/indifferent attitude toward race, see Edward R. Kantrowicz, *Polish American Politics in Chicago, 1888–1940* (Chicago, 1975), 149; Jean Scarpaci, "Immigrants in the New South: Italians in Louisiana Sugar Parishes, 1880–1910," *Labor History* 16 (Spring 1975): 175. For Park, see Robert E. Park and Herbert A. Miller, *Old World Traits Transplanted* (New York, 1921), 22.

CHAPTER 5

1. John I. H. Brown, *Philip Evergood* (New York, 1960), fig. 29; 9–20; Kendall Taylor, *Philip Evergood: Never Separate from the Heart* (London, 1987), 111; for Evergood and the "proletarian grotesque," see Michael Denning, *The Cultural Front: The Laboring of American Culture in the Twentieth Century* (London, 1997), 123. The epigraphs are from W.E.B. Du Bois, *An ABC of Color* (Berlin, 1964), 139; and Henry Pratt Fairchild, *Greek Immigration to the United States* (New Haven, 1911), 236–237.

2. See Matthew Jacobson, *Whiteness of a Different Color: European Immigrants and the Alchemy of Race* (Cambridge, Mass., 1998), 4, on "inconclusive" whiteness; on double V, see Ronald Takaki, *Double Victory: A Multicultural History of America in World War II* (Boston, 2000).

3. See Desmond King, *Making Americans: Immigration, Race, and the Origins of the Diverse Democracy* (Cambridge, Mass., 2000), 85–126, for the history of high and dashed hopes for changing immigrant culture during and after World War I. For a more optimistic reading, see Nancy Gentile Ford, *Americans All! Foreign-Born Soldiers in World War I* (College Station, Tex., 2001). On African Americans in World War II, see John Morton Blum, *V Was for Victory: Politics and American Culture During World War II* (New York, 1976), 182–220.

4. Philip Gleason, "Minorities (Almost) All: The Minority Concept in American Social Thought," *American Quarterly* 43 (September 1991): 392–397; Werner Sollors, ed., *The Invention of Ethnicity* (New York, 1989), xiii, and Chapter 1 in this book; Donald Young, *American Minority Peoples: A Study in Racial and Cultural Conflicts in the United States* (New York, 1932), the key text in introducing "minorities," offers an interesting move away from race as biology and to some extent from applying the language of "race" to new immigrants even as it insists on commonalities between the experiences of oppressed European races and those of Asian Americans and African Americans. See especially pages xi–xiii.

5. Nelson Algren, *Never Come Morning* (1942; New York, 1987), 74–75, 90–94, 183–184, 261, 272, 280. In discussing Algren, I am much in the debt of Todd Michney, "Nelson Algren's Fiction and the Shifting Terrains of Race and Class" (forthcoming).

6. David A. J. Richards, *Italian American: The Racializing of an Ethnic Identity* (New York, 1999), 225; Bruce Stave and John F. Sutherland with Aldo Salerno, *From the Old Country: An Oral History of European Migration to America* (New York, 1994), 209–212, 217–218; Emory S. Bogardus, *Immigration and Race Attitudes* (Boston, 1928), 245, 251; Jeff Kisseloff, *You Must Remember This: An Oral History of Manhattan from the 1890s to World War II* (New York, 1989), 189; David Roediger and James Barrett, "Irish Hosts and White Pan-Ethnicity," in Nancy Foner and George Fredrickson, eds., *Not Just Black and White: Immigration and Race, Then and Now* (New York, 2004).

7. Eric L. Goldstein, "'Different Blood Flows in Our Veins': Race and Jewish Self-Definition in Late Nineteenth-Century America," *American Jewish History* 85 (March 1997): 37, 44, 54–55. See also John J. Bukowczyk, "'Who Is the Nation?'—or, 'Did Cleopatra Have Red Hair?': A Patriotic Discourse on Diversity, Nationality and Race," *MELUS* 23 (Winter 1998): 9–11 on the ebb and flow of "race" among Polish Americans.

8. Jack D. Foner, *Blacks and the Military in American History* (New York, 1974), 133–175, esp. 146–147, 167–168, 173; on internment, compare Sarah Goodyear, "When Being Italian Was a Crime," *Village Voice*, April 18, 2000, 51–55; Morton Grodzins, *Americans Betrayed* (Chicago, 1949); Yasuko I. Takezawa, *Breaking the Silence: Redress and Japanese American Ethnicity* (Ithaca, N.Y., 1995), 30.

9. Quoted in Loren Baritz, *The Good Life: The Meaning of Success for the American Middle Class* (New York, 1982), 53; Dominic J. Capeci and Martha Wilkerson, *Layered Violence: The Detroit Rioters of 1943* (Jackson, 1991), 181, 185.

10. Lewis A. Erenberg, *Swingin' the Dream: Big Band Jazz and the Rebirth of American Culture* (Chicago, 1998), 188–189; Thomas Doherty, *Projections of War: Hollywood, American Culture, and World War II* (New York, 1993), 224–226.

11. Mike Davis, *Prisoners of the American Dream* (London, 1986), 89.

12. Jennifer L. Hochschild, *Facing Up to the American Dream: Race, Class, and the Soul of the Nation* (Princeton, 1995), 243.

13. Jacobson, *Whiteness of a Different Color*, 93.

14. Jacobson, *Whiteness of a Different Color*, 93, 94–135; James Baldwin, "On Being 'White' . . . and Other Lies," *Essence*, April 1984, 90–92.

15. John Higham, *Strangers in the Land: Patterns of American Nativism, 1860–1925* (New Brunswick, N.J., 1955), 320, 312–330.

16. Calvin Coolidge, "Whose Country Is This?" *Good Housekeeping*, February 1921, 13–14; citations from 14. Elaine Tyler May, *Barren in the Promised Land: Childless Americans and the Pursuit of Happiness* (New York, 1995), 102–103.

17. Hiram W. Evans, "The Klan's Fight for Americanism," *North American Review* 223 (March 1926): 33; Roberts, *Why Europe Leaves Home* (Indianapolis, 1922), as

excerpted in Lewis H. Carlson and George A. Colburn, eds., *In Their Place: White America Defines Her Minorities* (New York, 1972), 312; Higham, *Strangers in the Land*, 271–274, 186–199; Nancy MacLean, *Behind the Mask of Chivalry: The Making of the Second Ku Klux Klan* (New York, 1994), xi; Kenneth T. Jackson, *The Ku Klux Klan in the City, 1915–1930* (New York, 1967). On eugenics and the 1924 debates, see also Matthew Pratt Guterl, *The Color of Race in America, 1900–1940* (Cambridge, Mass., 2001), 46–48; King, *Making Americans*, 166–195; Ian Dowbiggin, *Keeping America Sane: Psychiatry and Eugenics in the United States and Canada, 1880–1940* (Ithaca, N.Y., 1997), 227; on Laughlin, see King, *Making Americans*, 173, 189, 131–138, 173–190 passim; Steven Selden, *Inheriting Shame: The Story of Eugenics and Racism in America* (New York, 1999), 43–44.

18. Higham, *Strangers in the Land*, 307, and above on the Klan.

19. Gerard Leeflang, *American Travels of a Dutch Hobo, 1923–1926* (Ames, Iowa, 1984), 85–86; James T. Farrell, *The Young Manhood of Studs Lonigan*, from the *Studs Lonigan* trilogy (1936; Urbana, Ill., 1993), 402.

20. Quoted in James Gardner, "'Our Native Clay': Racial and Sexual Identity and the Making of Americans in *The Bridge*," *American Quarterly* 44 (March 1992): 29.

21. Robert K. Murray, *Red Scare: A Study of National Hysteria, 1919–1920* (Minneapolis, 1955), 169, for the doggerel; Horace Kallen, *Culture and Democracy in the United States* (New York, 1924), 24. Alan Kraut, *Silent Travelers: Germs, Genes, and the "Immigrant Menace"* (Baltimore, 1995), 74–76; Stephen Jay Gould, *The Mismeasure of Man* (New York, 1981), 192–233. On kaffir, see Alan Dawley, *Changing the World: American Progressives in War and Revolution* (Princeton, 2003), 287.

22. Yerkes and Sheldon, as cited in Carlson and Colburn, eds., *In Their Place*, 333–334, 149–150. See also Stephen Jay Gould, *Hen's Teeth and Horse's Toes* (New York, 1983), 291–302; and Hamilton Cravens, "Scientific Racism in Modern America, 1870–1990s," *Prospect: An Annual of American Cultural Studies* 21 (1996): 480; Ford, *Americans All*, 16–111.

23. Stephen Meyer III, *The Five-Dollar Day: Labor Management and Social Control in the Ford Motor Company, 1908–1921* (Albany, 1981), 176–185; Keith Sward, *The Legend of Henry Ford* (New York, 1948), 108–118, 141–142; Sharon M. Leon, "Beyond Birth Control: Catholic Responses to the Eugenics Movement in the United States, 1900–1950" (Ph.D. diss., University of Minnesota, forthcoming); Kenneth M. Ludmerer, *Genetics and American Society: A Historical Appraisal* (Baltimore, 1972), 100–113.

24. Higham, *Strangers in the Land*, 226, 261–262, 316–317; Kallen, *Culture and Democracy*, 151; David Montgomery, *The Fall of the House of Labor: The Workplace, the State, and American Labor Activism* (Cambridge, 1987), 461–462.

25. On the daring and dedication of new immigrant unionists in the postwar strike wave, see David Saposs, "The Mind of Immigrant Communities in the Pittsburgh District," in Interchurch World Movement, *Report on the Steel Strike of 1919* (New York, 1920), esp. 239; David R. Roediger and Philip S. Foner, *Our Own Time: A History of*

American Labor and the Working Day (London, 1989), 217–226; on the AFL, see Quinn, "Americanism and Immigration," *American Federationist* 31 (April 1924): 295; for Gompers, see David Brody, *In Labor's Cause: Main Themes on the History of the American Worker* (New York, 1993), 117; on the American Legion, see William Pencak, *For God and Country: The American Legion, 1919–1941* (Boston, 1989).

26. Thomas G. Dyer, *Theodore Roosevelt and the Idea of Race* (Baton Rouge, 1980), 42–44, 130–131, and for "alchemy," 132. Higham develops the themes on which this conclusion centers in *Strangers in the Land*, especially with reference to Kellor's trajectory, 239–249, and Horace Kallen, *Culture and Democracy in the United States* (New York, 1924), 139 n. 1, but compare 149–150 for a more benign view. See also 234–330 passim, with the quoted passage on 262–263. Compare John F. McClymer, "The Americanization Movement and the Education of the Foreign-Born Adult, 1914–1925," in Bernard J. Weiss, ed., *American Education and the European Immigrant, 1840–1940* (Urbana, Ill., 1982), 96–116; and Gary Gerstle, "The Protean Character of American Liberalism," *American Historical Review* 99 (October 1994): 1055–1067; on War Plans White, see Dawley, *Changing the World*, 275, 272–274.

27. Gwendolyn Mink, "The Lady and the Tramp: Gender, Race, and the Origins of the American Welfare State," in Linda Gordon, ed., *Women, the State, and Welfare* (Madison, Wis., 1990), 93–94; Mae M. Ngai, "The Architecture of Race in American Immigration Law: A Reexamination of the Immigration Act of 1924," *Journal of American History* 86 (June 1999): 69–70, 74, 67–92 passim. Calculations from *Proclamation by the President of the United States*, no. 1872, March 22, 1929, 46 Stat. 2984; Karen Brodkin, *How Jews Became White Folks and What That Says About Race in America* (New Brunswick, N.J., 1998), 60.

28. *Ex parte Dow*, D.C., E.D.S.C., 211 Fed. 486 (1913); *In re Dow*, C.C.A., 226 Fed. 145 (4th Cir. 1915); *In re Balsara*, C.C., S.D.N.Y., 171 Fed. 294 (1909); *U.S. v. Balsara*, C.C.A., 180 Fed. 694 (2nd Cir. 1910); *Ozawa v. U.S.*, 260 U.S. 178 (1922) aptly summarizes precedents. See also *In re Akhay Kumar Mozumdar*, D.C., S.D. Cal., 296 Fed. 173 (1913); Ian Haney Lopez, *White by Law: The Legal Construction of Race* (New York, 1996), 67–68, 203–225; and Emory Bogardus, *Immigration and Race Attitudes* (Boston, 1928), 23–25.

29. See Laura Browder, *Slippery Characters: Ethnic Impersonators and American Identities* (Chapel Hill, 2000), 154.

30. Henry Pratt Fairchild, *The Melting Pot Mistake* (Boston, 1926).

31. Calculated from "Legal Immigration to the U.S. by Region of the World, 1820–1990," in Silvia Pedraza, "Origins and Destinies: Immigration, Race, and Ethnicity in American History," in Silvia Pedraza and Rubén G. Rumbaut, eds., *Origins and Destinies: Immigration, Race, and Ethnicity in America* (Belmont, Calif., 1996), 4; Mac H. Donaldson, *Labor Problems in the United States* (New York, 1939), 210.

32. Pedraza, "Origins and Destinies," 4; Niles Carpenter, *Immigrants and Their Children, 1920* (1927; New York, 1969), 62, 193.

33. Gary Gerstle, *American Crucible: Race and Nation Across the Twentieth Century* (Princeton, 2001), 97, 81–127; Feldman, *Racial Factors*, 174; Pedraza, "Origins and Destinies," 4.

34. Donaldson, *Labor Problems*, 210–211; Feldman, *Racial Factors*, 149; Joel Perlmann, *Toward a Population History of the Second Generation: Birth Cohorts of Southern-, Central-, and Eastern-European Origins, 1871–1970,* Working Paper no. 333 (Jerome Levy Economics Institute of Bard College, June 2001), table 6-A, unpaginated.

35. Gerstle, *American Crucible*, 95–127; Ngai, "Architecture of Race," 77.

36. Feldman, *Racial Factors*, 177; Ngai, "Architecture of Race," 77–80; King, *Making Americans*, 206–112; Higham, *Strangers in the Land*, 324; John Mack Faragher et al., *Out of Many: A History of the American People* (New York, 1998), 623; Robert Divine, *American Immigration Policy, 1924–1952* (New Haven, 1957), 26–51.

37. Feldman, *Racial Factors*, 186; Oscar Handlin, *The Uprooted: The Epic Story of the Great Migration That Made the American People* (1951; Boston, 1973), 262–263. On Klan membership, estimates of the organization's mid-1920s crest of membership range from 1.5 to 5 million. See Kenneth T. Jackson, *The Ku Klux Klan in the City, 1915–1930* (New York, 1967), xii, 236; and Nancy MacLean, *Behind the Mask of Chivalry: The Making of the Second Ku Klux Klan* (New York, 1994), 197 n. 2.

38. Donaldson, *Labor Problems*, 210; Feldman, *Racial Factors*, 144–145; William Leiserson, *Adjusting Immigrant and Industry* (New York, 1924), 255; David Fellman, "The Alien's Right to Work," *Minnesota Law Review* 22 (1938): 155–174.

39. Feldman, *Racial Factors*, 144–146; Richard W. Steele, "'No Racials': Discrimination Against Ethnics in American Defense Industry, 1940–42," *Labor History* 32 (Winter 1991): 66–90.

40. Donaldson, *Labor Problems*, 210–211; "Composition and Assimilation of Foreign Population of the United States," *Monthly Labor Review* 54 (1942): 74.

41. Browder, *Slippery Characters*, 146, quotes Hoover; Feldman, *Racial Factors*, 176–177; Young, *American Minority Peoples*, 152.

42. Feldman, *Racial Factors*, 186; Carpenter, *Immigrants and Their Children*, 266; Leiserson, *Adjusting Immigrants and Industry*, 70; Sinclair Lewis, *Babbitt* (1922; New York, 1942), 145.

43. Francis J. Brown and Joseph Slaney Roucek, eds., *Our Racial and National Minorities: Their History, Contributions, and Present Problems* (New York, 1937), 14. Carole Marks, *Farewell—We're Good and Gone: The Great Black Migration* (Bloomington, Ind., 1989), esp. 17; Gary B. Nash et al., *The American People: Creating a Nation and a Society* (New York, 1998), 816. For excellent analysis of immigration restriction and antiblack racism (including efforts to stall black immigration to the United States), see King, *Making Americans*, 138–164, 224–226.

44. Gladys L. Palmer, *Philadelphia Workers in a Changing Economy* (Philadelphia, 1956), 57–58. For an acute account of the ways such demographic changes

helped make the "race" problem hinge increasingly on color, see Guterl, *Color of Race in America*, 14–67.

45. Feldman, *Racial Factors*, 19, 105–107; Donaldson, *Labor Problems*, 211; Pedraza, "Origins and Destinies," 4; Jeremiah W. Jenks and W. Jett Lauck with Rufus D. Smith, *The Immigration Problem: A Study of American Conditions and Needs* (New York, 1926), chart II, appended; and Bureau of the Census, *Historical Statistics of the United States: Colonial Times to 1957* (Washington, D.C., 1960), 66; T. J. Woofter, *Races and Ethnic Groups in American Life* (New York, 1933), 43–44, 57, 62–63; Kathleen Mapes, "'A Special Class of Labor': Mexican (Im)migrants, Immigration Debate, and Industrial Agriculture in the Rural Midwest," *Labor* 1 (Summer 2004): 65–88; Gunther Peck, *Reinventing Free Labor: Padrones and Immigrant Workers in the North American West* (Cambridge, U.K., 2000), 228–230.

46. James Gregory, *American Exodus: The Dust Bowl Migration and Okie Culture in California* (New York, 1989); James Grossman, *Land of Hope: Chicago, Black Southerners, and the Great Migration* (Chicago, 1989); Rodolfo Acuña, *Occupied America: The Chicano's Struggle Toward Liberation* (New York, 1972), 121–126; Zaragosa Vargas, *Proletarians of the North: A History of Mexican Industrial Workers in Detroit and the Midwest, 1917–1933* (Berkeley, 1993).

47. Carpenter, *Immigrants and Their Children*, 5–9; Margo Anderson, *The American Census: A Social History* (New Haven, 1988), 90–92, 142–149.

48. Montgomery, *House of Labor*, 462; Mark Wyman, *Round-trip to America: The Immigrants Return* (Ithaca, 1993), 112, 205; Jenks and Lauck, *Immigration Problem*, 36–38; Gunther Peck, *Reinventing Free Labor: Padrones and Immigrant Workers in the North American West, 1880–1930* (Cambridge, U.K., 2000), 167–168.

49. Montgomery, *House of Labor*, 462; Feldman, *Racial Factors*, 149; compare Leiserson, *Adjusting Immigrant and Industry*, esp. 94–97, with Sanford Jacoby, *Employing Bureaucracy: Managers, Unions, and the Transformation of Work in American Industry, 1900–1945* (New York, 1985), 174–180; Elliott Robert Barkan, *And Still They Come: Immigrants and American Society, 1920 to the 1990s* (Wheeling, Ill., 1996), 20, 42, 199; Brown and Roucek, eds., *Our Racial and National Minorities*, 678; Woofter, *Races and Ethnic Groups*, 55; Candice Lewis Bredbenner, *A Nationality of Her Own: Women, Marriage, and the Law of Citizenship* (Berkeley, 1998), 93–96, 157–158, 161 (Breckinridge quotation); Donna Gabaccia, *From the Other Side: Women, Gender, and Immigrant Life in the U.S., 1820–1990* (Bloomington, Ind., 1994), 114.

50. Barkan, *Still They Come*, 42–43; Robert A. Slayton, *Empire Statesman: The Rise and Redemption of Al Smith* (New York, 2001), esp. 324–325.

51. Alan Dawley, *Struggles for Justice: Social Responsibility and the Liberal State* (Cambridge, Mass., 1991), 291–292.

52. Joshua A. Fishman, *Language Loyalty in the United States* (London, 1966), 379; Richard D. Alba, *Ethnic Identity: The Transformation of White America* (New Haven, 1990), 11; Kotaro Nakano, "Preserving Distinctiveness: Language, Loyalty,

and Americanization in Early Twentieth-Century Chicago" (section paper presented to the Kyoto American Studies Summer Seminar, Center for American Studies, Ritsumeikan University, Kyoto, 2000), 1–15.

53. Jane Perry Clark, *Deportation of Aliens from the United States to Europe* (New York, 1931), 250–296; Randy D. McBee, *Dance Hall Days: Intimacy and Leisure Among Working-Class Immigrants in the United States* (New York, 2000), 15, 32, 95–96; Donna Gabaccia, "Women of the Mass Migrations: From Minority to Majority, 1820–1930," in Dirk Hoerder and Leslie Moch, eds., *European Migrants: Global and Local Perspectives* (Boston, 1996), 90–114; Barbara Foley, *Spectres of 1919: Class and Nation in the Making of the New Negro* (Urbana, Ill., 2003), 122-158.

54. Ngai, "Architecture of Race," 90, 91, 68–92 passim; Clara Rodriguez, *Changing Race: Latinos, the Census, and the History of Ethnicity in the United States* (New York, 2000), 83, 101–102; Melissa Nobles, *Shades of Citizenship: Race and the Census in Modern Politics* (Stanford, Calif., 2000), 73–75. On the impact of debates over Mexican migration on the position of new immigrants, see also Clare Sheridan, "Contested Citizenship: National Identity and the Mexican Immigration Debates of the 1920s," *Journal of American Ethnic History* 21 (2002): esp. 8.

55. Feldman, *Racial Factors*, 107; Camille Guerin-Gonzalez, *Mexican Workers, American Dreams: Immigration, Repatriation, and California Farm Labor, 1900–1939* (New Brunswick, N.J., 1994); Ngai, "Architecture of Race," 91; Francisco Rodriguez Balderrama and Raymond Rodriguez Balderrama, *Decade of Betrayal: Mexican Repatriation in the 1930s* (Albuquerque, 1995).

56. E. San Juan Jr., *From Exile to Diaspora: Versions of the Filipino Experience in the United States* (Boulder, 1998), 151–152; Ngai, "Architecture of Race," 91–92.

57. Montgomery, *House of Labor*, 462; Roger Daniels, *The Politics of Prejudice: The Anti-Japanese Movement in California and the Struggle for Japanese Exclusion* (Berkeley, 1962), 92–105, esp. 98; Gerstle, *American Crucible*, 117–122; King, *Making Americans*, 201.

58. Gerstle, *American Crucible*, 121.

CHAPTER 6

1. The epigraphs are from Nadia Venturini, "'Over the Years People Don't Know': Italian Americans and African Americans in Harlem in the 1930s," in Donna Gabaccia and Fraser Ottanelli, eds., *Italian Workers of the World: Labor Migration and the Formation of Multiethnic States* (Urbana, Ill., 2001), 196, from a 1988 reminiscence on the interwar years by Pascale, a "lifelong" Harlem resident; and Charles Abrams, *Forbidden Neighbors: A Study of Prejudice in Housing* (New York, 1955), 138–139; Claude McKay, "White Houses," in Alain Locke, ed., *The New Negro* (1925; New York, 1969); William J. Maxwell, *Old Left, New Negro:*

African-American Writing Between the Wars (New York, 1999), 103; Barbara Foley, *Spectres of 1919: Class and Nation in the Making of the New Negro* (Urbana, Ill., 2003), 242, 294 n. 52.

2. Arnold R. Hirsch, *Making the Ghetto: Race and Housing in Chicago, 1940–1960* (Chicago, 1998), 187, 189; Kenneth T. Jackson, *Crabgrass Frontier: The Suburbanization of the United States* (New York, 1985), 288–290. Richard Harris, "Working-Class Home Ownership in the American Metropolis," *Journal of Urban History* 17 (November 1990): 46–69; David Montgomery, *Citizen Worker: The Experience of Workers in the United States and the Free Market During the Nineteenth Century* (Cambridge, U.K., 1993), 109.

3. Harris, "Working-Class Home Ownership," esp. 56, 40–55; Ewa Morawska, *For Bread with Butter: The Life-Worlds of East Central Europeans in Johnstown, Pennsylvania, 1890–1940* (Cambridge, U.K., 1985), 401, 205–206 ("expectedly"); Olivier Zunz, *The Changing Face of Inequality: Urbanization, Industrial Development, and Immigrants in Detroit, 1880–1920* (Chicago, 1982), 153–155, 390; Victor Greene, *For God and Country: The Rise of Polish and Lithuanian Ethnic Consciousness in America* (Madison, 1975), 38–39l; Josef Barton, *Peasants and Strangers: Italians, Rumanians, and Slovaks in an American City, 1890–1920* (Cambridge, Mass., 1975), 102. On the special case of Jews as successful but not likely to buy homes, see Stephen Steinberg, *The Ethnic Myth: Race, Ethnicity, and Class in America* (Boston, 1989), 98–106; and Stanley Lieberson, *Ethnic Patterns in American Cities* (New York, 1963), 206–218.

4. Zunz, *Changing Face of Inequality*, 161.

5. Peter Roberts, "Immigrant Wage-Earners," in Paul Underwood Kellogg, ed., *Wage-Earning Pittsburgh* (1914; New York, 1974) 53; Margaret F. Byington, *Homestead: The Households of a Mill Town* (1910; Pittsburgh, 1974), 155.

6. Louise Montgomery, *The American Girl in the Stockyards District* (Chicago, 1913), 3–4; Robert A. Slayton, *Back of the Yards: The Making of a Local Democracy* (Chicago, 1986), 30–31; Addams quoted in Hirsch, *Making the Second Ghetto*, 188; see also Joseph C. Bigott, *From the Cottage to the Bungalow: Houses and the Working Class in Metropolitan Chicago, 1869–1929* (Chicago, 2001), 2–4.

7. Abrams, *Forbidden Neighbors*, 138–139.

8. Upton Sinclair, *The Jungle* (1906; Urbana, Ill., 1988), esp. 44–46, 171–172, 207–214, 271; see also Nicholas Semmond and Chandra Mukerji, "'What You Are . . . I Wouldn't Eat': Ethnicity, Whiteness, and Performing 'the Jew' in Hollywood's Golden Age," in Daniel Bernardi, ed., *Classic Hollywood, Classic Whiteness* (Minneapolis, 2001), 4–14.

9. Michael Gold, *Jews Without Money* (New York, 1930), 113.

10. Hirsch, *Making the Second Ghetto*, 187 ("transfiguration"), 326 (citing Vecoli); Abrams, *Forbidden Neighbors*, 147 (Hoover); Slayton, *Back of the Yards*, 31 (polanis); Roberts, "Immigrant Wage-Earners," 45; Suzanne W. Model, "Work and Family: Blacks and Immigrants from South and East Europe," in Virginia Yans-

McLaughlin, ed., *Immigration Reconsidered: History, Sociology, and Politics* (New York, 1990), 135.

11. Model, "Work and Family," 134–135; Zunz, *Changing Face of Inequality*, 173; Byington, *Homestead*, 144–147; Slayton, *Back of the Yards*, 34; John Bodnar, *Workers' World: Kinship, Community, and Protest in an Industrial Society, 1900–1940* (Baltimore, 1982), 43–47, 105; Morawska, *For Bread with Butter*, 127, 128–130, 351.

12. Zunz, *Changing Face of Inequality*, 171, 170–173; Harris, "Working-Class Homeownership," 52, 54; Sinclair, *The Jungle*, 55; Dianne Harris, *The Ordinary Postwar House, 1945–1960: Fashioning Domesticity in an Era of Assimilation* (forthcoming).

13. Harris, "Working-Class Home Ownership," 47; Byington, *Homestead*, 144; Slayton, *Back of the Yards*, 34; use value and exchange value are taken from Karl Marx, *Capital: A Critique of Political Economy* (1867; Chicago, 1906), 1:42–43. See also Zunz, *Changing Face of Inequality*, 47, and, for a provocative attempt to consider late-nineteenth- and early-twentieth-century working-class home ownership from a Marxist point of view, Daniel D. Luria, "Wealth, Capital, and Power: The Social Meaning of Home Ownership," *Journal of Interdisciplinary History* 7 (Autumn 1976): 261–282.

14. On "ghetto," see especially Thomas Philpott, *The Slum and the Ghetto: Immigrants, Blacks, and Reformers in Chicago, 1880–1930* (1978; Belmont, Calif., 1991), 135–145, esp. 141; and Loic Wacquant, "A Black City Within the White: Revisiting America's Dark Ghetto," *Black Renaissance Noire* 2 (Fall–Winter 1998): 141–151. The classic University of Chicago study is Louis Wirth, *The Ghetto* (Chicago, 1928); on Wirth and the generalized use of "ghetto," see James B McKee, *Sociology and the Race Problem: The Failure of a Perspective* (Urbana, Ill., 1993), 129; on nonacademic usages, see Riv-Ellen Prell, *Fighting to Become Americans: Jews, Gender, and the Anxiety of Assimilation* (Boston, 1999), 21–57 ("ghetto girls"); Steven J. Ross, *Working-Class Hollywood: Silent Film and the Shaping of Class in America* (Princeton, 1998), 38, 44; Hutchins Hapgood, *The Spirit of the Ghetto* (1902; Cambridge, Mass., 1967). See also Jacob Riis, *How the Other Half Lives: Studies Among the Tenements of New York* (1901; New York, 1971), 115, 138, 85.

15. Henry Yu, *Thinking Orientals: Migration, Contact, and Exoticism in Modern America* (Oxford, 2001), 50, 54ff.

16. Nelli, *Italians in Chicago*, 45, 44–54; Philpott, *The Slum and the Ghetto*, 135–146, esp. 141, 143; Zunz, *Changing Face of Inequality*, 43–46; John Logan, *The Ethnic Neighborhood, 1920–1970*, Working Paper (Russell Sage Foundation, 1995), esp. 38.

17. Logan, "Ethnic Neighborhood," 21–41.

18. Philpott, *Slum and Ghetto*, 136, 375 n. 16; see also 137–144 passim.

19. Steinberg, *Ethnic Myth*, 53–55; on the Irish, see James Barrett and David Roediger, "Making New Immigrants Inbetween: Irish Hosts and White Pan-Ethnicity,

1890–1930," in Nancy Foner and George Fredrickson, eds., *Not Just Black and White: Historical and Contemporary Perspectives on Immigration, Race, and Ethnicity in the United States* (New York, 2004), 167–196; Steven Erie, *Rainbow's End: Irish Americans and the Dilemmas of Urban Machine Politics* (Berkeley, 1988), 69–41, 80, 88, 102–113.

20. Zunz, *Changing Face of Inequality*, 388, 390; Slayton, *Back of the Yards*, 33–34; Hirsch, *Making of the Second Ghetto*, 189–190; Greene, *For God and Country*, 54–57.

21. Philpott, *Slum and the Ghetto*, 144–145.

22. Randy D. McBee, *Dance Hall Days: Intimacy and Leisure Among Working-Class Immigrants in the United States* (New York, 2000), 175–176, 157–196, is the best recent evocation of gang or "social club" culture; see also Guglielmo, *White on Arrival*, 52–53. On deadlines, see Roediger and Barrett, "Making New Immigrants Inbetween," 175; William Z. Foster, *Pages from a Worker's Life* (New York, 1939), 17–18; Langston Hughes, *The Big Sea* (1940; New York, 1963), 33; Myron Davis, "Canaryville" (research paper, University of Chicago, 1927), 20–21; Frederick Thrasher, *The Gang: A Study of 1313 Gangs in Chicago* (1927; Chicago, 1963), 5–22, 62–63; Jeff Kisseloff, *You Must Remember This: An Oral History of Manhattan from the 1890s to World War II* (San Diego, 1989), 190, 268, 196; Thaddeus Radzialowski, "The Competition for Jobs and Racial Stereotypes: Poles and Black in Chicago," *Polish American Studies* 33 (Autumn 1976): 7–8; Caroline Ware, *Greenwich Village, 1920–1940* (Boston, 1935), 52, 131; Virginia Yans-McLaughlin, *Family and Community: Italian Immigrants in Buffalo, 1880–1930* (Ithaca, N.Y., 1982), 112–113; William Foote Whyte, *Steet Corner Society: The Social Structure of an Italian Slum* (Chicago, 1943), 195; Michael La Sorte, *La Merica: Images of Italian Greehorn Experience* (Philadelphia, 1985), 51, 139, 148–152; Niles Carpenter, *Nationality, Color, and Economic Opportunity in the City of Buffalo* (1927; Westport, Conn., 1970), 119; Ronald Bayor, *Neighbors in Conflict: The Irish, Germans, Jews, and Italians in New York City, 1929–1941* (Baltimore, 1978), esp. 3–4; Gamm, *Urban Exodus*, 227–228; Thomas A. Guglielmo, *White on Arrival: Italians, Race, Color, and Power in Chicago* (Oxford, 2003), 46; Bruce M. Stave and John F. Sutherland with Aldo Salerno, eds., *From the Old Country: An Oral History of European Migration to America* (New York, 1994), 89, 106–107. On the origin of the term "deadline," see Ted Collins, ed., *New York Murders* (New York, 1944), 47–48; and Randolph Lewis, "The Central Office," *Munsey's Magazine* 24 (February 1901): 721, both as cited and quoted in Peter Tamony's notes in the Tamony Papers at Western Historical Manuscripts Collections, University of Missouri, Columbia.

23. McGreevy, *Parish Boundaries*, 9–10 (for quotations), 7–54; see also 10–13, 34, 82–83, 100, 222, 261 on national and territorial perishes, and Everett Cherrington Hughes and Helen MacGill Hughes, *Where Peoples Meet: Racial and Ethnic Fron-*

tiers (Glencoe, Ill., 1952), 125; Kevin Kenny, *The American Irish: A History* (Harlow, U.K., 2000) 166–171; Richard M. Linkh, *American Catholicism and European Immigrants, 1920–1924* (Staten Island, 1975), 19–31; Delores Ann Liptak, *Immigrants and Their Church* (New York, 1989), 11, 62; Phillip Gleason, "Immigrant Assimilation and the Crisis of Americanization," in *Keeping the Faith: American Catholicism* (Notre Dame, 1987), 58–81; and Edward R. Kantowicz, "Cardinal Mundelein of Chicago and the Shaping of Twentieth Century American Catholicism," *Journal of American History* 68 (June 1981): 52–68.

24. McGreevy, *Parish Boundaries*, 11; Jeanie Wylie, *Poletown: Community Betrayed* (Urbana, Ill., 1989), 4, 15–20; Greene, *For God and Country*, 42–43; see also Joshua A. Fishman and Vladimir C. Nahirny, "The Ethnic Group School and Mother Tongue Maintenance"; and John E. Hofman, "Mother Tongue Retentiveness in Ethnic Parishes," in Fishman, *Language Loyalty in the United States* (London, 1966), 92–126, 127–155.

25. Barrett and Roediger, "Making New Immigrants Inbetween" (forthcoming); David W. Southern, *John LaFarge and the Limits of Catholic Interracialism, 1911–1963* (Baton Rouge, 1996), 251; McGreevy, *Parish Boundaries*, 10–11, 82–83.

26. Cohen, *Making a New Deal*, 94; Southern, *LaFarge*, 251 ("newer Catholic races"); Irvin L. Child, *Italian or American? The Second Generation Conflict* (1943; New York, 1970), 43; McGreevy, *Parish Boundaries*, 10.

27. On minstrelsy and the Church, see "Holy Rosary Minstrel Show," leaflet reprinted in Mayfield Murray District Council, *Bicentennial 1996, Cleveland, Ohio, Little Italy: A Pictorial History* (Cleveland, 1996), n.p. (with Italian American perfomers); "St. Andrews: A Community Center," *New World* (Chicago), April 22, 1921; Russell A. Kazal, "Becoming 'Old Stock': The Waning German–American Identity in Philadelphia, 1900–1930" (Ph.D. diss., University of Pennsylvania, 1998), 546; reports in the *Chicago Province Chronicle* from November 1936, 19 (on Chicago), from May 1937, 84 (on Cleveland); and "The Minstrel Show Must Go!" *Interracial Review,* May 1950, 68; Thomas A. Guglielmo, *White on Arrival: Italians, Race, Color, and Power in Chicago, 1890–1945* (Oxford, 2003), front cover photo. Thanks to Todd Michney and Steve Rosswurm for aid in this research.

28. Guglielmo, *White on Arrival*, 46; Southern, *LaFarge*, 251–257; Eileen M. McMahon, *What Parish Are You From? A Chicago Irish Community and Race Relations* (Lexington, 1995), 123–126; Hughes and Hughes, *Where Peoples Meet*, 127; McGreevy, *Parish Boundaries*, 37; Dominic Capeci and Martha Wilkerson, *Layered Violence: The Detroit Rioters of 1943* (Jackson, Miss., 1991), 25, 237.

29. On the arson and riot, see Chapter 4 in this book.

30. Langston Hughes, "Restrictive Covenants," 361.

31. See Clement E. Vose, *Caucasians Only: The Supreme Court, the NAACP, and the Restrictive Covenant Cases* (Berkeley, 1967), esp. 109–121, 205–210; and Philpott, *Slum and the Ghetto*, 193–194.

32. Abrams, *Forbidden Neighbors*, 217; Vose, *Caucasians Only*, 3–4, 17–19, 254 n. 17; Steve Grant Meyer, *As Long As They Don't Move In Next Door: Segregation and Racial Conflict in American Neighborhoods* (Lanham, Md., 2000), 24–28; Philpott, *Slum and the Ghetto*, 191–192 (constitution proof), 189.

33. Herman H. Long and Charles S. Johnson, *People vs. Property: Race Restrictive Covenants in Housing* (Nashville, 1947), 13.

34. Philpott, *Slum and the Ghetto*, 168, 196–197; Abrams, *Forbidden Neighbors*, 170–172.

35. Abrams, *Forbidden Neighbors*, 158, 157–160 passim; Philpott, *Slum and the Ghetto*, 191–192. On the long-standing view that immigrants threatened property values, see Jennifer Hochschild, *The American Dream and the Public Schools* (Oxford, 2003), 227.

36. Abrams, *Forbidden Neighbors*, 160–164, quoting Male.

37. Philpott, *Slum and the Ghetto*, 189 ("made to order"), 195 (quoting *Herald*); see also 188–197 passim; For "racial frontier," see Thrasher, *The Gang*, 102; Abrams, *Forbidden Neighbors*, 183.

38. Hennepin County (Minn.) register of deeds, Book 1312 of Deeds, p. 335, as Document no. 1961482, and Book 1450 of Deeds, p. 108, as Document 1967049; Abrams, *Forbidden Neighbors*, 170–175, 218; Long and Johnson, *People vs. Property*, 17–18; Philpott, *Slum and the Ghetto*, 351–356 (reprinting Chicago covenants and racial restrictions); Yu, *Thinking Orientals*, 48.

39. Long and Johnson, *People vs. Property*, 47; Philpott, *Slum and the Ghetto*, 196–198; on the exclusion of Jews, see Abrams, *Forbidden Neighbors*, 172, 218; Yu, *Thinking Orientals*, 48; Roger Daniels, *Not Like Us: Immigrants in America, 1890–1924* (Chicago, 1991), 131; Nancy Foner, *From Ellis Island to JFK: New York's Two Greatest Waves of Immigration* (New York, 2000); Karen Brodkin, *How Jews Became White Folks and What That Says About Race in America* (New Brunswick, N.J., 1998), 47; and Stanley Lieberson, *A Piece of the Pie: Blacks and White Immigrants Since 1880* (Berkeley, 1980), 270.

40. Abrams, *Forbidden Neighbors*, 146, 158–159, 161–162, 165; Philpott, *Slum and the Ghetto*, 163, 194; Vose, *Caucasians All*, 8 passim.

41. Cheryl Harris, "Whiteness and Property," *Harvard Law Review* 106 (June 1993): 1710–1793.

42. Abrams, *Forbidden Neighbors*, 219, 182; Philpott, *Slum and the Ghetto*, 191–199, esp. 191–192, 196; Vose, *Caucasians All*, 8–9; Capeci and Wilkerson, *Layered Violence*, 63; Meyer, *Move In Next Door*, 38–45; Johnson and Long, *People vs. Property*, 52, 83. On "pioneering," see Hirsch, *Making the Second Ghetto*, 194–195; on gangs and race, see Thrasher, *The Gang*, 191–193.

43. Abrams, *Forbidden Neighbors*, 183 (on democracy and covenants); Philpott, *Slum and the Ghetto*, 192; Johnson and Long, *People vs. Property*, 18, 39–55 (esp. 45); Thomas Sugrue, *The Origins of the Urban Crisis: Race and Inequality in Postwar Detroit* (Princeton, 1996), 44–46; Douglas S. Massey and Nancy A. Denton,

American Apartheid: Segregation and the Making of the Underclass (Cambridge, Mass., 1993), 34–35; and William A. Osborne, *The Segregated Covenant: Race Relations and American Catholics* (New York, 1967), 207 n. 1.

44. Vose, *Caucasians All*, 9; on "anticitizen," see David R. Roediger, *The Wages of Whiteness: Race and the Making of the American Working Class* (New York, 1991), 57; see also Lisa Lowe, *Immigrant Acts: Asian American Cultural Politics* (Durham, 1996).

45. Massey and Denton, *American Apartheid*, 24–34; Lieberson, *A Piece of the Pie*, 253–291; Barton, *Peasants and Strangers*, 21; Logan, "The Ethnic Neighborhood," passim; Philpott, *Slum and the Ghetto*, 116–146.

46. Abrams, *Forbidden Neighbors*, 172, 218; Vose, *Caucasians All*, 8–9; Johnson and Long, *People vs. Property*, 20–33.

47. Kevin Mumford, *Interzones: Black/White Sex Districts in Chicago and New York in the Early Twentieth Century* (New York, 1997), 76–90.

48. Johnson and Long, *People v. Property*, 33–38; Abrams, *Forbidden Neighbors*, 178; Denton and Massey, *American Apartheid*, 114–120.

49. Child, *Italian or American*, 76–117; see also Deborah Moore, *At Home in America: Second Generation New York Jews* (New York, 1981, esp. 8–9. Evelyn W. Hersey, "The Emotional Conflicts of the Second-Generation: A Discussion of the American-Born Children of Immigrant Parents," Interptreter Release Clip Sheet, July 10, 1934, as reprinted in Stanley Feldstein and Lawrence Costello, eds., *The Ordeal of Assimilation: A Documentary History of the White Working Class* (Garden City, N.Y., 1974), 398.

50. On "allrightnik," see Robert E. Park and Herbert A. Miller, *Old World Traits Transplanted* (New York, 1921), 101–103; and Marshall Berman, "Love and Theft: From Jack Robin to Bob Dylan," *Dissent* 49 (Summer 2002): 70. See also Howard F. Stein, *The Psychoanthropology of American Culture* (New York, 1985), 66–67.

51. Michael Alexander, *Jazz Age Jews* (Princeton, 2001), 167, 139–140; Thomas Doherty, "This Is Where We Came In," in Melvyn Stokes and Richard Matlby, eds., *American Movie Audiences: From the Turn of the Century to the Early Sound Era* (London, 1999), 159; Jeffrey Melnick, *A Right to Sing the Blues: African Americans, Jews, and American Popular Song* (Cambridge, Mass., 1999), 178, 102–113; Michael Rogin, *Blackface, White Noise: Jewish Immigrants in the Hollywood Melting Pot* (Berkeley, 1996), 3–5, 112–113, 126, 183–184, esp. 103. Quotes from the film are from the 1927 Warner Bros. production with Alan Crosland directing.

52. Rogin, *Blackface, White Noise*, 91, 112–113 passim. For critiques of Rogin, see Alexander, *Jazz Age Jews*, 171–172, 179; Seth Forman, *Blacks in the Jewish Mind: A Crisis of Liberalism* (New York, 1998), 14; and Thomas Cripps, "African Americans and Jews in Hollywood," in Jack Salzman and Cornel West, eds., *Struggles in the Promised Land: Toward a History of Black–Jewish Relations in the United States* (New York, 1997), 263; see also Berman, "Love and Theft," 71, for a friendly but bizarre caricature.

53. Alexander, *Jazz Age Jews*, 139–140; Wirth, *The Ghetto*, passim; for the quotations, see Moses Rischin's introduction to the Belknap Press edition of *The Ghetto* (Cambridge, Mass., 1967), xxix.

54. Desmond King, *Making Americans: Immigration, Race, and the Origins of the Diverse Democracy* (Cambridge, Mass., 2000), 43; Semmond and Mukerji, "'What You Are . . . I Wouldn't Eat,'" 3–30; Giorio Bertellini, "Italian Imageries, Historical Feature Films, and the Fabrication of Italy's Spectator in Early 1900s New York," in Stokes and Maltby, eds., *American Movie Audiences*, 29–45; Cohen, *Making a New Deal*, 120–128, 132–136; Rogin, *Blackface, White Noise*, 117–120, 190.

55. Judith Thissen, "Jewish Immigrant Audiences in New York City, 1905–14," in Stokes and Maltby, *American Movie Audiences*, 25, 15–28.

56. David Nasaw, *Going Out: The Rise and Fall of Public Amusements* (New York, 1993), 236–237; Daniel Bernardi, introduction to *The Birth of Whiteness and the Emergence of U.S. Cinema* (New Brunswick, N.J., 1996), 5; Rogin, *Blackface, White Noise*, 43 passim; see Gabriela Arredondo, "Negotiating Ethnicity and Race in Chicago, 1916–1935" (paper presented to the annual meeting of the Organization of American Historians Meeting, San Francisco, 1997), 10.

57. Miriam Hansen, *Babel and Babylon: Spectatorship in American Popular Film* (Chicago, 1991), 245–294; Rogin, *Blackface, White Noise*, 76–77, 128–136, 164; Michael Rogin, *Ronald Reagan: The Movie and Other Essays in Political Demonology* (Berkeley, 1987), 190–235; Bernardi, "Voices of Whiteness," 103–128; Hernan Vera and Andrew Gordon, "Sincere Fictions of the White Self in the American Cinema," in Bernardi, *Classic Hollywood, Classic Whiteness*, 266–171; Donald Bogle, *Toms, Coons, Mulattoes, Mammies, and Bucks: An Interpretive History* (New York, 1973), 4, 7, 16; Ross, *Working-Class Hollywood*, 38–39, 47–51; Dennis Hickey and Kenneth C. Wylie, *An Enchanting Darkness: The American Vision of Africa in the Twentieth Century* (East Lansing, 1993). On Burroughs, see John F. Kasson, *Houdini, Tarzan, and the Perfect Man: The White Male Body and the Challenge of Modernity in America* (New York, 2001), 164, 184, 218; and Harry Stecopoulos, "The World According to Normal Bean: Edgar Rise Burroughs' Popular Culture," in Stecopoulos and Michael Uebel, eds., *Race and the Subject of Masculinities* (Durham, 1997), 180–188, for readings of an immigrant working-class presence in Tarzan novels.

58. Alexander, *Jazz Age Jews*, 140.

59. Kevin Santiago-Valles, "'Still Longing for de Old Plantation': The Visual Parodies and Racial National Imaginary of U.S Overseas Expansion, 1893–1903," *American Studies International* 37 (October 1999): 26–30; Bruce Lenthell, "Outside the Panel: Race in America's Popular Imagination: Comic Strips Before and After World War II," *Journal of American Studies* 32 (1998): 39–61; Gary Cross, *Kids' Stuff: Toys and the Changing World of American Childhood* (Cambridge, Mass., 1997), 41, 68, 88, 92–94, 97–99; Miriam Formanck-Brunell, *Made to Play House: Dolls and the Commercialization of American Girlhood, 1830–1930* (Baltimore,

1993), 91–106, 127; Maurice Manring, *Slave in a Box: The Strange Career of Aunt Jemima* (Charlottesville, 1998), 76–77 passim; Kenneth Goings, *Mammy and Uncle Mose: Black Collectibles and American Stereotyping* (New York, 1994); Nasaw, *Going Out*, 93; Kasson, *Houdini, Tarzan, and the Perfect Man*, 84, 131, 134–135; Andrea Lewis, "An Exhibit of Distortions," *Progressive* 65 (February 2001): 39–40; Jackson Lears, *Fables of Abundance: A Cultural History of Advertising in America* (New York, 1994), 123–124.

60. Susan Smulyan, *Selling Radio: The Commercialization of American Broadcasting* (Washington D.C., 1994), 97, 103; Manring, *Slave in a Box*, esp. 115–121. On soap and race, see Anne McClintock, *Imperial Leather: Race, Gender, and Sexual Conquest* (New York, 1995), 31–36, 207–231.

61. For a foreign-language Aunt Jemima, see the April 13 and April 17, 1918, issues of *Jewish Journal*, clipped in the J. Walter Thompson collection at Duke University. Thanks to Maurice Manring for a copy of the ad.

62. Donna Haraway, "Teddy Bear Patriarchy: Taxidermy in the Garden of Eden, 1908–1936," in Donna Haraway, *Primate Visions: Gender, Race, and Nature in the World of Modern Science* (New York, 1989), 237–291; Loe D. Baker, *From Savage to Negro: Anthropology and the Construction of Race, 1896–1954* (Berkeley, 1998), 56–73; Robert Rydell, *All the World's a Fair: Visions of Empire at American International Expositions, 1876–1916* (Chicago, 1984); Burton Benedict, "Rituals of Representation: Ethnic Stereotypes and Colonized Peoples at World's Fair," in Robert Rydell and Nancy Gwinn, eds., *Fair Representations: World's Fairs and the Modern World* (Amsterdam, 1994), 37–46; Nasaw, *Going Out*, 74–79; Phillips Verner Bradford and Harvey Blume, *Ota: The Pygmy in the Zoo* (New York, 1992); Eric Breitbart, *A World on Display, 1904: Photographs from the St. Louis World's Fair* (Albuquerque, 1997), 59 passim; Laura Wexler, *Tender Violence: Domestic Visions in an Age of U.S. Imperialism* (Chapel Hill, 2000), esp. 262–290; Paul Kramer, "Making Concessions: Race and Empire Revisited at the Philippine Exposition, St. Louis, 1901–1905," *Radical History Review* 73 (Winter 1999): 101, 75–115.

63. Durante as quoted in Marybeth Hamilton, *When I'm Bad, I'm Better: Mae West, Sex, and American Entertainment* (Berkeley, 1997), 164; Nasaw, *Going Out*, 81.

64. Nasaw, *Going Out*, 113, 117–118; Elizabeth Ewen, *Immigrant Women in a Land of Dollars: Life and Culture on the Lower East Side, 1890–1925* (New York, 1985), 214; Elizabeth Beardsley Butler, *Women and the Trades, Pittsburgh, 1907–1908* (Pittsburgh, 1984), 324.

65. Nasaw, *Going Out*, 116, 113–118.

66. Mumford, *Interzones*, 85, 76–90; Hamilton, *When I'm Bad*, 164–165; Anzia Yezierska, *Bread Givers* (1925; New York, 1975), 193, 196.

67. Rhacel Salazar Parrenas, "'White Trash' Meets the 'Little Brown Monkeys': The Taxi Dance Hall as a Site of Interracial Alliances Between White Working Class Women and Filipino Immigrant Men in the 1920s and 1930s," *Amerasia* 24

(Summer 1998): 115–134; McBee, *Dance Hall Days*, 143–146; Joanne J. Meyerowitz, *Women Adrift: Independent Wage-Earners in Chicago, 1880–1930* (Chicago, 1988), 102.

68. Maria Damon, "Jazz-Jews, Jive, and Gender: The Ethnic Politics of Jazz Argot," in Jonathan Boyarin and Daniel Boyarin, eds., *Jews and Other Differences: The New Jewish Cultural Studies* (Minneapolis, 1997), 161, 150–175; Gary Boulard, *Louis Prima* (Urbana, Ill., 2002), esp. 8–9; Burton Peretti, *The Creation of Jazz: Music, Race, and Culture in Urban America* (Urbana, 1992), esp. 82–86, 205–206.

69. See note 84 below and Gayle Wald, "Mezz Mezzrow and the Voluntary Negro Blues," in Stecopoulos and Uebel, *Race and the Subject of Masculinities*, esp. 119 ("self-referential"); Werner Sollors, *Beyond Ethnicity: Consent and Descent in American Culture* (New York, 1986), 17; S. Oso, "Lots," in Tracy Kidder, ed., *Best American Essays, 1994* (New York, 1994), 269, 255–271.

70. Berman, "Love and Theft," 68–72; and Rogin, *Blackface, White Noise*, 152–156. See also Robert W. Snyder, *The Voice of the City: Vaudeville and Popular Culture in New York* (New York, 1989), 120.

71. Gold, *Jews Without Money*, 124–125; for didactic tales on visits by black fellow workers to Irish American homes, see Archie Green, *Calf's Head and Union Tales: Labor Yarns at Work and Play* (Urbana, Ill., 1996), 123–125; Sabatini, conversation with author, May 2002.

72. Child, *Italian or American*, 81, 154–158; Robert W. Creamer, *Babe: The Legend Comes to Life* (New York, 1974), 34, 38–39, 43, 185, 269–270; Stewart Bird, Dan Georgakas, and Deborah Shaffer, eds., *Solidarity Forever: An Oral History of the IWW* (Chicago, 1985), 14; Alexander, *Jazz Age Jews*, 141; McBee, *Dance Hall Days*, 175–176.

73. Nick Evans, "Racial Discourse in Ethnic Autobiography: 'Black' Self-Fashioning in Mezz Mezzrow's *Really the Blues*" (paper presented to the annual meeting of the American Studies Association, Pittsburgh, 1995); Gold, *Jews Without Money*, 36–51; McBee, *Dance Hall Days*, 145–146.

74. Bodnar, *Workers' World*, 122–125; Robert L. Chapman, *New Dictionary of American Slang* (New York, 1981), 128; Frederic C. Cassidy and Joan Houston Hall, eds., *Dictionary of American Regional English* (Cambridge, Mass., 1991), 2:336.

75. Emily Wortis Leider, *Becoming Mae West* (New York, 1997), 342; Hamilton, "When I'm Bad, I'm Better," 6, 153–172; Grace Abbott, *The Immigrant and the Community* (New York, 1921), 79, 71–77; Jane Addams, as quoted in Sylvia Hood Washington, *Packing Them In: An Archaelogy of Environmental Racism in Chicago, 1865–1954* (forthcoming).

76. On immigration and prostitution, see Ruth Rosen, *The Lost Sisterhood: Prostitutes in America, 1900–1918* (Baltimore, 1982), 44; David Langum, *Crossing the Line: Legislating Morality and the Mann Act* (Chicago, 1994), 16–19; Parrenas, "'White Trash' Meets the 'Little Brown Monkeys,'" 115–154; Val Marie Johnson, "Defining 'The Social Evil': Moral Citizenship and Governance in New York City,

1890–1920" (Ph.D. diss., New York School for Social Research, 2002); on "sneaking out," see McBee, *Dance Hall Days*, 208–214; for Chicago, see Gabriela Arredondo, "Navigating Ethno-Racial Currents: Mexicans in Chicago, 1916–1939," *Journal of Urban History* 30 (March 2004): 399–427; Meyerowitz, *Women Adrift*, esp. 102–113.

77. Lewis A. Erenberg, *Steppin Out: New York Nightlife and the Transformation of American Culture, 1890–1930* (Westport, Conn., 1981), 195; Judy Wu, *Doctor "Mom" Chung of the Fair-Haired Bastards* (forthcoming); Janice Okoomian, "Becoming White: Contesting History, Armenian American Women, and Racialized Bodies," *MELUS*, Spring 2002, 213–237; Prell, *Fighting to Become Americans*, 50, for the *Day* material.

78. Julie Willett, *Permanent Waves: The Making of the American Beauty Shop* (New York, 2000), 27–29, 46–50, with quotations from *Physical Culture* and Grant; Yezierska, *Bread Givers*, 4; Valerie Babb, *Whiteness Visible: The Meaning of Whiteness in American Literature and Culture* (New York, 1998), 119–125, esp. 122; Romano as quoted in Mary Ann Mannino, "Blurred Racial Borders in the Poetry of Marie Mazziotti Gillan and Rose Romano," in Ashyk, Gardaphe, and Tamburri, *Shades of Black and White*, 336–337. See also Maria Mazzioti Gillan, *Where I Come From: Selected and New Poems* (Toronto, 1995), 54–57. For Ross, see Julius Weinberg, *Edward Alsworth Ross and the Sociology of Progressivism* (Madison, Wis., 1972), 159.

79. The ads are all contained in the D'Arcy Collection on advertising history at University of Illinois, microfilm reel 138. They were clipped from the *Saturday Evening Post* (August 16, 1924), *American Weekly* (July 29, 1941), and *Ladies' Home Journal* (May 30, 1942). See also Anthony Sigismondi, "White or Inbetween? The Racial Identity of Italians in Chicago from 1890–1940" (seminar paper, Northern Illinois University, 2002), 6–31. For Zahller, see Linda Castrone, "Reviving Little Italy," *Denver Post*, November 2, 2003.

80. Antin in Babb, *Whiteness Visible*, 122; Park and Miller, *Old World Traits Transplanted*, 147–148.

81. Katrina Irving, *Immigrant Mothers: Narratives of Race and Maternity, 1890–1925* (Urbana, Ill., 2000), 40, 1–30.

82. Lieberson, *A Piece of the Pie*, 179; Steven Sage Burnett, "Women of Steel: Gender and Labor in the Great Steel Strike of 1919" (M.A. thesis, University of Missouri, 1995), 162; Sydney Stahl Weinberg, *The World of Our Mothers: The Lives of Jewish Immigrant Women* (Chapel Hill, 1988), 196; Byington, *Homestead*, 131.

83. Frank Julian Warne, *The Slav Invasion and the Mine Workers: A Study in Immigration* (Philadelphia, 1904), 70–71; Emory Bogardus, *Immigration and Race Attitudes* (Boston, 1928), 150.

84. Oscar Handlin, *The Uprooted* (1951; Boston, 1973), 252; William Leiserson, *Adjusting Immigrant and Industry* (New York, 1924), 312, 309–311, 101.

85. Alice M. Hoffman, "An Interview with David Saposs" (1967), Saposs Papers, State Historical Society of Wisconsin, Box 26 F5 (with thanks to Tom Mackaman); La

Sorte, *La Merica*, 51, 61, 132; Suellen Hoy, *Chasing Dirt: The American Pursuit of Cleanliness* (New York, 1995), 87–121.

86. Burnett, "Women of Steel," 86–87; Mary Heaton Vorse, *A Footnote to Folly: Reminiscences of Mary Heaton Vorse* (New York, 1980), 281–282.

87. Karen Brodkin, "Race, Class, and Gender: The Metaorganization of American Capitalism," *Transforming Anthropology* 7 (1998): 52–53; Brodkin, *How Jews Became White Folks and What That Says About Race in America*, 96–97; Linda Gordon, *Pitied But Not Entitled: Single Mothers and the History of Welfare* (New York, 1994), 48.

88. All of the Chicago material, including the quotations, is from Guglielmo, *White on Arrival*, 45–47; Byington, *Homestead*, 131; Vincenza Scarpaci, "Walking the Color Line: Italian Immigrants in Rural Louisiana, 1880–1910," in Jennifer Guglielmo and Sal Salerno, eds., *Are Italians White?* (New York, 2003), 60–76.

89. Stave and Sutherland, with Salerno, *From the Old Country*, 228–229, 26; Jennifer Mary Guglielmo, "Negotiating Gender, Race, and Coalition: Italian Women and Politics in New York City" (Ph.D. diss. University of Minnesota, 2003), 224.

90. Bogardus, *Immigration and Race Attitudes*, 66; Ivan Greenberg, "Class Culture and Generation Change: Immigrant Families in Two Connecticut Cities During the 1930s" (Ph.D. diss., City University of New York, 1990), 75–77, includes the remarkable quoted passage and an apt discussion of immigrants facing and parrying charges regarding their alleged dirtiness. On Mellone, see Guglielmo, "Negotiating Gender, Race, and Coalition," 224.

91. T. J. Woofter Jr., *Races and Ethnic Groups in American Life* (New York, 1933), 164–166; Jeremiah W. Jenks and W. Jett Lauck, *The Immigration Problem: A Study of American Immigration Conditions and Needs*, rev. and enl. Rufus D. Smith (New York, 1926), 353–357; Steven Selden, *Inheriting Shame: The Story of Eugenics and Racism in America* (New York, 1999), 14–15, 57–60; on failures, dropouts, and low grades among Italian Americans, see Joel Perlmann, *Ethnic Differences: Schooling and Social Structures Among the Irish, Italians, Jews, and Blacks in an American City, 1880–1935* (Cambridge, U.K., 1988), 90–95; Jean Anyon, *Ghetto Schooling: A Political Economy of Urban Educational Reform* (New York, 1997), 49–50.

92. Handlin, as cited in Peter Binzen, *Whitetown, U.S.A.* (New York, 1970), 47, 44–46; Jenks, Lauck, and Smith, *Immigration Problem*, 358–359; David B. Tyack, *The One Best System: A History of American Urban Education* (Cambridge, Mass., 1974), 231, 254 for the quotations for teachers; on "black marks," see Hoy, *Chasing Dirt*, 145; see also Myra Kelly, *Little Citizens: The Humors of Social Life* (New York, 1904), 184, 194, 141–142, 162, 167.

93. Louis Adamic, *What's Your Name?* (New York, 1942), 102; Hoy, *Chasing Dirt*, 125, 123–127 passim; cf. Peter Roberts, *The Problem of Americanization* (New York, 1920), 135; Anyon, *Ghetto Schooling*, 50.

94. Jenks, Lauck, and Smith, *Immigration Problem*, 358–360; Barton, *Peasants and Strangers*, 150; Jonathan Zimmerman, "Ethnics Against Ethnicity: European

Immigrants and Foreign-Language Instruction, 1890–1940," *Journal of American History* 88 (March 2002): esp. 1400; Steinberg, *Ethnic Myth*, 128–150, 228.

95. Whyte, *Street Corner Society*, 276; Stave and Sutherland with Salerno, *From the Old Country*, 179–180; Andrew Greeley, *Why Can't They Be Like Us? Facts and Fallacies About Ethnic Differences and Group Conflicts in America* (New York, 1969), 32; Carmen Leone, *Rose Street: A Family History* (Youngstown, 1996), 10–14; with thanks to Thomas Sabatini.

96. For Covello and the quotations, see Robert A. Orsi, *The Madonna of 115th Street: Faith and Community in Italian Harlem, 1880–1950* (1985; New Haven, 2002), 161, 196, 110–112; cf. Louis Adamic, *From Many Lands* (New York, 1940), 93.

97. David Herr, "Intermarriage," in *Harvard Encyclopedia*, 516.

98. John J. Bukowczyk, "'Who Is the Nation?'—or, 'Did Cleopatra Have Red Hair?' A Patriotic Discourse on Diversity, Nationality, and Race," *MELUS* 23 (Winter 1998): 11, 3–23; Joel Perlmann, *The Romance of Assimilation? Studying the Demographic Outcomes of Ethnic Intermarriages in American History*, Working Paper no. 230 (Jerome Levy Economics Institute of Bard College, June 2001), 1–22; see also William Z. Ripley, "Races in the United States," *Atlantic Monthly* 102 (December 1908): 751–754.

99. Perlmann, "Romance of Assimilation," 1, 3, 6, 9; Julius Drachsler, *Democracy and Assimilation* (New York, 1920), 120–124; Woofter, *Races and Ethnic Groups in American Life*, 204–209; Joel Perlmann, *Towards a Population History of the Second Generation: Birth Cohorts for Southern-, Central-, and Eastern European Origins, 1871–1970*, Working Paper no. 333 (Jerome Levy Economics Institute, 2001), table 7, table 8.

100. Drachsler, *Democracy and Assimilation*, 234–235, Stave and Sutherland with Salerno, *From the Old Country*, 153; Bodnar, *Workers' World*, 58; Sigismondi, "White or Inbetween," 18–19. See also Ray Stannard Baker's predictions on the "mingling white races" in Nasaw, *Going Out*, 48.

101. Barton, *Peasants and Strangers*, 164; Warne, *The Slav Invasion and the Mine Workers*, 79.

102. McGreevy, *Parish Boundaries*; Drachsler, *Democracy and Assimilation*, 124–125; Will Herberg, *Protestant-Catholic-Jew: An Essay in American Religious Sociology* (Garden City, N.Y., 1960), 32–34, 151–152. On the limits of Catholic intermarriage, see Harold Abramson, *Ethnic Diversity in Catholic America* (New York, 1973), 49–68.

103. Stave and Sutherland with Salerno, *From the Old Country*, 153, 185–187, 215; *L'Italia*, August 4, 1912 (thanks to Thomas Guglielmo for the citation); Child, *Italian or American*, 135–142; on Greek American intermarriage, see Ruth Cavan and Katherine Howland Ranck, *The Family and Depression: A Study of One Hundred Chicago Families* (Chicago, 1938), 38–39.

104. Ann Nichols, *Abie's Irish Rose: A Novel* (New York, 1927), 75–98, 101–106; Prell, *Fighting to Become Americans*, 72–77.

105. Woofter, *Race and Ethnic Groups in American Life*, 208; J. Douglas Smith, *Managing White Supremacy: Race, Politics, and Citizenship in Jim Crow Virginia* (Chapel Hill, 2002), 76–106; Renee C. Romano, *Race Mixing: Black–White Marriage in Postwar America* (Cambridge, Mass., 2003), 7.

CHAPTER 7

1. The epigraphs are from Mike Davis, *Prisoners of the American Dream: Politics and Economy in the History of the U.S. Working Class* (London, 1986), 89; Bob Dylan, "I Pity the Poor Immigrant," on *John Wesley Harding* (Columbia Records, 1967). For Randolph, Hillman, and LaGuardia, see Daniel Kryder, *Divided Arsenal: Race and the American States During World War II* (Cambridge, U.K., 2000), 59–63; Gary M. Fink, *Biographical Dictionary of American Labor* (Westport, Conn., 1984), 296; Philip S. Foner, *Organized Labor and the Black Worker, 1619–1973* (New York, 1976), 239, 241.

2. Gary Gerstle, *Working-Class Americanism: The Politics of Labor in a Textile City, 1914–1960* (Cambridge, U.K., 1989); Robert A. Slayton, *Empire Statesman: The Rise and Redemption of Al Smith* (New York, 2000), 237–328; Elliot Robert Barkan, *And Still They Come: Immigrants and American Society 1920s to the 1990s* (Wheeling, Ill., 1996), 43; Lizabeth Cohen, *Making a New Deal: Industrial Workers in Chicago, 1919–1939* (Cambridge, U.K., 1990) 275, 255, 259, 63; Bruce Nelson, *Divided We Stand: American Workers and the Struggle for Black Equality* (Princeton, 2001), 66; for Pennsylvania, see John Hinshaw, *Steel and Steelworkers: Race and Class Struggle in Twentieth-Century Pittsburgh* (Albany, 2002), 63.

3. Roger Daniels, *Coming to America: A History of Immigration and Ethnicity in American Life* (New York, 1990), 282 (Daniels paraphrases Cermak); Ross, as quoted in Harold J. Abramson, *Ethnic Diversity in Catholic America* (London, 1973), 18 n. 9; Ross, however, retained much of his anti–new immigrant and pro-restriction attitude. See Ross, *Seventy Years of It: An Autobiography* (New York, 1936), 223–325.

4. Steven Fraser, *Labor Will Rule: Sidney Hillman and the Rise of American Labor* (New York, 1991), 449, 493, 530; "He Called Me a Guinea," *Time*, December 15, 1940, 11.

5. Gary Gerstle, *American Crucible: Race and Nation in the Twentieth Century* (Princeton, 2001), 167–175; Silver, in Jeff Kisseloff, ed., *You Must Remember This: An Oral History of Manhattan from the 1890s to World War II* (San Diego, 1989), 205.

6. Edwin Amenta, *Bold Relief: Institutional Politics and the Origins of Modern American Social Policy* (Princeton, 1998), 157–158.

7. Patricia Sullivan, *Days of Hope: Race and Democracy in the New Deal Era* (Chapel Hill, 1996), 3 passim. Sullivan's work was anticipated by Harvard Sitkoff when he cast the New Deal as first embodying racist "Old Deal" elements and then progressing, in *A New Deal for Blacks* (New York, 1978), esp. 34–83.

8. Philip Rubio, *A History of Affirmative Action, 1619–2000* (Jackson, Miss., 2001), 90; and Craig Steven Wilder, *A Covenant with Color: Race and Social Power in Brooklyn* (New York, 2000), 178.

9. Linda Faye Williams, *The Constraint of Race: Legacies of White Skin Privilege in America* (University Park, Pa., 2003), 69–105; Frank Freidel, *FDR and the South* (Baton Rouge, 1965); Rubio, *History of Affirmative Action*, 98–99; Nancy Grant, *TVA and Black Americans: Planning for the Status Quo* (Philadelphia, 1990); Linda Gordon, *Pitied But Not Entitled: Single Mothers and the History of Welfare* (New York, 1994), 197.

10. Nancy J. Weiss, *Farewell to the Party of Lincoln: Black Politics in the Age of FDR* (Princeton, 1983), 212–214; Amenta, *Bold Relief*, 158. For fuller figures, see Michael K. Brown, *Race, Money, and the American Welfare State* (Ithaca, N.Y., 1999), 76–90.

11. Brown, *Race, Money, and the American Welfare State*, 64–65, 68–69, 70; Gordon, *Pitied But Not Entitled*, 196, 217–218; Roy Rosenzweig, "Organizing the Unemployed: The Early Years of the Great Depression, 1929–1933," *Radical America* 10 (July–August 1976): 47–60; Randi Jill Storch, "Shades of Red: The Communist Party and Chicago's Workers, 1928–1939" (Ph.D. diss., University of Illinois, 1998), 78–118; William A. Sundstrom, "Explaining the Unemployment Gap: Race, Region, and the Employment Status of Men, 1940," *Industrial and Labor Relations Review* 50 (April 1997): 460–476; Lois Rita Helmbold, "Downward Occupational Mobility During the Great Depression: Urban Black and White Working Class Women," *Labor History* 29 (Spring 1988): 135–175, esp. 155.

12. Brown, *Race, Money, and the American Welfare State*, 81, 76–89; Gordon, *Pitied But Not Entitled*, 88, 196.

13. Brown, *Race, Money, and the American Welfare State*, 71–72, 56–63; Nancy E. Rose, "Gender, Race, and the Welfare State: Government Work Programs from the 1930s to the Present," *Feminist Studies* 19 (Summer 1993): 326–327.

14. Suzanne Mettler, *Dividing Citizens: Gender and Federalism in New Deal Public Policy* (Ithaca, N.Y., 1998), 72 (quoting Douglas), 73–76; Phyllis Palmer, "Outside the Law: Agriculture and Domestic Workers Under the Fair Labor Standards Act," *Journal of Policy History* 7 (1995): esp. 420; Brown, *Race, Money, and the American Welfare State*, 90–94.

15. Gordon, *Pitied But Not Entitled*, 293, 287–306; Rose, "Gender, Race, and the Welfare State," 325–327; Mettler, *Dividing Citizens*, 129–139, 159–175; Brown, *Race, Money, and the American Welfare State*, 90–94.

16. As quoted in Ivan Greenberg, "Class Culture and Generational Change: Immigrant Families in Two Connecticut Industrial Cities During the 1930s" (Ph.D. diss., City University of New York, 1990), 78; Charles Abrams, *Forbidden Neighbors: A Study of Prejudice in Housing* (New York, 1955), 162, 231; Gunnar Myrdal, *An American Dilemma: The Negro Problem and Modern Democracy* (New York, 1944), 75–76; John Bodnar, *Workers' World: Kinship, Community, and Protest in an*

Industrial Society, 1900–1940 (Baltimore, 1982), 61–62. See also Susan Traverso, *Welfare Politics in Boston, 1910–1940* (Amherst, 2003), 118–119; Jonathan Rieder, *Canarsie: The Jews and Italians of Brooklyn Against Liberalism* (Cambridge, Mass., 1985), 27–28, 101–187.

17. Wilder, *Covenant with Color*, 130, 196–197, 209; Martha Biondi, *To Stand and Fight: The Struggle for Civil Rights in Postwar New York City* (Cambridge, Mass., 2003), 33–36; Herman David Bloch, *The Circle of Discrimination: An Economic and Social Study of the Black Man in New York* (New York, 1969), 107; Keith P. Griffler, *What Price Alliance? Black Radicals Confront White Labor, 1918–1938* (New York, 1995), 181–182; Fraser, *Labor Will Rule*, 374–378, esp. 478–480.

18. Biondi, *To Stand and Fight*, 16; Richard W. Steele, "'No Racials': Discrimination Against Ethnics in American Defense Industry, 1940–42," *Labor History* 32 (Winter 1991): 68–70, 66–89 passim; Andrew Edmund Kersten, *Race, Jobs, and the War: The FEPC in the Midwest, 1941–1946* (Urbana, Ill., 2000), 11, 138; John Morton Blum, *V Was for Victory: Politics and American Culture During World War II* (New York, 1976), 174.

19. See note 18 above; for the statistics and quotations, see Steele, "'No Racials,'" 67, 77–78.

20. Marion Crain, "Colorblind Unionism," *UCLA Law Review* 49 (2004): 1113, 1325–1326; Paul Moreno, "An Ambivalent Legacy: Black Americans and the Political Economy of the New Deal," *Independent Review* 6 (Spring 2002): 523; Foner, *Organized Labor and the Black Worker*, 215; Rubio, *History of Affirmative Action*, 88–89.

21. Robert Zieger, "Black and White, Unite and Fight? Race and Labor in Modern America," http://www.clas.ufl.edu/users/rzieger/labher814.html (October 2002), 6; Herbert R. Northrup, "Organized Labor and Negro Workers," *Journal of Political Economy* 51 (June 1943): 213–215; Herbert Hill, "Comment on Discrimination and Trade Unions," in Orley Ashenfelter and Albert Rees, eds., *Discrimination in Labor Markets* (Princeton, 1973), 121; Andrew Kersten, *Labor's Home Front: The American Federation of Labor During World War II* (forthcoming).

22. Myrdal, *An American Dilemma*, 285, 389–390; Hill, *Black Labor and the American Labor System*, 103–116.

23. Mettler, *Dividing Citizens*, 204, 198–205; Palmer, "Outside the Law," 420.

24. Foner, *Organized Labor and the Black Worker*, 231, 215–292; David Brody, "Labor," in Stephan Thernstrom, ed., *Harvard Encyclopedia of American Ethnic Groups* (Cambridge, Mass., 1981), 614–618; Hill, *Black Labor and the American Legal System: Race, Work, and the Law* (Madison, Wis., 1985), 376–377; Bruce Nelson, *Divided We Stand: American Workers and the Struggle for Black Equality* (Princeton, 2001), xxxii–xxxiv, 201; Robert Zieger, *The CIO, 1935–1955* (Chapel Hill, 1995), esp. 155–156; Judith Stepan-Norris and Maurice Zeitlin, *Left Out: Reds and America's Industrial Unions* (Cambridge, U.K., 2003), 232–265; Steve Rosswurm, introduction to *The CIO's Left-Led Unions* (New Brunswick, N.J., 1992), 3–5. On

McWilliams, see Daniel Geary, "Carey McWillams and Antifascism, 1934–1943," *Journal of American History* 90 (December 2003): 922–923.

25. Foner, *Organized Labor and the Black Worker*, 215; Nelson, *Divided We Stand*, xxiii–xxxiii; Zieger, *CIO*, 154–161; Robert Korstad and Nelson Lichtenstein, "Opportunities Found and Lost: Labor, Radicals, and the Early Civil Rights Movement," *Journal of American History* 75 (December 1988): 786–811.

26. Steven R. Scipes, "Trade Union Development and Racial Oppression in Chicago's Meatpacking Industries, 1933–1955," (Ph.D. diss., University of Illinois, 2004), 343, 322; Matthew L. Basso, "Metal of Honor: Montana's World War II Homefront, Movies, and the Social Politics of White Male Anxiety" (Ph.D. diss., University of Minnesota, 2001), 139–148; Stepan-Norris and Zeitlin, *Left Out*, 237; David Wellman, *The Union Makes Us Strong: Radical Unionism on the San Francisco Waterfront* (Cambridge, U.K., 1995), 53, 100–103; Nancy Quam-Wickham, "Who Controls the Hiring Hall? The Struggle for Job Control in the ILWU During World War II," in Rosswurm, *Left-Led Unions*, 67; on Republic Steel, see Thomas A. Guglielmo, *White on Arrival: Italians, Race, Color, and Power in Chicago, 1890–1945* (Oxford, 2003), 139; Moon-Kie Jung, "Interracialism: The Ideological Transformation of Hawaii's Working Class," *American Sociological Review* 68 (June 2003): 373–400; Stan Weir, *Singlejack Solidarity* (forthcoming); Foner, *Organized Labor and the Black Worker*, 224–225; Zieger, *CIO*, 281–282.

27. Zieger, "Black and White, Unite and Fight?" 1; Foner, *Organized Labor and the Black Worker*, front cover; Zieger, *CIO*, 160; Rick Halpern, *Down on the Killing Floor: Black and White Workers in Chicago's Packinghouses, 1904–54* (Urbana, Ill., 1997), 96–129. The extent to which the U.S. labor movement, including its mainstream elements, is rooted in syndicalist views has recently reemerged as an object of debate. See Howard Kimeldorf, *Battling for American Labor: Wobblies, Craft Workers, and the Making of the Labor Movement* (Berkeley, 1999); and Larry Isaac, "In Search of American Labor's Syndicalist Heritage," *Labor Studies Journal* 27 (Summer 2002): 21–25.

28. W.E.B. Du Bois, *Dusk of Dawn: An Essay Toward an Autobiography of a Race Concept* (1940; New York, 1971), 321, 206–207; Yuichiro Onishi, "Giant Steps of the Black Freedom Struggle: Trans-Pacific Connections Between Black America and Japan in the Twentieth Century" (Ph.D. diss., University of Minnesota, 2004).

29. Cohen, *Making a New Deal*, 202–203, 333–360; Roger Horowitz, *"Negro and White Unite and Fight": A Social History of Industrial Unionism in Meatpacking* (Urbana, Ill., 1997), 73–75; for a fierce critique of the limits of CIO policy on race, see Herbert Hill, "The Problem of Race in American Labor History," *Reviews in American History* 26 (1996): 199–203.

30. David Montgomery, "Empire, Race, and Working-class Mobilizations," in Peter Alexander and Rick Halpern, eds., *Racializing Class, Classifying Race: Labour and Difference in Britain, the USA and Africa* (Basingstoke, U.K., 1999), 16; Cohen, *Making a New Deal*, 333–334; Kimberly L. Phillips, *AlabamaNorth: African-American*

Migrants, Community, and Working-Class Activism in Cleveland, 1915–45 (Urbana, Ill., 1999), 235–237; Wilder, *Covenant with Color*, 170–172; Hill, *Black Labor and the American Legal System*, 334–372; Andrew Kersten, "Seeking Justice in the Sky: Racial Discrimination in the Airline Industry in the 1950s" (paper presented to the Organization of American Historians, Memphis, 2003), 2; Michelle Brattain, *The Politics of Whiteness: Race, Workers, and Culture in the Modern South* (Princeton, 2001), 109–110.

31. Myrdal, *American Dilemma*, 285, 389–390; see also David R. Roediger, *The Wages of Whiteness: Race and the Making of the American Working Class* (London, 1991), 144–145, 180.

32. Keith P. Griffler, *What Price Alliance? Black Radicals Confront White Labor, 1915–1938* (New York, 1995), esp. 15, 193; Kersten, *Labor's Home Front* (forthcoming); Herbert Hill, "Myth-Making as Labor History: Herbert Gutman and the United Mine Workers of America," *International Journal of Politics, Culture, and Society* 2 (Winter 1988): 132–200; Noel Ignatin, "A Golden Bridge: A New Look at William Z. Foster, the Great Steel Strike, and the 'Boring-from-Within' Controversy," in *Workplace Papers* (Chicago, 1980), 53–65; Philip S. Foner and Ronald Lewis, eds., *Black Workers: A Documentary History from Colonial Times to the Present* (Philadelphia, 1989), 237–248; Myrdal, *American Dilemma*, 1112–1115; Foner, *Organized Labor and the Black Worker*, 162; the quotation is from Bloch, *Circle of Discrimination*, 107.

33. Quoted in Nelson, *Divided We Stand*, 201; and Zieger, *CIO*, 159. See also David Brody, *In Labor's Cause: Main Themes on the History of the American Worker* (New York, 1993), 123; David Morgan Lewis-Coleman, "African Americans and the Politics of Race Among Detroit's Auto Workers, 1941–1971" (Ph.D. diss., University of Iowa, 2001), 58–59; Thomas J. Sugrue, *The Origins of the Urban Crisis: Race and Inequality in Postwar Detroit* (Princeton, 1996), 102; and Foner and Lewis, *Black Workers*, 446.

34. Myrdal, *American Dilemma*, 402; Foner and Lewis, *Black Workers*, 460–461 (Calloway); for White, see August Meier and Elliott Rudwick, *Black Detroit and the Rise of the UAW* (New York, 1979), 187–192; James Wolfinger, "The Rise and Fall of the Roosevelt Coalition: Race, Labor, and Politics in Philadelphia, 1932–1955" (Ph.D. diss., Northwestern University, 2003), chaps. 6–7.

35. Nelson, *Divided We Stand*, 206, 210; Michael Honey, "Racism, Organized Labor, and the Black Freedom Struggle," *Contours: A Journal of the African Diaspora* 1 (Spring 2003): 68, 73. See also Bruce Nelson, "Short but Sweet: The Brave Life of Local 22," *New Labor Forum* 13 (Summer 2004): 121–125. For the illusion that CIO unions worked as hard for civil rights as for trade unionism, see Melvyn Dubofsky, *Hard Work: The Making of Labor History* (Urbana, Ill., 2000), 134–135. See also James Loewen, *Sundown Towns* (forthcoming).

36. Stanley B. Greenberg, *Race and State in Capitalist Development: Comparative Perspectives* (New Haven, 1980), 335, 348–349; Zieger, *CIO*, 347; Wolfinger, "Rise

and Fall of the Roosevelt Coalition," chaps. 6–7; Bruce Nelson, "Organized Labor and the Struggle for Black Equality in Mobile During World War II," *Journal of American History* 80 (December 1995): 976–977; Robert J. Norrell, "Caste in Steel: Jim Crow Careers in Birmingham, Alabama," *Journal of American History* 79 (December 1996): 670–677.

37. Zieger, *CIO*, passim; Matthew Frye Jacobson, *Whiteness of a Different Color: European Immigrants and the Alchemy of Race* (Cambridge, Mass., 1998), 252–256, 263; Mark Solomon, *The Cry Was Unity: Communists and Africans, 1917–1936* (Jackson, Miss., 1998), 137–144.

38. Patterson, as quoted in Cohen, *Making a New Deal*, 339; "F.A. Robinett to Hon. Harold H. Burton," July 27, 1937, in Burton Papers, Western Reserve Historical Society, MS 3828.

39. On the Communists and baseball, see Irwin Silber, *Press Box Red: The Story of Lester Rodney, the Communist Who Helped Break the Color Line in American Sports* (Philadelphia, 2003), ix (from Jules Tygiel's foreword), 12–13, 148. Cf. the 1929 Communist Party report, "Instructions for Our Work in Non-Party Language Organizations," as quoted in Josephine Fowler, "'To Be Red and Oriental': The Experiences of Japanese and Chinese Immigrant Communists in the American and International Communist Movements, 1919–1933" (Ph.D. diss., University of Minnesota, 2003), 58; Dubofsky, *Hard Work*, 134; John Bodnar, *Immigration and Industrialization: Ethnicity in an American Mill Town* (Pittsburgh, 1977), 145–147; Bodnar, *Workers' World: Kinship, Community, and Protest in an Industrial Society, 1900–1940* (Baltimore, 1982), 139; Sherry Lee Linkon and John Russo, *Steeltown U.S.A.: Work and Memory in Youngstown* (Lawrence, 2002), 30. Thomas Gobel, "Becoming American: Ethnic Workers and the Rise of the CIO," *Labor History* 29 (Spring 1988): 176–182; Colette A. Hyman, *Staging Strikes: Workers' Theatre and the American Labor Movement* (Philadelphia, 1997), 69, 70–71.

40. Nelson, *Divided We Stand*, 157; James D. Rose, *Duquesne and the Rise of Steel Unionism* (Urbana, Ill., 2001), 73–74; Ewa Morawska, *For Bread with Butter: The Life-Worlds of East Central Europeans in Johnstown, Pennsylvania, 1890–1940* (Cambridge, Mass., 1985), 274; Brody, *In Labor's Cause*, 124–125.

41. Louis Adamic, *What's Your Name?* (New York, 1942), 95, 97, 130; Gobel, "Becoming American," 182.

42. *Oxford English Dictionary*, 1933 ed., 1:278; Gobel, "Becoming American," 195.

43. Quoted in Wolfinger, "Rise and Fall of the Roosevelt Coalition," chaps. 6–7.

44. *American Slav*, January 1942, front cover; Michael Denning, *The Cultural Front: The Laboring of American Culture in the Twentieth Century* (London, 1997), 63, 75; Michael Goldfield, *The Color of Politics: Race and the Mainsprings of American Politics* (New York, 1997), 195, 188–198.

45. Lewis A. Coser, ed., *Everett C. Hughes on Work, Race, and the Sociological Imagination* (Chicago, 1994), 122.

46. Nelson, *Divided We Stand*, 209, on Steelton; John Hinshaw, *Steel and Steelworkers: Race and Class Struggle in Twentieth-Century Pittsburgh* (Albany, 2002), 73–74; John S. Heywood, "Race Discrimination and Union Voice," *Industrial Relations* 31 (Fall 1992): 507; Brody, *In Labor's Cause*, 124–125; Greenberg, *Race and State*, 230.

47. Judith Stein, *Running Steel, Running America: Race, Economic Policy, and the Decline of Liberalism* (Chapel Hill, 1998), 99–100; Henderson and Buba's *Struggles in Steel* (Braddock Films) premiered in 1996.

48. Rose, *Duquesne*, 16, 189–193, 218–219.

49. Nowicki in Alice Lynd and Staughton Lynd, eds., *Rank and File: Personal Histories by Working-Class Organizers* (Boston, 1973), 85–86; Scipes, "Trade Union Development and Racial Oppression," 336, 340–343; Paul Street, "The 'Best Union Members': Class, Race, Culture, and Black Worker Militancy in Chicago's Stockyards During the 1930s," *Journal of American Ethnic History* 20 (Fall 2000): 27–29; Clement E. Vose, *Caucasians Only: The Supreme Court, the NAACP, and the Restrictive Covenant Cases* (Berkeley, 1967), 163.

50. Horowitz, "*Negro and White Unite and Fight*," 63; Abrams, *Forbidden Neighbors*, 92; Eileen M. McMahon, *What Parish Are You From? A Chicago Irish Community and Race Relations* (Lexington, 1995), 123–124; Arnold R. Hirsch, *Making the Second Ghetto: Race and Housing in Chicago, 1940–1960* (Chicago, 1998), 55–56. For a fine account of the Detroit riot and the difficulties in knowing how much to credit charges that it was led by new immigrants or by recently arrived white southerners, see Dominic Capeci Jr. and Martha Wilkerson, *Layered Violence: The Detroit Rioters of 1943* (Jackson, Miss., 1991), esp. 24–25, 62–81, 151. See also David Southern, *John LaFarge and the Limits of Catholic Interracialism* (Baton Rouge, 1996), 254–255. For an important explication of "plant friendships" and "socializing," see Bernice Anita Reed, "Accommodation Between Negro and White Employees in a West Coast Aircraft Industry, 1942–1944," *Social Forces* 26 (1947): 83, 76–84.

51. Foner, *Organized Labor and the Black Worker*, 256; Eileen Boris, "'You Wouldn't Want One of 'Em Dancing with Your Wife': Racialized Bodies on the Job in World War II," *American Quarterly* 50 (March 1998): 94, 77–108; Guglielmo, *White on Arrival*, 139, 141; Andrew Hurley, *Diners, Bowling Alleys, and Trailer Parks: Chasing the American Dream in Postwar Consumer Culture* (New York, 2001), 188–189; Joyce Shaw Peterson, *American Automobile Workers, 1900–1933* (Albany, 1987), 28. See also Kevin Boyle, "The Kiss: Racial and Gender Conflict in a 1950s Automobile Factory," *Journal of American History* 50 (September 1997): 496–523; and Patricia Cooper and Ruth Oldenziel, "Cherished Classifications: Bathrooms and the Construction of Gender/Race on the Pennsylvania Railroad During World War II," *Feminist Studies* 25 (Spring 1999): 7–41.

52. Cohen, *Making a New Deal*, 207; David Montgomery, *The Fall of the House of Labor: The Workplace, the State, and American Labor Activism, 1885–1925* (Cam-

bridge, U.K., 1987), 100; Wolfinger, "Rise and Fall of the Roosevelt Coalition," chaps. 6–7.

53. Cohen, *Making a New Deal*, 275; Sugrue, *Origins of the Urban Crisis*, 60; Sugrue, "Crabgrass-Roots Politics," 564.

54. Arnold R. Hirsch, "'Containment' on the Home Front: Race and Federal Housing Policy from the New Deal to the Cold War," *Journal of Urban History* 26 (January 2000): 158; Abrams, *Forbidden Neighbors*, 229; Singh, as quoted in Jacobson, *Whiteness of a Different Color*, 188.

55. Gail Radford, *Modern Housing in America: Policy Struggles in the New Deal Era* (Chicago, 1996), 198–199; Abrams, *Forbidden Neighbors*, 95.

56. Radford, *Modern Housing*, 191–198; Sugrue, *Origins of the Urban Crisis*, 63 ("feckless"); Stephen Grant Meyer, *As Long as They Don't Move Next Door: Segregation and Racial Conflict in American Neighborhoods* (Lanham, Md., 2000), 53–55; Myrdal, *American Dilemma*, 350; Sitkoff, *New Deal for Blacks*, 50.

57. Meyer, *Next Door*, 55; Radford, *Modern Housing*, 193, quoting the architect; Hirsch, "'Containment' on the Home Front," 158–162; Abrams, *Forbidden Neighbors*, 189–190; Thomas J. Sugrue, "Crabgrass-Roots Politics: Race, Rights, and the Reaction Against Urban Liberalism in the Urban North, 1940–1964," *Journal of American History* 81 (September 1995): 563; Sugrue, *Origins of the Urban Crisis*, 69–70; Myrdal, *American Dilemma*, 625. Herman H. Long and Charles S. Johnson, *People vs. Property: Race Restrictive Covenants in Housing* (Nashville, 1947), 70; Guglielmo, *White on Arrival*, 152; Wilder, *Covenant with Color*, 206, 209–210.

58. Abrams, *Forbidden Neighbors*, 234 ("extorted"), 229; Meyer, *Next Door*, 52; Douglas S. Massey and Nancy A. Denton, *American Apartheid: Segregation and the Making of the Underclass* (Cambridge, Mass., 1993), 52, 49–53; Kenneth T. Jackson, *Crabgrass Frontier: The Suburbanization of the United States* (New York, 1985), 196–201.

59. Meyer, *Next Door*, 53, quoting the NAACP official; Sitkoff, *New Deal for Blacks*, 50; Radford, *Modern Housing*, 180–181, 193–194, 199; David M. P. Freund, "Making It Home: Race, Development, and the Politics of Place in Suburban Detroit, 1940–1967" (Ph.D. diss., University of Michigan, 1999), 28 and passim.

60. Myrdal, *American Dilemma*, 348–349, 364–366; Abrams, *Forbidden Neighbors*, 162, 231; Massey and Denton, *American Apartheid*, 54; Cheryl Harris, "Whiteness as Property," *Harvard Law Review* 106 (June 1993): 1710.

61. Abrams, *Forbidden Neighbors*, 230–233.

62. Abrams, *Forbidden Neighbors*, 230–233, 297; Vose, *Caucasians Only*, 19, 168–169. Civil rights pressure on the FHA yielded limited results, especially after 1948. See Abrams, *Forbidden Neighbors*, 233–234; and Hirsch, "'Containment' on the Home Front," 162–172.

63. Hirsch, *Making the Second Ghetto*; Sugrue, *Origins of the Urban Crisis*; and Freund, "Making It Home" all start in the 1940s and typify the strength and the limits

of the approach. On racial and civic nationalism, see Gerstle, *American Crucible*, esp. 3–10, 153.

64. Quoted in Abrams, *Forbidden Neighbors*, 95. The best account of the deportation of Mexican Detroiters is Elena Herrada's film *Los Repatriados: Exiles from the Promised Land* (2001).

65. Abrams, *Forbidden Neighbors*, 95, 167, 230; Sugrue, "Crabgrass-Roots Politics," 564–565; Sugrue, *Origins of the Urban Crisis*, 63; Arnold Hirsch, "The Race Space Race," *Journal of Urban History* 26 (May 2000): 521. The best work in this regard is Theresa Mah's forthcoming study of race and housing in California, especially the chapter "Democracy in the Suburbs" with its acute dissection of the 1951 Freedom of Choice Initiative and "voting" on neighbors. See also Michael Omi and Howard Winant, *Racial Formation in the United States from the 1960s to the 1990s* (New York, 1994), 95.

66. James Baldwin, "On Being 'White' . . . and Other Lies," *Essence,* April 1984, 90, 92; Wilder, *Covenant with Color,* 187; Abrams, *Forbidden Neighbors,* 167.

67. Wilder, *Covenant with Color,* 190–193; Cohen, *Making a New Deal,* 274–276; Guglielmo, *White on Arrival,* 164 ("racial concentrations").

68. Meyer, *Next Door,* 53; Long and Johnson, *People vs. Property,* 72; Massey and Denton, *American Apartheid,* 54; Abrams, *Forbidden Neighbors,* 162–165, 230.

69. George Lipsitz, *The Possessive Investment in Whiteness: How White People Profit from Identity Politics* (Philadelphia, 1998), 6; Denton and Massey, *American Apartheid,* 54; Jackson, *Crabgrass Frontier,* 211; Jean Anyon, *Ghetto Schooling: A Political Economy of Urban Educational Reform* (New York, 1997), 63; Guglielmo, *White on Arrival,* 167; Freund, "Making It Home," 27–29; Lizabeth Cohen, *A Consumers' Republic: The Politics of Mass Consumption in Postwar America* (New York, 2003), 205. On Boyle Heights, see George Sanchez, "Working at the Crossroads: American Studies for the 21st Century," *American Quarterly* 54 (2002): 1–27.

70. Jackson, *Crabgrass Frontier,* 203–218; Mah, "Democracy in the Suburbs" (forthcoming); Abrams, *Forbidden Neighbors,* 163–164, 235. The *Time* quotation is from Reginald R. Isaacs, "Are Urban Neighborhoods Possible?" *Journal of Housing,* July 1948, 178, as cited in Mah. See also Cohen, *Consumers' Republic,* 194–256.

71. Wilder, *Covenant with Color,* 201–204; Biondi, *To Stand and Fight,* 116–117; Abrams, *Forbidden Neighbors,* 174–175. On anticommunism and race, see Mary Dudziak, *Cold War Civil Rights: Race and the Image of American Democracy* (Princeton, 2002).

72. David J. Hellwig, "Black Images of Jews: From Reconstruction to Depression," in Maurianne Adams and John Bracey, eds., *Strangers and Neighbors: Relations Between Blacks and Jews in the United States* (Amherst, 1999), 308; Guglielmo, *White on Arrival,* 149, 150–167; Paul Mishler, "How Did the Jews Become White?" (paper sent to author, 2000), 6.

73. Robert Orsi, "The Religious Boundaries of an Inbetween People: Street *Feste* and the Problem of the Dark-Skinned 'Other' in Italian Harlem," *American Quar-*

terly 44 (September 1992): 329; Freund, "Making It Home," 4–5, 9–11; Sugrue, *Origins of the Urban Crisis*, 23; Nikhil Singh, *Black Is a Country: Race and the Unfinished Struggle for Democracy* (Cambridge, Mass., 2004), 87–89.

AFTERWORD

1. Tom Kuntz and Phil Kuntz, eds., *The Sinatra Files: The Secret FBI Dossier* (New York, 2000), xv, 40, 87; Gerald Meyer, "The Popular Front and an American Icon," *Science and Society*, Fall 2002, 318–323. The RKO film *The House I Live In* was released in 1945. On popular music, the war, and challenges to segregation, see Lewis A. Erenberg, *Swingin' the Dream: Big Band Jazz and the Rebirth of American Culture* (Chicago, 1998), 188–210.

2. Kuntz and Kuntz, *Sinatra Files*, xv, 87; Jon Wiener, "His Way," http://jazzinstituteofchicago.org/jazzgram/features/sinatra/hisway.asp; Joshua B. Freeman, *Working-Class New York: Life and Labor Since World War Two* (New York, 2000), 34; Michael Denning, *The Cultural Front: The Laboring of American Culture in the Twentieth Century* (London, 1997), 35, 335; Thomas Cripps, "African Americans and Jews in Hollywood: Antagonistic Allies," in Maurianne Adams and John Bracey, eds., *Strangers and Neighbors: Relations Between Blacks and Jews in the United States* (Amherst, Mass., 1999), 466; Ralph Seliger, "Bad Friends and Fellow Travelers," *Forward*, July 2003, http://www.forward.com/issues/2003/03.07.18/arts4.html.

3. Jon Weiner, "'When Old Blue Eyes Was Red': The Poignant Story of Frank Sinatra's Politics," *New Republic*, March 31, 1986, 21–23; Meyer, "Popular Front and an American Icon," 318, 319 n. 5, 322–333 ("empty" at 328); Kuntz and Kuntz, *Sinatra Files*, 40–92, 130. For Meeropol's anger, see the recent film *Strange Fruit* (California Newsreel, 2003); Peter Dreier and Dick Flacks, "So Conservatives Wave the Flag While Liberals Burn It?" Center for History and New Media, September 24, 2003, http://hnn.us/articles/830.html.

4. Gerald Gamm, *Urban Exodus: Why the Jews Left Boston and the Catholics Stayed* (Cambridge, Mass., 1999), 227; Kitty Kelley, *His Way: The Unauthorized Biography of Frank Sinatra* (Toronto, 1986), 106–107; on wartime Communist policy on race, the extremes are defined by Earl Ofari Hutchinson, *Blacks and Reds: Race and Class in Conflict, 1919–1990* (East Lansing, Mich., 1995), 185; and the far more positive assessments of continued local struggles in Gerald Horne, *Black Liberation/Red Scare: Ben Davis and the Communist Party* (Newark, N.J., 1994). See also Judith E. Smith, *Visions of Belonging: Family Stories, Popular Culture, and Postwar Democracy, 1940–1960* (New York, 2004), 151, 140–165; and Cripps, "African Americans and Jews in Hollywood," 464–465.

5. See Charles E. Wynes, *Charles Richard Drew: The Man and the Myth* (Urbana, Ill., 1988), 66–74; Kelley, *His Way*, 106–107. On the riots, see Ronald Takaki, *Double Victory: A Multicultural History of America in World War Two* (Boston, 2000), 50–55, 106–110. On *Lone Journey*, see Smith, *Visions of Belonging*, 29. On popular

music, the war, and challenges to segregation, see Erenberg, *Swingin' the Dream*, 188–210.

6. Gerald Meyer, "When Frank Sinatra Came to Italian Harlem: The 1945 'Race Riot' at Benjamin Franklin High School," in Jennifer Guglielmo and Salvatore Salerno, eds., *Are Italians White? How Race Is Made in America* (New York, 2003), 173–174, 161–176. Meyer suggests (175) that Sinatra skipped singing "The House I Live In" at Franklin High; cf. Meyer, "Popular Front and an American Icon," 318–322.

7. Jennifer Guglielmo, "Negotiating Gender, Race, and Coalition: Italian Women and Working Class Politics in New York City, 1880-1945" (Ph.D. diss., 2003), 224 (quoting Mellone), 223–225; Meyer, "When Frank Sinatra Came to Italian Harlem," 170–171 (Marcantonio) and passim; Jane Dailey, "Sex, Segregation, and the Sacred after *Brown*," *Journal of American History*, June 2004, esp. 127–138.

8. Kuntz and Kuntz, *Sinatra Files*, 42–45; Meyer, "Popular Front and an American Icon," 320–322; Meyer, "When Frank Sinatra Came to Italian Harlem," 174, 161–174; Andrew Kersten, *Race, Jobs, and the War: The FEPC in the Midwest, 1941–46* (Urbana, Ill., 2000), 64; Ruth Needleman, *Black Freedom Fighters in Steel: The Struggle for Democratic Unionism* (Ithaca, N.Y., 2003), 83; John McGreevy, *Parish Boundaries: The Catholic Encounter with Race in the Twentieth Century Urban North* (Chicago, 1996), 89. The NAACP quotation is from Ronald D. Cohen, *Children of the Mill: Schooling and Society in Gary, Indiana, 1906–1960* (Bloomington, Ind., 1990), 179; Thomas Guglielmo, *White on Arrival: Italians, Race, Color, and Power, 1890–1945* (Oxford, 2003), 161, on Italian-American activism in a postwar student hate strike in Chicago in 1947; Kelley, *His Way*, 107–110.

9. Kelley, *His Way*, 110, 124–126. For *L'Unità del Popolo*, see Meyer, "Popular Front and an American Icon," 323; see also Wiener, "When Old Blue Eyes," 21–23; Kuntz and Kuntz, *Sinatra Files*, 87; and Lee Bernstein, *The Greatest Menace: Organized Crime in Cold War America* (Amherst, Mass., 2002). For Sinatra's troubles with both allegations of Mafia ties and charges of Communism and for his attempts to address them by moving to the right in union politics, see Gerald Horne, *Class Struggle in Hollywood, 1930–1950: Moguls, Mobsters, Stars, Reds, and Trade Unionists* (Austin, Tex., 2001), 211, 115, 201.

10. John Morton Blum, *V Was for Victory: Politics and American Culture During World War II* (New York, 1976), 151–154; Takaki, *Double Victory*, 134–135 (Warren and *Crisis*); Masumi Izumi, *Japanese American Internment and the Emergency Detention Act (Title II of the Internal Security Act of 1950), 1941–1971* (Doshisha University, 2004), 40, 44. Cf. Alan Dawley, *Changing the World: American Progressives in War and Revolution* (Princeton, 2003), 272–276.

11. Guglielmo, "Negotiating Race, Gender, and Coalition," 224; Meyer, "When Frank Sinatra Came to Italian Harlem," 167–168, 172.

12. Meyer, "Popular Front and an American Icon," 320–322; Meyer, "When Frank Sinatra Came to Italian Harlem," 174–175; for the steelworker, see Peter Tamony's

notes on "guinea" in the Tamony Collection, Western Historical Manuscripts Collection, University of Missouri at Columbia.

13. Guglielmo, "Negotiating Gender, Race, and Coalition," 224.

14. Todd Michney, "Changing Neighborhoods: Race and Upward Mobility in Southeast Cleveland, 1930–1980" (Ph.D. diss., University of Minnesota, 2004), chap. 4.

15. Denning, *Cultural Front,* esp. 466; Barbara Savage, *Broadcasting Freedom: Radio, War, and the Politics of Race, 1938–1948* (Chapel Hill, N.C., 1999); David Montgomery, "Racism, Immigrants, and Political Reform," *Journal of American History*, March 2001, 1271–1274.

16. "The House We Live In," *Ebony*, January 1946, 20, with thanks to Alex Lubin. For Sinatra and housing, see Kuntz and Kuntz, *Sinatra Files*, 47.

INDEX

Abbott, Grace, 90, 186
Abie's Irish Rose, 198
Abrams, Charles, 160, 172, 175, 225
Adamic, Louis, 28, 194, 195, 218, 219
Addams, Jane, 71, 93, 94, 102, 111, 117,
    128, 160, 186
Advertising, 181, 303n61
AEEAs (American of Eastern European
    ancestry), 30–31
Afghanis, 61
AFL (American Federation of Labor),
    6, 7, 15, 79, 80, 81, 82, 83, 84, 86,
    90, 92, 142, 149, 156, 200, 209,
    210, 213, 214, 215, 216, 219,
    272n52
Africa, 111, 114
African Americans, 9, 13, 14–15, 25, 30,
    31, 33, 36, 46, 60, 62, 66, 71,
    111–113, 116–121, 123, 124, 125,
    128, 136, 138, 140–144, 150, 151,
    156, 177, 202, 204, 224–227, 231,
    233, 237, 238, 244, 285n61,
    293nn43–44. *See also* Blacks;
    Negroes; "Nigger"
    housing and, 163–169, 170–173,
    176–178, 181, 182, 184, 185, 187,
    191–193
    inbetween jobs and, 72–78
    language and, 37, 39, 41, 44, 45

    music and, 100, 102, 104–108
    racial consciousness and, 93–100
    unions and, 82–92, 207, 209, 213,
    222–224
African Blood Brotherhood, 99
"Africani," 113
The African American United Mine
    Workers, 49
Afro-southerners, migration of, 150,
    165, 168, 170, 176
Agassi, Andre, 3, 4
Aid to Dependent Children (ADC), 206
Alba, Richard, 153
Albanians, 51, 122
Algren, Nelson, 43, 135
"Alien white races," 76
Allison, Mose, 101
Alpine, 50, 51, 60, 67, 141
Amalgamated Clothing Workers of
    America, 199
The Amboy Dukes (Shulman), 40
Amenta, Edwin, 202
*American Apartheid as Segregation and
    the Making of the Underclass*
    (Massey and Denton), 164
American Defense Society, 143
American Enterprise Institute, 30
American Federation of Labor. *See* AFL
American Federationist, 82

American Indians, 15, 17, 20, 33, 46, 96, 181, 230. *See also* Indians

American Jewish Committee (AJC), 16

American Legion, 142, 143

American Minority Peoples (Young), 24, 82

"American race," 20, 36, 52, 63, 139 "new immigrants" and, 64–72

American Scholar (Riesman), 26

American Slav, 219

American Sociological Review, 26

American Speech, 43

American Travels of a Dutch Hobo (Leeflang), 140

American Xenophobia and the Slav Immigrant (Wtulich), 43

An American Dilemma (Myrdal), 28, 95

The American Girl in the Stockyards District (Montgomery), 160

The American Scene (James), 5, 21

Americanization, 70, 79, 84, 94, 117, 143, 178, 189, 195, 217

Anglos, 74

Anglo-Saxons, 61, 63, 68, 69, 81, 85, 94, 95, 97, 99, 123, 126, 127, 137, 141, 143, 161, 189, 198, 208

Antin, Mary, 188, 189

Appointment in Samarra (O'Hara), 43

Arab Americans, 7, 46

"Aristocracy of labor," 90, 274n69

Armenian Americans, 4, 51, 96, 106

Arnold, Matthew, 21

Arredondo, Gabriela, 75, 122

Aryan, 25, 59

Asher, Robert, 80, 81

Asian Americans, 7, 27, 33, 36, 45, 91, 106, 120, 138

Asian Indians, 59, 60, 61

Asians, 31, 40, 51, 63, 79, 97, 104, 108, 109, 137, 150, 170, 173

Asiatics, 4, 6, 7, 51, 94, 115, 116

Ask the Dust (Fante), 42

Assimilation in American Life (Gordon), 29

Assimilation, of "new immigrants," 20

Assyrians, 51

Atlantic Monthly, 41, 141

Attaway, William, 39, 101, 102, 103

Aunt Jemima, 181

Austin High gang, 183

Austrians, 43, 126

Austro-Hungarian, 146, 147

The Autobiography of Malcolm X (Malcolm X), 103

Babb, Valerie, 71

Babbitt (Lewis), 10, 11, 12, 13, 149

Baldwin, James, 7, 12, 103, 104, 106, 107, 111, 112, 137

Baritz, Loren, 110

Barnes, Charles, 39

Barnhart, C. A., 42

Barrett, James, 126

Barton, Josef, 44, 197

Basques, 62

Bell, Thomas, 44, 123

Benedict, Ruth, 25, 26

Benton, Thomas Hart, 63

Berkson, Isaac, 22, 23, 49

Berman, Marshall, 105, 184

Bilbo, Theodore, 241, 242

Birth of a Nation, 91, 180

"Black guinea," 39

"Black Irish," 39

Black Metropolis (Cayton and Drake), 23

Black solidarity, 100–110

Blackface, 180, 184

Blacks, 51, 74, 82, 86, 87, 97, 100, 120, 122, 123, 128, 137, 165, 206, 207, 210, 226, 232, 233, 237, 244. *See also* African Americans; Negroes

Blauner, Robert, 31

Blood on the Forge (Attaway), 39, 101

Blues, 101
Blumenbach, Johann Friedrich, 14, 50
Boarders, 162
Boas, Franz, 69, 139
Bogardus, Emory, 192
Bohemians, 43, 72
"Bohunk," 43, 49, 51, 75
Bold Relief (Amenta), 202
Bramen, Carrie Tirado, 28
Bread Givers (Yezierska), 183, 188
Breckinridge, Sophonisba, 152, 160
Bridges, Harry, 211
Brodkin, Karen, 12
Brody, David, 88, 122
"Brotherhood of Man," 83
Brown, Francis, 150
Brown, Michael, 205
Brown, Sterling, 98
Buba, Tony, 221
Buchanan v. Warley, 170
Buff, Rachel, 61
Buff, Stephen A., 43
Bukowczyk, John, 196
Bulgarians, 59, 122, 219
Bunche, Ralph, 48, 60
Burke, Thomas A., 242
Burnett, Stephen Sage, 190
Bustamante, Antonio, 74

Cabán, Pedro, 70
Cable Act of 1922, 152
Califi, Michael, 124
Call, 98
Cantor, Eddie, 125
Carey, Archibald, 171
Carnegie Foundation, 167
Carpenter, Niles, 20, 75, 77, 130, 146
Catholics, 36, 65, 101, 124, 167–169,
    194–195, 221, 223, 236, 238,
    239
Caucasian, 7, 16, 26, 36, 45, 81, 87, 136,
    138, 173, 198, 241

The Causes of Race Superiority (Ross),
    7
Cayton, Horace, 23, 104
Celts, 61, 127
Cermak, Anton, 200, 201
Chafets, Ze'ev, 105
Chang, Michael, 4
"Changes in Bodily Form of
    Descendants of Immigrants"
    (Boas), 69
Changing Conceptions of Education
    (Cubberly), 19
Chicago Oral History Project, 75
Chicago School of Sociology, 28
Child, Irvin L., 25, 40, 177, 185
A Child of the Ghetto (Griffith), 163,
    180
The Children of the Ghetto (Zangwill),
    179
Chinatown, 163, 164
Chinese, 4, 5, 6, 13, 14, 17, 24, 46, 51,
    53, 61, 63, 72, 74, 79, 80, 81, 82,
    87, 89–90, 97, 106, 120, 165, 173,
    180, 230
"Chink," 45, 80
Christianity, ethnic religions v., 21
Christians, 174
Churchill, Winston, 133
CIO (Congress of Industrial
    Organizations), 148, 200, 209, 210,
    211, 212, 214–223, 224, 238, 239,
    240
Citizenship, 152–156
Civil liberties, 122
Civil rights, 9, 30, 121, 228, 232
Clemente, Egidio, 46
Code of ethics, 172
Cohen, Israel, 32
Cohen, Lizabeth, 179, 200, 212
Color, race v., 11, 13
"Color-races," 21, 28, 36
"Coloured," 6

Commander, Lydia Kingsmill, 72

Common Ground (Adamic), 28

Commons, John R., 54, 73, 76, 84

Communist/Communism, 204, 211,
    215, 216, 217, 232, 235, 238,
    313n39

"Conditionally white," 12

The Confidence Man (Melville), 38

Congress of Industrial Organizations.
    See CIO

Conrad, Joseph, 115

Contract Labor Law of 1885, 66

Coolidge, Calvin, 139

"Coolie," 79, 82

"Coon," 91, 171

Cope, E. D., 66

Cornell University Library Making of
    America, 18, 252n31

Courts, 59–64

Covello, Leonard, 192, 195, 238

Covenants, 169–177

Craigie, Sir William, 18

Crain, Marion, 208

The Crimes of the White Race, 96

Criminal Slang, 43

The Crisis, 94

Croats/Croatian Americans, 44, 50, 59,
    75, 108, 159, 197, 219

Cubans, 85

Cubberly, Ellwood, 19

Cultural organizations, 153–154

*Culture and Democracy in the United
    States* (Kallen), 143

Cultures, of ghetto, 163

Cunard, Nancy, 98

Curtis, L. Perry, 115

Czecho-Slovak, 59

Czechs, 99, 164, 171, 201, 219

"Dago," 40, 43, 45, 46, 47, 53, 75, 80,
    94, 96, 97, 99, 120, 217, 240, 241

Daily News, 238

Daily Worker, 217, 238

Damon, Maria, 183

"Dark white," 4, 36

Darwin, Charles, 68

Daughters of the American Revolution,
    143

Davis, Harry E., 209

Davis, Mike, 137, 138

Davis, Richard L., 49

Day, 187

Days of Hope (Sullivan), 202

De Caro, Lou, Jr., 113

Debs, Eugene V., 80, 214

DeForest, J. W., 41

Democracy and Assimilation
    (Drachsler), 197

Democrats, 200, 203, 204, 227

Demographics, of immigration, 149–156

Deniker, Joseph, 22

Denning, Michael, 242

Denton, Nancy, 176

Deportation Act of 1929, 155

Depression. *See* Great Depression

di Tommaso, Andrea, 113

Dialectics, of whiteness, 145–156

Dickstein, Samuel, 156

*Dictionary of American English on
    Historical Principles* (Craigie and
    Hulbert), 18

*Dictionary of American Regional
    English*, 42

Dictionary of Races or Peoples, 4, 16

Dillingham, William P., 16

The Dillingham Commission, 16, 21–22,
    52, 73

DiMaggio, Joe, 217

Discrimination, 75–78, 148, 207–224

Dollard, John, 13

Douglas, Paul, 205

Douglas, Stephen, 63

Douglass, Frederick, 101, 102, 103, 111

Down These Mean Streets (Thomas), 40

Drachsler, Julius, 22, 23, 197
Drake, St. Clair, 23, 104
Drew, Charles, 237
Du Bois, W.E.B., 80, 87, 93, 94, 95,
    102, 112, 115, 117, 122, 212
Dubofsky, Melvyn, 77, 78
Dunne, Finley Peter, 95
Durante, Jimmy, 182
Dutch, 52
Dziennik Chicagoski, 97
Dziennik ludowy, 97
Dziennik Zwiazkowy, 95, 129

Eastern Europeans. *See* Europeans
Ebony, 243
Edwards, Richard, 73
Ellis Island, 5, 9, 141
*The Encyclopaedia of the Social
    Sciences,* 23, 24
English, 70, 74, 156
English for Coming Americans
    (Roberts), 53
Entertainment industry, 177–184
Erenberg, Lewis, 137
Ethiopia, 111–112, 281n43
Ethnic(s)
    concentric circles of, 29
    Europeans as, 23
    groups of, 23
    invention of, 21–27
    race v., 22, 23, 27, 36
    "White," 18, 19, 27–34, 28, 30, 45
Ethnic Options (Waters), 32
"Ethnic race," 28
Ethnicity, 13
    absence of, 18
    definition of, 24, 25
    invention of, 21–27, 136
    language of, 18, 20, 25, 31
    "new immigrants" and, 18–21
    studies of, 28
"European Chinamen," 51

Europeans, 26, 33, 78, 79, 155
    central, 11
    divisions of, 17
    eastern, 4, 5, 9, 11, 18, 20, 30, 36, 43,
        45, 49, 50, 59, 64, 65, 75, 80, 83,
        91, 92, 116, 120, 123, 138, 145,
        146, 148, 151, 163, 200, 201, 218,
        221, 239, 244
    as ethnic, 23
    groupings of, 50
    immigration of, 145–147
    northern, 4, 6, 39, 139, 146, 172, 208
    race of, 12
    southern, 4, 5, 9, 11, 18, 20, 30, 36,
        39, 45, 50, 59, 64, 65, 70, 75, 80,
        83, 85, 91, 92, 120, 123, 138, 145,
        146, 148, 151, 200, 218, 221, 239,
        244
    western, 4, 6, 139, 146
Evergood, Philip, 133–134, 136

Fair Employment Practices Committee
    (FEPC), 208, 224
Fair Labor Standards Act (FLSA) of
    1938, 209, 210
Fairchild, Henry Pratt, 28, 46, 51, 58,
    145
Fante, John, 42
Farrell, James T., 140
Fascism, 25, 137
Federal Housing Authority. *See* FHA
"Federal race classifications," 15
Feldman, Herman, 75, 76, 99, 148, 149
FHA (Federal Housing Authority), 225,
    227, 228, 229, 230, 231, 232, 233
Fields, Mamie Garvin, 99
Filipinos, 15, 42, 46, 50, 51, 70, 150,
    155, 181, 183, 186, 198
Finns, 51, 53, 61, 62–64
Fishberg, Maurice, 22
Fishman, Joshua, 153
Fiske, John, 68

Fitch, John, 49, 91
Fitzpatrick, John, 86
Flynn, Elizabeth Gurley, 48
Foerster, Robert F., 39
Foley, Barbara, 154
Forbidden Neighbors (Abrams), 160
Ford, Henry, 49, 141
Foreign Affairs (Du Bois), 112
"Foreign stock," 65
"Foreign-Born White and Other Races,"
    23
The Fortunate Pilgrim (Puzo), 39,
    257n7
Foucault, Michel, 116
Fox, Clifton A., 39
Frank, Leo, 106
Fraser, Steven, 242
Frazier, E. Franklin, 117
Freie Arbeiter Stimme, 98
French, 7, 52
French Canadians, 51, 109
Freund, David, 228, 233
The Future of America (Wells), 6

Gabaccia, Donna, 116
Galt, Margot Fortunato, 113
Gambino, Richard, 77, 106
Gary, Indiana, strike in, 239
Gellert, Hugo, 98, 114
Georgakas, Dan, 45
Gerber, David, 29
German Jews, 126, 225
Germans, 21, 52, 53, 61, 71, 75, 116,
    126, 156, 208
Gerstle, Gary, 156, 200, 201, 242
Ghetto
    African Americans relating to,
        163–168, 177, 244
    Chinatown as, 163, 164
    cultures of, 163
    "deadlines" relating to, 167
    home ownership relating to, 163–169

houses of worship relating to,
    167–169
    Jews relating to, 163, 165
    Little Italy/Sicily, 163, 166
    Little Poland as, 166
The Ghetto (Wirth), 98, 163, 179
GI Bill of Rights, 224, 233
The Gift of Black Folk (Du Bois), 94, 95
Gilman, Sander, 69, 105
Giunta, Edvige, 113
Glazer, Nathan, 30, 31, 33
Gleason, Philip, 27, 70
Glos Polek, 128, 288n79
Gobel, Thomas, 219
Gold, Mike, 160, 185
Goldberg, Barry, 13
Goldfield, Michael, 219
Goldstein, Eric, 135–136
Gompers, Samuel, 66, 79, 81, 82, 83,
    84, 87, 142, 213, 214, 291n25
Good Housekeeping, 139, 174
The Good Life (Baritz), 110, 281n40
Goodman, James, 100
Gordon, David, 73
Gordon, Linda, 74, 205
Gordon, Milton, 29–30, 33
Government, 14–18
"Goy/goyim," 107, 114
Graham, A. A., 82
Gramsci, Antonio, 112
Grant, Madison, 67, 139, 140, 187
"Grease monkey," 42
"Greaser/greaseball," 36, 37–45, 50, 51,
    53, 54, 59, 64, 66, 258n12
"The Greaser" (Lighton), 41
The Greaser Bill, 41
Great Depression, 148, 149, 155, 204
Great Migration. *See* Migration
Greek Immigration to the United States
    (Fairchild), 46
Greeks, 4, 7, 42, 45, 46, 48, 50, 51, 53,
    58, 59, 61, 73, 87, 89, 94, 96, 108,

122, 124, 126, 152, 165, 172, 173, 198
Greeley, Andrew, 30
Greenberg, Stanley, 215
Griffith, D. W., 163
Griswold, John, 90, 91
Grossman, James, 128
Gruppo Diretto all' Esistenza, 96
Guggenheim, Simon, 16
Guglielmo, Jennifer, 111, 192
Guglielmo, Thomas, 12, 13, 27, 110
"Guinea/ginnies," 36, 37–45, 50, 51, 53, 59, 64, 86, 87, 127, 135, 148, 185, 242
Guterl, Matthew Pratt, 139
Gutman, Herbert, 76
Gypsies, 46, 115, 118

The Hairy Ape (O'Neill), 39
Haley, Alex, 103
Hall, Covington, 85
Halpern, Rick, 128
Handlin, Oscar, 9, 26, 147, 190, 194
Haney-Lopez, Ian, 62
Happy Tho' Broke (Fox), 39
Harper, Frances E. W., 38
Harpers Weekly, 124
Harris, Cheryl, 174
Harris, Dianne, 162
Harris, Richard, 162
Harte, Bret, 41
Hatred. *See* "Race hatred"
Hattam, Victoria, 22, 23
Haywood, William "Big Bill," 121
Hearn, Lafcadio, 23
Heart of Darkness (Conrad), 115
"Hebrew race," 16, 194
Hecht, Ben, 102
Hellwig, David, 233
Helmbold, Lois Rita, 204
Henderson, Ray, 221
Herr, David, 196

Heywood, John S., 220
Higham, John, 12, 13, 30, 39, 65, 79, 143, 282n26
Higher education, 9
Hill, Herbert, 105
Hillman, Sidney, 199, 201, 202, 207, 208
Hindus, 51, 53
Hinshaw, John, 221
Hirsch, Arnold, 158, 166
History
    of immigration, 9
    of "new immigrants," 7, 8, 31
A History of Affirmative Action (Rubio), 203
History of the American People (Wilson), 69
Hochschild, Jennifer, 120, 137, 138
Hoerder, Dirk, 90
HOLC (Home Owners Loan Corporation), 227, 230, 231
Holiday, Billie, 236, 237
Hollinger, David, 33
Hollywood, 179
Home Owners Loan Corporation. *See* HOLC
Home ownership
    boarders relating to, 162
    code of ethics relating to, 172
    covenants relating to, 169–177
    finances relating to, 162
    ghetto relating to, 163–169
    importance of, 161–162, 166
    for "new immigrants," 158–162
    "sweat equity" and, 162
Honey, Michael, 215, 216
Hoover, Herbert, 149, 161, 202, 205
Hope, John, II, 222
Hopper, Hedda, 240
Horowitz, Irving Louis, 27
Houdini, Harry, 181
Hourwich, Isaac, 52, 81

House Committee on Immigration and Naturalization, 141

The House I Live In, 235–243

Housing
  for African Americans, 163–169, 170–173, 176–178, 181, 182, 184, 185, 187, 191–193
  changes in, 8
  for Italians, 158, 159, 164–166, 171–173, 176
  for Jews, 163, 165, 171, 173, 174
  New Deal policies of, 9, 158, 198, 200–207, 224–234

Housing, 173

How Columbus and I Discovered America (Trees), 49, 53, 110

Howells, William Dean, 48

Hoyt, Homer, 172

Hughes, Everett and Helen, 26, 76, 220

Hughes, Langston, 170, 176

Huginnie, Yvette, 45

Hulbert, James R., 18

Hull House, 71, 93, 102

Hungarians, 43, 49, 50, 61, 71, 72, 81, 94, 114, 141, 152, 191, 239

"Hunky," 36, 37–45, 49, 50, 51, 53, 54, 59, 64, 74, 75, 86, 87, 88, 89, 90, 97, 99, 104, 120, 123, 127, 134, 148, 218, 220, 221, 242, 259n14, 279n22

"Huns," 43, 80, 142

Husband, W. W., 20

Hyde Park Herald, 172

Hyman, Colette, 218

Il Proletario, 96

ILGWU (International Ladies' Garment Workers Union), 97, 99, 214

"Illegal entry," 154

ILWU (International Longshoremen's and Warehousemen's Union), 211

Imagining the Balkans (Todorova), 116

"Immigrant problem," 8

Immigrant radicalism, 142

The Immigrant and the Community (Abbott), 90

The Immigrant Invasion (Warne), 6

Immigrants and Their Children (Carpenter), 20

Immigrants Protective League, 186

Immigration. *See also* "New immigrants"
  demographics of, 149–156
  European, 145–147
  history of, 9
  illegal, 148, 155–156
  racial politics of, 14
  restrictions on, 8, 10, 20, 36, 82, 133–138, 145–156

Immigration Act of 1924, 155

Immigration Commission, 4, 17

An Imperative Duty (Howells), 48

Inbetween nationalities, 45–50

"Inbetween peoples," 12, 13, 20, 37, 146, 154

"Inbetweenness," 8, 50–54, 57–59, 61, 67, 69, 71–78, 81, 82, 85, 88, 92, 94, 116, 119–130, 144

Independent, 142

Indians, 41, 61, 63, 64, 72, 151. *See also* American Indians; Asian Indians

Industrial unionism, 8, 200–201, 211

Industrial Workers of the World. *See* IWW

Intermarriage, 196–198

"International Fraternity of Labor," 82

International Ladies' Garment Workers Union. *See* ILGWU

International Longshoremen's and Warehousemen's Union. *See* ILWU

International Workers Order, 217

The International Jew (Ford), 49

Inter-Racial Council, 142, 143

Irish, 7, 21, 26, 27, 30, 39, 45, 46, 51,
    61, 62, 63, 65, 71, 74, 84, 86, 87,
    94, 100, 102, 111, 119, 120, 123,
    124, 126, 134, 158, 165, 167, 171,
    194, 198, 200, 231, 237
Irish People Monthly, 100
Irvine, Alexander, 47, 120
Irving, Katrina, 189
Italian Americans, 61, 62, 63, 66, 86, 87,
    97, 98, 106, 110, 112, 117, 119,
    120, 127, 128, 129, 136, 137, 164,
    168, 177, 179, 185, 186, 191, 192,
    196–197, 199, 211, 219, 223, 231,
    233, 238, 240, 241
Italian or American (Child), 177
Italian socialists, 83
Italians, 5, 6, 7, 10, 12, 25, 27, 30, 46,
    47, 48, 50, 51, 52, 53, 61, 94, 96,
    97, 99, 100, 120, 122, 123, 124,
    126, 127, 146, 149, 152, 238, 239
    housing and, 158, 159, 164–166,
        171–173, 176
    inbetweenness of, 58, 61, 67, 69,
        71–75, 77, 81, 82, 85, 88
    language and, 36, 38, 42, 45
    racialization relating to, 135, 141, 142
    unions relating to, 194, 198, 208
    WOA relating to, 111, 113, 116
Italy. *See* Little Italy/Sicily
IWW (Industrial Workers of the World),
    83, 85, 86, 89, 99, 121

Jackson, Kenneth, 227
Jacobson, Matthew Frye, 7, 8, 26,
    31–32, 50, 109, 138
James, C. L. R., 100
James, Henry, 4, 5, 21, 53, 58
"Jap," 45, 46, 80, 241
Japanese, 13, 50, 51, 53, 59, 61, 62, 79,
    87, 97, 108, 120, 156, 173
    internment of, 137, 241
Jazz, 101

The Jazz Singer, 102, 125, 178–17
Jefferson, Blind Lemon, 102
Jenks, Albert, 23, 99
A Jew in Love (Hecht), 102
Jewish Daily Courier, 98, 127
Jewish Daily Forward, 95
Jewish Educational and Charitable
    Association, 107
Jews Without Money (Gold), 160, 185,
    304n71
Jews/Jewish, 5, 7, 16, 17, 22, 25, 26, 27,
    30, 32, 48, 49, 51, 94, 98, 114,
    115–116, 123, 124, 125, 127, 128,
    146, 149, 191, 198, 236, 237, 238,
    240, 241. *See also* German Jews;
    Russian Jews
    housing relating to, 163, 165, 171,
        173, 174
    inbetweenness of, 58, 69, 71, 74, 81,
        94
    music relating to, 101, 102, 105,
        106–109
    racialization relating to, 135, 136, 140
    unions relating to, 199, 208, 213, 231
Jim Crow/Jim Crowed, 4, 12, 14, 45, 47,
    70, 71, 78, 91, 94, 100, 109, 136,
    141, 154, 170, 174, 175, 178, 180,
    182, 203, 209, 210, 213, 214, 215,
    217, 223, 226, 230, 232, 240
Johnson, Albert, 140
Johnson, Charles S., 173, 175
Johnson-Reed Act of 1924, 139–145
    immigration laws of, 139
    implementation of, 144, 147
    quotas in, 144–145, 147
Jolson, Al, 102, 125, 178–179, 180
Joseph's Trials in Egypt, 179
Joyce, James, 41
The Jungle (Sinclair), 160

"Kaffir," 141
Kafka, Franz, 115

Kallen, Horace, 22, 23, 71, 142, 143
Karpatho-Rus, 219
Katz, Daniel, 130
Kawakami, Kiyoshi Karl, 61
Kelley, Florence, 72
Kellor, Frances, 143
"Kikes," 49, 99, 135, 217
Kikta, Anna, 120
Killens, John Oliver, 104
Kimeldorf, Howard, 82, 99
King, Desmond, 122, 140
Kingsblood Royal (Lewis), 10, 12
Kline, Tiny, 125
Koukol, Alois, 44
Kraditor, Aileen, 72
Kraut, Alan, 66
Ku Klux Klan, 22, 59, 96, 99, 106, 126,
 139, 143, 147, 148, 171

La Questione Sociale, 96
La Sorte, Michael, 46, 126
Labels, of "new immigrants," 13
Labor force
 discrimination in, 75–78, 148,
 207–224
 divided by race, 72–78
 immigrant women in, 84, 189, 206
 inbetweenness relating to,
 123–130
 management in, 72–78, 80
 shortage of, 142
 socialist movement and, 91
 unions relating to, 78–92
Labriola, Arturo, 97
LaGuardia, Fiorello, 156, 199, 200, 202,
 207, 241
Lane, A. T., 82
Language
 African Americans and, 37, 39, 41,
 44, 45
 of ethnicity, 18, 20, 25, 31
 Italians and, 36, 38, 42, 45

of "new immigrants," 153–154
of race, 7, 13, 37–45, 50, 66, 92,
 134
Lapps, 62
Lasch-Quinn, Elizabeth, 71
Latinos, 6, 7, 30, 31, 33, 36, 85, 106,
 108, 120, 138, 151, 233
Latvians, 43
Laughlin, Henry, 140, 141
Laurino, Maria, 43
Lazarus, Emma, 106
"Le Razza di Colore e il Colore il
 Socialismo" (Labriola), 97
Lee, Erika, 51
Lee, Robert, 79
Leeflang, Gerard, 140
Legislation
 of New Deal, 209, 210
 "new immigrants" relating to, 66, 95,
 106, 138, 139–145
Leiserson, William, 85
Leonard, Oscar, 107
Leonardo, Micaela de, 18, 32
Leone, Carmen, 195
L'Era Nuova, 96
Lerner, Michael, 105, 116
LeRoy, Mervyn, 236
Letts, 51
Lewis, Austin, 6
Lewis, Sinclair, 10, 11, 149
Lieberson, Stanley, 78, 82, 176
Lietuva, 161
Life, 76
Lighton, William R., 41
Lincherei (Opatoshu), 98
L'Italia, 63, 128, 266n15
L'Italia barbara contemporanea
 (Niceforo), 112–113
Lithuanians, 50, 158, 169
Little Italy/Sicily, 163, 166
Little Poland, 166
Locke, Alain, 22, 157

Lodge, Henry Cabot, 14, 15, 17, 18, 27, 52, 80

Logan, John, 164, 165

Loguidice, Joseph, 58

Lombroso, Cesare, 112

London, Jack, 42, 46, 91, 275n72

Lone Journey, 237

"Long early twentieth century," 9, 244

Long, Herman H., 173, 175

Lopez, Ian Haney, 145

Los Angeles Sentinel, 225

Lots (Oso), 183

Luconi, Stefano, 112

L'Unitá del Popolo, 240

Lunt, Paul S., 25

Lynching, 52, 96, 97, 98, 106, 108, 109, 117, 122, 263n26

Lyons, Eugene, 48

MacChesney, William, 171, 173

MacIver, Robert, 26

Magyars, 43, 44, 62, 73, 115

Malays, 38

Malcolm X, 103, 120

Male, Charles, 172

Maltz, Albert, 236

Marcantonio, Vito, 238, 239, 241, 242

Margariti, Antonio, 127

Marine Transport Workers Local 8, 99

Martinelli, Phylis Cancilla, 85

Massey, Douglas, 176

McCaffery, Isaiah, 46

McClintock, Anne, 115

McDowell, Mary, 87, 160, 273n63

McGirr, Lisa, 99

McGouldrick, Paul, 77

McGovern, Michael, 81

McGreevy, John, 167

McKay Claude, 117, 157, 295n1

McKee, James B., 24

McSweeney, Edward F., 15, 95

McWilliams, Carey, 210

Mediterranean immigrants, 36, 42, 50, 60, 67, 80, 81, 93, 141

Meeropol, Abel, 235, 237

Mellone, Viola, 192, 238

Melnick, Jeffrey, 125

Melting pot, 60, 68, 70, 143, 145, 179, 232

The Melting Pot Mistake (Fairchild), 145

Melville, Herman, 37–38

Menorah Journal, 22

Mesaro, Stjepan, 108

"Mestizo," 41, 151

Mettler, Suzanne, 210

Mexican Americans, 13, 36, 41, 42, 45, 46, 50, 51, 74, 77, 85, 87, 91, 108, 122, 141, 150, 151, 154, 155, 170, 172, 173, 180, 205, 206, 210, 230, 237, 316n64

Meyer, Gerald, 236

Meyerowitz, Joanne, 187

Mezzrow, Mezz, 101–102, 183, 185

Migration, 146–147
  of Afro-southerners, 150, 165, 168, 170, 176
  of Mexicans, 151, 154–155, 170

The Militant Proletariat (Lewis), 6

Miller, Glenn, 137

Miller, Herbert, 189

Mink, Gwendolyn, 31, 71, 79, 80, 144

Minorities, 134, 289n4

Minstrel shows, 125, 180

Mitchell, John, 81

Mitigation, of "new immigrants," 6, 53

Model, Suzanne, 123

Mongolians, 51, 61, 62, 63, 173

Mongoloid, 26, 29, 51

"Mongrelization," 150

Montagu, Ashley, 25

Montgomery, David, 152, 155–156, 242, 243

Montgomery, Louise, 160

Moorish, 173
Morawska, Ewa, 159
Moreno, Paul, 209
The More Perfect Union (MacIver), 26
Morgan Journal-Tageblatt, 102
Morrison, Toni, 34, 102–103, 104
Mortimer, Lee, 239–240
Moynihan, Daniel Patrick, 30
Mulattos, 38, 46
Mumford, Kevin, 177, 182
Murray, Albert, 112
Music
  blues as, 101
  jazz as, 101
  "new immigrants" relating to,
    100–110
  second generation relating to,
    182–184
  "wailing" as, 101
"Mutts," 75
Myrdal, Gunnar, 28, 30, 33, 95, 117,
  210, 213, 228, 236

NAACP (National Association for the
  Advancement of Colored People),
  94, 99, 210, 226, 227, 237, 239, 241
Nana (Zola), 41
Narod Polski, 128
Nasaw, David, 180, 182
National Association for the
  Advancement of Colored People.
  See NAACP
National Labor Relations Act (NLRA)
  of 1935, 209
National Maritime Union, 215
National Negro Congress, 207
National Security League, 143
Nationalists, 143
"Nation-races," 11, 21, 25, 36
"Native Americans," 21, 31, 36, 41, 75,
  106, 205
"Native-White," 23, 135, 176

Naturalization
  of Irish, 61
  of Italians, 61
  of new immigrants, 59–64, 121,
    144–145
Naturalization law, 121
The Nature of Race Relations (Park), 25
Nazis/Nazism, 134, 137, 236, 237
Neather, Andrew, 79, 271n45
Negroes, 5, 6, 20, 23, 24, 25, 27, 47, 49,
  50, 58, 72, 76, 77, 78, 87, 92, 94,
  95, 97–100, 102, 108, 127–130,
  140, 150, 151, 172, 173, 175, 191,
  199, 212, 214, 216, 223, 225, 230,
  231, 237, 238, 241
Negroid, 26, 29
Nelli, Humbert, 164
Nelson, Bruce, 215
Never Come Morning (Algren), 135
New Deal, 8, 138, 153, 242–244
  housing policy of, 9, 158, 198,
    200–207, 224–234
  labor legislation of, 209, 210
  liberalism of, 201
  unions relating to, 200–203, 207–224
  welfare and, 203–207
  as "white," 203
"New immigrants," 4, 5
  American race and, 64–72
  assimilation of, 20
  black solidarity with, 100–110
  citizenship of, 152–156
  civil liberties of, 122
  courts and, 59–64
  cultural organizations of, 153–154
  ethnicity and, 18–21
  history of, 7, 8, 31
  home ownership for, 158–162
  inbetween jobs, 72–78, 92
  inbetweenness of, 50, 57–59,
    119–130, 144
  intelligence tests of, 141

labels of, 13
language of, 153–154
legislation relating to, 66, 95, 106, 138, 139–145
mass arrival of, 9
"mitigation of," 6, 53
music relating to, 100–110
naturalization and, 59–64, 121, 144–145
political power of, 201
prostitution relating to, 186–187
race and, 7, 18, 250n7
racial categorization of, 9–10, 11, 50, 64, 134–138
racial characteristics of, 19–20
racial consciousness of, 93–100, 135–136
racialization of, 37–45, 45–50, 50–54, 64–72, 134, 135, 136, 141, 142
as "racials," 75, 76, 208, 270n39
restrictions on, 64–72
second generation of, 177–184
unions and, 78–92, 207–224
work force of, 66–67
The New Negro (Locke), 157
New Sociology (Horowitz), 27
"New unionism," 86
New York Times, 111, 145
Ngai, Mae, 144, 147, 154, 155
Niceforo, Alfredo, 112–113
"Nigger," 44, 49, 80, 89, 91, 97, 99, 103, 104, 106, 114, 117, 120, 150, 185, 198, 213, 217
Non-Partisan League, 207
Nordics, 50, 67, 94, 97, 139, 141, 208, 216
Northern Europeans. See Europeans
Norwegians, 27, 52
Novak, Michael, 27
Nowicki, Stella, 222
NWNPs (native-born whites with native-born parents), 78

O'Hara, John, 43
Okoomian, Janice, 187
Old Labor and New Immigrants in American Political Development (Mink), 31
Old World Traits Transplanted (Park and Miller), 189
Omi, Michael, 31
O'Neill, Eugene, 39
Opatoshu, Joseph, 98
Orientals, 20, 51, 78, 80
Orsi, Robert, 12, 13, 108, 112, 119, 233
Oso, S., 183
Otis, Johnny, 124
Out of This Furnace (Bell), 44
"Overland" (DeForest), 41
Ovington, Mary White, 120
Oxford American Dictionary, 21
Oxford English Dictionary, 18, 21, 26, 42, 219
Ozawa case, 59, 154

Pacific Islanders, 31, 40, 150
Panunzio, Constantine, 47
Park, Robert, 24–25, 28, 128, 130, 189
Parrenas, Rhacel Salazar, 183
Passing of the Great Race (Grant), 139
Patterson, George, 216
Pearlman, David, 107, 108
Peck, Gunther, 45, 152
Peretti, Burton, 184
Perlmann, Joel, 15, 17, 20, 196, 197
Persians, 51
Persons, Stow, 28
Peterson, William, 27
Philpott, Thomas Lee, 164, 165
Physical Culture Magazine, 187
Pittinger, Mark, 68
Plessy v. Ferguson, 15
Podhoretz, Norman, 114
Pogroms, 22, 98, 104, 108, 128
"Polack," 53, 75, 84, 127, 213

Poles, 27, 30, 32, 37, 43, 44, 48, 49, 50, 53, 59, 61, 69, 72, 73, 75, 77, 97, 99, 100, 105, 109–110, 115, 116, 127, 130, 141, 152, 158, 161, 164, 165, 169, 171, 173, 219, 241

Polish Americans, 105, 128, 159, 168, 191, 196, 198, 222, 223, 231, 239

The Polish Peasant in Europe and America (Thomas and Znaniecki), 115

Portuguese, 59, 62, 109

Powderly, Terence, 14, 15, 17, 18, 32, 89

Pride, Charley, 103

Prima, Louis, 183

Principles of Real Estate Law (MacChesney), 173

Problems of Modern Industry (Webb), 6

Progressive Era, 110, 138

Progressive reformers, 9, 64–72, 86, 143, 175

Prohibition, 200

Prostitution, 186–187

Protestant, 238

Pryor, Richard, 104

Public Works Administration (PWA), 225, 226

Puerto Ricans, 15, 37, 46, 51, 70, 150, 207, 226, 232, 238

Puzo, Mario, 39

Quinn, John, 142

Quintance, Esther, 191

Quotas, 144–145, 147

Race
  as biological and cultural, 66
  as category, 8, 16, 35, 50–54
  color v., 11, 13
  as division of humanity, 14
  ethnics v., 22, 23, 27, 36
  of Europeans, 12
  fascism relating to, 25, 137
  government and, 14–18
  labor force relating to, 72–78
  language of, 7, 13, 37–45, 50, 66, 92, 134
  messiness of, 35–37
  "new immigrants" and, 7, 18, 250n7
  relations of, 8
  unions relating to, 78–92

Race and Nationality in American Life (Handlin), 26

"Race attitudes," 59

"Race hatred," 14, 67, 76, 116

"Race relations cycle," 28

"Race Relations in Industry" (Hughes), 220

"Race suicide," 7, 60, 68, 69, 70, 71, 72, 80, 83, 189

Race thinkers before coming. *See* RTBC

"Race-extraction," 27

Races and Ethnic Groups in American Life (Woofter), 23

The Races of Mankind (Benedict), 25, 26

Racial categorization, 9–10, 11, 50, 64, 134–138

Racial characteristics, 19–20

Racial consciousness, 93–100, 135–136

Racial Integrity Act of 1924, 198

"Racial longings," 161

"Racial occupancy," 229

Racial politics, 14

Racial slurs
  "Africani" as, 113
  "black guinea" as, 39
  "black Irish" as, 39
  "bohunk" as, 43, 49, 51, 75
  "chink" as, 45, 80
  "coolie" as, 79, 82
  "coon" as, 91, 171

"dago" as, 40, 43, 45, 46, 47, 53, 75, 80, 94, 96, 97, 99, 120, 217, 240, 241
"goy/goyim" as, 107, 114
"grease monkey" as, 42
"greaser/greaseball" as, 36, 37–45, 50, 51, 53, 54, 59, 64, 66, 258n12
"guinea/ginnies" as, 36, 37–45, 50, 51, 53, 59, 64, 86, 87, 127, 135, 148, 185, 242
"hunky" as, 36, 37–45, 49, 50, 51, 53, 54, 59, 64, 74, 75, 86, 87, 88, 89, 90, 97, 99, 104, 120, 123, 127, 134, 148, 218, 220, 221, 242, 259n14, 279n22
"huns" as, 43, 80, 142
"Jap" as, 45, 46, 80, 241
"kaffir" as, 141
"kikes" as, 49, 99, 135, 217
"mestizo" as, 41, 151
"mutts" as, 75
"nigger" as, 44, 49, 80, 89, 91, 97, 99, 103, 104, 106, 114, 117, 120, 150, 185, 198, 213, 217
"Polack" as, 53, 75, 84, 127, 213
"schwartzes" as, 114, 116
"sheeny" as, 84, 217
"tutsún" as, 113
"wobblies" as, 217
"wop" as, 45, 75, 99, 127, 185
"Zhid" as, 106
Racialization, 37–45, 45–50, 50–54, 64–72, 134, 135, 136, 141, 142
"Racials," 75, 76, 208, 270n39
Racism, 12, 141, 144
Radford, Gail, 225
Radzialowski, Thaddeus, 105, 109, 110
Ragen's Colts, 126, 128, 169
Ragusa, Kym, 113
Railway Labor Act of 1926, 209
Randolph, A. Philip, 199, 202, 207

Randolph's March on Washington movement (MOWM), 199
Real Estate Fundamentals (Male), 172
Really the Blues (Mezzrow), 101
Reich, Michael, 73
Republicans, 200, 204
Restrictions
  on immigration, 8, 10, 20, 36, 82, 133–138, 145–156
  on "new immigrants," 64–72
Reuther, Walter, 216
Richards, David A. J., 112
Riesman, David, 26
Riis, Jacob, 41–42, 53
Ripley, William Z., 32, 85
The Rise of the Unmeltable Ethnics (Novak), 27
Roberts, Kenneth, 139
Roberts, Peter, 52, 159
Robeson, Paul, 102, 236
Robinett, F. A., 217
Robinson, Earl, 235
Rocker, John, 4
Rodney, Lester, 217
Rogin, Michael, 125
"The Roll of Honor of the New York Police" (Roosevelt), 21
Romanians, 59, 73, 194, 197
Romano, Rose, 188
Ronning, Gerald, 64
Roosevelt, Franklin D., 199, 200, 201, 202, 207, 210, 219, 224, 227, 228, 234, 241
Roosevelt, Theodore, 7, 17, 21, 47, 52, 60, 63, 64, 65, 67, 68, 69, 70, 71, 84, 149
Ross, Edward A., 7, 42, 54, 66, 67, 68, 188, 201
Rossi, Adolfo, 114
Roucek, Joseph Slabey, 150
Rovnost L'udu, 98
Rowell, Chester, 46

RTBC (race thinkers before coming),
110
Rubio, Philip, 203
Russian Jews, 42, 49, 172, 179
Russians, 43, 48, 50, 51, 59, 61, 71, 97,
102, 107, 120, 141, 164, 171, 196,
219
Ruth, Babe, 185

Sabath, Adolph, 156
Sabatini, Thomas, 184
Sacco, Nicola, 48, 262n21
Salt of the Earth, 211
Sampras, Pete, 3, 4
Samson the Hero, 179
Saposs, David, 88, 89, 190, 274n66
Sargent, Frank, 89
Saturday Evening Post, 139
Saxton, Alexander, 31
Scandinavians, 53, 61, 99, 126, 231
Schmier, Louis, 107
Schools, 193–195
"Schwartzes," 114, 116
Scientific Monthly, 23
Scipes, Steven, 211
Scots/Scotch, 27, 71, 90
Scott-Childress, Reynolds, 11
Scottsboro Boys, 100
Second generation
advertising and, 181, 303n61
entertainment industry relating to,
177–184
intermarriage and, 196–198
Italian Americans relating to, 186
music relating to, 182–184
of "new immigrants," 177–184
schools and, 193–195
women, 186–193, 305n79
The Second-Story Man (Sinclair), 44
Segregation, 12, 227
Seles, Monica, 4
Semitic "races," 50, 67

Sen, Katayama, 118
Sennett, Richard, 18
Serbs/Serbian, 43, 44, 50, 59, 73, 108,
219
Seymour, Jim, 48
Shaler, Nathaniel S., 23
"Sheeny," 84, 217
The Sheik, 125
Sheldon, William A., 141
Shulman, Irving, 40
Sicilians, 37, 42, 51, 52, 69, 114, 127,
129, 135, 197
Silver, Lee, 202
Sinatra, Frank, 235–243, 317n3, 318n9
Sinclair, Upton, 44, 45, 160
Singing Jailbirds (Sinclair), 45
The Slav Invasion and the Mine Worker
(Warne), 84, 190
Slavs, 6, 7, 10, 30, 43, 49, 51, 52, 53, 54,
68, 72, 73, 76, 77, 80, 81, 88, 97,
99, 100, 115, 116, 128, 137, 141,
149, 158, 191, 197, 216
A Slav's a Man for All That (Koukol), 44
Slovak-Chinese, 51
Slovaks, 17, 43, 44, 73, 98, 123, 159,
171, 194, 197, 219
Slovenians, 44, 127, 219
The Slum and the Ghetto (Philpott), 164
The Smart Money, 42
Smith, Al, 153, 200
Smith, Bessie, 183
Smith, Judith, 237
Smith, Rogers, 61
Social Security Act of 1935, 205, 206
Socialist movement, 91
Socialists, Italian, 83
*The Social Systems of American Ethnic
Groups* (Warner and Lunt), 25
Sociology and the Race Problem
(McKee), 24
Sojourner Truth Homes, 223, 229
Sollors, Werner, 21, 25, 184

Somebody in Boots (Algren), 43
The Soul of an Immigrant (Panunzio), 47
South Sea Islander, 94
Southern Europeans. *See* Europeans
Spanish/Spaniards, 46, 74
Speek, Peter, 86
Speranza, Gino, 96
"Spiritualism: Old and New" (James), 21
State policies, changes in, 8
"State racism," 117
Steele, Richard, 208
Stein, Howard, 178
Stein, Judith, 221
Steinberg, Stephen, 105, 166
Stoddard, Lathrop, 140
Stoler, Ann Laura, 116
"Strange Fruit," 236
Straus, Oscar, 17
Street Corner Society (Whyte), 42, 195
Strikes, 100, 239
Struggles in Steel, 221
Sugrue, Thomas, 224
Sullivan, Patricia, 202
"Sweat equity," 162
Swede, Swedish, 52, 71
Swiss, 52
Syrians, 45, 50, 51, 61, 73, 96

Tamony, Peter, 42
Tannen, Michael, 77
Tartars, 46
"The Tenement House Blight" (Riis), 42
Teutonic, 68
Theories of Americanization (Berkson), 22
The Thind case, 59, 62, 140, 144, 145, 154
Thomas, Piri, 40
Thomas, William I., 115
Time, 232
Todorova, Maria, 116

Tolnay, Steward, 78
Toomer, Jean, 59
Trachtenberg, Alan, 5
Trade unions, 100
Trees, Daniel, 49, 53, 110–111
Trial and Trouble (Harper), 38
Triulzi, Alessandro, 112
Truman, Harry, 228, 234
Tucker, Sophie, 125, 187
Turks, 46, 51, 173
Turner, Frederick Jackson, 89
"Tutsún," 113
Tyrolean, 43

Ukrainians, 219
Ulysses (Joyce), 41
"The Un-Americanizing of America," 82–83, 272n54
Unionism
    industrial, 8, 200–201, 211
    new, 86
Unions. *See also* AFL; CIO
    The African American United Mine Workers, 49
    African Americans and, 82–92, 207, 209, 213, 222–224
    Amalgamated Clothing Workers of America, 199
    ILGWU, 97, 99, 214
    ILWU, 211
    immigrants and, 78–92, 207–224
    International Workers Order, 217
    Italians relating to, 194, 198, 208
    IWW, 83, 85, 86, 89, 99, 121
    Jews relating to, 199, 208, 213, 231
    labor force relating to, 78–92
    Marine Transport Workers Local 8, 99
    National Maritime Union, 215
    New Deal relating to, 200–203, 207–224
    "new unionism" of, 86

Unions (*continued*)
    race relating to, 78–92
    strikes relating to, 100
    trade, 100
    United Hebrew Trades, 83
    United Mine Workers of America, 81, 84
    United Textile Workers, 82
    UPWA, 222
    Waist and Dress Makers Union, 99
    WFM, 45, 87, 108
United Hebrew Trades, 83
United Mine Workers of America, 81, 84
United Packinghouse Workers of America. *See* UPWA
United Textile Workers, 82
UPWA (United Packinghouse Workers of America), 222
Urban League, 210
Urban race relations, 8
Urgo-Finns, 216
U.S. Census Bureau, 65
U.S. Department of Labor, 100
U.S. Housing Authority (USHA), 226
U.S. Immigration Commission, 15, 20, 43
U.S. Industrial Commission, 73
U.S. Supreme Court, 11, 59, 145, 170, 241
The Uses of Variety (Bramen), 28

VA (Veterans Administration), 227, 230, 231, 233
Valentino, Rudolph, 125, 180
Vanzetti, Bartolomeo, 48, 262n21
Vargas, Sylvia R. Lazos, 30
Vecoli, Rudolph, 95, 161
Veterans Administration. *See* VA
Visions of Belonging (Smith), 237
Vladeck, Baruch, 104, 105
Vorse, Mary Heaton, 190

Wacquant, Loic, 163
"Wailing," 101
Waist and Dress Makers Union, 99
Walker, Francis Amasa, 64, 65, 66, 69, 70
War Plans White initiative, 143
Ward, Robert, 140
Ware, Caroline, 24, 25
Warne, Frank Julian, 6, 51, 52, 53, 84–85, 190, 197
Warner, W. Lloyd, 25, 26
Warren, Earl, 241
Washington, Booker T., 92
WASP (white Anglo-Saxon Protestant), 5, 31, 75, 76
Waters, Mary, 32
Wattenberg, Ben, 30
WBC (white before coming), 110–119
Webb, Sidney and Beatrice, 6
Weir, Stan, 109
Weiss, Nancy, 204
Weiss, Richard, 52
Welfare, 203–207
Wells, H. G., 6, 90
West, Cornel, 105
West, Mae, 186, 187
Western Europeans. *See* Europeans
Western Federation of Miners. *See* WFM
WFM (Western Federation of Miners), 45, 87, 108
What's Your Name? (Adamic), 194, 218
Wheels of Victory (Evergood), 133–134, 136
White before coming. *See* WBC
"White ethnic," 18, 19, 27–34, 28, 30, 45
White house, 174, 177–184, 200
"White Houses" (McKay), 157, 158
White, Josh, 236
White on arrival. *See* WOA
White supremacy, 15, 211

Whiteness. *See also* WOA
  chronologies of, 134–138
  dialectics of, 145–156
  legality of, 59–64
  questioning of, 86, 145
  as situational, 135
  study of, 7
  tests for, 59
Whiteness of a Different Color
  (Jacobson), 7, 31–32
Whitening, 8, 9, 134, 203, 230
Whyte, William Foote, 42, 195
Wilder, Craig Steven, 203, 226, 230
Willett, Julie A., 187
Williams, Linda Faye, 203
Williams, Patricia J., 93
Williams, Serena, 4
Williams, Venus, 4
Wilson, Woodrow, 63, 69, 180
Winant, Howard, 31
Winkowski, Stefan, 118
Wirth, Louis, 98, 163, 179
WOA (white on arrival), 110–119
  inbetweenness relating to,
    119–130
"Wobblies," 217
Wolfe, Patrick, 12
Wolff, Larry, 116
Wolfinger, James, 224
Women
  in labor force, 84, 189, 206
  second generation of, 186–193,
    305n79
  suffrage of, 72
Woodbey, George Washington, 99

Woofter, T. J., Jr, 23, 24, 76, 78
"Wop," 45, 75, 99, 127, 185
Work force, 66–67
Works Progress Administration (WPA),
  204, 206
A World View of Race (Bunche), 48
World War I, 22, 43, 60, 80, 86, 88, 99,
  108, 116, 122, 129, 134, 137, 140,
  150, 154, 155, 200, 216, 244
World War II, 8, 25, 30, 103, 133, 136,
  137, 163, 199, 200, 207, 213, 220,
  229, 237
Wright, Carroll D., 109
Wtulich, Josephine, 43

Yankee City series, 25, 26
Yans-McLaughlin, Virginia, 88
Yerkes, Robert, 141
Yezierska, Anzia, 183, 188
Yiddish vaudeville, 179
Young, Donald, 20, 24, 25, 82
The Young Manhood of Studs Lonigan
  (Farrell), 140
Yu, Henry, 163
Yugoslav, 53

Zahller, Alisa, 188
Zangwill, Israel, 135, 145, 179
Zecker, Robert, 109
"Zhid," 106
Zieger, Robert, 212, 214, 216
Zionists, 22, 23
Znaniecki, Florian, 115
Zola, Emile, 41
Zunz, Olivier, 159, 162